THE CHRISTIAN MOSES

THE CHRISTIAN MOSES

FROM PHILO TO THE QUR'ĀN

EDITED BY

Philip Rousseau and Janet A. Timbie

The Catholic University of America Press
Washington, D.C.

Library of Congress Cataloging-in-Publication Data
Names: Rousseau, Philip, editor.
Title: The Christian Moses : from Philo to the Qur'ān / edited by
Philip Rousseau and Janet A. Timbie.
Description: Washington, D.C. : The Catholic University of America Press, 2019. |
Series: CUA studies in early Christianity | Includes bibliographical
references and index.
Identifiers: LCCN 2019010763 | ISBN 9780813231914 (cloth : alk. paper)
Subjects: LCSH: Moses (Biblical leader)
Classification: LCC BS580.M6 C485 2019 | DDC 222/.1092—dc23
LC record available at https://lccn.loc.gov/2019010763

produced with grant by

Figure Foundation

child of a sound world

CONTENTS

PREFACE

The chapters in this volume reproduce the bulk of the papers presented at a conference with the same title—"The Christian Moses: From Philo to the Qur'ān"—held at the Catholic University of America, May 31–June 3, 2012. Our purpose in creating the occasion and ordering the papers in the way we have was to examine how the figure of Moses was put to use, as it were, by Christians during the period suggested. There are no chapters devoted exclusively either to Philo or to Islam, but the allusions imply a recognizable set of centuries—roughly the first to the seventh C.E.—that were at the same time strikingly varied in their character and preoccupations. They cover not only the emergence of Christianity itself and its transition to toleration, dominance, and division, but also the journey of the Jews from a Hellenistic world that included and (at first) tolerated their Diaspora beyond their homeland and the development of rabbinic "formative" identity and practice, the creation of the Mishnah and its attendant traditions, and the Talmudic achievements of later centuries.

We open the book as we did the conference, with a chapter by Daniel Boyarin, which, with characteristic authority, freshness, and breadth, set a tone that lasted through the days that followed; an evening plenary session that brought together all those attending, after an opening dinner, and gave us a sense of collegiality and purpose. Professor Boyarin is naturally anxious to emphasize that his chapter has now been overtaken by subsequent published debate, the details of which are duly noted in the chapter itself; but it remains here as a record of his presence and impact. With some reluctance, we then arranged most of the other papers in two streams, in some cases brought together as panels under thematic headings; but we were careful to present seven plenary sessions, which everyone could attend without missing something else, and maintained an atmosphere of coherence and shared inquiry. Now they can be read as a single unit. There were long periods, at lunchtime and in the evenings, when participants could seek the culinary pleasures of Washington and continue the discussions of the day.

In the book, the material is presented in a different order. We start with a predominantly "New Testament" section, reflecting a period when Christians and Jews were very conscious of ambiguities in their relationships and growing distinctions. Here we see Moses moving through the imaginations of early writers and early Christian communities, with an interesting convergence on Corinth.

This is followed by a lynchpin plenary paper by Richard Layton, which ranges right across the early Christian era. Here Philo does make his appearance; but we are carried forward all the way to Augustine, via several other figures; and the author provides in many ways a framework within which to explore the details of later essays. It is as a sequel to that survey that we include the chapters touching upon that great movement of appropriation that reaches from the time of Clement of Alexandria and Origen to the writings of Eusebius.

From the dawning of the age of Constantine, we move to two papers focused on one peak period of Greek patristic literature, but from a distinctive angle—that of Gregory of Nyssa. Here Moses truly does, in Ann Conway-Jones's phrase, ascend to heaven. There is a feeling that his greatness, central in the Jewish mind, has been given not necessarily a more accurate but definitely a novel grandeur as underpinning the task of penetrating not only the deepest meaning of his own writings (as they were thought to be) but also the experience of knowing what it was to speak face to face with God.

This seemed the suitable moment, in the book, to present the two chapters with images, both based on plenary presentations, since they allow us to pick up more general threads in vivid form, deepening our awareness of the impact of the inventiveness we have witnessed so far on the imaginations of Christians who were able—had for a long time, in some cases, been able—to give tangible form to their shifting interpretation of texts, both within the texts themselves and on the surfaces of buildings within which they were read and pondered.

We then radiate outward to what was for Christians a new world—more contentious, more insecure, more fractured. This is also the point at which we venture more deeply into the Christian literature of the Latin West especially.

In some ways, this was where we might have ended, for divergent opportunities were undoubtedly opened to the Christian communities as the sixth century drew to a close.

But we decided to end the book where we ended the conference—and, by everyone's agreement, most fortuitously. John Reeves's closing plenary session summoned us all back to a big picture, or—putting it in the richer light it deserves—to a more subtle view of the whole we thought we had been looking at. The final chapter stands, therefore, as a reminder that, as we moved from phase to phase through our central threads, there was, as it were, a great body of outriders that accompanied us on the flanks of our advance, representing territory and traditions and exerting influences that we might otherwise have failed to attend to. It gave the conference, and we think it gives the book, a clear invitation to think about this species of thematic template, which comes nowhere near exhausting the reflections it induced, and provides a welcome warning that there is a great deal more to be made of it.

Producing this book has been, for a variety of (for the most part) justifiable reasons, a slow process, and we appreciate immensely the loyalty and patience of our contributors, who made this a memorable and, we confidently hope, a useful experience. Above all we value the interplay of cultures that inevitably resulted. Moses was a Jew, and the Jewish presence, then as now, hovered over the Christian experience inescapably. The motives for allowing that to happen (in the early Christian period itself) were not always tactful, or even humane; but the affinity implied was ancient, has been lasting, and remains a force today.

We would like to conclude with practical gratitude to the outside readers of our final manuscript and to our editorial colleagues at the Catholic University of America Press, whose encouragement and advice were a constant support and whose vigilance has saved us from rare obscurity and even the odd error. Special thanks are due to Louise Mundstock, senior graduate student in Greek and Latin, who prepared the index and provided other editorial assistance. The actual setting up of the original conference owed much to a generous donation from the Eugene and Emily Grant Family Foundation of New York, and without the conference there would have been, of course, no book.

Philip Rousseau and Janet A. Timbie

ABBREVIATIONS

We have kept these to a minimum. Each contributor has been consistent within his or her chapter. Abbreviations of primary sources, where they occur, follow the conventions of either *The Oxford Classical Dictionary*, 3rd edition revised, edited by Simon Hornblower and Antony Spawforth (Oxford University Press, 2003); or *The Oxford Dictionary of the Christian Church*, 3rd edition revised, edited by F. L. Cross and E. A. Livingstone (Oxford University Press, 2005).

In the general bibliography, the titles of all journals (to which contributors will have referred in their notes) have been entered in full.

Very common abbreviations have been listed here for further convenience:

ACW	Ancient Christian Writers
BHG	Bibliotheca Hagiographica Graeca
CC	Corpus Christianorum
CCSL	Corpus Christianorum, series latina
CCSG	Corpus Christianorum, series graeca
CSCO	Corpus Scriptorum Christianorum Orientalium
CSEL	Corpus Scriptorum Ecclesiasticorum Latinorum
DACL	*Dictionnaire d'Archéologie Chrétienne et de Liturgie*
DHGE	*Dictionnaire d'Histoire et de Géographie Ecclésiastiques*
Dict. Sp.	*Dictionnaire de Spiritualité*
FOTC	Fathers of the Church
GCS	Die griechischen christlichen Schriftsteller
MGH	Monumenta Germaniae Historica
PG	Patrologia Graeca, edited by J. P. Migne
PL	Patrologia Latina, edited by J. P. Migne
SC	Sources Chrétiennes
TU	Texte und Untersuchungen der altchristliche Literatur

THE CHRISTIAN MOSES

Daniel Boyarin

1. MOSES AND JESUS AGAINST THE PHARISEES

Mark and Paul on Moses

Joel Marcus has recently revived the argument that Mark is a disciple of Paul. Among the arguments for Pauline-Marcan religious intimacy, Marcus writes, "And both think that the widening of God's purposes to incorporate the Gentiles was accomplished by an apocalyptic change in the Law that had previously separated Jews from Gentiles, a change that included an abrogation of the OT food laws; in the new situation that pertains since Jesus' advent, all foods are pure (Mark 7:19; Rom 14:20)."[1] Without entering an opinion on the general question of Paul's impact on Mark, on this precise point—the relation between Mark 7 and Romans 14—I wish to contest most of the scholarly (and all of the Christian hermeneutic) tradition directly. Mark's Moses and Paul's could not be more different from—nor more in direct opposition to—each

Author's note: This paper is dedicated to my friends and colleagues Richard Hays and Joel Marcus. *Editors' note*: This paper is printed essentially in the form it was received in May 2013. Scholarship has meanwhile advanced, and Professor Boyarin has asked us to note here Joel Marcus, "Mark—Interpreter of Paul" in *Mark and Paul: Comparative Essays, 2, For and Against Pauline Influence on Mark*, ed. Eve-Marie Becker, Troels Engberg-Pedersen, and Mogens Müller (Berlin: De Gruyter, 2013), 29–49; and his own forthcoming paper, "Mark 7:1–23—Finally," in *Re-Making the World: Categories and Early Christianity: Essays in Honor of Karen L. King*, ed. Carly Daniel-Hughes, Benjamin Dunning, Laura Nasrallah, AnneMarie Luijendijk, and Taylor Petrey (Tübingen: Mohr Siebeck).

1. Joel Marcus, "Mark—Interpreter of Paul," *New Testament Studies* 46 (2000): 475–76.

other.[2] The overall approach of my work on Mark has been to show that there is no way that Marcan Christology, including Jesus' theology of the Law, constitutes a break with earlier Jewish tradition or the expectation of the Messiah's privileges and prerogatives.

I would propose that Mark is best read as a text of Second-Temple Judaism *simpliciter*, while Paul—also a Jew, of course—marks a much more radical swerve from what can be known and said about the Judaism of his time.[3] The old saw about Jesus not being a Christian because Paul hadn't invented Christianity yet has something to it. I would nonetheless modify this in two ways. First of all, I think Paul did not yet know that he was inventing Christianity, and second, the decisive move that would lead to the invention of Christianity had not been made in any of the Gospels. Especially for Mark, I would claim that Jesus is portrayed as defending the Torah—Moses—and not attacking it in any way. This has enormous historical consequences, especially since now it seems almost clear that Mark's is the first Gospel.

Many influential scholars (Bultmann and his students prominently among them) have insisted on a Jesus who is as un-Jewish as possible, explicitly articulating a principle of dissimilarity where only that which is supposedly antithetical to the "Judaism" of the time is taken as authentic words of Jesus.[4] This interpretation of the evidence would have the effect of rendering any appearance of similarity with Judaism (as New Testament scholarship has imagined that "religion") the product of an early church that was a Judaizing church (especially in Matthew), while the *original* message of Jesus is the idea that over time became "orthodox" within the historical Christian churches, to wit, that the Law was abrogated by Jesus entirely and quite without concern

2. I make no claims here as to the more general question of Marcan dependence on Paul. As Marcus has noted, Mark could easily have been a dissenting follower of Paul, after all. Another point of contrast between these two authors, however, has to do with the name of the Christ. For Mark, the proper title of the Christ is "Son of Man," while for Paul, of course, it is "Son of God." As I have argued recently, in the one-time usage of the term "Son of God" in Mark's Gospel—a usage that is in any case questioned on text-critical grounds—it is most plausibly interpreted as the human king Messiah expected by the Jews.

3. This is actually a deeply problematic formulation. See now my *Judaism: the Genealogy of a Modern Notion* (Rutgers University Press, 2018). I show that it is anachronistic to speak of "Judaism" at all for this period. What is printed here, however, provided convenient shorthand for the conference itself.

4. For an effective, concise example of how this works, in the writings of Ernst Käsemann, for example, see Jesper Svartvik, *Mark and Mission: Mk 7:1–23 in Its Narrative and Historical Contexts*, Conlectanea Biblica, New Testament Series (Stockholm: Almqvist & Wiksell, 2000), 22–23. I thank Paula Fredriksen for bringing this important (and frustrating) publication to my attention.

for continuity with traditional Israelite Torah.[5] Was the earliest Jesus movement a movement that began in utter rejection of Moses and his Torah, as
nearly all commentators on Mark would have it, or was it something quite different? To cite a recent author who has formulated this well: "We note that
the question of whether Jesus taught or fought the Law is essential."[6] (Paul,
I still think—although I'm wavering on this—fought the Law.) The example
of Mark 7:15–19 is a telling one. In this paper, I shall present my reading of
this passage and then contrast it with what seems, at first glance, to be a Pauline parallel, and then, finally, by considering the place of "Moses" in 2 Corinthians 3, draw a decisive contrast between Mark and Paul with respect to their
portrayals of Moses.

The whole context of Mark 7 suggests that, here, Jesus speaks from the
position of a traditional Galilean Jew whose community and traditional practices are being criticized and interfered with from outside, that is, from Jerusalem, by the Judeans, as is emphasized in the incipit of the story itself.[7] Jesus accuses these Pharisees of introducing practices that are beyond what is written
in the Torah, or even against what is written in the Torah, and fights against
their "tradition of the Elders [κατὰ τὴν παράδοσιν τῶν πρεσβυτέρων],"[8] which
they take to be as important as the Torah, or sometimes, in the eyes of their

5. For critical discussion of this "principle of dissimilarity," see John Gager, "The Gospels and Jesus:
Some Doubts about Method," *Journal of Religion* 54 (1974): 256–59. It is surely odd, or so it seems to me,
to decide in advance that what is authentically dominical is only that which is different from some reified
idea of ancient Judaism that doesn't include Jesus in it. What seems to me most troubling about the
"criterion of dissimilarity" is that it privileges as authentic in a portrait of Jesus precisely and only what
seemingly differs from his environment, thus thoroughly distorting the teaching of a(ny) teacher. Furthermore, it assumes that that which is different from some reified idea of Judaism must be authentically
from Jesus and could not itself be a product of a Christian group moving gradually away and distinguishing itself from another community of Jews. See also Peter J. Tomson, "Jewish Purity Laws as Viewed by
the Church Fathers and by the Early Followers of Jesus," in *Purity and Holiness: The Heritage of Leviticus*,
ed. M. J. H. M. Poorthuis and J. Schwartz, Jewish and Christian Perspectives Series, vol. 2 (Leiden: Brill,
2000), 85n46, for further sharp critique of the principle of dissimilarity.

6. Svartvik, *Mark and Mission*, 18.

7. "It seems that this is not the only occasion on which Jesus defends a conservative halakhic stand.
In the woe-sayings in Matt 23, Jesus twice rails against Pharisaic law and offers an alternative halakhic
opinion. In both matters, that of oaths (vv. 16–22) and the subject of purifying vessels (vv. 25–26), Jesus
objects to the leniency of the Pharisees and offers a stricter ruling. This point is stressed by K. C. G. Newport, *The Sources and Sitz im Leben of Matthew 23* (JSNTSup 117; Sheffield: Sheffield Academic Press,
1995), 137–45" (Yair Fürstenberg, "Defilement Penetrating the Body: A New Understanding of Contamination in Mark 7.15," *New Testament Studies* 54 [2008]: 178).

8. Albert I. Baumgarten, "The Pharisaic *Paradosis*," *Harvard Theological Review* 80 (1987): 63–77.

opponents such as Jesus, as uprooting or superseding the Torah.[9] I would assert, moreover, that Jesus' Galilean disciples were following their own accepted traditional practice in their refusal of the *nonbiblical* notion that impure foods could render the body impure and hence their refusal to wash their hands before eating. Jesus' disciples are upbraided by these upstarts from Jerusalem for not observing the purity strictures that they had introduced and demanded on the basis of the "traditions of the Elders." Jesus responds vigorously, accusing them of hypocrisy and of ascribing a self-importance to their own rulings and practices that is greater than the importance they ascribe to the Torah. There is, thus, nothing in this passage, even in the Marcan version, that suggests that Jesus is calling for abandoning the Torah at all. The Galileans were antipathetic to the urban Judaean/Jerusalemite Pharisaic innovations.[10]

The great advantage of this interpretation, I think, from a purely exegetical point of view, is that the narrative remains coherent from its beginning to its end. It begins with a controversy over a Pharisaic innovation, continues with Jesus' attack on the "tradition of the Elders," the set of practices and ideas that the Pharisees held and that were not in the written Torah (and that were the source of sharp controversy among Jews right through the Middle Ages), and ends with a rejection of an entire complex of Pharisaic stringency with regard to eating practices and purity that was the source of the requirement for a ritual hand washing before eating.[11] The development of Jesus' argument from hand washing, to other purity practices, to the allegedly Pharisaic innovation of vows that make it forbidden to care for one's parents, to a homily on

9. In support of this suggestion, I might cite Josephus *Ant.* 13.297, where we read, "νῦν δὲ δηλῶσαι βούλομαι, ὅτι νόμιμά τινα παρέδοσαν τῷ δήμῳ οἱ Φαρισαῖοι ἐκ πατέρων διαδοχῆς, ἅπερ οὐκ ἀναγέγραπται ἐν τοῖς Μωυσέως νόμοις, καὶ διὰ τοῦτο ταῦτα τὸ Σαδδουκαίων γένος ἐκβάλλει, λέγον ἐκεῖνα δεῖν ἡγεῖσθαι νόμιμα τὰ γεγραμμένα, τὰ δ' ἐκ παραδόσεως τῶν πατέρων μὴ τηρεῖν. [What I would now explain is this, that the Pharisees have delivered to the people a great many observances by succession from their fathers, which are not written in the laws of Moses; and for that reason it is that the Sadducees reject them, and say that we are to esteem those observances to be obligatory which are in the written word, but are not to observe what are derived from the tradition of our forefathers.]" Without, of course, suggesting that Jesus was a Sadducee—which he almost certainly was not—we surely see in his polemic against the Pharisees here an echo of the same controversy to which Josephus refers as well.

10. This is close to the view of Seán Freyne, *Galilee, from Alexander the Great to Hadrian, 323 B.C.E. to 135 C.E.: A Study of Second Temple Judaism*, University of Notre Dame Center for the Study of Judaism and Christianity in Antiquity 5 (Notre Dame, Ind.: University of Notre Dame Press, 1980), 316–18, 322.

11. On purely hermeneutic grounds, surely such a reading is preferable to one that must insist that the text is an "artificial" (whatever that might mean) construct, *pace* E. P. Sanders, *Jesus and Judaism* (Philadelphia: Fortress Press, 1985), 256, as well as many others.

the relative significance of pious practice and piety is perfectly coherent on this account, and we need ascribe no editorial intervention, quilting, or felting of sources to make perfectly good sense of the argument of the chapter. This is strong support for this reading, especially given that the received interpretation actually has Jesus arguing hypocritically or, at least, not in good faith, complaining that the Pharisees depart from Moses and then, himself, discarding Moses.[12]

While there are, indeed, some recent scholars who have seen that verse 15a is about purity and impurity and not kashrut,[13] virtually all of the modern commentators I have consulted take v. 15b to refer in its plain sense to something called "moral impurity"[14] and not Levitical or ritual impurity. Thus, for instance, Adela Y. Collins, who writes, "The 'not ... but' formula in v. 15 indicates that moral purity is given a higher priority than ritual priority."[15] Similarly Robert Gundry: "We should therefore take v. 15b as a statement about moral defilement."[16]

If, however, in verse 15 Jesus is already saying that ritual impurity does not contaminate, but only moral impurity from within contaminates, then it becomes virtually impossible to understand why the disciples refer to it as a parable. There is nothing whatever parabolic about it. It's also difficult to see what

---

12. For a very good explication of this argument, presented at greater length than would be appropriate in the present format, see Svartvik, *Mark and Mission*, 6.

13. Notably Menahem Kister, "Law, Morality and Rhetoric in Some Sayings of Jesus," in *Studies in Ancient Midrash*, ed. James L. Kugel (Cambridge, Mass.: Harvard University Center for Jewish Studies, Harvard University Press, 2001), 145–54.

14. Adela Yarbro Collins, *Mark: A Commentary*, ed. Harold W. Attridge, Hermeneia—a Critical and Historical Commentary on the Bible (Minneapolis, Minn.: Fortress Press, 2007), 353–54.

15. Collins, *Mark: A Commentary*, 355. For a very recent and innovative reading, on which I, in part, depend here, see Fürstenberg, "Defilement Penetrating the Body."

16. Robert H. Gundry, *Mark: A Commentary on His Apology for the Cross* (Grand Rapids, Mich.: Eerdmans, 2004), 366. With all due respect, I suggest that had Gundry understood the parable here, he would have been less inclined to dismiss out of hand the view of Schmitals and Boucher that both cola refer to ritual impurity. Schmitals was quite right to sense that the kind of antithesis that Jesus is using here ought to refer to the same sphere in both halves, even though he misunderstood the actual halakhic point. Gundry, on the other hand, is also quite mistaken in his comment that according to the "OT," eating nonkosher foods renders the body impure. Neither eating kosher food that has become impure nor nonkosher food renders the body impure. Carrion is the only exception, but that is a form of corpse impurity, not the eating of food that has become impure (see, on this topic, the clear statements of Kister, "Law, Morality and Rhetoric," 151–52). But even Kister takes 15b to be about moral defilement and not ritual purity (Kister, "Law, Morality and Rhetoric," 153). It is, of course, at this point that our ways part and mine converge with Fürstenberg. See below a fuller discussion of the historical stakes of this difference in interpretation.

precisely they would not understand in such an ostensibly plain-spoken homily. So Matthew Henry: "They asked him, when they had him by himself, concerning the parable (Mark 7:17); *for to them, it seems, it was a parable*" (emphasis added). One must assume a devastating inability to understand on the part of the disciples—much more than their usual thickness—if they heard Jesus' allegedly clear statement and didn't get the point. What on earth would have made them think there is a parable here?

Mark 7:16 is a phantom verse, lately honored more often by its absence than by its presence. Its absence in two very important early witnesses to the Gospel has led to its near complete occlusion in modern texts and translations.[17] Thus, for instance, the NRSV:

14 Then he called the crowd again and said to them, "Listen to me, all of you, and understand: 15 there is nothing outside a person that by going in can defile, but the things that come out are what defile." 16 17 When he had left the crowd and entered the house, his disciples asked him about the parable.

In the AV, v. 16 was included; nearly all translations since into English and all modern scholarly editions excise this verse.

Verse 16, "Let him who has ears hear!," whether "genuine" or "spurious," helps us to understand better the structure of the dominical argument. When it is present, as in most witnesses, it clarifies the text perfectly: Jesus made a statement of a literal halakhic (not moral, not tropological) nature in its plain sense, but Jesus then signified that it was a parable by using the formula, "Let him who has ears hear!" It is precisely the declaration of v. 16 that so mystifies the disciples. They have heard a simple, and as we shall see in a moment, quite accurate statement of the Torah against the Pharisees' alleged distortions of it, but then they have been informed that it (the Law itself) is a parable, and that is what they don't get. Note that this interpretation works well even without v. 16, since R. T. France makes the point that the contested v. 16 only makes explicit the parabolic nature of the discourse that is implicit in Jesus' call to hear in v. 14: "Καὶ προσκαλεσάμενος πάλιντὸνὄχλονἔλεγεν

---

17. The two witnesses were Vaticanus and Sinaiticus. This is my best reconstruction of the textual evidence as given in Nestle-Aland which cites this verse from nearly all of the Uncial and minuscule manuscripts "of the first order." I am grateful to Prof. Bart Ehrman for his guidance on this matter. Ehrman himself prefers the view that it is an addition in the other witnesses, which certainly seems more than possible to me as well.

αὐτοῖς· Ἀκούσατέ μου πάντες καὶ σύνετε [And he called to him the multitude again, and said unto them, Hear me all of you, and understand]." The call to hear and understand is itself a marker and signifier of a parable.[18] Verse 16 only makes absolutely explicit that which is already strongly indicated in v. 14. It is the signs of parabolic discourse that so puzzle them. Without these, they would have been not at all puzzled or troubled at Jesus' intervention; they would have had no reason to be, but then, Jesus would not have conveyed his message—his message that punctilious and correct observance of what the Torah actually says is what is necessary for us to understand its deeper significance. Let those who have ears, hear!

I have recently interpreted the actual halakhic issue here at some length,[19] referring as well to an article published by Yair Fürstenberg on the subject, so I will only quickly summarize the point.[20] According to the written Torah, it is indeed the case that foods that are impure (that is, that have been in contact with dead bodies or touched by people with various fluxes from the body) do not render the body impure; impurity is conveyed upon a human body through things that come out: genital blood, semen, and gonorrheal fluxes.[21] It is, therefore, only the Pharisaic tradition that showed concern for the purity of food by requiring ablutions before eating, suggesting that the food could become impure and render the body impure, as well.[22] Jesus thus, appropri-

---

18. R. T. France, *The Gospel of Mark: A Commentary on the Greek Text*, The New International Greek Testament Commentary (Grand Rapids, Mich.: Eerdmans, 2002), 184.

19. Daniel Boyarin, *The Jewish Gospel: The Story of the Jewish Christ* (New York: The New Press, 2012).

20. Fürstenberg, "Defilement Penetrating the Body." I regret that I had unfortunately overlooked the major contribution of Kister, "Law, Morality and Rhetoric," at the time of that writing. Below I will discuss this important paper at some length.

21. The only seeming exception to this rule has to do with carrion, which, if ingested, does make the body impure (Lv 17:15). This is, indeed, the proverbial exception that proves the rule; neither eating pork nor kosher food that has been contaminated by contact with impurities render a body impure, and in this the Pharisaic rulings certainly appear to depart from those of the "Written Torah," namely "Moses." In any case, of course, no washing of hands would ever "defend" against the impurity of carrion! For the absolutely clearest exposition of this distinction between purity and impurity and between kosher and forbidden, see Svartvik, *Mark and Mission*, 363–73. Especially relevant here are his conclusions that (1) "the Pentateuch itself upholds a difference between food laws and purity laws" (*Mark and Mission*, 365); and (2) "prohibited food as such does not render a person unclean" (*Mark and Mission*, 367); and (3) "contaminated food is to a much higher extent the result of a rabbinic interpretation" (*Mark and Mission*, 371). One of the most frustrating things about Svartvik's book is that, while 75 percent of it is irrelevant and 25 percent full of brilliant insight, he never actually interprets the pericope!

22. See also Kister, "Law, Morality and Rhetoric," 153.

ately for the context of the pericope as a whole, in verse 15 is still continuing his theme of Pharisaic distortions that interfere with or contradict the plain meaning of Torah.

But he informs them and us that the plain meaning of the purity practice enjoined by Scripture has a deeper, symbolic interpretation, a tropological reading, by telling us "Let those who have ears, hear!" If you distort and change the practice of the Law, you will not understand its inner meaning, either.[23]

A parable, by definition, has a literal and a figurative side. If Jesus talks about a vineyard, but means the Kingdom of Heaven, that is a parable. Consequently, if we have here a parable, it, too, must have a literal and figurative side. If, when Jesus said it is not what goes in that makes one impure but only what goes out, he was not declaring a literal fact, a fact of the Torah, but instead just making the moral point directly, then there would be here no parable at all, just a sermon.

That this point has been thoroughly missed by scholarly commentators is shown by the multiple approving citations of Westerholm's comment that 7:15 means that "a person is not so much defiled by that which enters him from outside as he is by that which comes from within."[24] Others argue against Westerholm's suggestion and say that Jesus meant to reject purity practices entirely, but all such discussion is actually otiose, once we understand that Jesus is simply offering the true, literal law of Moses, which is an absolute binary opposition:[25] only that which comes out defiles a body, not that which goes in. Henry, writing in the seventeenth century, got this point: "As by the ceremonial law, whatsoever (almost) comes out of a man, defiles him (Leviticus 15:2; Dt 23:13), so what comes out from the mind of a man is that which defiles him before God, and calls for a religious washing (Mark 7:21)." Once more, to make my interpretation crystal clear: Jesus asserts the law and then offers it up for a parabolic interpretation, as signified by "Hear me all of you, and under-

23. Cf. Collins, who writes: "Yet it is a significant difference that Jesus apparently did not present ritual purity as a symbol of moral purity, as Philo did" (*Mark: A Commentary*, 355). In my view as laid out in this brief communique, in contrast, such a symbolic interpretation is the exact meaning of "parable" here.

24. Robert A. Wild, "The Encounter between Pharisaic and Christian Judaism: Some Early Gospel Evidence," *Novum Testamentum* 27, no. Fasc. 2 (April 1985): 119, citing Stephen Westerholm, *Jesus and Scribal Authority*, Coniectanea Biblica (Lund: LiberLäromedel/Gleerup, 1978), 83.

25. See here also Kister, "Law, Morality and Rhetoric," 154n31.

stand" and ratified by (when it is there) "Let him who has ears, hear!" The disciples recognized through this phrase that a parable had been delivered, that is, they understood that the statement was literal and that there was a figurative second meaning, but they could not discern its meaning on their own. They did not understand the parable. I submit that this is the only reading (in both senses) that renders this sequence of verses intelligible.

The disciples were puzzled because they heard their rabbi making a straightforward point about the Law—the literal side of the parable—but didn't understand why he signified that this was a parable. They caught the literal sense, but needed help with the figure. And Jesus answered them. Why does the Torah render impure only that which comes out, and not that which goes in, if not to teach us something, namely, that matters of the heart that are externalized in evil behavior also confer "moral" impurity?

As Menahem Kister has pointed out, Jesus' statement is coherent only if he is speaking about *kosher* food that has become defiled, which, of course, is entirely consistent with the context of the narrative in which the disciples are being accused of eating not food that is not kosher, but food that is impure. And it is that impurity that Jesus declares invalid, not the distinction between kosher and nonkosher. In direct contradiction to the Pharisaic innovation of washing hands to prevent food from becoming impure, says Jesus: you may eat kosher food whether or not it has become defiled and impure, and you will not become impure, just as the written Torah explicitly teaches. But this has absolutely nothing to do with abrogating the Law; it is the finale of Jesus' answer as to why his disciples (and presumably he, too), following their own accepted traditional practice in their refusal of the (nonbiblical) notion that impure foods could render the body impure, need not perform a ritual ablution of the hands prior to eating. Follow Moses and not the human traditions of the Pharisees!

The consistent argument of the pericope is thus that the Pharisees who have come from Judea and Jerusalem seeking to impose their "tradition of the Elders" (in Hebrew, מסורת אבות) on the Jews of the Galilee, seek arrogantly, "hypocritically," to substitute their human tradition for divine doctrine, as they themselves concede by referring to it as traditions of the Elders. Jesus not only angrily rejects their attempt to replace the written Torah with traditions of human origin, but also explains why this is so dangerous a practice, because the Pharisaic attempt to add to the Torah in order to protect its rules ends up subverting God's intent as expressed in the Torah. No abrogation of the Law is thus comprehended here by Jesus or Mark. I take this conclusion to be virtually incontrovertible as a straightforward reading of the text as we have it.

According to the Talmud itself, it was the Rabbis (or the legendary Pharisees) who innovated the washing of the hands before meals, together with a set of other practices that together imply that the ingesting of defiled or polluted foods renders one impure. It was thus against those Pharisaic innovations, which they are trying to foist on his disciples, that Jesus railed, and not against the keeping of kosher.[26] This is a debate, however acrimonious, between Jews about the correct way to keep the Torah, and not an attack on the Torah.

Fürstenberg has brilliantly argued that, in its original sense, Jesus' attack on the Pharisees here is literal: They *have* changed the rules of the Torah. This is made clear in a rabbinic text that, while much later than the Gospel, ascribes a change in the halakha to the time of Mark:

These categories render the Priestly offering unfit [to be eaten by the Priests]: He who eats directly impure food; ... and he who drinks impure fluids; ... and the hands. (Zabim 5:12)

If someone eats or drinks impure food, then his touch renders the priestly portion unfit.[27] This innovative ruling is explicitly connected in the list with the "hands," as well, just as the Marcan Jesus associates them. These rulings are explicitly marked within the talmudic tradition as being of rabbinic origin and not as rulings of the Torah. That is to say, the classical Rabbis themselves maintained a distinction between that which was written in the Torah and that which had been added by them or by their Pharisaic forbears. They explicitly remark that we have here a Pharisaic extension of the Torah, just as Jesus said. According to the Torah, only that which comes out of the body (fluxes of various types) can contaminate, not foods that go in.[28] Thus, if the Pharisees argue that food itself contaminates, that is a change in the Law.

26. Fürstenberg, "Defilement Penetrating the Body," 178.

27. Tomson, "Jewish Purity Laws," 81, has brought this text to bear on Mark 7. It should be further pointed out that, according to the Babylonian Talmud Shabbat 14a, Rabbi Eliʿezer holds an even stricter standard than this, but it is still within the category of rabbinic (Pharisaic) innovation or the "traditions of the Elders," just as Jesus dubs it.

28. Fürstenberg, "Defilement Penetrating the Body," 200.

This interpretation has the great advantage of rendering the attack on handwashing consistent with the attack on the vow that releases one from supporting one's parents. They both represent instances in which the "Pharisees" apparently supplant the Torah with their "tradition of the Elders." Once again, Jesus and Mark have got it exactly right in terms of the Torah and the traditions. For Jesus (Mark) the "tradition of the Elders" is a *human* creation as opposed to the Written Torah, which is divine, hence the force of the citation from Isaiah: He said to them, "Isaiah prophesied rightly about you hypocrites, as it is written, 'This people honors me with their lips, but their hearts are far from me; in vain do they worship me, teaching human precepts as doctrines.' You abandon the commandment of God and hold to human tradition" (Mk 7:6–8). From Jesus' point of view (as well as from the point of view of Qumran and the Sadducees) the "tradition of the Elders"—later called the Oral Torah—consists of "human precepts" being taught as doctrines in precisely the way the prophetic formulation states. For the Pharisees, and later for the Rabbis, the "tradition of the Elders" is divine word, and not a collection of human precepts, transmitted orally, rather than scripturally.[29]

Contrast this perfectly coherent account with the currently regnant interpretation of this text. In it, Jesus starts out by complaining about the Pharisees' addition of handwashing, then accuses them of setting aside Moses in favor of their human traditions and practices, which makes them hypocrites, then offers another example of that (the law of supported parents), and then says, in a total volte-face: in fact, we don't need Moses at all, since it's all abrogated. I leave readers to decide on purely literary, hermeneutical grounds which interpretation is preferable.

However, a voice will ask at this point, what is to be done with verse 19c, "and thus he purified all foods [καθαρίζων πάντα τὰ βρώματα]"? I would assert, as a matter of principle, that it would be a bad reading practice to allow one admittedly difficult and syntactically awkward phrase in the entire passage, not to say the entire corpus, to control our reading of that passage and render that which is coherent incoherent. Following this principle, I will offer

29. Collins, *Mark: A Commentary*, 350. Given, however, that she so precisely articulates this, I cannot understand how on the next page she approves of Claude Montefiore's statement that "the argument in vv. 6–8 is not compelling." It is as compelling as can be, as described above: Why, Pharisees, are you setting aside the commandments of God in favor of the commandments of humans—handwashings, vows—as Moses prophesied?!

three different explanations for the verset. These are, to be sure, attempts to deal with a problem, but involve in my opinion considerably less special pleading than the other view, which essentially argues that the whole pericope is a patchwork.

The most obvious way to deal with this problem (and perhaps the most valid) would be simply to remark that verse 19c is a gloss in the text. Verse 19c is a strange plant here, one that interrupts and disrupts the logic of the dispute and its development, renders Jesus a hypocrite (accusing the Pharisees of departing from Moses when he, himself, is about to completely abrogate "Moses" himself), and, moreover, concludes with a total non sequitur. It would hardly be a stretch to consider it a gloss that was added by a Gentile Christian voice committed to the notion of a dominical permission to eat all foods. I need not argue whether "Mark" was the one who added this strange gloss or not, but if some "Mark" or other, then surely not the "Mark" who authored the entire, perfectly coherent, consistent, and logical discourse of Jesus in the entire pericope. In other words, if one claims that this is a Marcan gloss, then one would have to concede that the bulk of Mark's Gospel was not written by "Mark," and "Mark" contradicts the bulk of Mark. Whoever this glossator was, it would seem that he might have been the author of two other glosses in the pericope, as well, namely, the verse explaining that the Pharisees and all of the *Ioudaioi* do not eat bread unless they wash their hands with a fist, and the gloss explaining the term *korban* in v. 11, all of which suggests an author writing for the purposes of a Gentile church, but not the author of the first Gospel.

A second possibility would be to insist that καθαρίζων means "to declare pure," not "to permit the forbidden." Just as in Hebrew there is a distinction between לטהר and להתיר, this reasoning would propose that the Greek here is the equivalent of the first Hebrew term and not the second. And thus he purified all foods, that is—against the Pharisees—he declared all foods not capable of rendering the body impure, in accord with "Moses" and not the Pharisaic "traditions of the Elders." This, in my opinion, is a more than acceptable interpretation of v. 19c. It is not about kashrut, but about purity and impurity. Usage of this verb in general throughout the Septuagint and other NT passages suggests strongly that it is cleansing from (or declaring clean from) ritual impurity that is the sense required here. Since only kosher foods can become impure, a Jew would never speak about declaring nonkosher foods pure or impure, but only kosher ones. This consequently has absolutely nothing to do with abrogating the Law; it is the finale of Jesus' answer as to why his disciples (and presumably Jesus himself) do not perform a ritual ablution of the hands prior to eating. Menahem Kister has made this point: "The assumption that Jesus' saying applies exclusively to defiled kosher food is quite natural: In a Jewish context the expression 'defiled food' often means defiled kosher food (compare אוכלים טמאים ['defiled food'] in rabbinic literature in the sense of defiled kosher food) simply because kosher food is the only food eaten by Jews."[30] In this fashion, v. 19c can be read as part and parcel of the entire narrative and polemical logic of the whole piece.

There remains a third possibility, one that I will propose in a highly tentative fashion and as highly speculative, as well, namely, that καθαρίζων does not mean here "declared all foods pure" but indeed *purified* all foods. Once again, it is vital to emphasize that the purity of foods and their permissibility are not at all the same halakhic system, and the failure of many interpreters of Mark, traditional and modern, to understand this engenders much confusion.[31] Given that in Zekharia 13:2, God promises that "on that day, I will remove the spirit of impurity from the land," this, on this reading, would be part and parcel of Jesus' claiming his messianic office. Even more explicitly, in the same prophet at 14:20–21, we read: "On that day there shall be inscribed on the bells of the horses, 'Holy to the LORD.' And the cooking pots in the house of the LORD shall be as holy as the bowls in front of the altar; and every cooking pot in Jerusalem and Judah shall be sacred to the LORD of hosts, so that all who sacrifice may come and use them to boil the flesh of the sacrifice. And

---

30. Kister, "Law, Morality and Rhetoric," 152.

31. Including the famous conundrum that if Jesus so clearly permitted all "unclean" foods, how is it that in Acts, Romans, Galatians, there is an "extended debate" about the dietary laws; Robert A. Guelich, *Mark 1–8:26*, Word Biblical Commentary, vol. 34A (Dallas, Tex.: Word Books, 1989), 375. The answer is simply that this pericope had nothing to do with the laws of Leviticus 11, which Jesus upheld (or at any rate, did not challenge). Guelich himself comes to such a conclusion, assigning it, however, to the primitive church and not to Jesus, as if that church had simply misread Jesus (Guelich, *Mark 1–8:26*, 376), thus, in my view, turning the history exactly upside down! Gundry is an excellent example of confusion on these matters. He fails even to understand the correct interventions of his colleagues in New Testament studies, such as Räisänen, owing to this confusion on his part. Jesus eating with Jewish sinners does not imply at all that he is eating nonkosher foods! See Peter J. Tomson, *Paul and the Jewish Law: Halakha in the Letters of the Apostle to the Gentiles*, vol. 1 of *Jewish Traditions in Early Christian Literature*, Compendia Rerum Iudaicarum Ad Novum Testamentum (Minneapolis, Minn.: Fortress Press, 1990), 240–42, who nails this, as well as marking the utter muddle that attends most scholarship on this passage. I thank Ishai Rosen-Zvi for bringing the Tomson text to my attention.

there shall no longer be traders in the house of the LORD of hosts on that day."[32] Just as Jesus, following this verse, overturned the tables of the traders in the Temple as a signifier of his messianic office, so, on this reading, would be his removing of the spirit of impurity from the land. This would make our text parallel to the passage in chapter 2, where Jesus claims to be Lord of the Sabbath in his messianic role of Son of Man, but does not say that the Sabbath is no longer to be observed.[33]

My inclination now is toward the first explanation, the text-critical one, but I assert strongly, in any case, that any interpretation that takes v. 19c at face value as indicating that the point of the pericope is to explain Jesus' total abrogation of food prohibitions is forced to engage in much more special pleading than the perhaps somewhat forced readings suggested here for 19c.

There are other—powerful—arguments that Jesus was not understood in any quarter of the earliest church as having abrogated the rules of kashrut. Neither of the other synoptics understood him thus, nor did the disciples in Acts who entered into the agreement on foods, nor those Christian martyrs of Lyons who bought their kosher meat from Jews, according to Eusebius.[34] Moreover, Origen himself read the entire controversy as being about Pharisaic innovation and not an alleged dominical defalcation from the Law of Moses. As remarked by Svartvik, "It is important to Origen that the pharisees and the scribes accuse the disciples before their teacher for transgressing not a commandment of God, but only one tradition of the Jewish elders."[35] Svartvik goes on, in the next several pages of his book, to demonstrate that according to Origen, it is only in apostolic times, after the death and resurrection of Jesus, that the kashrut laws were abrogated, that is, only the suffering of Jesus on the Cross redeemed even the disciples from the "curse of the Law." He, obviously, read the Marcan text more or less in accord with the reading suggested herein. Svartvik also shows there, however, that Origen is not entirely consistent in this reading and is led into self-contradiction when he tries to reconcile the meaning of the Gospel text that he has accurately perceived and his Chris-

32. This would seem to be the verse that lies behind Jesus' Temple-aktion as well.

33. Daniel Boyarin, "The Talmud in Jesus: How Much Jewishness in Mark's Christ?" in *Envisioning Judaism: Studies in Honor of Peter Schäfer on the Occasion of His Seventieth Birthday*, ed. Ra'anan Boustan et al. (Tübingen: Mohr Siebeck, 2013).

34. W. H. C. Frend, *Martyrdom and Persecution in the Early Church: A Study of a Conflict from the Maccabees to Donatus* (New York: New York University Press, 1967), 18.

35. Svartvik, *Mark and Mission*, 175.

tian antinomian practice: "Thus, in a fascinating way he [Origen] outlines a Law-abiding Jesus within the boundaries of first-century Judaism, but also a justification for Christians' not observing Jewish halakhah. He tried to have it both ways, but can one?"[36]

Perhaps, however, the most interesting ancient testimonium for a literal reading of the parable (prior to its figurative resolution) comes from Athanasius, who, in his letter to Amoun, refers to a group of Egyptian Christian ascetics who have understood Jesus' declaration that what comes out of the body renders one unclean as a literal affirmation by Jesus of the Law of Leviticus and Deuteronomy to the effect that emissions render a body unclean, in accord with the literal sense of the parable.[37] As Svartvik concludes with respect to the addressees of Athanasius's letter, "Hence, we have come across proof that a group of Christians at the time of Athanasius argued that the saying, actually, reinforced Levitical purity laws—in Lev 15:16 words for 'going out' are actually being used: יצא (MT) and ἐξέρχεσθαι (LXX)."[38] This interpretation of the literal level of the dominical parable is in complete accord with the interpretation of the pericope offered here. Athanasius, needless to say, disagreed with this interpretation, taking Jesus' saying to be *abrogating* Levitical prohibitions on purity and on forbidden foods, and not supporting them.

From beginning to end, this pericope is a controversy between Jesus and the Pharisees about how correctly to observe and defend Moses's Torah, not a controversy between Christians and Jews as to whether "Moses" is still applicable. When Jesus explains the "parable" to his uncomprehending disciples, it is clear what he is doing. He is showing how the literal force of the halakha itself should be read as indicating its spiritual or moral meaning.[39] Indeed, it is

36. Svartvik, *Mark and Mission*, 201. It should be remarked that Svartvik's book is a major contribution to our understanding, appallingly marred, however, by the absence of any signs, whatsoever, of editing. In particular, Svartvik seems to be laboring under the misapprehension that the term *pace* means "in accord with, following the view of" and not its virtual opposite. Anyone can err, especially when not writing in one's native tongue, but did not anyone read this manuscript before it was published?

37. Svartvik, *Mark and Mission*, 182. See David Brakke, *Athanasius and the Politics of Asceticism* (Oxford: Clarendon Press, 1995), 90–99; and L. W. Barnard, "The Letters of Athanasius to Amoun and Draconius," *Studia Patristica* 26 (1993): 354–59; Tim Vivian, "'Everything Made by God Is Good': A Letter from Saint Athanasius to the Monk Amoun," *Église et théologie* 24 (1993): 75–108.

38. Svartvik, *Mark and Mission*, 182–83.

39. In chapter 2, there is also a passage that is, I think, illuminated by such a perspective. In vv. 18–22, some people wonder why other pietists (the disciples of John and the Pharisees) engage in fasting practices, while the disciples of Jesus do not. Jesus answers that they may not fast in the presence of the bridegroom, which is clearly a halakhic statement interpreted spiritually, as it were, to refer to the divine

not what goes into the mouth that renders one impure, but the impure intentions of a heart, as *signified* by the halakhic fact that things that go out of the body cause impurity. All of the practices to which Jesus refers as Pharisaic, the handwashing, the washing of vessels, all are connected with the particular traditions of the Pharisees regarding the encroachment of impure foods on the purity of the body. Those Pharisees who believe that impurity (literal, halakhic impurity) comes from without (or worse, add such impurity to the Torah's) do not comprehend (as, at first, neither do the disciples) what the spiritual import of the Torah's rule about impurity coming from within truly is. It follows from this that neither Jesus nor the Evangelist held, suggested, or implied that the new Jesus movement involved a rejection of traditional Jewish practices around eating, (Moses's Torah),[40] nor that it constituted a step out to form a new "religion." Mark's Jesus is defending the sanctity of the Law and its ultimate meaningfulness, not attacking them.

Menahem Kister, in the paper I have been citing here, considerably advanced the discourse on this text. Consistent with the approach of his great teacher, David Flusser, he argues for a genuinely Jewish substratum in the Gospel that has been reframed by the Evangelist himself in producing the antinomian Christian text. In my view, in contrast, the Gospel itself remains "Jewish," being Christianized, as it were, only in the hands of its Gentile readership. As I have remarked, Kister saw (even before Fürstenberg) that the first half of Jesus' quoted statement in v. 15a is a statement of the Torah's law—namely, that what goes into the body does not render it impure—arguing explicitly, however, that 15b is a moral statement and not a continuation of the literal halakhic point. (Here is where Fürstenberg has moved beyond Kister in my view.) For Kister, moreover, this is essentially a rhetorical artifice on the part of Jesus: "It appears that in these cases Jesus used a rhetorical device, attract-

---

Bridegroom of Israel. As Collins makes clear, this is another indirect claim on Jesus' part to be divine (Collins, *Mark: A Commentary*, 199). This is, by the way, entirely reminiscent of the way the Rabbis themselves read the purity system, seeing the impurities as consequences and symbols of moral fault: thus leprosy for slander. See, too, "In talmudic literature there are *ethical* sayings based on purity laws," Kister, "Law, Morality and Rhetoric," 149.

40. *Pace* John C. Poirier, "Why Did the Pharisees Wash Their Hands?" *Journal of Jewish Studies* 47 (1996): 226n43, a paper that in other ways has moved this discourse forward considerably. Poirier seems clearly correct in his argument against the commonly held position that the Pharisaic commitment to purity rules was understood as the application of priestly rules to eating in general. See also Thomas Kazen, *Jesus and Purity Halakhah: Was Jesus Indifferent to Impurity?* (Stockholm: Almqvist & Wiksell, 2002), 86, already cited by both Fürstenberg and Kister, "Law, Morality and Rhetoric."

ing the attention of his audience by raising what seemed to be a controversial halakhic issue, while his real concern was moral (although not antihalakic; compare Matt. 23:24)."[41] Kister further remarks that such an ethical extension of a point about purity is not at all unparalleled in other Jewish writings, from the Prophets to the rabbinical texts. He cites other examples of verses in which the first clause is halakhic and the second metaphorical or moral in its intent. This is fine as far as it goes and may very well be compelling in other cases that Kister cites.[42] In any case, it is a distinct improvement over the standard view that sees v. 15a as an attack on and not an assertion of "Moses."

I think I can best articulate my difference from Kister by quoting his conclusion at some length and then commenting on it:

The first half of Jesus' saying is based, then, on halakhic perception, whereas in the second half there is a shift to emphasize moral defilement, precisely in the same rhetorical manner as in the sayings of Jesus discussed earlier. Jesus criticizes the Pharisees for being concerned with problems of food purity, important as they might be, and less concerned (in his view) with moral purity, which is "the weightier matter of law." He makes his point with great wit, by using a halakhic statement, that no (kosher) food that has become impure can defile a man, at least according to the Torah as interpreted by the rabbis, and probably by their predecessors, the Pharisees. But, Jesus argues, moral impurity can, on another level, defile a man. This saying is not antinomistic, neither is it necessarily antihalakhic. Jesus severely criticizes the religious priorities of his Pharisaic opponents, using in his argument "rabbinic niceties" as a rhetorical device. Transmitted in a different, nonhalakhic and sometimes antinomisticcontext, this saying came to be the most radical antinomistic saying in the Synoptic Gospels.[43]

I differ with this statement of Kister's on two counts: his interpretation of Jesus' allegedly actual words and his interpretation of what the Gospel has done to them here.

For Kister, Jesus' invocation of the Law is not entirely in good faith, being only an ironic rhetorical ploy—to get his audience's attention, as it were. Jesus' original statement, while not antinomian, puts the Law in its place, that

---

41. Kister, "Law, Morality and Rhetoric," 149.

42. My analysis of the statement about straining out gnats while swallowing elephants would differ from Kister's; he gives it as an example in which the first stich is literal and halakhic while the second is "moral." In my view, in contrast, we have a single metaphor built on the allusion to the halakhic point about straining out gnats. In other words, both halves of the sentence perform the same figurative work. Be that as it may, I am arguing here that Mark 7:15 works quite differently.

43. Kister, "Law, Morality and Rhetoric," 153–54.

is, in a place decidedly inferior to some general ethical principles. After invoking the correct halakhic dictum that nothing that goes into the mouth makes one impure, Jesus immediately proceeds to its antithesis, that only immoral behavior that goes out from a person makes him or her impure. This is, in itself, a strange rhetoric, a thesis that is physical and literal and an antithesis that functions on an entirely different linguistic level. This is the reason that Fürstenberg's interpretation, that Jesus' statement was literal in both its thesis and antithesis, seems to me far preferable, especially since—as Matthew Henry already had seen centuries ago—it matches perfectly the actual purity law of the Torah. Jesus, on this level, would be countering the Pharisees' extensions of the Law with an argument from Moses, precisely and in good faith, just as is his argument against them vis-à-vis feeding parents.

Throughout the pericope, Jesus' argument against the Pharisees has been that they change the Torah's rulings ("Moses") in the name of their "tradition of the Elders." The interpretation that I have offered maintains that theme right through verses 15–17, explaining also why it is so crucial to observe the Law as written and not add to it what the later Rabbis would call "fences around it." The Law is a parable, and if you don't tell the story correctly, you cannot understand or interpret the parable properly. On the other hand, if Jesus intended, as Kister holds, to be merely rhetorically making a homiletic point that is not actually dependent logically on the claim that the Torah literally denies impurity from outside, his argument against the Pharisees is weakened considerably. Why not wash one's hands as well, as an indication of the need for moral purity? This objection is obviated on the usual Christianizing reading whereby Jesus is setting aside any rules about eating altogether, but then Jesus' claim against the Pharisees that they substitute human traditions for God's Law would be very nearly hypocrisy, or surely sophistry, in its bad faith.[44] This problem is solved on my interpretation that Jesus rejects the handwashing, a human tradition, as blurring or obscuring the ethical symbolism of the Torah's rule.[45] Finally, Kister's reading leaves unsolved the very

44. Tomson, in *Paul and the Jewish Law*, 241, argues correctly that it is impossible to imagine Jesus' defending the Torah from Pharisaic innovation in the same breath in which he will throw it all away!

45. I have argued elsewhere that Mark's πυγμῇ, "with the fist," indicates a great deal of intimate familiarity with Jewish practice. I have since noted that Martin Hengel, "Mc 7,3 *pugme*: Die Geschichte einer exegetischen Aproie und der Versuch ihrer Lösung," *ZNW* 60 (1969): 182–98, had preceded me here.

problem that I have set out to solve with my interpretation, namely, why this is called a parable. What comes out of the person literally confers ritual impurity in order to teach us symbolically that what comes out from the heart and mouth confers moral impurity. That is the parable. On these several grounds, then, I would deem preferable the interpretation that Jesus' statement is not only rhetorical, but logical, and insists on both a literal and moral reading of the Torah at once.

According to this reading, the import of the Marcan passage is substantially the same as the arguably more explicit parallel in Matthew 15:

Then Pharisees and scribes came to Jesus from Jerusalem and said, "Why do your disciples break the tradition of the elders? For they do not wash their hands before they eat." He answered them, "And why do you break the commandment of God for the sake of your tradition? For God said, 'Honor your father and your mother,' and, 'Whoever speaks evil of father or mother must surely die.' But you say that whoever tells father or mother, 'Whatever support you might have had from me is given to God,' then that person need not honor the father. So, for the sake of your tradition, you make void the word of God. You hypocrites! Isaiah prophesied rightly about you when he said: 'This people honors me with their lips, but their hearts are far from me; in vain do they worship me, teaching human precepts as doctrines.'" Then he called the crowd to him and said to them, "Listen and understand: it is not what goes into the mouth that defiles a person, but it is what comes out of the mouth that defiles." Then the disciples approached and said to him, "Do you know that the Pharisees took offense when they heard what you said?" He answered, "Every plant that my heavenly Father has not planted will be uprooted. Let them alone; they are blind guides of the blind. And if one blind person guides another, both will fall into a pit." But Peter said to him, "Explain this parable to us." Then he said, "Are you also still without understanding? Do you not see that whatever goes into the mouth enters the stomach, and goes out into the sewer? But what comes out of the mouth proceeds from the heart, and this is what defiles. For out of the heart come evil intentions, murder, adultery, fornication, theft, false witness, slander. These are what defile a person, but to eat with unwashed hands does not defile." (Mt 15:1–20)

It will be seen that given my interpretation of Mark 7, the Matthean version is a close match for it and not a "Judaizing" revision. Here there may be no question at all that the issue is purity rules (the washing of hands) and not kashrut: Jesus explicitly concludes: "These are what defile a person, but to eat with unwashed hands does not defile." In one respect, however, on the reading offered here, the reading of Mark is superior to the reading of Matthew, for by substituting "what comes out of the mouth" for what comes out of the person, Matthew has obscured the parable (one would imagine not deliberately, but through his own misunderstanding).[46] If my interpretation of Mark is acceptable, however, even that tampering has not succeeded in eradicating its meaning for those who have ears to hear. It is historically perverse, in my view, to assume that the Mark that Matthew read incorporated a dominical rejection of the food laws of the Torah that Matthew then neutralized for his own "Judaizing" purposes. Just saying it this way indicates, I think, how tendentious such a position is, how predetermined by later Christian theology, itself inflected by Paul.

It is here that we must look at the Pauline text. First of all, Paul's own reading of the sign "Moses" is in direct contrast to that of Mark. Where in Mark, Jesus defends Moses, the author, the text, and its literal meaning against the Pharisees, for Paul, "Moses" is a negative sign:

Indeed, what once had glory has lost its glory because of the greater glory; for if what was set aside came through glory, much more has the permanent come in glory! Since, then, we have such a hope, we act with great boldness, not like Moses, who put a veil over his face to keep the people of Israel from gazing at the end of the glory that was being set aside. But their minds were hardened. Indeed, to this very day, when they hear the reading of the old covenant, that same veil is still there, since only in Christ is it set aside. Indeed, to this very day whenever Moses is read, a veil lies over their minds; but when one turns to the Lord, the veil is removed. Now the Lord is the Spirit, and where the Spirit of the Lord is, there is freedom. And all of us, with unveiled faces, seeing the glory of the Lord as though reflected in a mirror, are being transformed into the same image from one degree of glory to another; for this comes from the Lord, the Spirit. (2 Corinthians 3:10–18)

For Paul's supersessionist—by which I do *not* mean anti-Judaic but anti-Mosaic—theology, Moses is a dead letter; whenever Moses is read, the same veil is there. Nothing could be further than this from Marcan Jesus' impassioned defense of Moses against Pharisaic *rejection* of Moses in the name of their oral traditions. Not surprisingly, it is in Paul that we find a reading of Jesus (Romans 14) that interprets him as setting Moses aside and, apparent-

46. This would not be the only place in which canonical Matthew is less conversant with Pharisaic, or Jewish, usage than Mark. See Daniel Boyarin, "'After the Sabbath, at the Moment When the First Day Was about to Shine,' (Matt. 28:1)—Once More Into the Crux," *Journal of Theological Studies* 52, no. 2 (2001): 678–88.

ly, declaring all foods acceptable, although it must be also mentioned that for Paul, too, the word used is "pure" and not a Greek term for "acceptable" or "permitted,"[47] thus weakening somewhat the lexical argument for my interpretation. Nonetheless, and *pace* Marcus,[48] I continue to insist that this reading of Mark's chapter is the one that makes best sense of the text as a whole, because, as said before, it does not render Jesus a hypocrite, and because the argument against the Pharisees is its theme from beginning to end. Nor is it a trivial matter, again *pace* Marcus ("the question throughout the chapter is only the technical one of whether or not impurity"), it goes to the very heart of the nature of Torah and its spiritual and ethical meanings and the ways that the Pharisees, in the view of Mark's Jesus, destroy them.[49] Marcus is incorrect in asserting that the Torah conflates the question of the purity of foods with that of whether or not they may be eaten.[50] The correct generalization is that the Torah (and indeed the Rabbis) occasionally uses the terms "pure" and "impure" to mean "kosher" and "not kosher"; the two systems remain absolutely distinct, nonetheless. Therefore, if "The Marcan Jesus says that *all* foods are pure, that *nothing* from outside of a person can pollute him—and *prima facie* that would seem to include non-kosher foods"—then he is saying no more than the Torah itself says, which is exactly my point.[51] No one had claimed differently, except apparently the Pharisees in their demand that people must pu-

47. Vis-à-vis the alleged Lukan parallel in Acts 10:34 ff., it seems clear to me that the issue is not, in fact, foods, nor is Jesus even portrayed as having permitted forbidden foods, but that the animals to be eaten (or not) are symbols of the Gentiles to be incorporated into salvation or not. As Randel Helms has argued persuasively—in my view—this "eating" of forbidden foods is a symbolic act on the order of God's demands of the prophets, especially Ezekiel, that they engage in strange eating practices as symbolic actions; Randel Helms, *Gospel Fictions* (Buffalo, N.Y.: Prometheus Books, 1988), 21. This suggests, as I have opined, that the issue of forbidden foods is not the point here; indeed, if Jesus had permitted such foods, then the symbolic act would be meaningless. Cf. Svartvik, *Mark and Mission*, 118–19, whose view is somewhat different from mine and also possible.

48. Joel Marcus, "Mark—Interpreter of Paul," in *Mark and Paul. Part II, For and Against Pauline Influence on Mark: Comparative Essays*, ed. Eve-Marie Becker, Troels Engberg-Pedersen, and Mogens Müller (Berlin: De Gruyter, 2014), 29–49. This is a reprint of Marcus's original essay, with a five-page appendix dedicated to the question of Mark 7 and Paul in response to my earlier publication.

49. I have not "unwittingly supplied an accurate description of Matthew's version of the story rather than Mark's" (Marcus, "Mark—Interpreter of Paul," 48): I have knowingly asserted that Matthew's version is substantially identical to Mark's when Mark's is read well.

50. Marcus, "Mark—Interpreter of Paul," 48.

51. This is where Kasper Bro Larsen, "Mark 7:1–23: A Pauline Halakah," in *Mark and Paul. Part II, For and Against Pauline Influence on Mark*, ed. Eve-Marie Becker, Troels Engberg-Pedersen, and Mogens Müller (Berlin: De Gruyter, 2014), 170, falters, in my opinion, assuming as well that in general the eating of nonkosher food defiles a person.

rify their hands before eating. This does not state *prima facie* or according to any other face that it is *permitted* to eat nonkosher foods. Finally, whether or not I am correct in the interpretation of Mark 7:19c, I remain adamant that to render the entire pericope (and Jesus himself) incoherent, illogical, and hypocritical for the sake of half of one verse, which might very well be a Pauline-inflected gloss, is profoundly erroneous methodologically.

The historical stakes are high. Robert H. Gundry writes openly that since Mark's is the earliest Palestinian witness to Jesus: "Mark, our earliest gospel, offers a more reliable standard; and it says that Jesus abrogated laws of food and purity and violated the Sabbath."[52] While Kister's reading certainly leads to the conclusion that the historical Jesus did not intend in any way through his logion to displace the Torah's Law, he, nonetheless, holds that such was indeed the interpretation given to the logion by Mark. I believe that the exact opposite is the case, claiming that in Mark, as well, when the passage is read as a whole, there is no reason at all to deem Jesus as being portrayed as abrogating the Law, but rather, doing exactly what he claims to be doing, defending Moses from the distortions and abrogations of the Law allegedly perpetrated by the Pharisees. This is, in Mark, Jesus and Moses against the Pharisees, not, as in Paul, Jesus against Moses. Jesus taught the Law, not fought the Law. According to the view that I offer here, Mark is no more antinomian than the alleged historical Jesus himself.[53]

If we take seriously the notion that Jesus' statement about purity and impurity means what it says and simply states what the Torah means, then it is clear that Jesus' commitment to Moses is not put into question by Mark. R. T. France considers that the conclusion that Jesus permitted all nonkosher foods is "a natural, indeed inevitable, deduction from the principle stated by Jesus in v. 15," and then refers to "the revolutionary significance of this declaration, and its relevance to the relations between Jews and Gentiles in the early years of the Christian movement."[54] In part relying on France's own insight above that we have here a parable, I hope to have shown that the revolutionary nature of the alleged declaration is far, far from a natural or an inevitable deduction, once we understand the import of Jesus' parable, the declaration of a literal

52. Gundry, *Mark: A Commentary on His Apology for the Cross*, 370.

53. I have treated the other case of an alleged break with the Law on the part of Jesus (Mark 2:10 on the Sabbath)—and again in disagreement with Kister—in another place.

54. France, *The Gospel of Mark: A Commentary on the Greek Text*, 292.

law with a figurative meaning. I agree with France that this matter of interpretation has enormous salience for the relations between Jews and Gentiles in
the so-called early church. The controversy here has little to do with the spe-
cifics of halakha, but, just as it says, with Pharisaic mutations of Moses in the
name of their tradition of the Elders, nothing less and nothing more. Mark
cannot be used, therefore, as a Gospel authorization for the abandonment of
kashrut on the part of the church. On this reading, Matthew is not a backslid-
ing Judaizer, but an exponent of the original meaning of his Marcan source.[55]

If, however, the lines between the literal and the figurative are blurred and
if, already in v. 15, Jesus is making a straightforward allegedly Christianizing
theological homiletical case, for some reason misunderstood as a parable by
his idiot disciples, then the pericope becomes available to the church as an authorization for the claim that Jesus meant that no foods are forbidden, and
then v. 19 is, of course, read to fit, as well. Another way of saying this would be
that in order to *understand* the parable and not pallidly interpret it as a *sort-
of* parable, something maybe a bit like a parable, or alternatively to ascribe its
parabolic nature to a mistake on the part of the foolish disciples, one would
have to admit that Jesus stood up for the literal sense of the Law, just as Leviticus and Deuteronomy prescribe. Moreover, one would have to be prepared
to recognize that Mark 7 is not a dominical authorization for the eating of
ham; indeed, that even Marcan Jesus kept kosher. When Jesus says, "Hear me
all of you, and understand" that's precisely what he is saying: This is the literal
meaning of the Torah, which the Pharisees have changed, and this literal sense
has a deeper, figurative meaning, as well; the literal meaning is thus asserted by
Jesus, not denied. If you mess with the literal law, then you have messed with
its parabolic meaning, as well. If we read the narrative Paulistically, the ele-
gance of the pericope is entirely undone.

The bottom line of my reading here is that Mark may be very Pauline in

---

55. *Pace*, for instance, Joel Marcus, *Mark 1–8: A New Translation with Introduction and Commentary* (New York: Doubleday, 2000), 447, who understands Mark's Jesus to have abrogated all rules about
forbidden foods and then, "Instead in his [Matthew's] narrative Jesus limits the implications of the saying to the conclusion that eating with unwashed hands does not defile a person. This toning down may
reflect Matthew's Law-observant, Christian Jewish perspective." In my view, Mark's Jesus was just as
law-abiding as Matthew's, and Matthew has read Mark well. On the other hand, and almost paradoxi-
cally, Matthew, by shifting Mark's "into the person" and "out of the person" to "into the mouth" and "out
of the mouth," seems to be understanding v. 15 (of the Marcan version) as already the moral statement
and not a statement of the halakha, which would explain also why there is no Matthean parallel of v. 16.

certain aspects of his soteriological thought, focusing, for instance, on the crucifixion more intensely than other early followers of Jesus, but on the question of the meaning of "Moses" and the alimentary canon in the new dispensation, Mark's Jesus, and thus Mark himself (save perhaps the glossator at 7:19c, but nothing else in the text), could not be more different from Paul.

Dulcinea Boesenberg

---

2. LUKE'S NARRATIVE CLAIM
ON MOSES, THE PERSECUTED
PROPHET

This paper will examine two passages from Acts to demonstrate that Luke has reconstructed the figure of Moses in an attempt to describe the relation of earliest Christianity to the people of Israel and the scriptural tradition. In Acts 3, Luke reconfigures the words of Moses in Deuteronomy to present Moses as saying that those who do not listen to Jesus are cut off from Israel, and in Acts 7, Luke reshapes the Exodus narrative to present Moses as a prophet rejected by his own people. Together, these two creative moves divide Moses both from his contemporary Israelites and from the nonbelieving Jews within the narrative world of Acts. Luke's presentation of Moses in Acts draws a boundary separating those Jews who follow Jesus, and thus Moses, from those who do not.

Acts 3: Whoever Does Not Listen to That Prophet
Will Be Cut Off from the People

In Acts 3:22–23, Peter reformulates Moses's own words in order to present Moses as saying that those who do not listen to Jesus, the prophet like Moses, will be cut off from Israel. In Acts 3, Peter heals a crippled man, drawing a large crowd. Peter capitalizes on this attention by delivering a speech about Jesus, the one whom the Jews[1] "rejected (ἠρνήσασθε)" (3:13 and 3:14), but "whom God raised from the dead (ὃν θεὸς ἤγειρεν ἐκ νεκρῶν)" (3:15). Having thus identified Jesus, Peter provides evidence that God's raising of Jesus was foretold: "Moses said, 'The Lord your God will raise up for you from your own people a prophet like me. You must listen to everything he says to you. And it will be that everyone who does not listen to that prophet will be utterly rooted out of the people'" (3:22–23).[2] Here in Acts 3:22–23, Peter condenses Dt 18:15–19 and combines it with a common Pentateuchal consequence for disobedience to the law, so that Luke does not cite a single text directly from the Septuagint but has essentially created his own prophecy.[3]

Acts 3:22 and Deuteronomy 18:15, 18

In Dt 18:15, Moses says to the people Israel, "The Lord your God will raise up for you from your own people a prophet like me. You must listen to him." Peter's statement in Acts 3:22 is very similar to this, though there are some minor differences in vocabulary and word order.

Both texts include the words or phrases προφήτην, ἐκ τῶν ἀδελφῶν, ὡς ἐμὲ, ἀναστήσει, κύριος ὁ θεός, and αὐτοῦ ἀκούσεσθε, though in differing orders. As is demonstrated by table 2-1, the only words in Dt 18:15 that do not appear in Luke's text are the three second singular pronouns: σου, σοι, and σου.[4] Instead, Luke uses three second person plural pronouns: ὑμῖν, ὑμῶν, and ὑμῶν.

Luke's use of plural pronouns in his citation likely results from conflat-

1. The subject of the verb ἠρνήσασθε is not "Jews" but "you." Because, at this point in the narrative of Acts, the apostles are preaching the news of Jesus only to other Jews, it is clear that Luke presents Peter as accusing the Jews of rejecting Jesus.

2. Luke is one of many authors who interprets Dt 18:15–18 as a prophecy of a future prophet. See 1 Macc 4:46; 14:41; 1QS 9.9–11; and 4Q175. In the Gospel of John (1:21; 4:19; 6:14; and 7:40) and the Testaments of the Twelve Patriarchs (T. Benj. 9:3–5 and T. Levi 8:11–15), the coming prophet is identified with Jesus. On the expectation of a coming prophet in John, see Wayne A. Meeks, The Prophet-King: Moses Traditions and the Johannine Christology (Leiden: Brill, 1967), 21–57.

3. The author of Luke-Acts, whom I refer to as Luke, for simplicity, uses the masculine participle παρηκολουθηκότι in describing his preparation for writing (Luke 1:3). See Mary Rose D'Angelo, "Women in Luke-Acts: A Redactional View," Journal of Biblical Literature 109 (1990): 443. Given Luke's knowledge of Greek, his regular citation of the Septuagint in preserved versions, and his dependence (in some places—e.g., Acts 15:16–17) on the Septuagint (hereafter LXX) rather than on the Masoretic Text (hereafter MT), I assume that Luke is working with a Greek version of the text, comparable to LXX. LXX contains, albeit in Greek translation, elements of the Hebrew legacy not included in the later Rabbinic MT (which is entirely in Hebrew and Aramaic).

4. These three second singular pronouns are also present in the MT. The verse is not preserved at Qumran.

TABLE 2-1. COMPARISON OF ACTS 3:22 AND DEUTERONOMY 18:15

Acts 3:22	Deuteronomy 18:15
Μωϋσῆς μὲν εἶπεν ὅτι	
προφήτην ὑμῖν <u>ἀναστήσει κύριος ὁ θεὸς</u> ὑμῶν	<u>προφήτην ἐκ τῶν ἀδελφῶν</u> σου <u>ὡς ἐμὲ ἀναστήσει</u>
<u>ἐκ τῶν ἀδελφῶν</u> ὑμῶν <u>ὡς ἐμέ·</u>	σοι <u>κύριος ὁ θεός</u> σου,
<u>αὐτοῦ ἀκούσεσθε</u>	<u>αὐτοῦ ἀκούσεσθε.</u>
κατὰ πάντα ὅσα ἂν λαλήσῃ πρὸς ὑμᾶς.	

TABLE 2-2. COMPARISON OF ACTS 3:22 AND DEUTERONOMY 18:18

Acts 3:22	Deuteronomy 18:18
Μωϋσῆς μὲν εἶπεν ὅτι	
<u>προφήτην</u> ὑμῖν <u>ἀναστήσει</u> κύριος ὁ θεὸς ὑμῶν	<u>προφήτην ἀναστήσω</u> αὐτοῖς
<u>ἐκ τῶν ἀδελφῶν</u> ὑμῶν <u>ὡς ἐμέ·</u>	<u>ἐκ τῶν ἀδελφῶν</u> αὐτῶν ὥσπερ σὲ
αὐτοῦ ἀκούσεσθε κατὰ πάντα ὅσα	καὶ δώσω τὸ ῥῆμά μου ἐν τῷ στόματι αὐτοῦ
ἂν <u>λαλήσῃ</u> πρὸς ὑμᾶς.	καὶ <u>λαλήσει</u> αὐτοῖς καθότι ἂν ἐντείλωμαι αὐτῷ.·

ing Dt 18:15 with 18:18 (see table 2-2). In Dt 18:15, Moses declares to Israel, "The Lord your God will raise up for you [σοι] from your own [σου] people a prophet like me." In Dt 18:18, the promise is repeated with the Lord as the speaker and Moses as the addressee. Here the pronouns are third person plural: God says to Moses, "I will raise up for them [αὐτοῖς] a prophet like you from their own [αὐτῶν] people." Luke's citation in Acts 3:22 is influenced by the second person pronouns of Dt 18:15 and the plural pronouns of Dt 18:18. In Acts 3:22, Luke seems to be condensing Dt 18:15–18, eliminating verses 16–17, which recall the people's fear at hearing directly from God—recorded in Dt 5:22–29 (cf. Ex 20:18–21)—and focusing on the promise of a prophet.

While Luke appears to have borrowed nearly all of his vocabulary from Dt 18:15, it seems that his word order is influenced by Dt 18:18. Further, in Dt 18:18, unlike in 18:15, God's action of raising up (ἀναστήσω) the prophet is placed near the beginning of the verse. Luke likewise places the verb ἀναστήσει early in his citation, capitalizing on the Septuagint's word choice and emphasizing the raising up of the prophet like Moses.

Luke presents the prophecy of Dt 18:15 as uniquely and doubly fulfilled in Jesus, the only prophet who is not only sent by God to the people, but also literally raised from the dead by God. The fulfillment of this promise is echoed in the last, climactic sentence of Peter's speech: "God, having raised up [ἀπέστειλεν] his servant, sent him first for you" (Acts 3:26). Peter's statement is understood: the priests, temple captain, and Sadducees are annoyed because the disciples "proclaim in Jesus the resurrection of the dead" (4:2).

Acts 3:22b–23, Deuteronomy 18:19, and ἐξολεθρευθήσεται

Luke continues his "citation" of Moses in Acts 3:22b–23: "You must listen to everything he says to you. And it will be that everyone [πᾶσα ψυχὴ] who does not listen to that prophet will be utterly rooted out [ἐξολεθρευθήσεται] of the people." Some of the vocabulary in this verse matches what is found in Dt 18:19, which reads, "And the person who does not listen to whatever the prophet says in my name, I will exact vengeance from him" (table 2-3).

Both Deuteronomy and Acts use ἐὰν μὴ ἀκούσῃ to describe the punishable act. Both use the noun προφήτης, though in different cases because of their different constructions, to identify the person to whom the hearers should listen. Additionally, both books use a relative clause with the verb λαλέω in the aorist subjunctive. In Dt 18:19, the hearers are warned against not listening to ὅσα ἐὰν λαλήσῃ, while in Acts 3:22, the crowd of Israelites is commanded to listen to ὅσα ἂν λαλήσῃ.

However, there is some vocabulary in Acts 3:23, which, while conveying an idea similar to that in Dt 18:19, is not present in that verse from Deuteronomy, but is present elsewhere in the LXX Pentateuch. In Acts 3:23, Moses is quoted as saying, "ἔσται δὲ πᾶσα ψυχὴ ἥτις ἐὰν μὴ ἀκούσῃ τοῦ προφήτου ἐκείνου ἐξολεθρευθήσεται ἐκ τοῦ λαοῦ." Similar constructions are commonly used in the Pentateuch to describe what will happen to the soul (ψυχή) who does or does not do what is required by the law: the soul will be cut off (ἐξολεθρευθήσεται) from its people (λαός), its kin, or Israel.[5]

Starting from the beginning of the Pentateuch, this construction first appears in Genesis 17:14. In establishing the covenant with Abraham, God announces the law of circumcision, and concludes by saying, "As for an uncircumcised male, who is not circumcised in the flesh of his foreskin on the

---

5. Mishnah Kerithoth 1.1 lists thirty-six acts for which a person is cut off (כרת).

TABLE 2-3. COMPARISON OF ACTS 3:22B–23 AND DEUTERONOMY 18:19

Acts 3:22b–23	Deuteronomy 18:19
αὐτοῦ ἀκούσεσθε κατὰ πάντα ὅσα ἂν λαλήσῃ πρὸς ὑμᾶς.	
ἔσται δὲ πᾶσα ψυχὴ ἥτις ἐὰν μὴ ἀκούσῃ	καὶ ὁ ἄνθρωπος, ὃς ἐὰν μὴ ἀκούσῃ
	ὅσα ἐὰν λαλήσῃ
τοῦ προφήτ ου ἐκείνου ἐξολεθρευθήσεται ἐκ τοῦ λαοῦ.	ὁ προφήτης ἐπὶ τῷ ὀνόματί μου, ἐγὼ ἐκδικήσω ἐξ αὐτοῦ.

TABLE 2-4. COMPARISON OF ACTS 3:23 AND EXODUS 31:14B

Acts 3:23	Exodus 31:14b
ἔσται δὲ πᾶσα ψυχὴ ἥτις ἐὰν μὴ ἀκούσῃ τοῦ	πᾶς, ὃς ποιήσει ἐν αὐτῷ ἔργον,
προφήτου ἐκείνου ἐξολεθρευθήσεται	ἐξολεθρευθήσεται ἡ ψυχὴ ἐκείνη
ἐκ τοῦ λαοῦ.	ἐκ μέσου τοῦ λαοῦ αὐτοῦ.

eighth day, that soul (ψυχὴ) will be utterly rooted out (ἐξολεθρευθήσεται) of its kin, for he scattered my covenant."

A similar construction appears four times in Exodus, twice in reference to Passover (12:15, 19), once concerning sacrificing to other gods (22:20), and once concerning the sabbath (31:14). This final occurrence is most similar to Acts 3:23: the Lord tells Moses, "Everyone who does work on it, that soul will be utterly rooted out from the midst of his people" (Ex 31:14b) (table 2-4).

Not surprisingly, this legal construction appears most frequently in Leviticus, where it occurs nine times. The construction describes what will happen to someone who slaughters an animal somewhere other than at the door to the tent of witness (17:4, 9), who eats blood (17:14), engages in sexual misconduct (18:29; 20:17, 18), eats a sacrifice of deliverance on the third day (19:8), comes near to sacred items (22:3), or does not observe the Day of Atonement (23:29). The construction and vocabulary of this final verse is most similar to Acts 3:23. According to Leviticus 23:29, "Every soul that does not humble itself on that day will be utterly rooted out of its people." Two phrases from this verse have parallels in Luke's account: πᾶσα ψυχὴ ἥτις and ἐξολεθρευθήσεται ἐκ τοῦ λαοῦ (table 2-5).

The construction is found three times in Numbers. The one who does not

TABLE 2-5. COMPARISON OF ACTS 3:23 AND LEVITICUS 23:29

Acts 3:23	Leviticus 23:29
ἔσται δὲ <u>πᾶσα ψυχὴ ἥτις ἐὰν μὴ ἀκούσῃ</u> τοῦ προφήτου ἐκείνου	<u>πᾶσα ψυχή, ἥτις μὴ</u> ταπεινωθήσεται ἐν αὐτῇ τῇ ἡμέρᾳ ταύτῃ,
<u>ἐξολεθρευθήσεται ἐκ τοῦ λαοῦ.</u>	<u>ἐξολεθρευθήσεται ἐκ τοῦ λαοῦ</u> αὐτῆς.

observe the Passover, even though he is not on a journey (9:13), the one who intentionally sins (15:30), and the one who is not purified after contamination from a corpse (19:20) will be cut off from the people.

The verb ἐξολεθρεύειν also occurs in Deuteronomy, but it does not appear in this same construction. Often the verb describes what God will do to the inhabitants of the land. Even when it is the Israelites who will be destroyed, the construction is different: the verb is active rather than passive, it is never a "soul" that is destroyed, and the Israelites are not cut off "from the people."

While Luke's language is closest to Leviticus 23:29 and also quite similar to Exodus 31:14, it is unlikely that he was drawing vocabulary from either of these verses in particular.[6] Rather, Luke uses a common construction to describe what happens to someone who does not observe the specific prescriptions of Moses. Luke applies this punishment to the one who does not listen to the prophet like Moses. Perhaps Luke imagines that if one is cut off from the people for not observing the law of Moses, then all the more should this happen to one who does not listen to the prophet like Moses.[7]

By appending this consequence to the act from Dt 18:19, Luke replaces an unspecified sentence ("I will exact vengeance") with a particular and harsh one ("will be utterly rooted out of the people"). According to Luke, Moses himself claimed that those Jews who do not listen to Jesus, the prophet like

6. Of Acts 3:22–23, Richard F. Zehnle writes, "Deut 18:15, 19 is combined with Lev. 23:29"; see *Peter's Pentecost Discourse: Tradition and Lukan Reinterpretation in Peter's Speeches of Acts 2 and 3* (Nashville, Tenn.: Abingdon, 1971), 86. Similarly, Hans Conzelmann states without explanation, "Here scriptural proof is presented from Deut 18:15, 18–19 and Lev 23:29"; *Acts of the Apostles* (Philadelphia: Fortress Press, 1987), 29. C. K. Barrett claims that "in ἐξολεθρευθήσεται ἐκ τοῦ λαοῦ Luke is using the language of Lev. 23.29"; *The Acts of the Apostles* (Edinburgh: T&T Clark, 1994), 1:209. Richard I. Pervo follows Barrett here; see *Acts: A Commentary*, (Minneapolis, Minn.: Fortress Press, 2009), 109. I argue that this language is not unique to Lev 23:29.

7. In Rabbinic exegesis, this method of reasoning is referred to as *qol va-homer*. It is possible that Luke is not responsible for the citation preserved in Acts 3:23, but has inherited it from an earlier exegete.

Moses, will be cut off from the people.[8] Obedience to Jesus is directly connected to membership in the people of God.

Defining Israel

By creatively incorporating into the promise of Deuteronomy 18 the threat of being cut out of Israel, Luke uses the figure of Moses to redefine the boundaries around Israel. Peter, addressing "all the people" (πᾶς ὁ λαὸς) (3:11), presents Moses as an ancient witness[9] testifying that those who do not listen to Jesus will be cut out of the people Israel. In 3:25, Peter identifies his audience as "descendants of the prophets and of the covenant" (οἱ υἱοὶ τῶν προφητῶν καὶ τῆς διαθήκης) with Abraham. Ethnic language connects them to Moses, the other prophets, and Abraham, and Peter offers them the possibility of maintaining that connection by listening to Jesus, the prophet like Moses.[10] The hope remains that they will accept Peter's message and follow Jesus. Yet, according to Luke, if they do not follow Jesus, their ancestral connection to Abraham will no longer matter. Listening to the prophet like Moses is now determinative for membership in Israel.[11] Even this was predicted in and is a fulfillment of Scripture.

8. Zehnle and Jürgen Roloff take Acts 3:23 at face value. Zehnle writes, "whoever does not listen to his words will be cut off from the people and will not participate in the days of refreshment" (*Peter's Pentecost Discourse*, 90). Roloff interprets Peter's citation to mean that the Jew who does not listen to the voice of Jesus "ceases to be a member of Israel"; *Die Apostelgeschichte*, (Göttingen: Vandenhoeck & Ruprecht, 1981), 78. Barrett recognizes that this is the meaning of the words, but says, "Whether Luke meant so much is doubtful. He probably thought the verse a powerful means of expressing in negative terms what is positively stated in 4.12" (*The Acts of the Apostles*, 1:210). Pervo apparently disagrees with Barrett; he writes, "those who do not listen to Jesus and heed the call to repent will be expelled from the people of God" (*Acts: A Commentary*, 109) and adds, "the threat of 3:23 will be, in retrospect, a foreshadowing of the ultimate Jewish reaction to the message" (110).

9. Both Aristotle and Cicero speak well of ancient witnesses. According to Aristotle, they are more trustworthy than their modern counterparts because "they cannot be corrupted" (*Rhet.* 1.15.17). Cicero claims that ancient witnesses are most convincing (*Verr.* 2.3.209).

10. In *Why This New Race?: Ethnic Reasoning in Early Christianity*, Denise Kimber Buell explores the mutability of ethnic language and the ways "early Christians capitalized on this dynamic character of ethnicity/race as being both fixed and fluid" in their own descriptions of group membership (New York: Columbia University Press, 2008), 3. Luke is an early example of the creative use of ethnic language to redraw the boundaries around Israel.

11. Jacob Jervell distinguishes between the repentant and unrepentant portions of Israel. See "The Divided People of God: The Restoration of Israel and Salvation for the Gentiles," in *Luke and the People of God: A New Look at Luke-Acts* (Minneapolis, Minn.: Augsburg, 1972), 41–74, esp. 43 and 54.

Acts 7: Reshaping Moses as
a Persecuted Prophet

In Stephen's speech before the council, in Acts 7, Luke presents a brief and highly selective history of Israel, the bulk of which focuses on the character of Moses. Though Luke's text often directly parallels the text of Exodus at the level of phrases and complete verses,[12] his retelling of Moses's life is no neutral endeavor.[13] In particular, Luke reshapes the stories of Moses's killing of the Egyptian and the worship of the golden calf in order to present Moses as a prophet rejected by his own people, the very ones he came to save.[14]

Killing the Egyptian

Luke's presentation of Moses as a rejected prophet depends primarily on his retelling of Exodus 2:11–15.[15] In the Exodus account, Moses leaves the Pharaoh's house and visits his kin in their forced labor. Seeing an Egyptian beating a Hebrew, he kills the Egyptian and buries him in the sand. The following day, Moses sees two Hebrews fighting and questions the one in the wrong. The

---

12. For an extensive treatment of the use of scriptural material in Stephen's speech, see Earl Richard, *Acts 6:1–8:4: The Author's Method of Composition* (Missoula, Mont.: Scholars Press, 1978), 33–155.

13. Scholars who claim that Acts 7 is a neutral telling of history include Martin Dibelius, "The Speeches in Acts and Ancient Historiography," in *Studies in the Acts of the Apostles*, ed. Heinrich Greeven (London: S. C. M. Press, 1956), 167–170, and Ernst Haenchen, *The Acts of the Apostles* (Philadelphia: Westminster, 1971), 288. More recently, scholars have argued for the polemical nature of the speech. See Earl Richard, "The Polemical Character of the Joseph Episode in Acts 7," *Journal of Biblical Literature* 98 (1979): 255–67; and T. L. Donaldson, "Moses Typology and the Sectarian Nature of Early Christian Anti-Judaism: A Study in Acts 7," *Journal for the Study of the New Testament* 12 (1981): 27–52.

14. On Moses as a rejected prophet, see Luke Timothy Johnson, *The Acts of the Apostles* (Collegeville, Minn.: Liturgical Press, 1992), 135–38.

15. This portion of Moses's life, in which he sees an Egyptian beating a Hebrew and responds by killing the Egyptian and burying him in the sand, was of particular concern to many Jewish interpreters. Jewish authors were commonly concerned to avoid the presentation of Moses as a shamed murderer who flees out of fear. While Jubilees and Ezekiel the Tragedian, for very different reasons, maintain this portion of the Exodus narrative, other authors rewrite this portion of Moses's life. Philo maintains much of the Exodus account, but he adjusts elements of it in order to validate Moses's action. Philo claims that the Egyptian whom Moses kills is the cruelest of all the cruel taskmasters who were working the Hebrew slaves to death, and Moses did a righteous deed in killing him (*On the Life of Moses* 1.44). Artapanus maintains Moses's killing of the Egyptian but nothing else about Exodus 2:11–15. He places the killing in an entirely new scenario such that Moses kills, in self-defense, an Egyptian who is wrongly plotting to kill him (*Praep. ev.* 9.27.18). By contrast, both Josephus and Pseudo-Philo eliminate the incident. Luke's approach is closest to Philo's; he maintains the killing, but justifies it. See John M. G. Barclay, "Manipulating Moses: Exodus 2:10–15 in Egyptian Judaism and the New Testament," in *Text as Pretext: Essays in Honour of Robert Davidson*, ed. Robert P. Carroll (Sheffield, U.K.: JSOT Press, 1992), 28–46.

TABLE 2-6. COMPARISON OF ACTS 7:27–28 AND EXODUS 2:14

Acts 7:27–28	Exodus 2:14
ὁ δὲ ἀδικῶν τὸν πλησίον ἀπώσατο αὐτὸν	ὁ δὲ
εἰπών,	εἶπεν
Τίς σε κατέστησεν ἄρχοντα καὶ δικαστὴν ἐφ' ἡμῶν; μὴ ἀνελεῖν με σὺ θέλεις ὃν τρόπον ἀνεῖλες ἐχθὲς τὸν Αἰγύπτιον;	Τίς σε κατέστησεν ἄρχοντα καὶ δικαστὴν ἐφ' ἡμῶν; μὴ ἀνελεῖν με σὺ θέλεις ὃν τρόπον ἀνεῖλες ἐχθὲς τὸν Αἰγύπτιον;

Hebrew replies, "Who appointed you ruler and judge over us? Do you wish to kill me as you killed the Egyptian yesterday?" (2:14). Moses realizes that the murder has become known, and he flees.

According to Luke, when Moses visits his relatives and sees one of them being mistreated by an Egyptian, "he came to the aid of the oppressed man and avenged him, striking down the Egyptian" (Acts 7:24). Luke claims that Moses "reckoned that his kin would understand that God, through his hand, was giving salvation to them" (7:25). Long before the episode at the burning bush, Moses already understands himself as a deliverer sent by God. The next day, Moses sees two Israelites fighting.[16] Moses attempts "to reconcile them to peace" (7:26), but "the one who had been wronging his neighbor rejected [ἀπώσατο] [Moses], saying, 'Who appointed you ruler and judge over us? Do you wish to kill me as you killed the Egyptian yesterday?'" (Acts 7:27–28). Hearing this rebuff and determining that his offer of salvation has been misunderstood, Moses flees to Midian.

Luke's account follows the basic plot of the Exodus account and even cites Exodus 2:14, the Israelite's question to Moses (table 2-6). Luke gives a new and creative interpretation of the episode and of this verse in particular. With three interpretive moves, Luke presents Moses as a rejected deliverer, and thus in the pattern of Jesus.[17]

16. The participle (μαχομένοις) in 7:26 specifies neither that they are Israelites nor that there are precisely two of them, but this is required by 7:26–27.

17. Pervo notes that through Luke's unique interpretation of the murder of the Egyptian, "Luke transforms Moses into a prototype of Jesus" (*Acts: A Commentary*, 185). Luke's presentation of Jesus as a prophet, and specifically as a prophet like Moses, is well documented. See, for example, Paul S. Minear, *To Heal and to Reveal: The Prophetic Vocation according to Luke* (New York: Crossroad, 1976), 102–21; and David L. Tiede, *Prophecy and History in Luke-Acts* (Philadelphia: Fortress Press, 1980). On the parallels between Jesus and Moses, see David P. Moessner, "Luke 9:1–50: Luke's Preview of the Journey of the Prophet Like Moses of Deuteronomy," *Journal of Biblical Literature* 102 (1983): 575–605; and Robert F. O'Toole, "The Parallels between Jesus and Moses," *Biblical Theology Bulletin* 29 (1990): 22–29.

First, Luke reshapes the narrative so that Moses understands himself as a deliverer. In Exodus, after Moses kills the Egyptian, he looks around, implying that he is ashamed of his action and wants to be sure there are no witnesses. Luke, by contrast, specifies that Moses seeks "vengeance [ἐκδίκησιν]" (Acts 7:24) and expects the killing will become known so that "his kin would understand that God, through his hand, was giving salvation to them" (Acts 7:25). Moses's killing of the Egyptian serves as an announcement that Moses is a means of salvation for the Israelites.

Second, according to Luke, Moses flees because he realizes that the Israelites do not understand that he has come to bring them salvation.[18] In Exodus 2:14, when the Israelite says to Moses, "Who appointed you ruler and judge over us? Do you wish to kill me as you killed the Egyptian yesterday?," Moses discovers that his killing of the Egyptian has become known, and he flees because Pharaoh seeks revenge. In Luke's retelling, Moses assumes that the killing is known and understood as an announcement of the salvation which he brings. Thus, when the Israelite asks, "Do you wish to kill me?" (7:28), Moses realizes that the Israelite does not understand his offer of salvation.

Third, Luke presents Moses as not only misunderstood but also rejected by the Israelites. Luke introduces the Israelite's question to Moses with the words, "the one who had been wronging his neighbor rejected [ἀπώσατο] Moses" (7:27). By not understanding that Moses killed the Egyptian on behalf of the Israelites, the Israelite rejects him as a deliverer appointed by God. This rejection prompts Moses's flight to Midian. It is noteworthy that Luke indicates that this Israelite who rejects Moses is "the one who was wronging [ἀδικῶν] his neighbor" (7:27); it is an unjust Israelite who rejects Moses. Later in the narrative, Luke applies this accusation to the Israelites as a whole. In Acts 7:35, Luke writes, "This is the Moses whom they denied [ἠρνήσαντο], saying [εἰπόντες], 'Who appointed you ruler and judge?'" Luke claims that the Israelites as a group reject Moses's offer of salvation. Thus, Luke reworks the episode in which Moses kills the Egyptian in order to present Moses as a deliverer who is misunderstood and rejected by the very people he came to save, and he reinterprets Exodus 2:14 as the Israelites' corporate rejection of Moses.

18. According to Barrett, "Such complete failure to understand his intentions (οἱ δὲ οὐ συνῆκαν, v. 25) was too much for Moses, who *fled* (ἔφυγεν)" (*The Acts of the Apostles*, 1:359).

The Golden Calf

Luke presents the Israelites rejecting Moses a second time through his brief report of their construction and worship of the golden calf. In Exodus the people reject the commands of the Lord, and there is a suggestion that their lawlessness is directed toward Moses. Luke reshapes the account so that the Israelites reject Moses rather than the commandments.

In Exodus 32, when Moses delays on the mountain, the people ask Aaron to make gods for them. Aaron obliges, forming a molten calf from their gold earrings. Meanwhile, the Lord alerts Moses to the danger: "Descend quickly from here, for your people [ὁ λαός σου], whom you brought out of [ἐξήγαγες] the land of Egypt, have acted lawlessly. They have quickly turned aside from the way that you commanded [ἐνετείλω] them"[19] (32:7–8). Exodus presents the people as acting "lawlessly" and deviating from the commands Moses has passed on to them. The emphasis is on the people turning from or rejecting the commands. Yet, there is a hint that the Israelites reject not only the commands, but Moses himself. When God warns Moses about the golden calf, God says "*your* people ... have quickly turned aside from the way that *you* commanded them" (32:7–8; italics mine).

Luke appears to have identified this suggestion in the Exodus account and amplified it.[20] He claims that the Israelites have explicitly rejected Moses. In Acts 7, Luke identifies Moses as the one to whom the angel spoke at Mount Sinai, "to whom our ancestors did not wish to be obedient, but they rejected [ἀπώσαντο], and in their hearts they turned back to Egypt, saying to Aaron, 'Make gods for

---

19. The Hebrew text is ambiguous at this point. The unpointed text of צום could be read as either "I commanded them" or "you commanded them." The majority of Greek manuscripts as well as the Latin Vulgate translate "you commanded them." This translation is unsurprising given that in the Hebrew of Exodus 32:7, God speaks to Moses about "your people whom you brought up from the land of Egypt." Yet, the Hebrew was also read as "I commanded them." This is the pointing preserved in BHS, and this reading is witnessed in Pseudo-Philo's *Biblical Antiquities*, which is preserved only in Latin, but was originally composed in Hebrew. See D. J. Harrington, "Pseudo-Philo (First Century A.D.)," in *Old Testament Pseudepigrapha*, ed. James H. Charlesworth (New York: Doubleday, 1985), 2:298–99. Pseudo-Philo presents God as saying that the people "have turned aside from my ways that I commanded them [*vias meas, quas precepi eis*]" (12:4).

20. That Luke's reading of the golden calf is not the only possible interpretation of the LXX Exodus account is suggested by Philo's *On the Life of Moses*. In that text, the Israelites appear to reject God, "forgetting the piety they owed to the One Who Is" (2.161), and Moses is presented as an attentive leader (2.163–66).

us who will lead the way for us'" (7:39–40). The object of ἀπώσαντο is unstated in the Greek text, but the closest possible antecedent is Moses, "to whom our ancestors did not wish to be obedient" in the earlier part of verse 39.[21] Luke uses the verb ἀπωθέομαι, the same verb he used in Acts 7:27, to present the people's demand as a rejection not of the commands but only of Moses.

The verb ἀπωθέομαι is used in the LXX of the Israelites' rejection not of Moses but of the law. While ἀπωθέομαι occurs most frequently in the LXX with God as the subject, there are a few instances in which Israel, or the people, is the subject. In nearly all of these cases, Israel rejects the commands of the Lord.[22] In Amos 2:4, Judah rejects the law of the Lord (τὸν νόμον κυρίου). In Jeremiah 6:19, Israel rejects the law (τὸν νόμον μου), and in 23:17, the word of the Lord (τὸν λόγον κυρίου). In Ezekiel 5:6, 20:13, and 20:16, Israel rejects the Lord's statutes (τὰ δικαιώματά μου); in 20:24, they reject the Lord's ordinances (τὰ προστάγματά μου). By contrast, this verb is never used of Israel's rejection of Moses in the LXX.

Thus, the use of the verb ἀπωθέομαι with Israel as the subject and Moses as the object is Luke's special formulation to reshape the narrative in such a way that the people are made to reject not God's commands but Moses's. This reinforces the picture of Moses as a rejected prophet, which Luke constructs primarily through his telling of Moses's killing of the Egyptian.

Having identified Moses as the object of the Israelites' rejection, Luke presents their words from Exodus 32:1 and 32:23 as the means by which the Israelites reject Moses: "Make for us gods who will go before us; as for this Moses, who led us out of the land of Egypt, we do not know what happened to him" (Acts 7:40). Luke then offers the construction of the calf (ἐμοσχοποίησαν) as evidence of their rejection (Acts 7:41), drawing on vocabulary from Exodus 32:4, 8, 20, and 35.[23]

Further, in Exodus, immediately after hearing that the people have turned from the commandments, Moses begs God not to destroy them but rather to

21. Barrett, following Gerhard Schneider, *Die Apostelgeschichte* (Freiburg: Herder, 1980), 1:464n 176, concedes that Moses is the "probable" object of ἀπώσαντο, but gives living oracles (λόγια ζῶντα) as "a possible alternative" (*The Acts of the Apostles*, 366). By contrast, Pervo argues that the relative pronoun at the beginning of 7:39 indicates that the "disobedience was directed toward Moses rather than God" (*Acts: A Commentary*, 188).

22. One exception is LXX 4 Kingdoms (2 Kings) 17:20, in which Judah not only breaks the Lord's commandments but even rejects the Lord (ἀπεώσαντο τὸν κύριον).

23. Richard, *Acts 6:1–8:4*, 118.

TABLE 2-7. COMPARISON OF ACTS 7:40 AND EXODUS 32:1, 23

Acts 7:40	Exodus 32:1, 23
ποίησον ἡμῖν θεοὺς οἳ προπορεύσονται ἡμῶν	ποίησον ἡμῖν θεούς, οἳ προπορεύσονται ἡμῶν
ὁ γὰρ Μωϋσῆς οὗτος,	ὁ γὰρ Μωυσῆς οὗτος ὁ ἄνθρωπος,
ὃς ἐξήγαγεν ἡμᾶς ἐκ γῆς Αἰγύπτου, οὐκ οἴδαμεν τί ἐγένετο αὐτῷ.	ὃς ἐξήγαγεν ἡμᾶς ἐκ γῆς Αἰγύπτου, οὐκ οἴδαμεν τί γέγονεν αὐτῷ.

remember his promise to Abraham (32:11–13), and God is persuaded (32:14). In Luke's version, there is no mention of Moses's pleading with God to remember mercy and give the Israelites a second chance. Moses's intercession on behalf of the people is a regular occurrence in the Exodus narrative,[24] but it is omitted by Luke. Rather, the Israelites' single turn from God immediately results in God's turning away from them: "But God turned away from them and handed them over to worship the host of heaven" (Acts 7:42). Thus, the divide between Moses and the Israelites at their rejection of him is not mended.

In summary, in Acts 7, Luke reworks two episodes—Moses's killing of the Egyptian and the Israelites' worship of the golden calf—in order to present the Israelites as rejecting Moses. In so doing, Luke creates a division between Moses and the Israelites.

Identifying "the Jews" with the Ancient Israelites

Luke does not leave this division between Moses and the Israelites in the past. Rather, this reconceived relationship between Moses and the Israelites, between the rejected prophet and the rejecting people, is brought into Stephen's, and Luke's, present.

At the end of his speech, Stephen shifts his attention from the ancient Israelites to his Jewish audience, the council which is examining him (cf. Acts 6:12, 15). He directly condemns them: "You stiff-necked people, uncircumcised in heart and ears, you are always opposing the Holy Spirit, just as *your* ancestors [οἱ πατέρες ὑμῶν] used to do. Which of the prophets did *your* ancestors [οἱ πατέρες ὑμῶν] not persecute?" (7:51–52a; italics mine). Stephen identifies his Jewish audience with *their* ancestors, the Israelites who rejected the prophet Moses and persecuted the subsequent prophets. Stephen continues,

24. For example, see Ex 32:11–14; Nm 11:1–2; 11:10–15; 12:13–14; 14:11–24.

"They killed those who foretold the coming of the Righteous One, and now you have become his betrayers and murderers" (7:52b). Stephen accuses his Jewish audience of following in the footsteps of their ancestors by killing the Righteous One, the prophet Jesus. Stephen's use of ethnic language redefines his opponents' ancestry and separates them from Moses, as well as from himself and the others who have believed. This is a sharp contrast to the end of Peter's speech in which the possibility remained open that his Jewish audience, not only the leaders but "all the people" (3:11), would listen to Jesus.

The Jewish council's response to Stephen's speech is a narrative demonstration of Stephen's status as a persecuted prophet. As Stephen's audience listened to him, they became "enraged" (7:54), and "they dragged him out of the city and began to stone him" (7:58). Stephen's persecution identifies him with the rejected Moses and Jesus.

The condemnatory conclusion of Stephen's speech functions to draw a boundary between the Jews who follow Jesus and those who do not, effectively co-opting Moses from some of his own people. Luke constructs a dichotomy in which Stephen's audience, the Jewish council, can no longer claim Moses as their ancestor. They are the descendants of the rejecting Israelites, and not the descendants of the rejected Moses. Luke does not allow Moses to be an ancestor to those Jews who do not follow Jesus.

Conclusion

In two different ways, Luke reshapes the Pentateuchal image of Moses in order to divide persecuted prophets from their persecutors. In Acts 3, Luke reconfigures the promise of Deuteronomy 18 in order to present Moses as claiming that those who do not listen to Jesus, the prophet like Moses, will be cut out of the people Israel. In Acts 7, Luke retells the narrative of Moses's life to present Moses as a prophet rejected by his own people, thus building a wall between Moses and the ancient Israelites. Luke then extends this division into the present by identifying Stephen's Jewish audience as the descendants of the ancient Israelites who rejected Moses, using their killings of Jesus and Stephen as evidence of this alignment. Both reconfigurations of the image of Moses create a boundary between (1) those Jews who follow Jesus and are thus aligned with Moses and the other persecuted prophets, and (2) those who do not follow Jesus and are identified with those who persecuted the prophets.

Emmanuel Nathan

3. THE PAULINE MOSES
AT CORINTH

Indications of a Transformation

Paul's depiction of Moses in the Corinthian correspondence is quite striking. In 1 Cor 10 he curiously speaks of ancestors "baptized into Moses," while in 2 Cor 3 he portrays Moses in more deprecating terms, as one whose glory had been set aside and whose donning of a veil indicated a lack of boldness. Traditional Pauline scholarship has generally agreed that in the two instances Paul was relying upon distinct traditions about Moses even though it is noteworthy that in both chapters Paul was alluding to the same episode from Exodus 32–34 (the incident of the golden calf in 1 Cor 10:7 and the radiant face of Moses in 2 Cor 3:7–18). Greater attention has of course been spent on Paul's more extensive treatment of Moses in 2 Cor 3 and rarely has a link between the two depictions of Moses in either epistle been drawn.

In this short paper, I will suggest a link that serves to avoid the more hypothetical speculations that result from sleuthing for parallels. And so, while I am aware of discussions of Moses by Paul's Jewish contemporaries, Philo (*Vit. Mos.* 2.67–70) and Josephus (*Ant.* 3.75–92) in particular, or even Greek and Roman treatments of Moses (Hecataeus of Abdera, Diodorus Siculus, Tacitus, and Juvenal, to name a few), these will not be the focus of my contribution. I will instead argue that Paul reconfigured Moses from being on par with Christ in 1 Cor 10 to being on par with διάκονος in 2 Cor 3. It is my contention that Paul's divergences from the original Exodus narrative, in particular his negative characterization of Moses, can be better explained in terms of the equally negative assessment he made of his own life, prior to his "turning to the Lord." For this reading I will rely on Paul's choice of the aorist subjunctive of the verb ἐπιστρέφω ("turning") in 2 Cor 3:16 as an indication that Paul was here considering his own conversion experience rather than simply engaging in an exegesis of Exodus 34:34.

The Typological Use of Moses in 1 Corinthians 10:2 and 2 Corinthians 3:7–18

In an extended section containing warnings and models from Scripture against idolatry and immoral behavior (1 Cor 10:1–13), Paul mentions that all the people who passed through the sea ("our fathers [πατέρες ἡμῶν]") were "baptized into Moses [εἰς τὸν Μωϋσῆν ἐβαπτίσθησαν]" (10:2). Time and space do not allow me to enter into an extensive discussion on whether Paul was here relying on a preexisting tradition or coining one of his own, but the point I do wish to make is that here, in this passage, Moses is very Christ-like, indicating a usage by Paul along the lines of a Moses-Christ typology. The people of Moses ate and drank supernatural food and drink (1 Cor 10:3–4), which clearly parallels the "cup of blessing" and bread that is broken, which are the participation in the blood and body of Christ (10:16–17). Similarly, when, in 10:7, Paul quotes from Exodus 32:6 that "the people sat down to eat and drink, and they rose up to play [Ἐκάθισεν ὁ λαὸς φαγεῖν καὶ πεῖν, καὶ ἀνέστησαν παίζειν]," it is a warning from Scripture against idolatrous practices in Paul's own time. Paul, in 1 Cor 10:11, gives the eschatological justification for drawing a contemporary lesson from Scripture:[1] "These things happened to them to serve as an example, and they were written down to instruct us, on whom the ends of the ages have come [ταῦτα δὲ τυπικῶς συνέβαινεν ἐκείνοις, ἐγράφη δὲ πρὸς νουθεσίαν ἡμῶν, εἰς οὓς τὰ τέλη τῶν αἰώνων κατήντηκεν]." The illustrations of idolatry in Moses's time serve to warn against idolatry in Paul's time: "You

---

1. Albert L. A. Hogeterp, *Expectations of the End: A Comparative Traditio-Historical Study of Eschatological, Apocalyptic and Messianic Ideas in the Dead Sea Scrolls and the New Testament*, Studies on the Texts of the Desert of Judah 83 (Leiden: Brill, 2009), 215: "1 Cor 10:11 voices an eschatological orientation to the reading of Scripture as contemporary model."

cannot drink the cup of the Lord and the cup of demons. You cannot partake of the table of the Lord and the table of demons" (10:21).

By the time Paul introduces Moses again in 2 Cor 3:7–18, however, a conflict had erupted that caused Paul to adapt his use of Moses. The debate about competence in ministry that was occurring between Paul and rival missionaries at the time of his writing 2 Cor caused Paul to focus on the "ministry" of Moses. At the same time, this new situation provided Paul an opportunity to present a different understanding of Moses than that in 1 Cor. Of note too is the Adam-Christ typology that Paul articulated in 1 Cor 15:22 ("for as all die in Adam, so all will be made alive in Christ") and also in 15:42–50. That the Adam-Christ typology also operates in 2 Cor is evident in 2 Cor 3:18 and 4:4. As van Kooten notes, "The glory of this Christ (2 Cor 3.18, 4.4), thus, is the glory of the second Adam, just as the first Adam was God's image and glory (1 Cor 11.7)."[2] That Paul incorporates echoes from his own usage in 1 Cor 15:45 can be seen from Paul's use of the "life-giving spirit [πνεῦμα ζῳοποιεῖ]" in 2 Cor 3:6c.[3] Similarly, Paul incorporates changes into his use of Moses in light of the Adam-Christ typology he has developed. He "refracts" the Moses typology in a new way, no longer in comparison with Christ, but in comparison with himself, as minister and apostle, relativizing the position of Moses in the process. The conflict situation at Corinth at the time of the writing of 2 Cor thus provided Paul the opportunity to localize his new understanding of Moses within another, thematically related, Exodus narrative.[4] It is also worth-

2. G. H. van Kooten, "Paul's Anti-Sophistic Interpretation of the Narrative of Moses' Shining Face (Exod 34) in 2 Cor 3: Moses' Strength, Well-being and (Transitory) Glory, according to Philo, Josephus, Paul, and the Corinthian Sophists," in his *Paul's Anthropology in Context: The Image of God, Assimilation to God, and Tripartite Man in Ancient Judaism, Ancient Philosophy and Early Christianity*, Wissenschaftliche Untersuchungen zum Neuen Testament (WUNT) 232 (Tübingen: Mohr Siebeck, 2008), 313–339, at 338.

3. John W. Yates, *The Spirit and Creation in Paul*, WUNT II/251 (Tübingen: Mohr Siebeck, 2008), 110: "This description of the spirit as 'life-giving' does not, however, come from Ezekiel 36.… Although 'spirit' and 'life' are joined together in the tradition of the placement of πνεῦμα as the subject of ζῳοποιεῖς probably original to Paul.… Paul echoes his own description from 1 Cor 15:45 … Paul's development of Gen 2:7 in that passage appears to have been his own, and the phrase πνεῦμα ζῳοποιοῦν is surely distinctive. This is a phrase that would have been familiar to Paul's Corinthian readers, and strikingly so as it occurred at a climactic point in an earlier letter to them."

4. As C. J. A. Hickling points out, in "Paul's Use of Exodus in the Corinthian Correspondence," *The Corinthian Correspondence*, ed. Reimund Bieringer, Bibliotheca Ephemerium Theologicarum Lovaniensum 125 (Leuven: Leuven University Press, 1996), 367–68: "Paul has used material at the beginning and the end respectively of a single continuous section of the text of Exodus, namely 32,1–34,35. The modern critical student identifies these chapters as a single unit. But some of the reasons suggesting this

while to point out significant Pauline additions to that narrative. The Exodus narrative does *not* (a) mention the glory on Moses's face fading, (b) suggest that the Israelites were unable to look at Moses's face, (c) link the putting on of the veil to their inability to gaze at Moses, or (d) provide a motive for the veiling.[5] These are distinctly Pauline accents.

Paul as a Second Moses

I am arguing that Paul's typological refraction of Moses in terms of διακονία introduced a correspondence with Paul's own status as a διάκονος of the καινή διαθήκη. This lends support to the view that Paul was portraying himself as a "second Moses" in 2 Cor 3:7–18. Here are two further considerations to support such a view.

First, it is known that, when comparing Qumran, Hellenistic Jewish, and Samaritan literature, there were many "second Moses" expectations held by eschatologically minded groups. These mostly were divided between messianic, or royal, and non-messianic prophetic types. Of these, the latter non-messianic second Moses traditions held at Qumran were most similar to Paul's portrayal, particularly that of the Teacher of Righteousness who, like Paul, compared and contrasted himself with Moses. Added to that, Paul seems to have been heavily influenced by the Isaianic *ebed Yhwh,* who was also believed to be the second Moses in certain Jewish circles. "Paul's awareness of fulfilling the mission of the Servant is further evidence of his conscious assumption of the role of the second Moses."[6]

Second, an extensive analysis of 2 Cor 3 shows the importance of Moses as a counterpart, role model, and foil for Paul. "The argument of II Corinthians 3 as a whole now appears based on Moses and several stories about his life and activity prototypical for Christian life and the activity of the Christian minister or apostle."[7] Yet, it is clear that Paul adjusted the Moses model

---

identification would surely be noticed by an attentive reader at any period in history.... Paul will surely have read them as a discrete, continuous section of the sacred text."

5. Linda L. Belleville, "Tradition or Creation? Paul's Use of the Exodus 34 Tradition in 2 Corinthians 3.7–18," in *Paul and the Scriptures of Israel,* ed. Craig A. Evans and J. A. Sanders, Journal for the Study of the New Testament, Supplement Series 83 (Sheffield, United Kingdom: JSOT, 1993), 165–86, at 185.

6. Peter R. Jones, "The Apostle Paul: A Second Moses according to II Corinthians 2:14–4:7" (PhD thesis, Princeton Theological Seminary, 1973), 376.

7. Carol K. Stockhausen, *Moses' Veil and the Glory of the New Covenant: The Exegetical Substructure*

through the use of prophetic texts, among them Ezekiel, in order to make the reading more easily intelligible to his own contemporaries.[8]

Moses as Person and Text

To aver that Paul portrays himself as a second Moses should not, however, overshadow the fact that the problem confronting all exegetical studies of 2 Cor 3:7–18 is that Paul casts himself as both similar *and* dissimilar to Moses in this passage. For instance, commenting on the *dissimile* in 2 Cor 3:12–18, Richard Hays is only too aware of opposing crosscurrents:

> On the surface, Moses is a figure not like Paul, because he is veiled and mysterious, not disclosing all that he knows.... By contrast, Paul has nothing to hide.... Below the surface, however, the current flows in the opposite direction, because Moses did, after all, encounter God face to face. Thus he becomes a symbol of unveiling as well as of veiling. The seductive power of the metaphor exerts so much pressure on Paul's exposition of the figure that in verse 16–18 Paul finds himself writing that he and other Christians are more like Moses than unlike him.[9]

For Hays, Paul's reliance on Moses is not just a straightforward reliance on stories of Moses in Exodus. It is in fact a complex parable that defies explanation in terms of an allegorical scheme. In 2 Cor 3:13–15 Moses appears to represent the old covenant, but in 3:16–18 he seems to be a paradigm for Christian believers. Herein lies the tension: Moses is both person and text, with differing significance to each dimension. "Moses prefigures Christian experience, but

---

of II Cor. 3,1–4,6, Analecta Biblica 116 (Rome: Pontifical Biblical Institute, 1989), 153. On pp. 169–75, Stockhausen reflects on Paul as a second Moses in 2 Cor 4:1–6. In sum, "II Cor. 3:1–4:6, is in fact a reflection of some aspect of Moses' actions in Exodus, particularly Exodus 33–34" (p. 172).

8. Stockhausen, *Moses' Veil*, 153: "For example, because the promised new covenant has arrived with its gift of the spirit, Paul no longer must display the humility of his predecessor Moses. Moses could not reveal everything. Paul may. Paul need not veil his face and may behave with the boldness and freedom characteristic of the full-fledged member of Greek society. Furthermore, Paul knows through the prophet Isaiah that the 'sons of Israel' were not only hampered in their vision of the glory of the old covenant, but still possess hardened hearts which cannot understand the glory of the new. These 'hardened minds' in Israel stand in direct contrast to the soft and fleshly hearts promised by Ezekiel and given to Paul, which are able to receive the spirit which unveils and reveals and enlivens. In Moses' day, according to II Cor. 3:14, it had not been revealed that *in Christ* the covenant, ministry and glory of Moses would be brought to an end (μὴ ἀνακαλυπτόμενον ὅτι ἐν Χριστῷ καταργεῖται). This is what unbelieving, veiled Israel could not see in Moses' day and still cannot see in Paul's."

9. Richard B. Hays, *Echoes of Scripture in the Letters of Paul* (New Haven, Conn.: Yale University Press, 1989), 142–43.

he is not a Christian. He is both the paradigm for the Christian's direct experience of the Spirit and the symbol for the old covenant to which that experience is set in antithesis."[10]

I believe that Hays has managed to articulate the tension aptly. However, his foray into metaphor, as an attempt to dissolve that tension, might fail to persuade others.[11] In what follows, I will argue that Paul's double uses of Moses, both as person and as text, should be retained without seeking to harmonize them.

Moses as Paul

In a discussion on narrative localization, Anthony Le Donne has argued that (mnemonic) refractions are articulated into narratives that follow stereotypical patterns. Classic examples would be Johann Kessler and John Bunyan, who structured their biographies on biblical accounts. A more contemporary example would be the immortalization of a Jewish military hero of the Zionist movement, Yoseph Trumpeldor (1880–1920) who was recast in modern Israeli consciousness as a modern-day Bar Kochba (d. 135 C.E.). The point here is that the influence does not run in only one direction. "When Trumpeldor's generation evoked Bar Kochba to interpret his character, they inevitably reinterpreted Bar Kochba in light of Trumpeldor. [Modern] Israel had to reinvent her tradition (however slightly) to accommodate for the new addition of Trumpeldor."[12]

I would like to take up this insight with regard to Paul's introduction of Moses in 2 Cor 3:7–18, and press the point a little further as follows: First, let

10. Ibid., 144.

11. Daniel Boyarin, *A Radical Jew: Paul and the Politics of Identity* (Berkeley: University of California Press, 1994) feels that Hays let Paul off the supersessionist hook too easily: "Thus, the move of the modern readers of Paul, such as Hays, who deny the allegorical and supersessionist movement of Paul's text is ultimately not convincing" (p. 104). N. T. Wright, *The Climax of the Covenant: Christ and the Law in Pauline Theology* (Minneapolis, Minn.: Fortress, 1992), 180n20, felt that Hays did not give any attention to Paul's argument on boldness: "Hays 1989, 142f., reads the passage [3:12–17] as though a submerged parallel between Moses and Paul breaks out from under the argued contrast. I think this puts it, if anything, the wrong way round, and helps to explain why Hays does not, in my view, give sufficient weight to Paul's argument about 'boldness', which does not appear (for instance) in his otherwise fine summary of the thrust of the passage (153)."

12. Anthony Le Donne, *The Historiographical Jesus: Memory, Typology, and the Son of David* (Waco, Tex.: Baylor University Press, 2009), 58, commenting on Yael Zerubavel, "The Historical, the Legendary and the Incredible: Invented Tradition and Collective Memory in Israel," in *Commemorations: The Politics of National Identity*, ed. J. R. Gillis (Princeton, N.J.: Princeton University, 1994), 105–25.

it be recalled that the typological refraction of Moses in terms of διακονία introduced a correspondence with Paul's own status as a διάκονος of the καινή διαθήκη. Second, as a result of this conflation, let it be argued that Paul inevitably reinterprets Moses in light of his own experience. Third, let it be contended that this results in a Moses whose contours—in particular, his διακονία— resemble those of the "pre-Christian" Paul.[13]

Viewed this way, Paul's narrative conflation of his own διακονία within a typological narrative of Moses's glory represents none other than an evaluation of his own life prior to conversion in much the same way that he did in Phil 3:3– 11.[14] This is not to argue that the narrative of Moses's fading glory should be seen merely as an allegory on Paul's own pre-Christian life. Instead, it is my contention that the divergences of Paul's retelling from the original Exodus narrative, and the negative characterization of Moses in 2 Cor 3:7–18 in particular, can be better explained in terms of the negative characterization Paul had come to give his former ministry and life prior to "turning to the Lord."

"When Anyone Turns to the Lord": Conversion before Transformation in 2 Corinthians 3:16

At 2 Cor 3:16, "but when one turns to the Lord, the veil is removed [ἡνίκα δὲ ἐὰν ἐπιστρέψῃ πρὸς κύριον, περιαιρεῖται τὸ κάλυμμα]," Paul removed reference to Moses where such might have been expected. He had, in 2 Cor 3:15, just spoken of the veil lying upon contemporary Israelites' minds whenever "Moses" is being read. Sze-Kar Wan has helpfully drawn up a synopsis of the original text to which Paul was alluding in 2 Cor 3:16:[15]

---

13. My uses of the term "Christian" or "pre-Christian," here as elsewhere, are merely referring to Paul's life prior to, and subsequent to, being "in Christ." In a similar way, I understand Paul's own reference to his "earlier life in Judaism [τὴν ἐμὴν ἀναστροφήν ποτε ἐν τῷ Ἰουδαϊσμῷ]" (Gal 1:13) as referring simply to his life prior to following Christ.

14. It will be recalled that E. P. Sanders, *Paul, the Law, and the Jewish People* (Philadelphia: Fortress, 1983), 137, had already made a similar observation, albeit from a different perspective: "In two passages Paul directly compares, in an evaluative way, the old dispensation and the new. These passages are 2 Cor. 3:4–18 and Phil. 3:3–11."

15. Sze-Kar Wan, "Charismatic Exegesis: Philo and Paul Compared." In *The Studia Philonica Annual: Studies in Hellenistic Judaism*, vol. 6, ed. David T. Runia, Brown Judaic Studies 299 (Atlanta, Ga.: Scholars Press, 1994), 77. Margaret E. Thrall, *A Critical and Exegetical Commentary on the Second Epistle to the Corinthians*, (Edinburgh: T&T Clark, 1994), 268, agrees that Paul is loosely quoting or paraphrasing Exodus 34:34 but cautions that there are several differences between the two texts, which have led some to claim that Paul is not here relying on the OT text at all.

TABLE 3-1. COMPARISON OF EXODUS 34 AND 2 CORINTHIANS 3:16

LXX Exodus 34:34	2 Corinthians 3:16
ἡνίκα δ᾽ ἂν <u>εἰσεπορεύετο</u> Μωυσῆς	ἡνίκα δὲ ἐὰν <u>ἐπιστρέψῃ</u>
ἔναντι κυρίου <u>λαλεῖν αὐτῷ</u>,	πρὸς κύριον,
περιῃρεῖτο τὸ κάλυμμα	<u>περιαιρεῖται</u> τὸ κάλυμμα.
<u>ἕως τοῦ ἐκπορεύεσθαι</u>.	

In removing references to specific actions of Moses, Paul has turned the biblical text into a general statement about encountering the Lord. The change from the more general ἰσεπορεύεσθαι to ἐπιστρέψειν, the more technical term for conversion, further underlines Paul's concern to shift the focus to "Christian conversion" or ecstatic experience, but what enables Paul to state this with confidence is most likely his own conversion experience.[16]

I would agree that 2 Cor 3:16 is a reference to Paul's own conversion experience. However, I am not entirely persuaded by those who see a need to link this conversion with ecstatic experience. There are currently three main ways of analyzing Paul's conversion: (1) in terms of mystical experience, (2) from a psychological perspective, and (3) in terms of a sociological explanation. The first approach was spearheaded by Alan Segal, for whom 2 Cor 3:18–4:6 was a key text for Paul's use of mystical vocabulary.[17] The second was defended by Gerd Theissen, whose reading of 2 Cor 3:4–4:6 includes text, tradition, and psychological analyses.[18] The third option has been proposed by Troels Engberg-Pedersen, whose sociological model of conversion was applied only to Philippians, Galatians, and Romans.[19]

16. Wan, "Charismatic Exegesis," 77. Cf. Gordon Fee, *God's Empowering Presence: The Holy Spirit in the Letters of Paul* (Peabody, Mass.: Hendrickson, 1994) 310 who agrees that ἐπιστρέψῃ was a quasi-technical term for conversion. So too does Victor Paul Furnish, *II Corinthians* (Garden City, N.Y.: Doubleday, 1984), 211, but he argues that it is arbitrary to suggest that Paul had his own conversion specifically in mind. Thrall, *A Critical and Exegetical Commentary*, 271, maintains that the subject is Moses, but Moses seen as the type of the Christian convert. Against the conversion reading, Ralph R. Martin, *2 Corinthians* (Waco, Tex.: Word, 1986), 70, prefers to see the verse in its simple sense "whenever there is a turning to the Lord."

17. Alan F. Segal, *Paul the Convert: The Apostolate and Apostasy of Saul the Pharisee* (New Haven, Conn.: Yale University, 1990), 58–61.

18. Gerd Theissen, *Psychological Aspects of Pauline Theology*, trans. John P. Galvin (Edinburgh: T&T Clark, 1987), 117–75.

19. Troels Engberg-Pedersen, *Paul and the Stoics: An Essay in Interpretation* (Edinburgh: T&T Clark, 2000), 81–292.

My objections to the mystical approach to Paul are its overemphasis on the individual at the cost of communal dimensions. With regard to the psychological approach, I am not alone when I say that I fear it runs the risk of being anachronistic. I therefore choose to pursue Engberg-Pedersen's sociological approach to conversion and apply it to 2 Cor 3:7–18.

Let me briefly state the key elements of Engberg-Pedersen's model. The first is his insight that conversion is conceptualized as a story in time (before-now-after). The narrative of Moses in 2 Cor 3:7–18 is such a story, in which "before" is represented by the veiled Moses, "now" by the moment of turning, and "after" by the moment of transformation once the veil has been removed upon turning.

Engberg-Pedersen further argues that the new conversion experience brings about a reinterpretation of one's pre-conversion existence. I would go further and say that this interpretation bears similarities to what Terence Donaldson has termed the "reconfiguration" of Paul's convictional world. It can be argued that Paul's conversion has brought about a reinterpretation, or reconfiguration, of his pre-conversion existence, which is typologically represented by the Mosaic διακονία, a διακονία of death and condemnation (2 Cor 3:7, 9).

In terms of identity, Engberg-Pedersen had argued that the individual transfers between states of membership. One is "taken over" by something (God, Christ, or reason) and "relinquishes" one's former self in the process. Engberg-Pedersen argued that it is an uncompromising change, an all or nothing affair. Certainly, the Mosaic διακονία, characterized as being one of death and condemnation, in comparison to the διακονία of righteousness (and life by implication; cf. 2 Cor 3:6c: πνεῦμα ζῳοποιεῖ) would lend itself to such a view. But Paul does maintain that this same Mosaic διακονία came ἐν δόξῃ, "in glory." And, when transformation takes place in 3:18, it is a change ἀπὸ δόξης εἰς δόξαν, "from glory to glory." In that sense, Paul's own understanding challenges Engberg-Pedersen's notion that transference of identity signals a break with one's former existence.[20] It is for this reason that rather than speak of "trans-

<hr />

20. See Jörg Frey, "Paul's Jewish Identity," In *Jewish Identity in the Greco-Roman World / Judische Identität in der griechisch-römischen Welt*, ed. Jörg Frey, Daniel R. Schwartz, and Stephanie Gripenrung (Leiden: Brill, 2007), 285–321, at 321: "Paul never converted from 'Judaism' to 'Christianity'. If—in spite of Paul's preference for the calling terminology—the term 'conversion' may be used for his Damascus experience, it may be seen as a conversion from one type of Judaism to another." *Pace* Paul Brooks Duff, "Transformed 'from Glory to Glory': Paul's Appeal to the Experience of His Readers in 2 Corinthians

ference of identity," I prefer to think in terms of "transformation of identity" and maintain that one's past identity is reconfigured rather than completely altered in the process.

Nonetheless, the community-oriented feature of Engberg-Pedersen's model of conversion is still pertinent, since I agree with him that Paul is offering his addressees an understanding of themselves as part of the specific way of life he is directing them to live out. Thus, when applying his model to the Philippian case, Engberg-Pedersen finds that, key to the model, working effectively among the Philippians requires an explicit exhortation from Paul to become co-imitators of him (Συμμιμηταί μου γίνεσθε, ἀδελφοί, καὶ σκοπεῖτε τοὺς οὕτω περιπατοῦντας καθὼς ἔχετε τύπον ἡμας; Phil 3:17).[21] A similar mimetic program had already been put in place by Paul among the Corinthians, in 1 Cor 4:16 (μιμηταί μου γίνεσθε) and 1 Cor 11:1 (Συμμιμηταί μου γίνεσθε, καθὼς κἀγὼ Χριστοῦ).[22] Likewise, as Jan Lambrecht points out, when it comes to the metamorphosis of 2 Cor 3:18: "We might note that Paul himself appears to be a clear example of such a metamorphosis. He had been a fanatical Pharisee, persecuting the young church. His metamorphosis was not only some inner change, nor simply an external change. It was both."[23]

3:18," *Journal of Biblical Literature* 127 (2008): 759–80, who takes the expression ἀπὸ δόξης εἰς δόξαν to mean a radical change from death to life; this interpretation is based on an earlier argument he developed that the Gentiles knew the Law but were under sentence of condemnation and death for not observing it (see Duff, "Glory in the Ministry of Death: Gentile Condemnation and Letters of Recommendation in 2 Cor 3:6–18," *Novum Testamentum* 46 [2004], 313–37).

21. Engberg-Pedersen, *Paul and the Stoics*, 114: "That is, imitators *of* him who join *with him* in what he is himself imitating, and that they take him as their model (*typos*)." A similar argument is developed along different lines by Bruce Longenecker on the purpose of Paul's autobiography in Galatians; see Longenecker, *The Triumph of Abraham's God: The Transformation of Identity in Galatians* (Edinburgh: T&T Clark, 1998), 149.

22. As highlighted by Henry T. Nguyen, *Christian Identity in Corinth: A Comparative Study of 2 Corinthians, Epictetus and Valerius Maximus* (Tübingen: Mohr Siebeck, 2008), 191, who chooses to connect this imitation motif to Paul's suffering and afflictions in 2 Cor. See also J. Brian Tucker, *'You Belong to Christ': Paul and the Formation of Social Identity in 1 Corinthians 1–4* (Eugene, Ore.: Pickwick Publications, 2010), 312–13, who connects the mimesis motif of 1 Cor 4:16 more closely to Paul's program of social identity formation in 1 Cor 1–4.

23. Jan Lambrecht, "Transformation in 2 Corinthians 3,18," in Reimund Bieringer and Jan Lambrecht, *Studies on Second Corinthians*, 305.

"Whenever Moses Is Read" (2 Cor 3:15)

I have so far argued that the portrayal of Moses in 2 Cor 3:7–18 represents Paul's understanding of his former life prior to it being transformed "in Christ." What, then, of the mention of Moses in 2 Cor 3:15? Here I maintain that the metonymic force of the equating of Moses with the Torah, or Law, stands. This threatens to weaken my argument to read all the other instances of Moses as an implicit reference to Paul's "pre-conversion" life, because it makes Paul appear inconsistent in his usage. This charge can be responded to in several ways, and I shall list three of them. First, allow me to quote Morna Hooker:

> From our point of view, his [Paul's] exposition is inconsistent. His arguments do not stand up logically, and he juxtaposes conflicting images and interpretations of the biblical text. Yet I have no doubt whatever that from his point of view, Paul's argument seemed proper and acceptable.... In our terms, Paul's own arguments about glory do not hold together; in his terms, both are valid interpretations of the text of Exod. 34. New Testament scholars perhaps need to take warning from this example of one of the dangers into which we easily fall when we are interpreting Paul, the danger of presupposing that all his exegesis will be consistent, and furthermore, that *his* form of consistency will be similar to our own.[24]

Second, in 2 Cor 3:15, the reading of Moses is by contemporaries of Paul (non-believing Jews) who have not yet encountered Christ as he has. Third, both Moses as person (i.e., the pre-converted Paul) and Moses as text (i.e., the Torah) are covered with a veil until the veil is removed through turning to Christ. The problem, then, is not Torah but an unconverted mind unable to understand its true significance in Christ.

Conclusion

To sum up, I have argued in this short paper that Paul's typological refraction of Moses in the Corinthian correspondence (from 1 Cor 10:2 to 2 Cor 3:7–18) led Paul not only to cast himself as a second Moses but, more importantly, to recast Moses as the "pre-Christian" Paul, that is to say, the Paul pri-

---

24. Morna D. Hooker, "Beyond the Things That Are Written? St. Paul's Use of Scripture," in *From Adam to Christ: Essays on Paul* (Cambridge: Cambridge University Press, 1990), 139–54, at 150–51.

or to his being "in Christ." In this reading, Moses came to represent Paul before the latter's "turning" to the Lord. That this turning, or conversion, had implications for identity transformation was argued on the basis of Engberg-Pedersen's sociological model of conversion, on the mimetic program that was developed by Paul in 1 Cor 4:16 and 11:1, and, finally, on Paul's own motif of transformation in 2 Cor 3:18. In short, I have argued that 2 Cor 3:7–18 represents not a negative assessment of Judaism or the Law, as it has traditionally been understood, nor even a negative assessment of Moses. Rather, it represents a reflection on Paul's own life prior to, during, and after conversion, in which an aspect of Moses's life was instrumental as a model. It can be only as a second step that the narrative in 2 Cor 3:7–18 was understood as representing a separation process from "Judaism."

Virginia Wayland

4. FOLLOWING PAUL, FOLLOWING MOSES

*Moses as Exemplar in Clement of Rome's
Letter to the Corinthians*

The reception of Moses and the Law in early Christianity, particularly in the Gentile churches associated with the Pauline missions, has been a prominent issue over the past several decades.[1] The letter known as *First Clement* was sent from the Roman church to the Corinthian church advising the Corinthian church to resolve a conflict arising from the expulsion of estab-

---

1. The most relevant studies for this paper are Mary Rose D'Angelo, *Moses in the Letter to the Hebrews* (Missoula, Mont.: Scholars, 1979); and John G. Gager, *Reinventing Paul* (New York: Oxford University Press, 2000); Gager, *The Origins of Anti-Semitism: Attitudes toward Judaism in Pagan and Christian Antiquity* (New York: Oxford University Press, 1983); Daniel Boyarin, *A Radical Jew: Paul and the Politics of Identity* (Berkeley: University of California, 1994), esp. 39–56; Krister Stendahl, *Paul among Jews and Gentiles, and Other Essays* (Philadelphia: Fortress Press, 1976). On the one hand, attention has focused on what Paul said or meant, through reinterpretation of his letters, and reconstruction of his historical and religious context. See James D. G. Dunn, *The New Perspective on Paul: Collected Essays*, Wissenschaftliche Untersuchungen Zum Neuen Testament (Tübingen: Mohr Siebeck, 2005); Dunn, *Paul and the Mosaic Law* (Grand Rapids, Mich.: Eerdmans, 2001); E. P. Sanders, *Paul: A Very Short Introduction* (New York: Oxford University Press, 2001); Sanders, *Paul, the Law, and the Jewish People* (Philadelphia: Fortress Press, 1983). On the other hand, the association of Paul and various "heresies" of the second century and later, such as Marcianism, has motivated some interest in the reception of Paul. See the papers collected in Michael F. Bird and Joseph R. Dodson, eds., *Paul and the Second Century*, Library of New Testament Studies (New York: T&T Clark, 2011). Much of this work has been stimulated by Walter Bauer, Robert A. Kraft, and Gerhard Krodel, *Orthodoxy and Heresy in Earliest Christianity* (Philadelphia: Fortress Press, 1971).

lished presbyters.[2] It reflects a sense of community and mutual responsibility between members of a community of communities,[3] rather like the leagues of ancient Greek city-states. The letter also preserves one early expression of Pauline tradition.[4] The admonishment to the Corinthians that their schism has turned aside many,[5] and reference to "a shameful report ... that the steadfast and ancient church of the Corinthians is being disloyal [στασιάζειν] to the presbyters"[6] reminds us that Paul called the Corinthian church "the seal of my apostleship" (1 Cor 9:2), his "letter of recommendation" (2 Cor 3:2–3). Peter and Paul are named in *1 Clement* 5.1, 4–5, as "noble examples of our own generation [τῆς γενεᾶς ἡμῶν τὰ γενναῖα ὑποδείγματα]." In addition, direct reference to Paul's letter to the Corinthians in *1 Clement* 47.1 suggests that one basis for this sense of community may be common adherence to "Paul's gospel."[7]

2. The letter does not include the name of its author. It is addressed from the church at Rome to the church at Corinth and, consistent with its address, refers to its writer in the first person plural, rather than the singular (e.g., *1 Clem.* 7.1; 59.1–2). This gives the entire assembly a single voice, which I will call Clement for simplicity. The letter itself belongs to the genre of deliberative rhetoric, intended, as are others from the Greek literature of antiquity, to promote concord and to warn of the disastrous consequences of internal discord. It is unusual that Clement draws on the scriptures and history of the Jews rather than on the wealth of examples from Greek history and literature built up by prior use. See Odd Magne Bakke, *"Concord and Peace": A Rhetorical Analysis of the First Letter of Clement with an Emphasis on the Language of Unity and Sedition*, Wissenschaftliche Untersuchungen Zum Neuen Testament (Tübingen: Mohr Siebeck, 2001), 33–62, especially 54–61 and 324–26; W. C. Van Unnik, "Studies on the So-Called First Epistle of Clement, the Literary Genre," in *Encounters with Hellenism*, ed. Cilliers Breytenbach and Laurence L. Welborn (Leiden: Brill, 2004), 115–81, especially 165–66.

3. The strong feeling of association communicated to the Corinthian church through this letter suggests a "league" of "Pauline" churches, which serves as a basis for an early edition of Paul's letters arranged as "letters to seven churches." See Harry Y. Gamble, *Books and Readers in the Early Church: A History of Early Christian Texts* (New Haven, Conn.: Yale University Press, 1995), 59–62.

4. Daniel Marguerat, "Paul après Paul: Une histoire de réception," *New Testament Studies* 54, no. 3 (2008): 317–37, has described the reception of Paul in terms of three "poles": a documentary pole, consisting of the letters of Paul; a biographical pole, consisting of traditions about his life and work; and a doctoral pole, consisting in his permanent authority for the church. Traditions concerning Paul's life and work form a major influence on the construction of the image of Paul in the first century, and perhaps into the second century. I would argue that *1 Clement* represents another significant piece of evidence for the reception of Paul within the body of early Christian literature.

5. *1 Clem.* 46.9. All translations of *1 Clement* are the author's unless otherwise noted; passages from Scripture are taken from the NRSV.

6. *1 Clem.* 47.6–7.

7. Clement's use of Paul and other New Testament writings has been found clearest for 1 Corinthians and Romans, but knowledge of other letters is probable. Andreas Lindemann, "Paul's Influence on 'Clement' and Ignatius," in *Trajectories through the New Testament and the Apostolic Fathers*, ed. Andrew F. Gregory and Christopher M. Tuckett (Oxford: Oxford University Press, 2005), 9–24; Donald Alfred Hagner, *The Use of the Old and New Testaments in Clement of Rome*, Supplements to Novum Testamentum, 5.34 (Leiden: Brill, 1973), 176–271, especially 195–222; Andrew F. Gregory and C. M. Tuckett, eds.,

At the same time, *1 Clement* frequently refers to as "Old Testament"[8] people who are now associated with Christian tradition. The author calls them "ancient examples [ἄρχαια ὑποδείγματα]" in contrast to the "noble examples of our own generation."[9] These are examples demonstrating a particular quality, not types foreshadowing future action. Most of these occur in lists of examples arranged in generally historical order.[10] By including a few figures in more than one list or context, the letter continually brings the figure to mind. Uniquely, Moses is named five times, usually as the "faithful [or "trustworthy"] servant of the Lord," at intervals that span most of the body of the letter.[11] This paper seeks to elucidate the special significance of Moses for this early tradent of Paul. I will first examine in the letter the parallels constructed between Moses and the apostles, particularly Paul, then elucidate the consequences that the letter anticipates for its audience as a result of these parallels. Finally, I will draw some conclusions about the way that imitation and precedent function in *1 Clement* to construct citizenship in the community of the elect people of God.

Trajectories through the New Testament and the Apostolic Fathers (New York: Oxford University Press, 2005); Oxford Society of Historical Theology, *The New Testament in the Apostolic Fathers* (Oxford: Oxford University Press, 1905).

8. Hagner finds more than seventy quotations within the letter: Hagner, *The Use of the Old and New Testaments in Clement of Rome*, 21–33. Among the apostolic fathers, only the *Epistle of Barnabas* has more quotations. Robert A. Kraft, *Barnabas and the Didache*, vol. 3 of *The Apostolic Fathers: A New Translation and Commentary*, ed. Robert M. Grant (New York: Nelson, 1965), 179–182, available online at http://ccat.sas.upenn.edu/rak//publics/barn/barndidintro.htm.

9. There are thirty-one named figures in *1 Clement*. Only the apostles Peter and Paul are named among the examples of the contemporary γενεά. Among the remaining twenty-nine, only a handful are named more than once. These are Noah (7.4; 9.4); Abraham (10.1–7; 17.2; 31.1); Jacob (4.8; 31.3ff); Moses (4.10–12; 17.5–6; 43.1–6; 51.3–5; 53.2–4); and David (4.13; 18.1ff). Among these, Moses is unique in that he is referenced in five places, and in that he is referenced in the section of the letter that applies specifically to the Corinthian situation (44.2–58.2). It is the use of the examples in the first general section of the letter that reflects a particular view of history.

10. The rhetorical impact of the lists in *1 Clement*, as compared to the list in Hebrews 11, is often broken by the inclusion of long quotations from the biblical texts. The most significant examples are quotation of most of the story of Cain and Abel in the list in *1 Clement* 4.1–6; citations of all the promises to Abraham in *1 Clement* 10.1–6; and citation of Psalm 51 (50 LXX) for David's repentance. Michael R. Cosby, "The Rhetorical Composition of Hebrews 11," *Journal of Biblical Literature* 107, no. 2 (1988): 257–73; and more explicitly Cosby, *The Rhetorical Composition and Function of Hebrews 11 : In Light of Example Lists in Antiquity* (Macon, Ga.: Mercer University Press, 1988), 148–62. In each of these cases, the text is recognizably quoted, not paraphrased. I suggest that the long citations serve two purposes. First, they emphasize the importance of a particular topic. Second, they ensure that the Corinthians actually have the relevant text.

11. *1 Clem.* 4.10–12; 17.5–6; 43.1–6; 51.3–5, 53.2–4.

The Example of Moses

The example of Moses appears twice in a complex series of parallels in
1 Clement 40–44, which form the transition from the thesis to the hypothesis, from the general standards of Christian behavior to the specific situation
in Corinth.[12] Two distinct parallels are invoked to demonstrate that an ecclesiastical hierarchy is a manifestation of the divine will: a parallel between the
Levitical priesthood and the bishops and deacons of the church; and a parallel between Moses and the apostles. The parallels are clearest beginning with *1
Clement* 43.1:

And what wonder is it if those who were in Christ, and were entrusted by God
[πιστευθέντες παρὰ θεοῦ] with such a duty, established [καθιστάναι] those who have
been mentioned? Since the blessed Moses also "a faithful servant in all his house" [ὁ
μακάριος πιστὸς θεράπων ἐν ὅλῳ τῷ οἴκῳ Μωϋσῆς] noted down in the sacred books
all the injunctions [διατεταγμένα] which were given him; and the other prophets followed him, bearing witness with him to the laws which he had given.

This passage refers back to an earlier passage in the letter, in which the bishops
and deacons were established by the apostles in accordance with the instructions transmitted to them with the Gospel, as indicated below:

The Apostles received the Gospel [εὐηγγελίσθησαι] for us from the Lord Jesus Christ,
Jesus the Christ was sent from God.... Having therefore received their commands
[παραγγελία],... They preached from district to district, and from city to city, and they
appointed [καθιστάναι] their first converts [ἀπαρχή], testing [δοκιμάζειν] them by the
Spirit, to be bishops and deacons of the future believers [τῶν μελλόντων πιστεύειν].[13]

The establishment of these offices for future believers is presented as parallel to the commands that Moses noted down in the sacred books. The importance of doing what is commanded is established in *1 Clement* 40.1–3. The
social order established by the divine commands to Moses is given in 40.5; the
services commanded are outlined in 41.2:

Since then these things are manifest to us, and we have looked into the depths of the
divine knowledge [γνώσεως], we ought to do in order all things which the Master
commanded [κελεύειν] us to perform [ἐπιτελεῖν] at appointed times. He commanded
[κελεύειν] us to celebrate [ἐπιτελεῖσθαι] sacrifices [προσφορά] and services [λειτουργία],

12. Cosby, "The Rhetorical Composition of Hebrews 11," 259–61.
13. *1 Clem.* 42.1, 3a, 4.

and that it should not be thoughtlessly or in a disordered way, but at fixed times and hours. He has fixed [ὁρίζειν] by his supreme will the places and persons whom he desires for these celebrations [ἐπιτελεῖσθαι], in order that all things may be done piously according to his good pleasure and be acceptable to his will.[14]

For to the High Priest his proper ministrations [λειτουργία] are allotted [δεδομέναι εἰσίν], and to the priests the proper place [τόπος] has been appointed [προστέτακται], and on Levites their proper services [διακονία] have been imposed [ἐπίκεινται]. The layman [λαϊκός] is bound [δέδεται] by the ordinances [προστάγμα] of the laity.[15]

Not in every place, my brethren, are the daily sacrifices offered or the free-will offerings, or the sin-offerings and trespass-offerings [προσφέρονται θυσίαι ἐνδελεχισμοῦ ἢ εὐχῶν ἢ περὶ ἁμαρτίας καὶ πλημμελείας], but only in Jerusalem; and there also the offering is not made [προσφέρεται] in every place, but before the shrine, at the altar, and the offering is first inspected by the High Priest and the ministers already mentioned.[16]

The essential and fundamental concept is that the Master commands the services, and appoints the persons who are to perform them. The order of the Levites and their services were appointed through the commands given to Moses and recorded by him.[17] This passage in *1 Clement* 40.5 is the earliest known occurrence of the term "laity" to reflect a rank in an ecclesiastical hierarchy.[18] It reflects an understanding of the whole Mosaic Law as commanding services.[19] Clement speaks of the priestly order as a present reality.[20] The commands recorded by Moses were confirmed by the prophets who followed after him and are still in effect. They were perpetual ordinances. However, the commands of the Master are also to "us," the Roman and Corinthian churches. They include the instructions given to the apostles in 42.3. By implication, the instructions of the apostles are founding an order of worship in Christ, or

14. *1 Clem.* 40.1–3.

15. *1 Clem.* 40.5.

16. *1 Clem.* 41.2.

17. *1 Clem.* 40.5, 41.2, 43.1.

18. Annie Jaubert, *Épître aux Corinthiens Clemens Romanus*, Sources Chrétiennes, no. 167. (Paris: Éditions du Cerf, 1971), 163–66. Robert M. Grant and Holt H. Graham, eds., *First and Second Clement*, vol. 2 of *Apostolic Fathers: A New Translation and Commentary*, ed. Robert M. Grant (New York: T. Nelson, 1965), 69.

19. For Clement, obedience to commandments is an important aspect of righteous behavior. When he refers to specific requirements (*1 Clem.* 13.38), however, the references are not drawn from the Mosaic Torah.

20. This is true also in *1 Clement* 32.2, where the priests and Levites, all those serving (λειτουργοῦντες) the altar of God, are descendants of Jacob.

they are locating the believers in Christ within the order established by Moses, or both. In *1 Clement* 47.1, he refers the Corinthians to Paul's letter: "Take up the epistle of the blessed Paul the Apostle. What did he first write to you at the beginning of the gospel?"[21] Paul claims that he has laid the foundation in 1 Corinthians 3:10: "According to the grace of God given to me, like a skilled master builder, I laid a foundation, and someone else is building on it. Each builder must choose with care how to build on it."[22] He continues the admonition to the Corinthians by saying: "I sent to you Timothy, my beloved and faithful child in the Lord, to remind you of my ways in Christ, as I teach them everywhere in every church,"[23] and concludes the first letter to the Corinthians with: "When Timothy comes … "[24] and, "Now, brethren, you know that the household of Stephanus were the first converts in Achaia, and they have devoted themselves to the service of the saints; I urge you to be subject to such men and to every fellow worker and laborer."[25]

Clement interprets Paul's foundation to include the establishment of bishops and deacons.[26] He also appears to consider Paul's letters the record of that foundation.

For Clement, λειτουργία is acceptable only if performed by persons acceptable to the Father.[27] This can lead to jealousy and strife unless each member of the community submits himself to the requirements of his own rank.[28] Such jealousy and strife arose in the time of Moses,[29] and Clement gives a synopsis of the series of rebellions recounted in Numbers 16–17, with a particular focus on the incident of Aaron's budding rod.[30] The account related by Clem-

---

21. *1 Clem.* 47.1–2: τί πρῶτον ὑμῖν ἐν ἀρχῇ τοῦ εὐαγγελίου ἔγραψεν.

22. 1 Cor 3:10.

23. 1 Cor 4:17.

24. 1 Cor 16:10.

25. 1 Cor 16:15–16.

26. The first letter to the Corinthians presents the authority of Paul in tension with the authority of other apostles, particularly Peter. That tension is reflected in *1 Clement* as well. The construction of apostolic authority in *1 Clement* 43–44 does not name any specific apostle, but all apostles, generally. In *1 Clement* 5 both Peter and Paul are named. In contrast, Marguerat ("Paul après Paul," 328–29) points out that when the pastoral Epistles pseudepigraphically construct Paul as founder and organizer of the church, he is represented as the sole author and only named apostle and model (ὑποτύπωσις) (2 Tm 1:13).

27. *1 Clem.* 40.1–3.

28. *1 Clem.* 41.1.

29. *1 Clem.* 43.2.

30. *1 Clem.* 43.3–5.

ent differs from the account in Numbers 17:6–10 in several details,[31] as shown by the comparison below:

For when jealousy arose concerning the priesthood, and the tribes were quarreling as to which of them was adorned with that glorious title, Moses commanded the rulers of the twelve tribes to bring him rods, with the name of a tribe written on each; and he took them, and bound them, and sealed them with the rings of the rulers of the tribes, and put them away in the Tabernacle of Testimony on the table of God. And he shut the Tabernacle, and sealed the keys, as he had done with the rods, and he said to them, "Brethren, of whichever tribe the rod shall bud, this has God chosen for his priesthood and ministry." And when it was daylight he called together all Israel, six hundred thousand men, and showed the seals to the rulers of the tribes, and opened the Tabernacle of Testimony, and took forth the rods, and the rod of Aaron was found not only to have budded, but also to be bearing fruit.[32]

Moses spoke to the Israelites; and all their leaders gave him staffs, one for each leader, according to their ancestral houses, twelve staffs; and the staff of Aaron was among theirs. So Moses placed the staffs before the LORD in the tent of the covenant. When Moses went into the tent of the covenant on the next day, the staff of Aaron for the house of Levi had sprouted. It put forth buds, produced blossoms, and bore ripe almonds. Then Moses brought out all the staffs from before the LORD to all the Israelites; and they looked, and each man took his staff. And the LORD said to Moses, "Put back the staff of Aaron before the covenant, to be kept as a warning to rebels, so that you may make an end of their complaints against me, or else they will die."[33]

Clement describes an elaborate procedure of binding and sealing of the rods, then the sealing and barring of the Tabernacle. The opening of the tent and bringing forth of the rods is performed in the sight of the whole congregation of Israel. It is a public demonstration that no one has interfered with the test of the Lord's will. Numbers 17:7–8 finds it sufficient to state that the staffs were placed before the Lord in the Tabernacle, and Moses goes into the tent alone. For Clement, the incident is an example of public test and demonstration of divine sanction, witnessed by the whole congregation. Moses performed this public testing to avert disorder in Israel. The apostles tested their

---

31. Some of the details of the story from Numbers are present in other Hellenistic authors, particularly Philo of Alexandria (*Vit. Mos.* 2.178ff) and Josephus (*Ant.* 4.63ff). Clement's presentation as a whole has no known precedent, and may be original. See Andreas Lindemann, *Die Clemensbriefe*, vol. 17, Handbuch Zum Neuen Testament (Tübingen: Mohr Siebeck, 1992), 129. Jaubert, *Épître aux Corinthiens Clemens Romanus*, 170–71.

32. *1 Clem.* 42.2–5.

33. Nm 17:6–10.

appointees in the Spirit, thus a public test in Corinth would avert the disorder there. The example of Moses gives a procedure for such a test.

Clement depicts Moses describing the sign for the people when the tent is sealed. In Numbers 17:5, the Lord describes the sign to Moses, but the people are not told beforehand. Clement has shaped his version to emphasize the foreknowledge of Moses. He goes on to assert that the foreknowledge of the apostles, through Jesus Christ (not through Scripture!), is the basis for appointing bishops and deacons:

Our Apostles also knew through our Lord Jesus Christ that there would be strife for the title of bishop. For this cause, therefore, since they had received perfect foreknowledge [πρόγνωσις], they appointed those who have already been mentioned, and afterwards added the codicil that if they should fall asleep, other approved men [δεδοκιμασμένοι ἄνδρες] should succeed to their ministry [λειτουργία].[34]

In addition, instead of a progression from bud to blossom to almond, Aaron's rod is said to have budded, and also to be bearing fruit (καρπόν).[35] Clement goes on to speak of presbyters who obtain a fruitful and perfect release as blessed.[36] Aaron's rod "bearing fruit" points toward a productive ministry. The testing in the Spirit of the apostolic appointees and their successors is not a list of criteria, but an affirmation of the blessing of God upon the work and the worker. Like Moses, the apostles received instructions and tested their appointees. Like Moses, the apostles had foreknowledge. The precedent of Moses confirms the apostles as servants of God, carrying out the divine will with respect to the social ordering of the church. But the social order of the church is parallel, not identical, to the order established by Moses.

The incident of Aaron's budding rod follows and concludes the description of the Korahite rebellion in Numbers 16–17.[37] Clement summarizes this

---

34. *1 Clem.* 44.1–2.

35. The concept of "fruitfulness" reflected in the New Testament writings is too complex to develop in detail here. However, it is relevant that Paul uses the expression "to bear fruit [ἔχειν καρπόν]" in the subjunctive to express his desire to preach in Rome (Rom 1:13). In that context, a ministry that serves to convert and nurture believers "in Christ" bears fruit (cf. Rom 15:28; 1 Cor 14:14; Gal 5:22; Eph 5:9; Phil 1:11; 4:17; Col 1:6, 10; Heb 12:11; 13:15).

36. *1 Clem.* 44.5.

37. This complex pericope sees Korah, a Levite, and fellow Levites, accompanied by Dathan and Abirim of the tribe of Reuben, protesting the special status of Aaron as priest. Korah, and the Levites, are consumed by fire which comes out from the Lord. Dathan and Abirim "go down into Hades alive." The demonstration with the rods is a response to the protest of the remaining Israelites in reaction to the deaths of so many of their fellow tribesmen.

complex situation with the statement that "when all the tribes were in rebellion over the question which one of them should be adorned with the glorious title."[38] The incident forms a model for the current situation in Corinth.[39] This incident provides Clement not only with an example of a public testing that resolves conflict, but also with an example of the danger of doing anything against the will of God expressed in the commandments to Moses and the apostles:

Those therefore who do anything contrary to that which is agreeable to his will suffer the penalty of death. You see, brethren, that the more knowledge we have been entrusted with [κατηξιώθημεν γνώσεως], the greater risk do we incur.[40]

Divine judgment is introduced as a key aspect of the depiction of Moses, the servant of the Lord, through the accusation of a fellow Israelite:

Jealousy made Moses flee [φυγεῖν ἀναγκάζειν] from the presence of Pharaoh, king of Egypt,[41] when he heard a fellow tribesman say [Ex 2:14], "Who made [καθιστῆναι] you a judge [κριτής] or assessor [δικαστής] over us? Do you mean to kill me, as you killed the Egyptian yesterday?" Because of jealousy Aaron and Miriam were excluded from the camp.
    Jealousy brought about the swallowing up of Dathan and Abirim in Hades because they rebelled against Moses the servant of God.[42]

The modified quotation of Exodus 2:14 replaces "ruler [ἄρχων]" with "judge [κριτής]," foreshadowing judgment through Moses. Miriam and Aaron,[43] then

38. *1 Clem.* 43.2.

39. Lindemann, *Die Clemensbriefe*, 129.

40. *1 Clem.* 41.3–4.

41. Both Artapanus (cited in Eusebius, *Praeparatio Evangelica* 9.27.7, 17) and Josephus (*Ant.* 2.254–255) imply that Moses fled from the jealousy of Pharaoh or members of his court. James L. Kugel, *Traditions of the Bible : A Guide to the Bible as It Was at the Start of the Common Era* (Cambridge, Mass.: Harvard University Press, 1998), 511–12. Clement does not appear to be drawing on this tradition. Clement implies that it is the fellow Israelite who is jealous of Moses, that is, of the privileges that Moses enjoys. The interpretation is closer to that reflected in Acts 7:23–29, 35 (the speech of Stephen). That passage emphasizes the rejection of Moses, not jealousy of Moses. See chapter 2 of this volume, Dulcinea Boesenberg "Luke's Narrative Claim on Moses, the Persecuted Prophet." Hebrews 11:24–25 may allude to Exodus 2:14 as a renunciation of the pleasures of sin for the reward of seeing the invisible. D'Angelo, *Moses,* 17–64.

42. *1 Clem.* 4.10–12.

43. In Numbers 12:15, only Miriam is shut outside the camp. The designation of Jesus Christ as high priest is used both in the letter to the Hebrews (2:17; 5:1,10; 6:20; 7:26; 8:3; 9:7, 11, 25) and in *1 Clement* (36.1; 61.3; 64.1). It is not present in the letters of Paul. Hagner, *The Use of the Old and New Testaments in Clement of Rome*, 179–84; Gareth Lee Cockerill, "Heb 1:1–14, *1 Clem.* 36:1–6 and the High Priest Title,"

Dathan and Abirim are examples of those who incurred judgment for their jealous rebellion against Moses.[44] The judgment that Dathan and Abirim "go down into Hades alive" is specifically applied to the Corinthians as an appeal to repent their transgression:

And those who were the leaders [ἀρχηγοί] of sedition [στάσις] and disagreement [διχοστασία] are bound to consider the common hope. For those who live in fear and love are willing to suffer torture themselves rather than their neighbors, and they suffer the blame of themselves, rather than of our tradition of noble and righteous harmony, for it is better for man to confess his transgressions than to harden his heart, even as the heart of those was hardened who rebelled against God's servant Moses, and their condemnation [κρίμα] was made manifest, for "they went down into Hades alive" and "death shall be their shepherd." Pharaoh and his army and all the rulers of Egypt, "the chariots and their riders," were sunk in the Red Sea and perished for no other cause than that their foolish hearts were hardened, after the signs and wonders had been wrought in the land of Egypt by God's servant Moses.[45]

Opposition to Moses, the servant of the Lord, brought divine judgment, and opposition to the apostolic order will bring judgment. Judgment through Moses is also an issue in the example of Moses in *1 Clement* 17.5–6:

Moses was called "Faithful with all his house," and through his ministry [ὑπηρεσία] God judged [κρίνειν] Egypt with their scourges and torments; but he, though he was given great glory [δοξασθεὶς μεγάλως], did not use great words, but, when an oracle was given to him from the bush, said: "Who am I that thou sendest [πέμπειν] me? Nay, I am a man of feeble speech, and a slow tongue." And again he says, "But I am as smoke from a pot."[46]

In Numbers 12:8, it is God himself who calls Moses "faithful with all his house." Moses is glorified by this commendation and by the ministry of judgment that God brings on Egypt through him. Moses is the agent (ὑπηρεσία), but God is the judge. The authority of Moses derives from his status as the faithful servant. Pharaoh and all of Egypt with him perish for their rejection of the message delivered through the signs performed by the servant, Moses. If

---

Journal of Biblical Literature 97, no. 3 (1978): 437–40. It suggests that Clement's conception of ecclesiastical offices in relation to the Aaronic priesthood is not derived from Paul or his letters alone. The reference to Aaron's being lodged outside the camp is the only indication in the letter that Jesus Christ displaces the Aaronic high priest.

44. Jaubert, *Épître aux Corinthiens Clemens Romanus*, 107n3.
45. *1 Clem.* 51.1b–4.
46. *1 Clem.* 17.5–6.

Dathan and Abirim represent those within the chosen people who reject the commands of Moses, Pharaoh and the Egyptians represent those outside the household of God who reject the commands of Moses.

Averting judgment and promoting the common hope is the occasion for the final reference to Moses in *1 Clement* 53–54. This is a composite quotation of Deuteronomy 9:12–14 and Exodus 32:31–32, reminding the Corinthians of Moses's intercession for the Israelites after the incident of the golden calf. Moses would rather be blotted out of the book of the living with the people, than see them blotted out and their inheritance forfeit.[47] Moses places the common hope above his own life, exactly the attitude that Clement appealed to the Corinthians to adopt.[48] Clement exhorts the Corinthians to intercede for those who have committed any transgression,[49] just as the servant Moses asked forgiveness for the people.[50] The Corinthians are to imitate Moses.

Clement exhorts the Corinthians in *1 Clement* 54.2–4 that flight, not self-sacrifice, is better than contention:

Who then among you is noble, who is compassionate, who is filled with love? Let him cry:—"If sedition and strife and divisions [στάσις καὶ ἔρις καὶ σχίσματα] have arisen on my account, I will depart, I will go away whithersoever you will, and I will obey the commands [προστασσόμενα] of the people; only let the flock of Christ have peace with the presbyters set over it. He who does this will win for himself great glory [κλέος] in Christ, and every place will receive him.[51]

Clement has opened his example of Moses with flight in the face of challenge to his authority by a fellow Israelite (*1 Clem.* 4.10). In this Moses follows the example of Jacob (*1 Clem.* 4.8; 31.4), who greatly glorified by God despite his exile:

Through jealousy our father Jacob ran from the face of Esau his brother.[52]

---

47. The use of Moses's intercession to preserve the inheritance of Israel is opposed in early Christian literature by use of the incident of the golden calf to indicate rejection of Moses (Acts 7:39–43) and rejection by God (*Epistle of Barnabas* 4.7–8; 14.3–4). Kraft, *Barnabas and the Didache*, 90, 125; Boesenberg, "Narrative Claim." 10–12.

48. See *1 Clem.* 51.2, above.

49. *1 Clem.* 56.1.

50. *1 Clem.* 53.5.

51. *1 Clem.* 54.2–4.

52. *1 Clem.* 4.8.

Jacob departed from his country in meekness because of his brother, and went to Laban and served him, and to him was given the scepter of the twelve tribes of Israel.[53]

But it also points toward the example of Paul:

Through jealousy [ζῆλος] and strife [ἔρις] Paul showed the way to the prize of endurance; seven times he was in bonds, he was exiled [φυγαδευθῆναι], he was stoned, he was a herald both in the East and in the West, he gained the noble fame [κλέος] of his faith, he taught righteousness to all the world, and when he had reached the limits of the West he gave his testimony before the rulers, and thus passed from the world and was taken up into the Holy Place—the greatest example [ὑπογραμμός] of endurance.[54]

Paul became fugitive, but because of his exile, he became a herald in East and West, taught righteousness to all the world, and reached the limits of the West. He was received in every place, even the Holy Place. He becomes not only an example but a model. Clement concludes: "Those governing the life of the citizens of God for themselves without regret did and will do these things."[55]

Conclusion

In *1 Clement*, the primary designation of Moses is the "servant of God." Moses serves within the letter from the church at Rome to the church at Corinth as an example not primarily for the Corinthians, but for the apostles. The apostles became imitators of Moses, their actions are like those of Moses, in the sense that in serving God through Jesus Christ, they became like Moses. The likeness between Moses and the apostles functions to authorize the appointment of bishops and deacons to perform the services commanded of those "in Christ,"[56] and the writing of Paul. However, rather than investing Moses with authority over the apostles,[57] the likeness to Moses extends the authority of Moses to the apostles through a pattern of the servant of the

53. *1 Clem.* 31.4.
54. *1 Clem.* 5.5–7.
55. *1 Clem.* 53.4: ταῦτα οἱ πολιτευόμενοι τὴν ἀμεταμέλητον πολιτείαν τοῦ θεοῦ ἐποίησαν καὶ ποιήσουσιν (translation mine).
56. James S. Jeffers, *Conflict at Rome: Social Order and Hierarchy in Early Christianity* (Minneapolis, Minn.: Fortress Press, 1991), 145; John G. Gager, *Kingdom and Community: The Social World of Early Christianity*, Prentice-Hall Studies in Religion Series (Englewood Cliffs, N.J.: Prentice-Hall, 1975), 70.
57. Elizabeth A. Castelli suggested that Paul's use of imitation in 1 Corinthians 4:16 and 11:1, and in Philippians 3:17, promotes Paul's own authority, and also a culture of sameness; *Imagining Paul: A Discourse of Power* (Louisville, Ky.: Westminster/John Knox, 1991), 95–117.

Lord. Both apostolic authority and Mosaic authority are derived from the divine authority. The apostolic order exists alongside the Mosaic order, which is depicted as a present reality.

The Corinthians are exhorted to be obedient to the instructions of the apostles and imitators of the life of the apostle(s) and Moses. The "Christian Moses" constructed in the letter known as *1 Clement* uses biographical incidents from the life of Moses, allusion to the writings attributed to Moses, and the reputation of Moses as the teacher and instructor of Israel to provide a precedent for constructing the authority of the apostle(s), particularly Paul, as teachers and instructors of the communities "in Christ." The construction of the reception of Paul, along the three poles of literature, biography, and teaching, follows the example and model of the reception of Moses as literature, biography, and instructor available to the Christians in the first century.

David A. Smith

5. "A SERVANT IN GOD'S HOUSE"

Competing Roles of Moses in 1 Clement
and the Epistle to the Hebrews

Theories of an early "parting of the ways" between church and synagogue depend upon particular readings of ancient texts, even as they shape the interpretation of these texts in light of the interpreter's governing historical model. While the theory of an early parting of the ways between Jewish and proto-orthodox Christian communities in Rome has been the dominant scholarly view for some time, recent challenges to this consensus invite a reexamination of the key texts relevant to the question of Jewish and Christian identities.[1] In the cases of *1 Clement* and the letter to the Hebrews, two such texts frequently used as evidence for reconstruction of Christian communities in Rome at the end of the first century, a description of the thought of these texts and their use for the writing of social history is governed not only by what Hebrews and *1 Clement* say individually but particularly by an understanding of the inter-

---

1. In his extensive study of Jewish Christianity, Reidar Hvalvik depends on particular readings of Hebrews and *1 Clement* as part of his case for an early break between church and synagogue in Rome. Reidar Hvalvik, *Jewish Believers in Jesus: The Early Centuries*, ed. Oskar Skarsaune and Reidar Hvalvik (Peabody, Mass.: Hendrickson, 2007), 205–11. See also Peter Lampe, *From Paul to Valentinus: Christians at Rome in the First Two Centuries*, trans. Michael Steinhauser, ed. Marshall D. Johnson (Minneapolis, Minn.: Fortress Press, 2003), 11–18. For a quite different reading of the evidence, which finds the origins of "Christianity" and "Judaism" to have been closely intermingled, "twins joined at the hip," see Daniel Boyarin, *Border Lines: The Partition of Judaeo-Christianity* (Philadelphia: University of Pennsylvania Press, 2006), 5.

textual relationship that exists between these two texts.[2] The dominant view, at least as early as Eusebius, is the straightforward supposition that the several instances of conspicuous verbal correspondence indicate that *1 Clement* utilized Hebrews as a literary source. However simple this solution may appear, it does not account for the most striking differences between these texts but rather tacitly encourages a harmonization of their distinctive thought-patterns and hermeneutical orientations in a manner that may obscure their true historical relationship, particularly on the question of the orientation of each author toward Judaism. The present article challenges this dominant viewpoint, suggesting an alternative relationship between these important texts that allows their distinctive visions to stand in their natural contrast to one another. When the distinctive voices of these documents are heard, it should be apparent that the greatest conceptual difference between these texts is focused upon their quite different orientations toward the figure of Moses, and that this difference has important implications for an historical appraisal of early Christian relations to Jewish identity.

The Traditional View: The Author of *1 Clement* Read and Used Hebrews

The traditional understanding of the verbal parallels between these documents as indicating *1 Clement*'s use of Hebrews as a written source dates to Eusebius in the fourth century. The bishop writes, regarding Clement's letter,

> In this he has many thoughts parallel to the Epistle to the Hebrews, and actually makes some verbal quotations from it showing clearly that it was not a recent production, and for this reason, too, it has seemed natural to include it among the other writings of the Apostle. For Paul had spoken in writing to the Hebrews in their native language, and some say that the evangelist Luke, others that this same Clement translated the writing. And the truth of this would be supported by the similarity of style preserved by the Epistle of Clement and that to the Hebrews, and by the little difference between the thoughts of both writings.[3]

2. In Raymond Brown's reconstruction, Hebrews is treated along with 1 Peter as representative of the "Second Generation" in the development of Roman Christianity, with *1 Clement* giving evidence of the "Third Generation." Raymond E. Brown, *Antioch and Rome: New Testament Cradles of Catholic Christianity*, ed. Raymond E. Brown and John P. Meier (New York: Paulist Press, 1982), 128ff.

3. Eusebius, *Hist. Eccl.*, trans. Kirsopp Lake, Loeb Classical Library 153 (Cambridge, Mass.: Harvard University Press, 1926), 3.38.1–3.

Following Eusebius (and the textual similarities he cites), most scholars
have seen in *1 Clement* a use of Hebrews that is "overwhelming and undeni-
able."[4] This allegedly indisputable relationship has provided a geographical
and chronological anchor for Hebrews, which is otherwise not early attested
in the Western church.[5] Although older scholarship, perhaps following Eusebius, understood the later ascription "to the Hebrews" to indicate an original Palestinian readership,[6] a growing number of modern scholars understand Hebrews to have been written to the church in Rome.[7] This modern
view depends largely on the assumption that the author of *1 Clement* read and
used Hebrews, as well as on an interpretation of "those from Italy" who send
their greetings in Hebrews 13:24 as displaced Romans greeting those in their
hometown. An originally Roman audience for Hebrews offers an historical
explanation for the verbal similarities with *1 Clement* and allows Hebrews to
be utilized as an additional source for the reconstruction of social history and
theology in early Christian Rome.[8]

The *Prima Facie* Problem with the Traditional View: Difference in Theological Outlook

While most modern scholars accept Eusebius's view of Clement's textual
dependence on Hebrews, Eusebius's assertion of "the little difference between
the thoughts of both writings" has received more varied treatment. As Ray-

---

4. J. B. Lightfoot, *The Apostolic Fathers*, (London: Macmillan, 1890), 1:353. See also Harold Attridge, *The Epistle to the Hebrews*, Hermeneia (Philadelphia: Fortress Press, 1989), 6; Edgar J. Goodspeed,
"First Clement Called Forth by Hebrews," *Journal of Biblical Literature* 30, no. 2 (1911): 157.

5. Horacio Lona astutely observes that, on grounds of late Roman canonical acceptance, the notion that *1 Clement* used Hebrews is problematic. See *Der Erste Clemensbrief. Kommentar zu den Apostolischen Vätern*. (Göttingen: Vandenhoeck & Ruprecht, 1998), 53.

6. For example, George Wesley Buchanan, *To the Hebrews: Translation, Comment and Conclusions*.
(Garden City, N.J.: Doubleday, 1981), 255–68.

7. See Goodspeed, "First Clement Called Forth by Hebrews," 157–60; Brown, *Antioch and Rome*,
149; Hvalvik, *Jewish Believers in Jesus*, 207; and, cautiously, Attridge, *Epistle to the Hebrews*, 9–10.

8. In view of certain non-scriptural verbal parallels discussed below, as well as a common use of biblical tradition shared with *1 Clement*, it is indeed tempting to conclude that Hebrews circulated in and
around Rome. While this is certainly *possible*, we should approach such a judgment with caution, for the
imperial city's importance and central location within the network of maritime trade routes must have
made Rome a natural place where many early Christian writings converged, including those with origins
far from Rome. We must distinguish between the geographical movement of texts and ideas and the precise literary relationship between the documents in question.

mond Brown has perceived, the conception of the levitical cult in *1 Clement* takes the author "in a direction quite opposite to the one urged by Hebrews."[9] While difference in theological outlook does not in principle exclude the possibility of textual dependence, in the case of *1 Clement* and Hebrews the thematic and theological differences between the works are so pronounced as to call into question the traditional view of the textual relationship. In Hebrews, the priestly self-sacrifice of Jesus has sanctified God's people definitively, demonstrating the insufficient, temporary, and typological character of the sacrificial system of the Torah.[10] For Hebrews, the priesthood of Jesus means that the levitical system is no longer necessary or valid: "He abolishes the first in order to establish the second."[11] By contrast, *1 Clement* speaks with unqualified approval of Temple worship, seeing the levitical cult as a model of order and piety:

Those who make their sacrificial offerings at the arranged times are acceptable and blessed. And since they follow the ordinances of the Master, they commit no sin. For special liturgical rites have been assigned to the high priest, and a special place has been designated for the regular priests, and special ministries established for the Levites.[12]

This levitical system is not, in *1 Clement*, superseded by a theology of Jesus' high-priesthood,[13] but applied directly to the church leaders: "Brothers, let each of us be pleasing to God by keeping our special assignments with a good conscience not violating the established rule of his ministry."[14] Whereas the argument in Hebrews is shaped by the author's Christology, resulting in the interpretive subordination of Israel's cult to Jesus, the author of *1 Clement* seems unaffected by this Christological concern and free to speak in a quite

9. Brown, *Antioch and Rome*, 169.

10. Heb 10:1–14.

11. Heb 10:9b.

12. *1 Clem.* 40.4–5, in *The Apostolic Fathers*, vol. 1, *I Clement. II Clement. Ignatius. Polycarp. Didache*, ed. and trans. Bart D. Ehrman, Loeb Classical Library 24 (Cambridge, Mass.: Harvard University Press, 2003). The reference to the Temple service in the present tense should not be read as indicative of a pre-70 C.E. situation. Decades after the destruction, Josephus speaks of the Temple in the present tense (*Ant.* 4.9.1–7).

13. Like the letter to the Hebrews, *1 Clement* refers to Jesus as high priest (61.3, 64.1), but only in conjunction with the title "guardian" in a manner suggesting dependence upon a liturgical tradition—in both cases, "διὰ τοῦ ἀρχιερέως καὶ προστάτου [τῶν ψυχῶν] ἡμῶν Ἰησοῦ Χριστοῦ." The priestly title receives none of the attention it does in Hebrews.

14. *1 Clem.* 41.1.

independent voice regarding his admiration for a system that hardly appears theologically "obsolete."[15]

This lack of Christological focus in *1 Clement*, relative to Hebrews, is pervasive. Both Hebrews and *1 Clement*, in deep dependence upon Jewish tradition, mine the Jewish Scriptures for biblical prototypes of Christian faithfulness. However, the centerpiece of each author's hermeneutic is markedly different. In Hebrews 11, the array of faithful individuals cited from the Scriptures reaches a climax in the call to follow the example of Jesus.[16] Despite its much greater length, however, *1 Clement* does not appeal to Jesus in this way.[17] Rather, Clement multiplies countless moral exemplars from Scripture, with Moses as the crowning embodiment of piety, wisdom, and sacrificial love. As we shall see, it is precisely this sort of veneration of Moses, particularly Clement's lack of Christological focus,[18] that Hebrews has sought to undermine. But before gaining a clear view of the distinctive presentations of Moses in these two works, we should first examine the evidence for a literary dependence between them.

Common Language Not Related to Scriptural Citation

While the greatest verbal correspondences between *1 Clement* and the letter to the Hebrews involve the citation of common biblical sources, several passages display common language not borrowed from the Scriptures. These

15. cf. Heb 8:13.

16. Heb 12:1–3.

17. The one exception to this statement begins at *1 Clement* 16.2, "The scepter of God's majesty, the Lord Jesus Christ, did not come with an ostentatious show of arrogance or haughtiness—even though he could have done so—but with a humble mind," and finishes several lines later, "You see, beloved men, the example that he has given us" (16.17). The humble nature of Christ's incarnation, as understood through Isaiah 53 (*1 Clem.* 16.3ff) is intended as a model for humility among church leaders in Corinth, "For Christ belongs to those who are humble minded, not those who vaunt themselves over his flock" (*1 Clem.* 16.1). The lengthy quotation from Isaiah that constitutes most of *1 Clement* 16 reveals that Clement's appeal to Christ as an example is subordinate to his larger project of presenting biblical precedent.

18. Christology is certainly important to Clement, and the influence of Pauline tradition is evident: *1 Clement* speaks of Christ as the "first fruit of the resurrection from the dead" (24.1, cf. 1 Cor 15:20), of sharing in the blood of Christ (21.6, cf. Rom 3:25; 1 Cor 10:16), and gives a parting benediction in Pauline terms: "the grace of the Lord Jesus Christ be with you" (65.2, cf. 2 Cor 13:13). However, Christology does not exercise a dogmatic influence over Clement's hermeneutic, as it does in Hebrews.

passages evidence the close connection between these texts, though it is not possible from these to specify the literary relationship between them.

Two passages state with nearly identical language the conviction that it is impossible for God to lie: οὐδὲν γὰρ ἀδύνατον παρὰ τῷ Θεῷ, εἰ μὴ τὸ ψεύσασθαι;[19] ἀδύνατον ψεύσασθαι τὸν θεόν.[20] Although the verbal correspondence is close, the assertion is so basic—neither author feels compelled to defend it—that we may assume it was generally accepted. More difficult to explain is the reference to "sheepskins and goatskins" in both texts. In Hebrews, those who set an example by their faith "went about in skins of sheep and goats [περιῆλθονὲν μηλωταῖς, ἐν αἰγείοις δέρμασιν]."[21] Clement also urges his readers to "become imitators also of those who went about in the skins of goats and sheep [οἵτινες ἐν δέρμασιν αἰγείοις καὶ μηλωταῖς περιεπάτησαν] proclaiming the coming of Christ. We mean Elijah and Elisha, and also Ezekiel, the prophets...."[22] The combination of these words (δέρμασιν, αἰγείοις, μηλωταῖς) does not appear outside these two texts, and commentators have frequently seen here a definitive confirmation of textual dependence.[23] While this is certainly plausible, it may be more likely, in view of the forthcoming analysis, that this odd similarity may be explained as a common tradition of glorifying the suffering of the prophets.

Common Language Involving Scriptural Citation

A comparison of biblical citations found in both *I Clement* and Hebrews suggests an exegetical tradition common to both. (See figure 5-1; in the comparisons illustrated here, language common to *I Clement* and Hebrews is in bold, while biblical material is underlined.) The strongest verbal correspondence between these two texts is the similarity between the citations from the Psalms in *I Clement* 36 and Hebrews 1. The two documents share quotations from Psalms 2, 103, and 109, as well as the introductory phrase indicating the disparity between Christ and the angels, in accordance with the superiority

19. *I Clem.* 27.2.
20. Heb 6:18.
21. Heb 11:37.
22. *I Clem.* 17.1.
23. Thus, Lightfoot asserts, "The whole passage is borrowed from the opening of the Epistle to the Hebrews, from which expressions, arguments, and quotations are taken," *The Apostolic Fathers*, 2:112. See also Attridge, *Epistle to the Hebrews*, 6.

of the inherited name. Furthermore, Christ is named as high priest, who is either helper (*1 Clement*) or sympathizer (Hebrews) with weakness, and he is variously described using the phrase "being the brightness [ὢν ἀπαύγασμα]." Moreover, both texts include a contrast between Psalm 2, which speaks of the son, and Psalm 103, which speaks of the angels.

Commentators regularly observe these similarities and rightly infer that these verbal correspondences require the postulation of a relationship of literary dependence between *1 Clement* and Hebrews.[24] However, the tendency (from Eusebius onward) has been to overlook the differences between these passages and so to assume a simple relationship of direct dependence. The differences between the two texts are substantial. In addition to the different order of the three common citations, Clement includes Psalm 2:8, which is not cited by Hebrews, and omits at least four citations that are preserved in Hebrews 1 (including 2 Sm 7:14, Dt 32:34, Ps 44:7, and Ps 101:26–28). Most importantly, the authors develop this common biblical material for markedly different purposes. The author of Hebrews utilizes the contrast between the psalm citations to introduce an extended warning against confusing the role of Christ with that of the angels.[25] The author of *1 Clement*, however, is uninterested in the relationship of Christ to the angels, but instead develops the reference to "enemies" in Psalm 109 to call the Corinthian Christians to an orderly battle modeled on the organization of the Roman legions.[26] While the contrast between the angels and the son is central to the Christology of Hebrews, it appears in *1 Clement* as a mere repetition, unrelated to that author's larger rhetorical aims, which are primarily ecclesiological. The absence of any apparent rhetorical purpose for the contrast between angels and the son in *1 Clement*, suggests that in *1 Clement* this contrast is a fossil of a prior tradition. The fact that in Hebrews the same contrast is central to the author's theological argument has led the majority of interpreters to conclude that the author of Hebrews was the originator of this tradition, rather than one of its early perpetuators.[27]

24. See Attridge, *Epistle to the Hebrews*, 6–7; Gareth Lee Cockerill, *The Epistle to the Hebrews*, New International Commentary on the New Testament (Grand Rapids, Mich.: Eerdmans, 2012), 34; Paul Ellingworth, *The Epistle to the Hebrews: A Commentary on the Greek Text*, NIGTC (Grand Rapids, Mich.: Eerdmans, 1993), 29.
25. Heb 2:1ff.
26. *1 Clem.* 37.
27. It is crucial for the right appraisal of the historical relationship of these texts to recognize the

Figure 5-1. Comparison of *1 Clement* with Hebrews 1

1 Clement 36.2-6

...Ἰησοῦν Χριστόν, τὸν ἀρχιερέα τῶν προσφορῶν ἡμῶν, τὸν προστάτην καὶ βοηθὸν τῆς ἀσθενείας ἡμῶν...διὰ τούτου ἠθέλησεν ὁ δεσπότης τῆς ἀθανάτου γνώσεως ἡμᾶς γεύσασθαι· ὃς ὢν ἀπαύγασμα τῆς μεγαλωσύνης αὐτοῦ / τοσούτῳ μείζων ἐστὶν ἀγγέλων, ὅσῳ διαφορώτερον ὄνομα κεκληρονόμηκεν.

Ps 103.4 — 3 γέγραπται γὰρ οὕτως· Ὁ ποιῶν τοὺς ἀγγέλους αὐτοῦ πνεύματα καὶ τοὺς λειτουργοὺς αὐτοῦ πυρὸς φλόγα.

Ps 2.7-8 — 4 Ἐπὶ δὲ τῷ υἱῷ αὐτοῦ οὕτως εἶπεν ὁ δεσπότης· Υἱός μου εἶ σύ, ἐγὼ σήμερον γεγέννηκά σε· αἴτησαι παρ' ἐμοῦ, καὶ δώσω σοι ἔθνη τὴν κληρονομίαν σου, καὶ τὴν κατάσχεσίν σου τὰ πέρατα τῆς γῆς.

Ps 109.1 — 5 καὶ πάλιν λέγει πρὸς αὐτόν· Κάθου ἐκ δεξιῶν μου, ἕως ἂν θῶ τοὺς ἐχθρούς σου ὑποπόδιον τῶν ποδῶν σου.

6 Τίνες οὖν οἱ ἐχθροί; οἱ φαῦλοι καὶ ἀντιτασσόμενοι τῷ θελήματι αὐτοῦ.

Hebrews 1.3-13, 4.15a

3 ὃς ὢν ἀπαύγασμα τῆς δόξης καὶ χαρακτὴρ τῆς ὑποστάσεως αὐτοῦ... 4 τοσούτῳ κρείττων γενόμενος τῶν ἀγγέλων ὅσῳ διαφορώτερον παρ' αὐτοὺς κεκληρονόμηκεν ὄνομα. — Ps 2.7

5 Τίνι γὰρ εἶπέν ποτε τῶν ἀγγέλων· υἱός μου εἶ σύ, ἐγὼ σήμερον γεγέννηκά σε; καὶ πάλιν· ἐγὼ ἔσομαι αὐτῷ εἰς πατέρα, καὶ αὐτὸς ἔσται μοι εἰς υἱόν; — 2 Sam 7.14

6 ὅταν δὲ πάλιν εἰσαγάγῃ τὸν πρωτότοκον εἰς τὴν οἰκουμένην, λέγει· καὶ προσκυνησάτωσαν αὐτῷ πάντες ἄγγελοι θεοῦ. — Deut 32.43

7 καὶ πρὸς μὲν τοὺς ἀγγέλους λέγει· ὁ ποιῶν τοὺς ἀγγέλους αὐτοῦ πνεύματα καὶ τοὺς λειτουργοὺς αὐτοῦ πυρὸς φλόγα... — Ps 103.4

13 πρὸς τίνα δὲ τῶν ἀγγέλων εἴρηκέν ποτε· κάθου ἐκ δεξιῶν μου, ἕως ἂν θῶ τοὺς ἐχθρούς σου ὑποπόδιον τῶν ποδῶν σου...4.15a οὐ γὰρ ἔχομεν ἀρχιερέα μὴ δυνάμενον συμπαθῆσαι ταῖς ἀσθενείας ἡμῶν. — Ps 109.1

However, the assumption that *1 Clement* was directly dependent upon Hebrews instead of a common tradition is not, in fact, the simple solution that it appears. To begin, it is unclear why, if the psalm citations in *1 Clement* 36 are derived from Hebrews 1, Clement would have selectively excluded the reference to Psalm 44:7, which would have supported his concern with the order of God's rule. This omission is striking when one considers that the author of *1 Clement* was apparently not concerned to be succinct and regularly quotes long selections of Scripture. If Clement elsewhere is so verbose in his citations, and if in this chapter he is so dependent upon his written source that he includes that source's introductory material to the psalm citations—material that is entirely unrelated to his rhetorical purpose—then the absence of important citations from Hebrews 1, the addition of material from Psalm 2:8, and the reordering of the citations included all require explanation.[28] This is particularly the case if the use of these common citations by the two writers differs substantially in both form and content and if these structural and conceptual differences are not limited to the present instance but, rather, may be shown to be a persistent feature of the relationship between *1 Clement* and Hebrews.

Both *1 Clement* and Hebrews quote Proverbs 3:12 to encourage their readers to endure discipline as a sign of God's parental love (figure 5-2). However, the citations differ significantly. Hebrews 12:5–6 includes Proverbs 3:11, whereas *1 Clement* 56 prefaces Proverbs 3:12 with a quotation from Psalm 117:18 (LXX), and follows it with Psalm 141:5, blending these three citations to create a single "holy word." Clement then proceeds to quote an extended section of the book of Job.[29] The combination of the text from Proverbs with other biblical texts suggests that, in this instance, Clement may be combining these texts freely and is here no more dependent on Hebrews than on the Septuagint. The shared text and the common paraenetic tone do suggest that the Prov-

---

traditional nature of this contrast between angels and the son as it appears in *1 Clement*. The standard interpretation of *1 Clement* as dependent upon Hebrews, the purported originator of the contrast, cannot be simply reversed, for *1 Clement* cannot reasonably be thought to have originally composed this contrast.

28. As Martin C. Albl observes, "If one assumes *1 Clement*'s dependence on Hebrews, no clear rationale or pattern for *1 Clement*'s abbreviations and adaptations *vis à vis* Hebrews is evident" (*"And Scripture Cannot Be Broken": The Form and Function of the Early Christian* Testimonia *Collections*, Novum-Testamentum, Supplements 96 [Leiden: Brill, 1999], 204).

29. *1 Clem.* 56.6ff.

Clement 56.3-5		Hebrews 12.5-6	
	οὕτως γὰρ φησιν ὁ ἅγιος λόγος·	ἐκλέλησθε τῆς παρακλήσεως, ἥτις	
Ps 117.18	Παιδεύων ἐπαίδευσέν με ὁ Κύριος,	ὑμῖν ὡς υἱοῖς διαλέγεται·	
	καὶ τῷ θανάτῳ οὐ παρέδωκέν με. ὃν	υἱέ μου, μὴ ὀλιγώρει παιδείας κυρίου	Prov
	γὰρ ἀγαπᾷ Κύριος παιδεύει,	μηδὲ ἐκλύου ὑπ᾽ αὐτοῦ ἐλεγχόμενος·	3.11-12
Prov	μαστιγοῖ δὲ πάντα υἱὸν ὃν	ὃν γὰρ ἀγαπᾷ κύριος παιδεύει,	
3.12	παραδέχεται. Παιδεύσει με γάρ,	μαστιγοῖ δὲ πάντα υἱὸν ὃν	
	φησίν, δίκαιος ἐν ἐλέει καὶ ἐλέγξει	παραδέχεται.	
Ps 141.5	με, ἔλεος δὲ ἁμαρτωλῶν μὴ λιπανάτω		
	τὴν κεφαλήν μου.		

Figure 5-2. Comparison of *1 Clement* with Hebrews 12

erbs passage was part of a shared tradition, but nothing indicates that Clement learned the tradition from the letter to the Hebrews.

The comparison of the interpretation of Numbers 12:6–7 in *1 Clement* and in Hebrews places the theological outlook of these two works in sharpest relief. Both authors are clearly dependent upon the traditions that honors Moses above other prophets in Israel:

If a prophet of the Lord arises from you, I will be known to him in a vision, and in his sleep I will speak to him. Not so with my servant Moses; he is faithful in all of my household [οὐχ οὕτως ὁ θεράπων μου Μωυσῆς ἐν ὅλῳ τῷοἴκῳ μου πιστὸς ἐστιν]. I will speak to him face to face.[30]

In Hebrews this special status of Moses is undermined by the assertion that "Christ, however, was faithful over God's house *as a son*," and so "Jesus is worthy of more glory than Moses, just as the builder of a house has more honor than the house itself."[31] The characterization of Moses as a servant (ὡς θεράπων) is moved to the end of the citation to emphasize its contrast with sonship (ὡς υἱὸς). Relative to the son, θεράπων would connote not honor but servitude, and the author's conviction of the categorical supremacy of Jesus neutralizes any suggestion that Moses (and, in view of Heb 10:1, the Torah, which he delivered) should be understood as anything other than preparatory for Jesus and the "new covenant" of which he is mediator.[32] Clement, on the other hand, employs the title θεράπων throughout the letter to portray Moses

30. Nm 12:6–7.
31. Heb 3:6a, 3. All English quotations of the Bible are taken from the New Revised Standard Version.
32. Heb 9:15.

<table>
<tr><td></td><td style="text-align:center">1 Clement 17.5, 43.1</td><td style="text-align:center">Hebrews 3.2, 5-6</td><td></td></tr>
</table>

	1 Clement 17.5, 43.1	Hebrews 3.2, 5-6	
Num 12.7	17:5 **Μωϋσῆς πιστὸς ἐν ὅλῳ τῷ οἴκῳ αὐτοῦ** ἐκλήθη…43:1 Καὶ τί θαυμαστόν εἰ οἱ ἐν Χριστῷ πιστευθέντες παρὰ Θεοῦ ἔργον τοιοῦτο κατέστησαν τοὺς προειρημένους; ὅπου καὶ ὁ μακάριος **πιστὸς θεράπων ἐν ὅλῳ τῷ οἴκῳ Μωϋσῆς** τὰ διατεταγμένα αὐτῷ πάντα ἐσημειώσατο ἐν ταῖς ἱεραῖς βίβλοις, ᾧ καὶ ἐπηκολούθησαν οἱ λοιποὶ προφῆται συνεπιμαρτυροῦντες τοῖς ὑπ' αὐτοῦ νενομοθετημένοις.	**πιστὸν** ὄντα τῷ ποιήσαντι αὐτὸν **ὡς καὶ Μωϋσῆς ἐν [ὅλῳ] τῷ οἴκῳ αὐτοῦ**…καὶ **Μωϋσῆς μὲν πιστὸς ἐν ὅλῳ τῷ οἴκῳ αὐτοῦ ὡς θεράπων** εἰς μαρτύριον τῶν λαληθησομένων, Χριστὸς δὲ ὡς υἱὸς ἐπὶ τὸν οἶκον αὐτοῦ· οὗ οἶκός ἐσμεν ἡμεῖς, ἐάν[περ] τὴν παρρησίαν καὶ τὸ καύχημα τῆς ἐλπίδος κατάσχωμεν.	Num 12.7

Figure 5-3. Comparison of *1 Clement* with Hebrews 3

in a positive light and cites Numbers 12:7 without any qualification of Moses's status.[33] In 17.5, Clement lifts up Moses as an example of meekness, reminding his readers that, even though he was honored by the statement of Numbers 12:7 (and, according to *1 Clem.* 43.6, had knowledge of the future), he was humble before God (figure 5-3). In 43.1, Moses—described as blessed—becomes a typological example to the Corinthian church for the orderly passing on of apostolic tradition, for he recorded his message in books and was succeeded by the prophets. This difference of disposition toward Moses undermines the suggestion that *1 Clement* is here dependent upon Hebrews, for Clement evidences no knowledge of Hebrew's Christological exegesis and treats Numbers 12:7 in a vastly different way.[34]

The contrast between Hebrews and *1 Clement* is all the more striking when one examines the marked contrast in the role Moses plays in each author's hermeneutic. For Hebrews, Moses's primary function as God's θεράπων is "to testify to the things that would be spoken later [εἰς μαρτύριον τῶν λαληθησομένων]"[35]—by which that author surely intends the speech spo-

---

33. *1 Clem.* 4.12; 43.1; 51.3, 5; 53.5.

34. If we were forced (as we are not) to posit a direct relationship between the two works, the most natural conclusion, given the sharpness with which Hebrews is opposed to the interpretation of Moses given in *1 Clement*, would be that Hebrews is a polemical response to *1 Clement's* lack of a clear and governing Christology, with regard to the interpretation of Numbers 12:7 and more broadly. However, as has been discussed (see note 27 above), the fact that much of the shared material in *1 Clement* exhibits a traditional character urges us to look for an explanation of the relationship between Hebrews and *1 Clement* in terms of dependence upon a common tradition.

35. Heb 3:5.

ken through the son in these last days.[36] For Clement, however, the message of "the rest of the prophets" apparently does not point *forward* to Christ but *backward* to Moses, for they "together testified to the laws he laid down."[37] For *1 Clement*, this preeminence of Moses in the biblical narrative—a preeminence that exists without any Christological reinterpretation—is perhaps best summarized by Clement's praise of Moses's self-sacrificial intercession for the people after the incident of the golden calf at Sinai: "O great love! O incomparable perfection!"[38] One can hardly imagine that the author of Hebrews, for whom Christology is a primary concern and Moses's distinctive status a threat, could approve of this superlative praise.[39] Rather, Hebrews stresses the unique supremacy of Jesus' intercession over that of any other figure, since, by virtue of his resurrection, "he always lives to make intercession for them."[40]

The Use of *Testimonia*

The foregoing analyses reveal a substantial contrast between the outlooks of these two documents. The author of *1 Clement* sees Moses as a venerable

---

36. Heb 1:1.

37. *1 Clem.* 43.1b. This assertion must not be taken as a strictly held hermeneutical *credo*, however, since the author employs prophetic passages with Christ as a messianic referent (e.g., Is 53 in *1 Clem.* 16). Nevertheless, Clement's explicit hermeneutical reflection is the mirror opposite of the outlook in Hebrews, as well as that of the first gospel, for whom "all the prophets *and the law*" are said to have "prophesied" of what was to be fulfilled only in the coming of Christ (Mt 11:13). If that which would become the dominant Christian position involved placing the center of gravity upon the christologically interpreted prophetic writings as the lens through which the Torah should be understood, Clement's thought appears to run in the opposite direction. In this respect *1 Clement* appears to be more closely aligned with a Jewish (or perhaps Jewish-Christian) hermeneutical outlook.

38. *1 Clem.* 54.5.

39. I deal here only with the strongest evidences of textual dependence. Considering additional instances of shared language does not alter this argument. *1 Clement* 23.5 and Hebrews 10:37, despite their similarity, are not parallel. The statement of *1 Clement*—Ταχὺ ἥξει καὶ οὐχρονιεῖ—is a citation from Is 13:22, whereas the similar phrase in Hebrews—ὁ ἐρχόμενος ἥξει καὶ οὐ χρονίσει—corresponds to Habakkuk 2:3. The common phrase μετανοίας τόπον (*1 Clem.* 7.5 // Heb 12:17) is utilized by the two authors to make opposite theological points and appears in Wisdom 12:10. References to Abraham as the inheritor of the promises of God (*1 Clem.* 10.1–2 // Heb 6:12–13, 15) are found in other literature (Rom 4:13, Gal 3:18, 22, Jas 2:5), as is the praise of Rahab's faith (*1 Clem.* 12.1, 8 // Heb 11:31; cf. Jas 2:25). Attridge's observation that the variant πυρος φλογα is shared by Hebrews and *1 Clement* against πυρ φλεγον of LXX Psalm 103 does not necessitate the use of Hebrews by Clement. The variant is attested in the Lucianic text family, and in the Bohairic and Sahidic versions, and its common use may be explained by its presence in a shared *testimonia* (*pace* Attridge, *Epistle to the Hebrews*, 54).

40. Heb 7:25.

leader whose intercessory love for his people knows no rival and whose laws
formed the core message of the later prophets. As the foundational leader of
biblical Israel, he is a prototype not of Jesus but of the apostles, and the Mosaic
economy provides the model for the orderly institution founded on the apostles' testimony. He is therefore worthy of unqualified praise. Hebrews, however,
is restlessly alert, lest Moses, the angels, the levitical priests, or Melchizedek
replace the unique place occupied by the exalted Jesus. Although this author
respects the role of Moses in the history of Israel, he is preoccupied with the
new Christological turn that this history has taken, so that the Mosaic covenant is growing old and is now about to vanish.[41] The fact that Hebrews has
appealed to Numbers 12:7 only to undermine its praise of Moses by contrasting Moses's subordinate role with the unique identity of the son suggests that
the author may be aware of a practice of appealing to this passage to support a
view of Moses as having an authority that rivaled or at least paralleled that of
Jesus.[42] By citing Numbers 12:7 in Hebrews 3, the author is able to critique such
a viewpoint by appealing to the superior status of the son figure. Hebrews is
thus engaged in a deliberate textual contradiction, in which the opposing interpretation of Scripture finds its position undermined by other carefully chosen authoritative passages. What is striking about this is that, while Hebrews is
carefully guarded against any tendency to read Numbers 12:7 as undermining
the superiority of Christ, *1 Clement* seems entirely unaware of any such danger.
His references to Numbers 12:7 underwrite a narrative of Moses's unparalleled
greatness, apparently oblivious of any potential challenge that Moses's preeminence might present to the unique place of Jesus.

The common explanation of the intertextual relationship between *1 Clem-
ment* and Hebrews as one of direct dependence of *1 Clement* on Hebrews thus
faces the challenge of accounting for *1 Clement*'s complicated redactional procedure. If the author of *1 Clement* used the text of Hebrews, he seems to have
been strangely unaware of its ideas. He has reworked the text's example of

41. Heb 8:13.

42. The viability of the figure of Moses as a symbol of Jewish challenge to Jesus' authority was likewise felt by the author of the fourth gospel (Jn 5:45, 6:32, 9:28). In the Pseudo-Clementine literature, Moses and Jesus share an apparently equal status: "Jesus is concealed from the Hebrews who have received
Moses as their teacher, and Moses hidden from those who believe Jesus. For since through both one and
the same teaching becomes known, God accepts those who believe in one of them." *Pseudo-Clementines*
H 8.6.1–2, trans. Johannes Irmscher, "The Pseudo-Clementines," in *The New Testament Apocrypha*, vol.
2, ed. Edgar Hennecke and Wilhelm Schneemelcher (Philadelphia: Westminster Press, 1976), 563–64.

Moses drawn from Numbers 12 in order to produce a rhetorical effect near-ly the opposite of that in Hebrews, yet without any indication of a polemical posture toward argument in Hebrews; he simply seems unaware of it. When we consider that the theory of the use of Hebrews by *I Clement* depends on the assumption that Hebrews was read and, at least to some degree, appreciated in the church in Rome, the likelihood that *I Clement* could be dependent upon Hebrews as a textual guide but so ignorant of its Christological rein-terpretation of those texts—particularly of Numbers 12:7—strains the limits of belief. Even if some scholars can posit such ambivalence in Clement's re-dactional activity,[43] this solution to the intertextual riddle hardly seems to be the most natural. If, however, through a careful comparison of the alleged ci-tations, we observe that, despite verbal agreements, the author of *I Clement* appears unfamiliar with the distinctive theology of Hebrews and its subjuga-tion of the status of Moses, then it seems much more probable that both docu-ments utilize a common tradition of scriptural interpretation.

This explanation of the intertextual relationship between *I Clement* and Hebrew thus fits broadly within the "testimony book" thesis advanced by Ren-dell Harris in the early twentieth century.[44] Although Harris's eccentric for-mulation of the *testimonia* hypothesis has been duly challenged,[45] the notion that collections of scriptural citations lie behind our extant texts seems to be a reasonable explanation of the data presented in this study. Indeed the *testimo-nia* form appears to have some precedent among the Qumran scrolls—*4QFlo-rilegium*, for example, includes multiple short biblical citations organized

43. Paul Ellingworth's observation that textual dependence does not exclude the possibility of mis-apprehending the meaning of the source text, while formally correct, requires us to imagine Clement's operating with deeply conflicting (and unexplained) redactional tendencies. See Ellingworth, "Hebrews and *I Clement*: Literary Dependence or Common Tradition?" *Biblische Zeitschrift* 23 (1979): 262–69.

44. See J. Rendel Harris, *Testimonies: Part I* and *Part II* (Cambridge: Cambridge University Press, 1916/20). For the use of *testimonia* by Hebrews, see Harris, *Testimonies*, 2:44.

45. C. H. Dodd challenged Harris's theory of *written* testimony documents in the production of the New Testament in favor of the notion that "New Testament writers were guided in their use of the Old Testament by certain agreed principles or conventions" and "that there were some parts of Scripture which were early recognized as appropriate sources from which *testimonia* might be drawn." C. H. Dodd, *According to the Scriptures: The Sub-Structure of New Testament Theology* (New York: Scribner's, 1953), 59–60. Dodd's caution is a welcome counter to Harris's forceful claims, but his alternative raises the ques-tion of how "principles or conventions" may have been transmitted across diverse communities apart from any written form. If we agree generally with Dodd's insights and critiques of Harris, we may still be justified in appealing to the existence of written testimonies when the evidence before us favors such a conclusion. For a more recent study of the issue of *testimonia*, see Albl, *"And Scripture Cannot Be Broken."*

around a common theme and presented with polemical, theologically interpretive editorial comments linking the various citations.[46] Thus the statement
in both Hebrews and *1 Clement* that the son is superior to the angels in accordance with the superiority of his inherited name—a statement that interprets
a collage of biblical citations—may have existed originally in a preexistent text
form. This suggestion of a common written tradition does not imply, however, that the authors of *1 Clement* and Hebrews worked from testimony documents that were identical; we need only posit that their sources must have
shared the common characteristics we have observed.

Jews and Christians at the Border

If recognizing the textual distance between *1 Clement* and Hebrews allows us to perceive the distinctive concerns of each document in sharper relief, how are we to account for the two texts' markedly different attitudes
toward Moses and the Temple cult? Specifically, why is *1 Clement* (unlike Hebrews) so unconcerned that the writer's overflowing admiration of the Jerusalem cult and the figure of Moses will rival the primacy of Jesus and his priesthood? The standard answer has been that a definitive break between church
and synagogue had occurred a generation or so before *1 Clement* was written,
such that nostalgia for the church's Jewish heritage was no longer a threat to
its distinctive identity.[47] This view of the rapid demise of Jewish Christianity
in Rome, however, depends primarily upon an argument from silence—the
absence of debate over the relation between Christianity and Judaism in texts
from the first half of the second century[48]—and upon a comparison of two
brief comments from Roman sources. Comparing Suetonius's report of the
edict of Claudius (*Claudius* 25.4) and Tacitus's report of Christian persecution under Nero (*Annals* 15.44), numerous scholars of early Roman Christian-

---

46. See especially the comments of J. M. Allegro, "Fragments of a Qumran Scroll of Eschatological
Midrashim," *Journal of Biblical Literature* 77 (1958): 350–54. Allegro judges that "the scroll was apparently devoted to a collection of *midrashim* on certain biblical texts, compiled perhaps for their common
eschatological interest. It must have formed part of a fairly extensive Essene *testimonia* literature" (350).

47. Thus Peter Lampe: "Once integrated into the Christian life, the synagogal tradition was carried
by people who themselves were no longer rooted in the synagogue: the Gentile Christian Clement seems
to have been an early example" (*From Paul to Valentinus*, 78).

48. "How completely insignificant [Jewish Christianity] was is shewn not only by the limited polemics of the Church Fathers, but perhaps still more by their silence." Adolf Harnack, *History of Dogma*,
vol. 1, trans. Neil Buchanan, (Boston, Mass.: Little, Brown and Company, 1905), 291.

ity find decisive evidence for the early social fissure between Jews and Christians.[49] Whereas Suetonius's claim that in 49 C.E. "Claudius expelled Jews from Rome because of their constant disturbances impelled by Chrestus"[50] is understood to refer to disputes about Christ internal to the *Jewish* community, Tacitus in 64 C.E. identified the "Christians" as a group that, though originating in Judea, was distinguishable from Jews. The dominant scholarly view is that, in Tacitus's report, "we have an indication that in the eyes of the Romans the Christian community clearly was distinguishable from the Jewish community.... Consequently in the 60s the links between the Jewish and the Christian community in Rome seem to have become almost invisible."[51]

If this view of an early "parting of the ways" is correct, then *I Clement* and Hebrews typify two sides of a theological dialectic that, from ancient times, has marked Christian reflection upon the continuity and discontinuity between the "old" covenant of Moses and the "new" covenant of which Jesus is mediator.[52] If, on the other hand, the comment of Tacitus, while differentiating the traditional Jewish community from the new groups of Jews and Gentiles that met together in the name of Jesus,[53] should not be understood to imply the early development of the categorically non-Jewish religious identity that Western intellectual tradition has come to attach to the words "church" and "Christian"—that is, if we do not from these two sources adopt the presupposition of an early decisive break in "Jewish" and "Christian" religious identities, then we may be free to imagine these documents inhabiting quite different social realities than have previously been assumed.

49. Stephen Spence, *The Parting of the Ways: The Roman Church as a Case Study*, Interdisciplinary Studies in Ancient Culture and Religion 5 (Leuven: Peeters, 2004), 9; Lampe, *From Paul to Valentinus*, 11–16; Hvalvik, *Jewish Believers in Jesus*, 197–99.

50. *Claud.* 25.4. This Latin spelling of "Christ" with an "e" is attested in the second century at the time Suetonius wrote. See Brown, *Antioch and Rome*, 101; Lampe, *From Paul to Valentinus*, 12–13.

51. Hvalvik, *Jewish Believers in Jesus*, 199. See also Lampe: "The most plausible solution is that in the wake of these events, urban Roman Christianity separated itself from the synagogue," *From Paul to Valentinus*, 15.

52. For Brown, Hebrews reacts against "a deeper commitment to the values of the Jewish cult, with the concomitant tendency to fit Jesus into an uninterrupted schema of salvation history, subsequent to the angels and Moses as revealers of God's will" (*Antioch and Rome*, 156). This view, which Hebrews negates, seems precisely that of *I Clement*, which stresses the value and usefulness of that cult as a prototype of the Christian church.

53. The need by outside observers to designate the early followers of Jesus with a non-ethnic term is attested as early as Acts 11:26. A simple act of distinction between "Christians" and Jews sheds little light, however, on the relation of these groups or their internal sense of identity. This is particularly the case for Jewish Christians.

The present article is no place to attempt the reconstruction of Jewish and Christian identities in first-century Rome. However, it is precisely the import of the present argument that the historiography of Jewish-Christian relations depends upon readings of texts in relation to one another, readings that are often shaped by erroneous assumptions about the origins of these texts and by the conceptual frameworks with which historians presume ancient authors to have worked. In the latter case, the anachronistic assumption that "Judaism" and "Christianity" were distinct, meaningful terms in antiquity has been forcefully called into question in recent scholarship. Advancing the compelling thesis that Jews and early Christians were engaged in the construction of these categories as they negotiated social and theological differences, Daniel Boyarin helpfully urges the hermeneutical point that "a perspective that refuses the option of seeing Christian and Jew, Christianity and Judaism, as fully formed, bounded, and separate entities and identities in late antiquity" allows the textually sensitive historian "to perceive more fully the work of those early Christian and Jewish writers as they were making the difference."[54] In the case of *1 Clement* and Hebrews, the divergent interpretations of the figure of Moses in Numbers 12:7 may signify not an abstract, minor difference over the role given to Moses in an early Christian biblical theology but rather the rhetorical clash between two different modes of valuing and relating to the fountainhead of Israelite identity—modes of relating that may have had significant sociological correlates.

54. Boyarin, *Border Lines*, 7.

Richard A. Layton

6. THE MAKING OF A CLASSIC

Moses as Author

"For us," Clement of Alexandria declared, "Moses is prophet, legislator, tactician, general, statesman, philosopher."[1] Moses, in Clement's index, represents the culmination of both the active and the contemplative lives, the political and the philosophical, uniting in one person the two modes of living that in Aristotle's ethics pertain to human fulfillment.[2] Clement curiously omits one facet of Moses's variegated perfection: the significance to Christian readers of Moses as an author. Early Christians regarded Moses as one of the most prolific of all writers of Scripture. Some commentators argued for Moses as the author of the book of Job.[3] Psalm 89 (LXX) was widely considered to be written by Moses. Diodore of Tarsus attempted to debunk this attribution,

---

1. Clement of Alexandria, *Stromateis* 1.24.158, ed. Otto Stählin, in *Clemens Alexandrinus, Werke*, GCS 52 (Berlin: Akademie Verlag, 1985), 99. Translation my own.

2. Aristotle, *Nicomachean Ethics* 1.5 (1095b–1096a) and 10.7–8 (1177a–1179a). Philo, *De Vita Mosis* (henceforward *Life of Moses*) 2.2, assimilates Moses to the Platonic ideal of the philosopher-king as an expression of the consummate Stoic sage. The translations of Philo's works are taken (sometimes slightly adapted) from the Loeb Classical Library's 10 vols. (London: Heinemann; New York, Putnam, 1929–1962). For discussion, see Albert C. Geljon, *Philonic Exegesis in Gregory of Nyssa's De Vita Moysis*, Studia Philonica Monographs 5 (Providence, R.I.: Brown Judaic Studies, 2002), 9–10.

3. Dieter Hagedorn, *Der Hiobkommentar des Arianers Julian*, Patristische Texte und Studien (PTS) 14 (Berlin: Walter de Gruyter, 1973), 1–4. Julian recognizes, but dismisses, potential objections to this attribution. Some rabbis also argued for Mosaic authorship of Job; see BT Baba Bathra 14b–15b, in J. Epstein, *The Babylonian Talmud. Seder Nezikin. Baba Bathra I* (London: Soncino Press, 1935), 71–73.

but Gregory of Nyssa held fast to the traditional view.[4] In some circles, magical treatises gained authority by the Mosaic label, a reputation based largely, as John Gager suggests, on the tradition that Moses received the secret of the divine name.[5] Of course, Moses's prestige as author was based primarily on the tradition that he composed the Pentateuch. This tradition was sanctified by longstanding synagogue practice, so that Paul could refer to Torah reading as simply reading "Moses."[6]

The composition of the Pentateuch through the hand of Moses was unquestioned in antiquity by Christians, Jews, or outside critics. This universal acceptance can obscure, however, a more elusive question: what interpretive work did the attribution of Mosaic authorship do for early Christian readers? How did Moses's authorship shape Christian views of his identity, and conversely, how did Mosaic authorship shape the interpretation of what he had written? In rabbinic tradition, the Torah existed as a heavenly prototype independent of and prior to Moses's own activity. The rabbis commonly depicted the production of the Mosaic Law in one of two ways to emphasize the fidelity of the written Torah to its prototype. In one model, Moses transcribed the words of God as they were spoken to him, the written Torah becoming an exact and permanent replica of divine speech. In the second model, Moses ascended to heaven and reproduced the Torah, descending again to Israel with the written Torah over angelic objections.[7] The prophet is critical to the Torah's appearance

---

4. On Diodore, see Louis Mariès, *Études préliminaires à l'édition de Diodore de Tarse sur les Psaumes* (Paris: Société d'Édition "Les Belle Lettres," 1933), 89–90; Gregory of Nyssa, *In Inscriptiones Psalmorum* (*Inscr. Pss.*) 1.7, in Gregorii Nysseni Opera (GNO), vol. 5, ed. J. McDonough and P. Alexander (Leiden: Brill, 1962), 43, 45–47. For translation, see Ronald E. Heine, *Gregory of Nyssa's* Treatise on the Inscriptions of the Psalms (Oxford: Clarendon Press, 1995), 101–5. BT Baba Bathra 14b (Epstein, *The Babylonian Talmud*, 71), attributes some psalms to Moses, presumably with Ps 90 in mind. Eusebius, *Comm. in Pss.* Pref. (PG 23:74CD) adduces Mosaic authorship of individual psalms without indicating any reservation of the attribution. Augustine, *Enarrationes in Psalmos* 89 (sermo 1), CCSL 39 (Turnhout: Brepols, 1956), 244f., holds that the psalm should be read in light of the dispensation established through Moses, but a reader should not presume that Moses personally (*ab ipso*) wrote the psalm.

5. John G. Gager, *Moses in Greco-Roman Paganism* (Nashville, Tenn.: Abingdon Press, 1972), 142–44; PGM 13 (4th cent.), in *The Greek Magical Papyri in Translation, Including the Demotic Spells*, ed. Hans Dieter Betz, 2nd ed. (Chicago: University of Chicago Press, 1986), 172, 172n2.

6. 2 Cor 3:15, cf. Acts 15:21. Origen, *Hom. in Genesim* 7.1, ed. W. A. Baehrens, in *Origenes Werke, Homilien zum Hexateuch in Rufins Übersetzung*, GCS 29 (Leipzig: J. C. Hinrichs'sche Buchhandlung, 1929), 30, no doubt alludes to 2 Cor 3:15 when he begins his homily: *Moyses nobis legitur in ecclesia*, a statement that might refer both to the individual lection he expounds and more generally to ecclesiastical practice.

7. Abraham Joshua Heschel, *Heavenly Torah as Refracted through the Generations* (New York:

in Israel, but the text is not imbued with the author's own intention.[8] God's word sounds from eternity, and to preserve its transcendence above history, the role of the human author is effaced to that of either scribe or deliverer.

Christian writers also employed this rhetoric. The author of *1 Clement* bears witness to the dictation model in the assertion that Moses "recorded in the sacred books all the orders given to him."[9] In his pentateuchal homilies, Origen refers to the Holy Spirit as the "writer" of the Law; God "writes the Law of the letter through Moses."[10] John Chrysostom compares the Pentateuch to correspondence sent from God:

> At the beginning, therefore, God would converse directly with humans, to the extent they were able to listen. In this way, God came to Adam, in this way he reproached Cain, in this way he conversed with Noah, in this way he was hosted by Abraham. Since, however, our nature has declined to evil, and has, as it were, separated itself to some distant country, and yet further, remains in distant exile, God sends letters, to revive the ancient friendship toward us through a kind of correspondence. While God sent these letters, Moses conveyed them. What, then, do the letters say? "In the beginning God created the heaven and the earth."[11]

This quaint homiletic image presents God as the author and Moses as the postman. As does the rabbinic tradition, Chrysostom maximizes the transparency of the written word to the divine speech and consequently minimizes the agency of the mediator. The tendency in Christian homiletics is to depict the text itself as an act of God's self-revelation; that is, the text does not only point to God's eternal will, it embodies that will. The role of Moses is to mediate and conserve that revelation, not to produce it. While the prophet certainly had intentions, the reader need only take account of the author's own experience in order to resolve particular difficulties and problems in the text.[12]

Continuum, 2007), 538–51. Examples of Moses's descent from heaven with the Torah can be found in Ex Rabbah 28.1, 42.4 and Lv Rabbah 1.3; BT Baba Bathra 15a (Epstein, *The Babylonian Talmud*, 72) attests to the dictation model.

8. Rabbinic tradition, e.g., Nm Rabbah 19.33, could also depict Moses as influencing the language of Torah, as God alters the diction of the text to account for a point Moses raises. For discussion, see Heschel, *Heavenly Torah*, 488–89.

9. *1 Clem.* 43.1.

10. Origen, *Hom. in Gen.* 15.5, ed. Baehrens, GCS 29:134. Translation my own. See also *Hom. in Gen.* 4.3, GCS 29:53, and *Hom. in Exodum* 4.2, GCS 29:172.

11. John Chrysostom, *Sermones in Genesim* 1.2, ed. Laurence Brottier, in *Jean Chrysostome: Sermons sur la Genèse*, Sources Chrétiennes (SC) 433 (Paris: Éditions du Cerf, 1998), 148–50. Translation my own.

12. The primary appeal to author intentionality in homiletics occurs in apologetic contexts. For

Philo: Moses the Hierophant

In both rabbinic and Christian tradition, it was possible to assign Moses a preeminent role in the delivery of the Pentateuch without regarding the prophet as crucial to its production. One emphatic exception to this hermeneutic of prophetic transparency is Philo, who offers, in the second book of his *Life of Moses*, a theory of Moses's authorial activity. He begins by presenting Moses in the Hellenistic tradition of the legislator who establishes the founding constitution of a nation. Moses is similar to Solon and other traditional figures, but superior to any legislator of either Greeks or barbarians. In this apologetic context, Philo makes the innovative move to take up the problem of the Law's literary structure: why is it that the lawgiver begins with a history before delivering the commands to the people? In response to his own question, Philo extends Moses's authorial identity to include that of "historian" (συγγραφεύς). As a historian, Moses approaches the task of recording the past not to provide mere entertainment, but to show two essential principles: first, that the father and maker of the world was also its lawgiver "in the truest sense," and second, that whoever observes the Mosaic Law would consequently live in harmony with the ordering of the universe as a whole.[13]

Philo builds his theory of Moses's authorial agency to link the Genesis narrative with the Sinai revelation. One result is that for Philo, the Law of Moses is not reducible, as Hindy Najman aptly notes, to a code of precepts, but includes both the creation account as a mirror of the natural law and the lives of the patriarchs as exemplars of the unwritten law.[14] As narrative, Genesis is not merely prefatory to Sinai, but also displays the permeation of nature and the moral life by the true lawgiver. To read the Pentateuch with Philo is to discern an intentional design inhabiting the structure of the Pentateuch as the author unfolds the logic of God's Law manifest in nature, in the lives of the ancestors, and in the constitution bequeathed to Israel through Moses. Moses

---

example, Origen, *Hom. in Gen.* 2.2, GCS 29:27–30, responds to doubts about the sufficiency of the ark to hold all the animals by appeal to the distinctive mathematical conventions in Egypt in which Moses the author would have been educated.

13. Philo, *Life of Moses* 2.12, 2.47, 2.48. Page citations refer to the edition of Leopold Cohn and Paul Wendland, *Philonis Alexandrini Opera Quae Supersunt* (Berlin: Georgii Reimeri, 1896–1930).

14. Hindy Najman, *Seconding Sinai: The Development of Mosaic Discourse in Second Temple Judaism*, Supplements to the Journal for the Study of Judaism 77 (Leiden: Brill, 2003), 70–107, esp. 82–89.

is not only a figure within the drama of Israel's history, his structuring of the Pentateuch displays God's sovereignty and rational ordering of the cosmos.

Philo's construction of an intrinsic narrative unity between Genesis and Exodus had a far-reaching impact on the imagining of Moses's authorial activity. As a historian, Moses linked the Sinai revelation to the constitution of the natural order and delineated God as the sovereign lawgiver of both the physical and the moral universes. At the outset of his history of Jewish *Antiquities*, Josephus echoes Philo by introducing the pentateuchal narrative with an explanation of Moses's formation as an author. Moses undertook his history after careful study (κατανόησις) of God's nature and the manifestation of that nature in the visible works of God, because it is the first duty of a writer to imitate this best possible model in nature. This disciplined cultivation of knowledge, moreover, cohered with the prophet's core purpose: to educate Israel to conform to the natural constitution, by "guiding their thoughts up to God and the construction of the world."[15] The words of the Pentateuch are not simply oracular, they reflect the author's careful contemplation of the structure of the world, which both precedes the writing of the Law and underlies its historical design.

This same discernment of authorial design is evident in the hexaemeral tradition. In his homilies on the six days work, Basil of Caesarea introduces his topic with a direct attribution of authorial agency: "It is Moses who composed this narrative." Moses took up his pen after his forty-year sojourn in Ethiopia, during which he contemplated creation, instructed by God "face to face" (Nm 12:7–9) in direct, plain speech without dark sayings.[16] Moses replicates this style in his account of the creation. Unlike the loquacious pagan philosophers, Moses avoids speculation and passes over in silence matters that do not contribute to the reader's moral progress. His narrative is devoid of artifice, but still "gentle and pleasant to the mind of all who prefer truth to plausibility."[17] Mosaic style, in Basil's view, is governed by a particular intention:

---

15. Josephus, *The Jewish Antiquities*, 1.4.19–21, trans. H. St. J. Thackeray, LCL 242 (New York: Putnam, 1930), 4.11.

16. Basil of Caesarea, *Hom. in hexaemeron.* 1.1, in *Basilius von Caesarea*, Homilien zum Hexaemeron, ed. Emmanuel Amand de Mendieta and Stig Y. Rudberg, GCS neue folge, Bd. 2 (Berlin: Akademie Verlag, 1997), 2f. See also *Hom. in hex.* 6.1, GCS n.f. 2:87f. For translations, see Stanislas Giet, *Basile de Césarée: Homélies sur l'Hexaéméron*, SC 1 (Paris: Éditions du Cerf, 1949); Agnes Clare Way, *Saint Basil: Exegetic Homilies*, The Fathers of the Church (FOTC) 46 (Washington, D.C.: The Catholic University of America Press, 1963), 3–150.

17. Basil, *Hom. in hex.* 3.1, GCS n.f. 2:38, trans. Way, *Saint Basil: Exegetic Homilies*. See also *Hom. in hex.* 9.1 (GCS n.f. 2:147).

to steer the reader from pagan error, which founds its moral universe on weak and insubstantial principles, a "spider's web" easily shaken by the breeze. Basil presents Moses as the author whose rhetorical economy exposes pagan sophistry. In their vain speculation, pagan philosophers have constructed a multitude of theories, none of which has stood "unmoved and unshaken."[18] As author, Moses provides a stable structure that stands athwart the fluid world of appearances and opinion.

One dimension of Philo's hermeneutic is ontological; the Mosaic narrative corresponds to and mirrors the structure of reality itself. Josephus and Basil continue the legacy of Philo to articulate a correspondence between narrative structure, authorial style, and moral purpose, all of which belong to the human effort to fashion a language that reflects the natural law. A second dimension to Philo's conception of Mosaic authorship is mystagogic, in which the narrative conducts the reader to a vision of eternity itself. Philo often presents the relationship between author and reader as analogous of that of teacher to student. A reader of the Law becomes a "student [γνώριμος]"[19] of Moses and is enrolled among those who "philosophize in the school of Moses [τοῖς κατὰ Μωυσῆν φιλοσοφοῦσιν]."[20] It is the first virtue, Philo holds, of students "to desire that their imperfections may imitate as far as possible the perfection of the teacher."[21]

Moses's function as a teacher reduces the gap between author and reader. To Philo, Moses not only instructs the students in a subject matter, but also initiates them into the divine mysteries. Moses is the sacred guide, the hierophant (ἱεροφάντης), who leads the student to the transcendent realities beyond the world of sense.[22] All progress toward virtue and transcendence of the material world requires a guide. Abraham and Isaac, for example, each had a guide on the path toward virtue. Moses transcends them in that he *is* a guide, both for Israel on its path from Egypt and in the gift of the Law for future

18. Basil, *Hom. in Hex.* 1.2. Translation is my own.

19. Philo, *Quod deterius potiori insidiari solet* (*Det.*) 86 (1.277); *De posteritate Caini* (*Post.*) 12 (2.3); *De confusione linguarum* (*Conf.*) 39 (2.237); *De migratione Abrahami* (*Migr.*) 201 (2.308); and *Quis rerum divinarum heres* (*Her.*) 81 (3.19).

20. Philo, *De mutatione nominum* (*Mut.*) 223 (3.195).

21. Philo, *De sacrificiis Abelis et Caini* (*Sacr.*) 65 (1.228); trans. F. H. Colson and G. H. Whitaker, *Philo*, vol. 2, LCL 227 (London: William Heineman, 1929).

22. Philo, *Post.* 16 (2.4), 173 (2.38); *Conf.* 95 (2.247); *Migr.* 14 (2.271); *De somniis* (*Somn.*) 2.29 (3.263), 2.109 (3.276); *De Decalogo* (*Decal.*) 18 (4.272); *De specialibus legibus* (*Spec.*) 1.41 (5.10).

Israel.[23] The prophets and the Psalmist are likewise disciples of Moses, who continue not just the legacy of Moses but speak in the Mosaic spirit. Philo holds that he also was initiated into the greater mysteries by Moses, the friend of God, who ushers Philo into the presence of the divine.[24] Moses still occupies the "inner sanctum," the heavenly holy of holies, where he awaits the readers and guides them on the path to this innermost reality.

Moses is uniquely suited as hierophant because he is unique among all humanity, by virtuous disposition, by inspiration, and by his particular cultivation. In the *Life of Moses*, Philo holds that Moses received not only training in mathematical subjects from Egyptian masters, but also received premier instruction in the Greek curriculum and Chaldean astronomic lore.[25] Philo's point is that even as a schoolboy, Moses was cultivated to fulfill his destiny as a κοσμοπολίτης, a world-citizen, capable of producing the legislation that would suit all of humanity, regardless of ethnicity or culture.[26] Such citizenry is the privilege that Adam enjoyed in his created state, the city of the cosmos, the constitution of which is "the right reason of nature [ὁ τῆς φυσεῶς ὀρθὸς λόγος], which is named with a more appropriate title 'ordinance' [θεσμός], a divine law, according to which obligations and rights have been distributed to each creature."[27]

The authorship of the Law is the means by which Moses draws all humanity to this state as "world citizen" that he already enjoys, as a servant of the truly existent one. All who aspire to this same service look to Moses as a pioneer: "It is their task to ascend in their thoughts to the ethereal height, Moses, the race [γένος] beloved of God, whom they set before themselves, the leader on the way. For then, this place—which truly is the Word—they will see, the place in which the unswerving and immutable God stands."[28] Moses is a universal figure, embodying in himself the *genos* of all the perfect. Philo elsewhere

23. Abraham and Isaac have a guide (ἡγεμών) (Philo, *Somn.* 1.168); Moses is a guide (ἡγεμών) (*Conf.* 95).

24. Philo, *Conf.* 39 (Psalmist), *Conf.* 62 (Prophet—ἑταῖρος), *De Cherubim* (*Cher.*) 49 (Philo himself).

25. Philo, *Life of Moses* 1.23–24.

26. Philo, *Conf.* 106 (2.249).

27. Philo, *De opificio mundi* (*Opif.*) 19.143, trans. David T. Runia, in *Philo of Alexandria: On the Creation of the Cosmos according to Moses* (Leiden: Brill, 2001), 84–85. See also Runia's commentary on the passage, pp. 339–40.

28. Philo, *Conf.* 95–96 (2.247), trans. Colson and Whitaker, in *Philo*, vol. 4, LCL 261 (London: William Heineman, 1932).

suggests even this label does not suffice to define Moses. As one who attains perfect virtue, Isaac embodies the *genos* of all who are incorruptible and fully perfect. By contrast, Moses transcends even the category of *genos*, so that his kinship is more with God than with humanity:

> There are still others, whom God has advanced even higher, and has trained them to soar above species and *genos* alike and stationed them beside himself. Such is Moses to whom he says, "You, stand here with me" [Deut. 5:31]. And so when Moses was about to die we do not hear of him "leaving" and "being added" like those others, but through the Word of the Cause he is "translated" [Deut. 34:5], the same word through which also the whole cosmos was created, so that you may learn that God considers the sage to be of equal honor with the cosmos.[29]

Moses has departed. His departure, however, is not an absence but a translation to the presence of eternity; all those who venture to eternal reality will find him there. The Pentateuch is not simply a remnant of Moses's virtue, it is an authentic and perfect expression of his mind, which ushers all readers to participation in his own journey. Philo praises the *Therapeutae* as a community that exemplifies this reading practice:

> To these people the whole law book appears to resemble a living creature with the literal ordinances [τὰς ῥητὰς διατάξεις] for its body and for its soul the invisible mind laid up in its wording. It is in this mind especially that the rational soul begins to contemplate the things akin to itself [τὰ οἰκεῖα θεωρεῖν] and looking through the words as through a mirror beholds the marvelous beauties of the concepts, unfolds and removes the symbolic coverings and brings forth the thoughts and sets them bare to the light of day.[30]

This hermeneutical summation reflects, I would suggest, Philo's ideal for a doctrine of Scripture, even if we harbor reservations about the nature and identity of the *Therapeutae* as a historical community.[31] The immediate con-

---

29. Philo, *Sacr.* 8 (1.205), trans. Colson and Whitaker, *Philo*, vol. 2, LCL 227. See also Philo, *Post.* 28 (2.7), *De gigantibus* 49 (2.51), *Somn.* 2.227 (3.295). For discussion of Philo's use of the term γένος in this context, see Anita Méasson, *De Sacrificiis Abelis et Caini*, Les Ouevres de Philon d'Alexandrie 4 (Paris: Éditions du Cerf, 1966), 191–93.

30. Philo, *De vita contemplativa* 78 (6.67), trans. F. H. Colson, *Philo*, vol. 9, LCL 363 (London: William Heineman, 1941). The *Therapeutae* were a Jewish sect prominent in Alexandria at the end of the Second Temple period, but also recorded elsewhere. They adopted a predominantly contemplative life, interpreted as a healing of their own souls and the souls of others.

31. Troels Engberg-Pedersen, "Philo's *De Vita Contemplativa* as a Philosopher's Dream," *Journal for the Study of Judaism* 30 (1999): 40–64, proposes that Philo's depiction of the *Therapeutae* should be read as a "utopian fantasy" (p. 43) to advance a philosophical ideal. Mary Ann Beavis, "Philo's Therapeu-

text is a justification for allegorical interpretation. For our purposes, however, the key point is the conviction that the Law has a "mind." For Philo, this mind is nothing other than Moses, author of the Law.[32] Authentic reading, in turn, strives to gaze into the "mirror" of this mind, and to see those thoughts that this mind has garbed in symbolic clothing. Philo depicts the author as present within the text, and thus authorship is not simply a process of originating a text but also one of clothing the author's mind within the written word.

Both Josephus and Basil take up Philo's search to detect the human intelligence that structures the text, and they find it particularly evident in the creation account. Basil's brother, Gregory of Nyssa, takes up this supplementary concept that the author also serves as guide to the spiritual realities indicated in his narrative. In his treatise on the psalm titles, Gregory suggests that each division of the Psalms represents a grade in the spiritual ascent, and Psalm 89, the "prayer by Moses, the man of God" begins the fourth step of the five-stage ascent. The prayer, Gregory holds, is spoken by one who, as Philo had suggested, "stands as a kind of boundary between the changeable and unchangeable nature and mediates, as it is appropriate, between the two poles."[33] Moses is both the voice that speaks in the psalm and also the guide of the aspirant to higher union with God, as he lifts "the understanding of those ascending with him."[34]

Philo's hermeneutical turn placed emphasis on the function of Genesis. Our final example of Philo's lineage shows the attempt to link Moses's activity as hierophant directly to the composition of Genesis. Didymus the Blind finds the inspiration for the book Genesis in a particular moment in Moses's life: God's demurral of Moses's request that God reveal his "glory" to the prophet. God offers, instead, to set Moses in the protective shelter of a cleft in a rock and to allow Moses to see "my back." For, God says, "you cannot see

---

tai: Philosopher's Dream or Utopian Construction?," *Journal for the Study of Pseudepigrapha* 14 (2004): 30–42, argues that Philo depicts an idealized conception of an actual community within his experience. Joan E. Taylor and Philip R. Davies, "The So-Called Therapeutae of *De Vita Contemplativa*: Identity and Character," *Harvard Theological Review* 91 (1998): 3–24, likewise argue for an actual community composed of a small group of men and women who withdrew from Alexandria to practice a philosophical Judaism.

32. See Philo, *Life of Moses* 2.40.

33. Gregory of Nyssa, *Inscr. Pss.* 1.7 (GNO 5:45), trans. Heine, *Gregory of Nyssa's Treatise on the Inscriptions of the Psalms*.

34. Gregory of Nyssa, *Inscr. Pss.* 1.7 (GNO 5:51), trans. Heine, *Gregory of Nyssa's Treatise*.

my face; for no one shall see me and live."[35] In his *Commentary on Zachariah*, Didymus relates the prophet's vision in Zechariah 1:8 to Moses's petition to God in Exodus 33:

Moses, the great teacher of sacred doctrine [ὁ μέγας ἱεροφάντης], while he was not yet able intelligibly [γνωστῶς] to see the "face" of God (cf. Exod. 33:13, 20), was placed in a position to see the things behind God [τὰ ὀπίσω αὐτοῦ] (cf. Exod. 33:23), that is, the things that come after God, which are nothing other than God's creation. And, indeed, when the things after God, which are called the things "behind" him, were shown to him, he wrote the creation account, which begins from "in the beginning God created the heaven and the earth."[36]

Moses's vision takes place while the prophet was still in a state of moral progress. Although he was superior to human beings, he had not yet attained the purity necessary to see the "face" of God. The prophet wrote Genesis at this frontier between moral purification and contemplative insight. In lieu of revealing the divine face, God promises to reveal to the prophet the "the things that come after me [(τὰ ὀπίσω μου]". For Didymus, the things Moses sees after God are neither God nor an aspect of God, they are not God's hindquarters. It is not a revelation of God that Moses receives, but rather a flash of recognition of a truth *about* God, and, more particularly, about the world.

The attribution Didymus makes of Moses as hierophant should alert us that Philo lurks in the background. Philo, like Didymus, takes this moment to be the point at which Moses reaches the limit of human knowledge. Even the consummate human must be satisfied with knowledge of God's effects, and accept the inability to know God's essence:

It is quite enough for human thought to go so far as to apprehend that God is and subsists as the cause of the entirety. But it is childish folly to strive to learn yet further, so as to inquire concerning the essence or quality of God. God did not accord this even to the all-wise Moses, and this even though he had made a myriad of prayers to him. Rather, a divine oracle was issued to Moses, "you will see the things after me, but my

---

35. Ex 33:17–23.

36. Didymus, *Commentary on Zachariah* 1.23, ed. Louis Doutreleau, in *Didyme l'Aveugle: Sur Zacharie*, SC 83 (Paris: Éditions du Cerf, 1962), 202 (translation is my own). Didymus offers an identical reading of Exodus 33 in a comment to Ps. 20:13 (LXX). See Didymus, *Commentary on the Psalms* 20:13, in *Didymos der Blinde: Psalmenkommentar (Tura-Papyrus). Teil 1: Kommentar zu Psalm 20–21*, ed. Louis Doutreleau, Adolphe Gesché, and Michael Gronewald, Papyrologische Texte und Abhandlungen 7 (Bonn: Rudolf Habelt, 1969), 88.

face you will not see," which means that everything that comes after God can be apprehended by the virtuous person, and God alone surpasses apprehension.[37]

Philo takes God's words to define the horizon of human apprehension, restricting the human quest for knowledge to the world of created phenomena. While it is clear that Philo is the source underneath Didymus's exegesis, it is significant that Philo does not define this moment as productive of Moses's activity as an author.[38] Didymus advances the Philonic conception of Moses as hierophantic author by conceiving the book of Genesis itself as a human response to a moment of *theoria*, not as a dictation of God. The cosmogony is the precipitate of a reaction—to make an analogy to chemistry—the product of an experience and not the record of that experience. Didymus suggests that the author's experience is vital to the understanding of Genesis. If Moses is the hierophant, ascending with the sacred guide involves retracing the prophet's footsteps. To read through Mosaic eyes requires the effort to return to that cleft in the rock and to visualize the things that come "after" God. Mosaic authorship constitutes not only a fact of the book's sacred origin, but also an invitation to enter into Moses's formative moment.

The Elusive Moses: Augustine and Authorial Intention in *Confessions*

Philo established a foundation for interpretation in which authorial intention is indispensable for complete understanding of the Pentateuch. By entering into the design of the narrative, the student both comprehends the structure of reality and ascends along with the master to the brink of eternity. By perceiving the structure of God's reason within the material world, the student of Moses overcomes the flux of the world of appearances, and, in this way, Moses mediates not only between God and humanity but also between the transience of the material world and the eternality of intelligible reality. Basil also links Mosaic discourse to the desire for a stable ontological foundation that undergirds the moral structure of the cosmos. It is unnecessary,

37. Philo, *Post.* 16, translation modified from Colson, *Philo*, vol. 2, LCL 227. See also Philo, *De fuga et inventione* 165, and *De mutatione nominum* 9.

38. Philo, *Spec.* 1.49–50, expands on this exchange in Exodus 33 to have God instruct Moses to contemplate the universe, but this does not quench the prophet's desire for the "invisible" (τοῖς ἀόρατοῖς) realities.

Basil declares, to refute the cosmogonies of the pagan philosophers (a point
we touched upon earlier), for each one overturns its predecessor.[39] By contrast,
the unadorned speech of Moses transcends the flux of vain opinion, his style
perfectly adapted to the unshakeable foundation of God's sovereignty over the
cosmos.

In this way, the lineage descending from Philo had placed authorial intention at the center of interpretation of the Mosaic narrative. A critical element
to this model was the confidence that the reader had reliable access to those
intentions, either by understanding the network of symbols that Philo undertook in his allegorical exposition, or by acceptance of the plain meaning of
Moses's speech. Basil professed that Moses's language pointed to a clear referent within the natural world. When Moses uses a word such as "grass,"[40] Basil
holds, "I think of grass, and likewise a plant, a fish, a wild beast, cattle—I take
everything just as it is said."[41] Basil's immediate concern here is to keep figurative exegesis on a short leash, but his argument also has hermeneutic implications. It presupposes that the stability of Mosaic language relates to its clarity
in signification. The author clearly relates his diction to identifiable referents
and the task of interpretation proceeds by accurately connecting the sign to its
signified.

What happens, however, if the relationship between sign and signified
cannot be univocally identified? In such a case, where does Mosaic discourse
find its stability above the erosion of time? Readers, Augustine judged, seek
"nothing else than the thoughts and will of the authors who wrote the scripture, to find through the scriptures the will of God, in accordance with which,
we believe, such men spoke."[42] To efface the mind of the author threatened
to introduce a fissure between the author and the meaning of the text. How
could the reader proceed to understand the will of God without also understanding the "thoughts and will" of Moses?

This is the question Augustine takes up in books 11 to 13 of his *Confessions*. The particular issue in this extended commentary on the first chapter

39. Basil, *Hom. in Hex.* 1.2, GCS n.f. 2:3f.
40. Gn 1:11–12.
41. Basil, *Hom. in Hex.* 9.1. Translation is my own.
42. Augustine, *De doctrina Christiana* 2.5.6, ed. Joseph Martin, CCSL 32 (Turnhout: Brepols,
1962), 35. Translation is my own; I consulted translations by D. W. Robertson Jr., *Saint Augustine: On
Christian Doctrine* (New York: Bobbs Merrill, 1958), and R. P. H. Green, *Augustine: De doctrina christiana* (Oxford: Clarendon Press, 1995), but vary somewhat from both.

of Genesis concerns the proper referent to the terms "heaven and earth" in Genesis 1:1, which itself connects, web-like, to several broader problems—the creation of spiritual beings, the nature of time, time's distinction from eternity, and the nature of God's creative activity.[43] In *Confessions*, Augustine expands upon a position he had previously tested in his unfinished commentary on Genesis.[44] In the *Liber imperfectus*, Augustine ventured the interpretation that in Genesis 1:1, "earth" refers to material reality, while "heaven" refers to non-corporeal, intelligible being. This exegesis was not wholly without precedent. It was, however, significant because it forged a path by which a reader might discern at the *literal level* of the narrative—and not as an allegorical extrapolation—the creation of angelic beings and intelligible, non-material reality in the creation account.

To understand the significance of Augustine's proposal we have to take a brief detour into late fourth century exegetical disputes. The absence of the spiritual order from the creation account was adduced by the emperor Julian as a critical weakness of the Mosaic account. Moses, he claims, "does not mention the birth or creation of the angels or in what manner they were brought into being but deals only with the heavenly and earthly bodies."[45] Most Christian interpreters accepted Julian's premise that the creation account passed over the origin of the angels and other spiritual powers. The exegetical debate in Christian circles concerned how to explain this silence. Basil, for one, commended the propriety of Moses in leaving without narration (ἀνιστόρητον) the existence of this transcendent condition of being, because the narrative was intended for novices unprepared for this knowledge.[46] The ever-recalcitrant Theodore of Mopsuestia was, by contrast, willing to take the

---

43. For detailed discussion of these three books of *Confessions* and also of their place in Augustine's Genesis interpretation, see E. P. Meijering, *Augustin über Schöpfung, Ewigkeit und Zeit: Das elfte Buch der Bekenntnisse* (Leiden: Brill, 1979); Marie-Anne Vannier, *"Creatio", "Conversio", "Formatio" chez S. Augustin*, Paradosis 31 (Fribourg: Éditions Universitaires, 1991); and James O'Donnell, *Augustine: Confessions*, 3 vols. (Oxford: Clarendon Press, 1992).

44. Augustine, *De Genesi ad litteram imperfectus liber* 3.6–10, CSEL 28/1. Translation by Roland J. Teske, *St. Augustine on Genesis: Two Books on Genesis against the Manichees and On the Literal Interpretation of Genesis: An Unfinished Book*, FOTC 84 (Washington D.C.: The Catholic University of America Press, 1991).

45. Julian, *Contra Galilaeos*, 49D–E (translation is my own). Julian's treatise is extant only in fragments quoted in Cyril of Alexandria's polemical response. See Cyril of Alexandria, *Contra Julianum* 2.19, ed. Paul Burguière and Pierre Évieux, *Cyrille d'Alexandrie, Contre Julien*, 2 vols., SC 322, 582 (Paris: Éditions du Cerf, 1985, 2016), 1:244.

46. Basil of Caesarea, *Hom. in Hex.*1.5, GCS n.f. 2:8.

Genesis account at face value; he expressed dismay that those who professed
to believe the Scriptures would so confidently assert that invisible powers pre-
existed the visible order, since "they are not able to supply any evidence of this
from the divine Scripture."[47] Theodore's critique focused more on proper exegetical method than on theological substance; he contested not the existence
of the invisible order but rather the ability to infer anything about spiritual beings on the basis of the Genesis account. Interpreters, such as Theodore's bête
noire, Origen, had resorted to allegorical readings in order find the transcendent, spiritual order as present at the outset of creation.

Theodore's materialistic understanding of the literal meaning of Genesis
1:1 had a strong pedigree by the time Augustine undertook his first attempt at
a literal interpretation of the creation account. His innovation was to propose
that the term "heaven" in Genesis 1:1 refers—and refers *literally*—to the formation of non-material creation. As a result, one might understand the collective "heaven and earth" as embracing all of creation in both its material and
spiritual orders. In the *Liber imperfectus*, Augustine defined his position tentatively, advancing "by way of inquiry" rather than "by way of assertion," and ultimately deferred any firm judgment, as none of the possible readings of Genesis 1:1 "could be affirmed without hesitation."[48]

When he revisits the issue in *Confessions*, Augustine does not offer new
options on the menu of possibilities. He instead attempts to explain the irre-
ducible diversity of interpretation on this point. On what grounds can a valid
interpretation be substantiated if readers appealing to author's intention arrive
at incompatible interpretations? The inability to determine one interpretation
at the literal level of the narrative provokes Augustine to undertake an extensive meditation on the relationship between Moses as author and himself as
reader. At the outset of book 11, Augustine addresses a prayer to God, asking
for illumination:

---

47. Theodore of Mopsuestia, apud John Philoponos, *De opificiomundi* 1.8, ed. Walther Reichardt
(Leipzig: Teubner, 1897). Translation is my own. I have used the edition of Clemens Scholten, *Johannes
Philoponos, Die Opificio Mundi: Über die Erschaffung der Welt*, 3 vols. (Freiburg: Herder, 1997), who re-
produces Reichardt's edition with translation (quote from vol. 1, p. 106). For discussion of this valuable
Theodore fragment, see Robert Devreessee, *Essai sur Théodore de Mopsueste* (Vatican: Biblioteca Apos-
tolica Vaticana, 1948), 8f.

48. Augustine, *De Genesi ad litteram imperfectus liber* 1.1, 3.10, trans. Teske.

May I hear and understand how in the beginning you made heaven and earth. Moses wrote this. He wrote this and went his way, passing from this world from you to you, and he is not now in my presence. If he were, I would take hold of him and ask him and through you beg him to explain these things to me.... If he spoke Hebrew, he would in vain make an impact on my sense of hearing, for the sounds would not touch my mind at all. If he spoke in Latin, I would know what he meant. Yet how would I know whether or not he was telling the truth? If I did know this, could I know it from him? No. Within me, within the abode of my thought, a truth would speak that is neither Hebrew nor Greek nor Latin nor any barbarian tongue and that uses neither mouth nor tongue as instruments and utters no audible syllables. It would say: "What he is saying is true." Being immediately certain, I would say with confidence to your man: "What you say is true." But since I cannot question him, I ask you by whom he was filled when he spoke truly. You, O Truth, my God, I ask: pardon my sins, and give to me, you who have granted to your servant to say these things, grant also to me the power to understand them.[49]

Augustine identifies the barriers that inhibit the communication of meaning in a written text: the absence of the author and difference of language between the author and the reader. Both of these are familiar problems that require the activity of the exegete, but Augustine does not rest at this point.[50] Even were Moses physically present to address the reader's questions, and even were he able to speak in Augustine's own tongue, the reader would need an interior illumination. The author could not supply an assurance that is unmediated and that transcends the sequential sounds of human language (*sine strepitu syllabarum*), but only selfsame Truth that fills both "him who spoke truly" and also the reader who is granted the power of understanding.[51] Author and reader, separated by the intervals of time and space, are joined in the eternal Truth that does not lodge in time or speak in divisible sounds.

Augustine's opponents resist his equation of "heaven" in Genesis 1:1 with the intelligible creation. They counter that although the intelligible and material orders both were created by God, "Moses did not have these two in mind when he said by the revealing spirit, 'In the beginning God made heaven and earth.' Rather, Moses intended first to signify in general and concise terms the

---

49. Augustine, *Confessiones* 11.3.5, CCSL 27 (Turnhout: Brepols, 1981), 196f. Unless noted otherwise, translations of Augustine's *Confessions* (sometimes modified) are taken from Henry Chadwick, *Saint Augustine, Confessions* (Oxford: Oxford University Press, 1991).

50. O'Donnell, *Augustine: Confessions*, 3:263, notes that Augustine raises these interpretive issues frequently in other contexts.

51. Augustine, *Conf.* 12.15.18, 12.16.23, returns to this theme.

entire visible world."[52] Augustine's opponents defend their more convention-
al fourth-century exegesis, adopted as well in Basil's homilies on the Hexaemeron, by situating Moses's utterance in the historical context of the Exodus:
"since he was speaking to a crude people of a carnal disposition, he judged
only the visible works of God should be entrusted to them."[53] Augustine's opponents apply the concept of authorial intention to govern this dispute: first,
that Moses had a specific corresponding referent in mind when he wrote, and
secondly, that intention is to be understood in the context of his target readership—the Israelites of his own day. In this model, the written word is a me-
morial of, and a substitute for, a speech act; it is the means by which the author transmits a particular intention to another person from whom the author
is separated by temporal or spatial distance, and the meaning of the text resides in that intention conveyed by the words. Interpretation proceeds by reconstruction and recovery of that originating moment in which the speech
occurs. Thus, the criterion for valid interpretation is established by the near-
est historical and literary context in which the communication originally took
place.

In *Confessions*, the adequacy of this hermeneutical framework becomes
subject to searching consideration. Augustine shifts the issue from articulating the proper exegesis of Genesis 1:1 (what are the referents of "heaven and
earth"?) to examining the interpretive process (how can a reader be assured
of a valid interpretation when exegesis yields different results?). Augustine is
confident in the truth of his own reading of Moses, since all particular truths
participate in the fullness of God's divine truth. God utters truth in Augustine's "inner mind," and, consequently, he can be assured of its truthfulness,
or, perhaps as importantly, he cannot be shaken from his confidence in it. But
how can Augustine convince his unnamed opponents of the validity of his interpretation? Augustine sets a rather modest goal. He does not aim to convince the opponents that his interpretation of Genesis 1:1 is the only correct
one. Rather, he appeals to the wide-encompassing nature of Truth—how can
they refuse to admit the truth of what Truth itself has disclosed to him:

What does it matter to me if what I think the author thought is different from what
someone else thinks he thought? Indeed, all of us who read seek to investigate and

---

52. Augustine, *Conf.* 12.17.24, CCSL 27:228. Translation is my own.
53. Ibid.

understand this: what the author whom we read wanted [*voluit*]. Since, moreover, we believe him to be truthful, we do not dare to judge him to have spoken anything that we either know or believe to be false. Therefore, as long as each reader seeks to perceive in the holy scriptures what the author perceived in them, what harm is it, if he perceives what you, light of all truth-speaking minds, show to be true, even if the author, whom he reads, did not perceive this, which, although true, he nevertheless did not perceive thus.[54]

Responding to the opponents' presuppositions, Augustine shifts attention away from the criteria for "right interpretation" to consideration of the risk of "wrong interpretation." This redirection opens an alternative path by which the "true meaning" of a text might be disclosed. In considering the possibility of a direct illumination by God to the reader, Augustine squarely confronts the consequence: this truth is not dependent on the author's conscious intention. He differentiates between his confidence in the *doctrine* and his own uncertainty in valid interpretation of Scripture:

Behold, I, who say with complete confidence, that in your immutable Word you made all things invisible and visible [cf. Col. 1:16], cannot so confidently say that Moses directed his attention [*attendisse*] to nothing other than this truth when he wrote "In the beginning God made heaven and earth." Although in your truth, I see this to be certain, I cannot see with equal certainty that this is what he was thinking when he wrote these words.[55]

The author's mind ultimately remains opaque and elusive to the reader. Augustine's language is circumspect; the appeal to authorial intention cannot rule out either of the readings proposed by Augustine and his opponents. The problem is that while Moses certainly intended his words to speak truth, it cannot be determined with certainty what particular truth Moses had in view (*attendisse*) with his words. For this reason, authorial intention cannot serve as a regulative principle to distinguish one truth to the exclusion of another. Augustine consequently proposes a principle for regulating interpretation; an interpretation directed toward sustaining the community:[56] "May all of us who,

54. Augustine, *Conf.* 12.18.27, CCSL 27:229–30. Translation is my own.

55. Augustine, *Conf.* 12.24.33, CCSL 27:234. In addition to having modified Chadwick's translation, I am indebted here to the translation of Maria Boulding, *The Confessions* (Hyde Park, N.Y.: New City Press, 1997), 332.

56. Paige E. Hochschild, *Memory in Augustine's Theological Anthropology* (Oxford: Oxford University Press, 2012), 179–82, rightly places emphasis on Augustine's hermeneutical principle of unity as a means to truth in this section of *Confessions*.

as I acknowledge, discern and speak true things in these texts, love one another and equally may we love you, our God, fount of truth—if truth is what we are thirsting after and not vanity."[57]

It is impossible for one reader to demonstrate to another an exclusive claim about Moses's intended meaning. The author's mind is less accessible to the reader than is the divine light. Indeed, the mind of the author is knowable only in and through divine illumination. The principle of authorial intention cedes primacy of place as a regulative interpretive principle. One reason for this is the surplus of meaning in a text beyond what the author intends; as Augustine concedes that he cannot know the contents of Moses's mind as he penned the first words of Genesis, it also means that the critical tools to determine this intention cannot be the ultimate judge of Scripture's meaning. But Augustine goes further and posits that the reader meets the mind of the author, and the minds of other readers, mutually in the divine light that illumines both author and reader. The community of readers is already prefigured in the community of author with reader, which is founded upon the indwelling of the eternal Word.[58]

In Augustine's argument, love is more than an ethical imperative; it is also an ontological foundation for valid interpretation as the condition for and medium of knowledge. Perhaps love here is already modeled in the inscrutability of the author.[59] The author cannot be mastered by the reader. Both are understood, and understand, only in the reality of illuminating Truth. Authorship signifies for Augustine by establishing the community of reader and author in the mutual quest for divine understanding. Moses is not a guide to, but a fellow supplicant from, the fount of Truth. He is a speaker of the truth, but the interpretive process starts by the reader's belief that his words *stem from* the truth. The good reader, in other words, will keep in mind that the truth of what he says is contingent upon—and reposes in (to use an Augustinian phrase)—its relation to the uncreated Truth.[60]

57. Augustine, *Conf.* 12.30.41 (CCSL 27:240), trans. modified from Chadwick.

58. On this point, see Isabelle Bochet, "Le fondement de l'herméneutique augustinienne," in *Saint Augustin et la Bible: Actes du colloque de l'université Paul Verlaine-Metz (7–8 avril 2005)*, edited by Gérard Nauroy and Marie-Anne Vannier (Bern: Peter Lang, 2008), 37–57, esp. 52–53.

59. Luigi Gioia, *The Theological Epistemology of Augustine's* De Trinitate (New York: Oxford University Press, 2008), 170–89, makes a similar argument with respect to Augustine's treatise *On the Trinity*, but does not extend the discussion to the hermeneutical process.

60. Vannier, *"Creatio", "Conversio", "Formatio"*, 159–72, argues that the metaphor of repose, taken

Conclusion

Ancient readers accepted without reservation that the Pentateuch entered into human experience through Moses's hands. This conviction, however, did not convey to interpreters what significance they ought to assign to the lawgiver's authorial agency. The authority of the divine speech frequently took precedence over the contributions of the human mediator. The Pentateuch conveyed divine speech to humanity, and it was not clear that the prophet's own intention assisted the reader in understanding the divine will.

Augustine and Philo both assigned hermeneutical significance to Mosaic authorship, in that as author Moses made manifest the boundary between the created and the uncreated, between time and eternity. For Philo, the process of reading aims for moral assimilation of the reader to Moses. Through identification with Moses, the reader gradually learns to assume the Mosaic identity and in this *persona* to enter into the heavenly sanctuary and enjoy the same vision of God that Moses beheld. For Augustine, the inability to fix the meaning of the first words of Genesis highlights the instability of language and reinforces the gap between time and eternity. Augustine ultimately turns to the community of reader, author, and mutually indwelling Truth to provide the place of repose that unstable and elusive words fail to secure.

---

from the Sabbath rest of God in Genesis 1, comes to occupy more importance to Augustine as an epistemological image than does the ocular metaphor of illumination.

Kathleen Gibbons

7. RIGHT REASONING AND THE INTERPRETATION OF THE MOSAIC LAW IN CLEMENT OF ALEXANDRIA

Clement of Alexandria's allegorical exegesis has sometimes come under fire as excessively speculative or arbitrary. As Alexander Roberts and James Donaldson conclude their description of the erudition of Clement's work in their introduction to the Ante-Nicene Fathers volume, "Of course throughout there is plenty of false science, and fanciful and frivolous speculation."[1] More recently, readers of Clement have been receptive to making sense of his methodological madness. David Dawson, for instance, has argued that Clement's interpretative approach is governed by an intertextual hermeneutic that strives to reconcile the Hebrew scriptures with what he takes to be the text of the New Testament.[2] Here, I would like to develop further the idea that Clement's allegorical exegesis aims to reconcile the two testaments, by

1. Alexander Roberts and James Donaldson, *Clement of Alexandria: Ante-Nicene Christian Library* (New York: Christian Literature Publishing Co., 1908), 15. Translations of Clement are my own, though I have benefited from the Roberts-Donaldson translation; the Greek text used is the edition by O. Stählin, *Clemens Alexandrinus*, Kirchenväter-Commission der Königl. Preussischen Akademie der Wissenschaften (Leipzig, 1905–1936).

2. David Dawson, *Allegorical Readers and Cultural Revision in Ancient Alexandria* (Berkeley: University of California Press, 1992); see also Judith Kovacs, "Divine Pedagogy and the Gnostic Teaching according to Clement of Alexandria," *Journal of Early Christian Studies* 9 (2001): 3–25. On ancient biblical exegesis, see also Daniel Boyarin, "By Way of Apology: Dawson, Edwards, Origen," *Studia Philonica*

examining in particular his understanding of the status of the Mosaic law. I propose that we can understand there to be not only two modes of interpretation, the literal and the allegorical, but also two senses in which one can obey the Mosaic law. On the one hand, we find the Christian learner following the commandments of the Mosaic law as a list of deontic rules, and on the other, the gnostic, whose right reason, or ὀρθὸς λόγος, leads him or her to act in accordance with the ethical implications of the providential theology implied by the very existence of a divine law. In making this distinction, we can make sense of Clement's perhaps seemingly contradictory commitments of holding the law of Moses as of enduring significance for Christians while, at the same time, as propaedeutic and therefore in some way surpassed by the revelation of the Logos of God.[3]

As is well-known to readers of Clement, the figure of Moses played a central role in his construction of Christianity and of the relationship between Jews and Christians. Yet whether the Mosaic law would have any particular kind of status for Christianity was, at the period in which Clement was writing, a far-from-settled question.[4] Against a backdrop of early discussion about the status of Moses and the Mosaic law, a discussion that included such wide-ranging views as those found in the different gospels, the various letters of Paul, the Epistle to the Hebrews, the *Epistle of Barnabas*, the works of Marcion, Ptolemy's *Epistle to Flora*, and Justin Martyr's *Dialogue with Trypho*, Clement argued that Moses was a forerunner to Christ, and that his writings prepared their readers for the coming revelation of the Word.[5] For Clement, following Paul, the law served as a tutor to prepare human beings for the incarnation of the Logos.[6] Yet in mapping his construction of Christianity onto the Hebrew scriptures, is Clement engaging in anything other than brute apologetic rhetoric, or is there an internal logic to his intertextual interpreta-

---

Annual 16 (2004): 188–217; Jean Daniélou, *From Shadows to Reality: Studies in the Biblical Typology of the Fathers* (London: Burns and Oates, 1960), esp. 217–26.

3. For a discussion of Clement's views on providence, see Silke-Petra Bergjan, *Der fürsorgende Gott: Der Begriff der Pronoia Gottes in der apologetischen Literatur der Alten Kirche* (Berlin: De Gruyter, 2002), 328–30.

4. The status of Moses in Judaism was, of course, also contested in antiquity. On the role of the figure of Moses in Enochian Judaism, see Andrei Orlov, *The Enoch-Metatron Tradition* (Tübingen: Mohr Siebeck, 2005), 254–303.

5. For a full-length treatment, see Daniel Ridings, *The Attic Moses: The Dependency Theme in Some Early Christian Writers* (Göteborg: Acta Universitatis Gothoburgensis, 1995).

6. Gal 3:24; cf. Clement, *Strom.* 1.167.2–3.

tion here? In answering this question, I would like to focus in particular on Clement's exegesis of the Decalogue in *Stromateis* 6.16, and how it relates to what Clement says elsewhere about Moses as one who engages in right reason or ὀρθὸς λόγος.[7] In drawing on the Stoic concept of law as the ability to reason rightly, Clement follows Philo's own reworking of the figure of Moses. Understanding how this concept fits into his discussion of the Mosaic commandments helps illuminate the ultimate role of the law in what Clement understands to be true Christianity.

Below, I will argue that, in offering his allegorical reading of the Mosaic law, Clement claims that the person who fully grasps the Mosaic law is the person who reasons rightly about the nature of God, and whose actions reflect the moral implications of that understanding. In particular, I suggest that for Clement, an understanding of the implications of the fact that the supreme God is the providential creator of the cosmos, who governs the created world through his Logos[8]—itself a contested theological claim in Clement's time from many quarters, including Marcion and Valentinus—will shape one's behavior in the way prescribed by the Decalogue. Here, I argue that Clement's interpretation and defense of the Mosaic law depends upon an understanding of the prescriptions and proscriptions given in the law as, in some sense, a direct consequence of the very idea that God is a lawgiver, and, like any good lawgiver, concerned with the well-being of and promotion of virtue in human beings. On this interpretation, the allegorical reading of Mosaic law requires one to reason rightly about God and his Logos as responsible for the governance of the cosmos. The person who understands the allegorical reading will obey the Mosaic law out of a reasoning process significantly different from the one who obeys the literal interpretation of the law, a difference that has implications for understanding the status of the law in Christianity.

---

7. Max Pohlenz, "Klemens von Alexandria und sein hellenisches Christentum," *Nachrichten von der Akademie der Wissenschaften in Göttingen* phil-hist. Kl (1943): 103–80, at 143, takes Clement's use of the Stoic concept of right reason to derive from Chrysippus; Salvatore R. C. Lilla, *Clement of Alexandria: A Study of Christian Platonism and Gnosticism* (Oxford: Oxford University Press, 1971), 73–76, suggests that Philo is a more likely source, while Annewies van den Hoek, *Clement of Alexandria and His Use of Philo in the Stromateis: An Early Christian Reshaping of a Jewish Model* (Leiden: Brill, 1988), 59, suggests that the terminology is widespread enough that we need not identify a unique source.

8. Cf. Clement, *Strom.* 5.103.

Rules, Reasoning, and the Stoics

In considering the Mosaic law to function on these two levels, it is illuminating to take stock of the Stoic background for ideas about law and right reason. While it has long been recognized that the concept of law played a central role in Stoic ethics, what the Stoics mean by the "natural law" has been debated. As we find Marcianus recording the opening of Chrysippus's *On Law*, "Law is king of all things human and divine. Law must preside over what is honourable and base, as ruler and as guide, and thus be the standard of right and wrong, prescribing to animals whose nature is political what they should do, and prohibiting them from what they should not do."[9] There are, however, different interpretations of what this assertion meant and of how later Stoics, such as Seneca and Epictetus, understood it. Philip Mitsis and Gisela Striker have both claimed that, for the Stoics, the law of nature consisted of a set of deontic principles.[10] Mitsis, for instance, has argued that in Seneca we find a theory of how moral reasoning is primarily a matter of applying certain rules to certain circumstances, in a manner that anticipates Kant in several salient respects. In his discussion of Seneca's distinction between *praecepta*, instructions about individual circumstances, and *decreta*, general moral principles, Mitsis claims that Seneca's concern with understanding how the rules of the *praecepta* flesh out the guiding norms of the *decreta* likely reflects a debate about the role of rule-following dating back to ancient Stoicism.[11]

Against this reading, Brad Inwood and Paul Vander Waerdt have argued

---

9. *Stoicorum Veterum Fragmenta* (henceforward *SVF*), compiled by Hans Von Arnim (Leipzig: Teubner, 1903–1905), 3.314, trans. A. A. Long and D. N. Sedley, *The Hellenistic Philosophers* (Cambridge: Cambridge University Press, 1987), 432. For discussion, see Paul A. Vander Waerdt, "Philosophical Influence on Roman Jurisprudence? The Case of Stoicism and Natural Law," *Aufstieg und Niedergang der Römischen Welt (ANRW)* 2.26.7 (1994): 4856–58.

10. Phillip Mitsis, "Seneca on Reason, Rules, and Moral Development," in *Passions and Perceptions: Studies in Hellenic Philosophy of Mind*, ed. Jacques Brunschwig and Martha C. Nussbaum (Cambridge: Cambridge University Press, 1993), 285–312; and Gisela Striker, "Origins of the Concept of Natural Law," and "Following Nature: A Study in Stoic Ethics," in *Essays on Hellenistic Epistemology and Ethics* (Cambridge: Cambridge University Press, 1996), 209–21, and 221–80; see also Joseph G. DeFilippo and Phillip Mitsis, "Socrates and Stoic Natural Law," in *The Socratic Movement*, ed. Paul Vander Waerdt (Ithaca, N.Y.: Cornell University Press, 1994), 252–71.

11. In commenting on Seneca's discussion of how rules guide our behavior with other people, Mitsis points out how Seneca "argues that the *praecepta* concerned with various helping actions are governed by a *decretum* enjoining that we respect other persons as mutually related parts of God and nature." In Mitsis, "Seneca on Reason," 303.

that the Stoics take a procedural, rather than deontic, interpretation of the law of nature.[12] Rather than taking the natural law as primarily a set of rules to be followed, following nature consists in reasoning rightly.[13] What is law-like about this law is not that it gives a set of commandments that must always be obeyed, but that its content has a prescriptive force. Inwood has emphasized the contextual reasoning of the sage in determining the actions appropriate to one's particular social role and circumstance, such as we might find described in Seneca's famous discussion of the javelin thrower in *Epistulae Morales* 94:[14]

Just as the student of javelin-throwing keeps aiming at a fixed target and thus trains the hand to give direction to the missile, and when, by instruction and practice, he has gained the desired ability, he can then employ it against any target he wishes (having learned to strike not any random object, but precisely the object at which he has aimed), so he who has equipped himself for the whole of life does not need to be advised concerning each separate time, because he is now trained to meet his problem as a whole; for he knows not merely how he should live with his wife or son, but how he should live aright.[15]

The suggestion that we find in Seneca an understanding of the sage's way of reasoning not as the application of a set of rules to any given circumstance, but as a way of reasoning about a particular situation in light of an understanding of the good, is borne out in Seneca's exhortation that, in moral deliberation, what matters is whether any particular thing we pursue is useful for us in light of the highest good: "Whenever you want to know what is to be avoided or what is to be sought, look to the highest good, the purpose of your entire life. For whatever we do ought to agree with that. Only someone who has before him a general purpose for his whole life will put individual things in order."[16] For the non-sage, this process requires the rules of thumb laid out in

---

12. Brad Inwood, "Rules and Reasoning in Stoic Ethics" and "Natural Law in Seneca," in *Reading Seneca: Stoic Philosophy at Rome* (Oxford: Clarendon Press, 2005), 95–131, and 224–48; Vander Waerdt, "Philosophical Influence," and "Zeno's *Republic* and the Origins of Natural Law," in Vander Waerdt, *The Socratic Movement*, 272–308.

13. Stobaeus 2.66.14–67.4; Diogenes 7.85–86.

14. On the difficulty with understanding Stoic law as deontic in light of the craft analogy, see Brad Inwood, "Goal and Target in Stoicism," *Journal of Philosophy* 83 (1986): 547–56; see also Striker, "Following Nature," 243.

15. Seneca, *Ep.* 94.3, in *Ad Lucilium epistulae morales*, vol. 3, trans. Richard Gummere (Cambridge, Mass.: Harvard University Press, 1925).

16. Seneca, *Epistola* 71.2, in *Selected Philosophical Letters*, trans. Brad Inwood (Oxford: Clarendon Press, 2007).

the *praecepta* and *decreta*, but the sage will understand that occasionally, there will be reason to violate these rules, such as in the case of suicide.[17] A sage will be able to gauge what best to do by adopting what Julia Annas has referred to as the "point of view of the universe"—the perspective from which one judges circumstances by acting in accordance with the rationality that governs the cosmos.[18] "Let a great mind obey god and let it endure without hesitation whatever the law of the universe demands. Either it is realized into a better life, to live more clearly and calmly among the divine, or at least it will be free of any future inconvenience if it is mixed again with nature and returns to the cosmos."[19]

For those who have grasped the norms of cosmic reason imperfectly, the rules of thumb found in the *praecepta* are useful for providing some sort of moral guidance. The sage, however, will understand that there are exceptions to these rules, because the sage's moral reasoning will be informed by the perspective that the things that lie outside of our capacities for choice are, in some sense, indifferents, whose value is to be judged from the perspective of the highest good (i.e., virtue).[20] While this particular reading of Stoicism allows the sage to make exceptions to rules, this reading also places a particular emphasis on a certain kind of reasoning—reasoning from a proper understanding of the cosmic order and one's place within it, rather than from an application of rules to circumstances. The non-sage might strive to imitate this reasoning, but will ultimately have to rely on rules to inform his or her behavior.

This idea that the sage, by adopting the cosmic perspective, is capable of forming moral judgments that are informed by an adequate grasp of the significant role that preferred indifferents play in our lives, is likewise found in Epictetus as well:[21]

---

17. On the prohibitions against suicide, see *SVF* 3.10.11. As Inwood writes, "suicide is permissible in early Stoicism, but only when a clear and correct judgment can be made about one's situation in life. No one but a wise person can do so; so only a wise person ought to commit suicide... there is a general rule against suicide, based on our natural preference for life, but it is [no more than] a defensible rule of thumb. Still, only a truly wise man can be relied on to make the decision well." Inwood, *Reading Seneca*, 113.

18. Julia Annas, *The Morality of Happiness* (Oxford: Oxford University Press, 1993), 159–79.

19. Seneca, *Epistola* 71.16, trans. Inwood, p. 28.

20. In the complex historical debates about ancient goods, see Inwood, "Ancient Goods: The Tria Genera Bonorum in Ethical Theory," chapter 11 in *Strategies of Argument: Essays in Ancient Ethics, Epistemology, and Logic*, ed. Mi-Kyoung Lee (Oxford: Oxford University Press, 2014).

21. Anthony Long, *Epictetus: The Stoic and Socratic Guide to Life* (Oxford: Clarendon Press, 2004), 153–56.

you are a citizen of the world, and a part of it, not one of the parts destined for service, but one of primary importance; for you possess the faculty of understanding the divine administration of the world, and of reasoning upon the consequences thereof. What, then, is the profession of a citizen? To treat nothing as a matter of private profit, not to plan about anything as though he were a detached unit, but to act like the foot or the hand, which, if they had the faculty of reason and understood the constitution of nature, would never exercise choice or desire in any other way but by reference to the whole.[22]

The Stoic understanding of law as a matter of right reason influenced Philo of Alexandria, who offered his own theory of the deontic rules of the Mosaic law; in developing his understanding of their significance, however, he draws on the Stoic conception of law in arguing that Moses, who dispenses with the law, possesses the capacity for right reasoning.[23] In his discussion of the laws in *De spec. leg.* 4.134, Philo describes the laws laid out in the commandments as preparatory for virtue.[24] Like Philo, Clement drew on the Stoic theory of law as right reason in his analysis of Moses. In examining what right reason means for Clement, I will argue that the gnostic's grasp of and obedience to the Mosaic law entails not, first and foremost, obedience to a set of deontic rules, but the adoption of a particular theological perspective that informs moral action.[25] In suggesting that the procedural interpretation of Stoic ideas of natural law informs Clement's ideas about the Mosaic law, I do not mean to suggest that Clement understands there to be exceptions to the commandments given in the Mosaic law. At no time is it ever permissible to commit adultery, murder, theft, and so forth. What I mean to suggest, however, is that the gnostic—the one who truly understands the Mosaic law on not only its literal but also its allegorical level—is the person whose actions will be in conformity with the literal content of the Mosaic law, because such a

22. Epictetus, *Diss.* 2.10.3–6, in *The Discourses as Recorded By Arrian*, vol. 1, trans. William Oldfather (London: W. Heinemann, 1926–1928).

23. Philo, *Mos.* 1.48; cf. *De spec. leg.* 1.191 and 2.29–31.

24. As Annas writes, "Philo appeals to the idea of virtue as a disposition not merely to act in certain ways, but to do so for certain reasons, and to have one's feelings and emotions in harmony with this." Julia Annas, "Virtue and Law in Plato," in *Plato's Laws: A Critical Guide*, ed. Christopher Bobonich (Cambridge: Cambridge University Press, 2010), 82n51. On the idea of the Logos in ancient Judaism, see Daniel Boyarin, *Border Lines: The Partition of Judaeo-Christianity* (Philadelphia: University of Pennsylvania Press, 2006), 112–27.

25. I suspect, *mutatis mutandis*, that much of my interpretation of Clement would apply to Philo as well; I leave this discussion, however, for another occasion.

person, in adequately grasping an appropriate understanding of the relationship between God and the universe, will not be inclined to perform the sorts of behaviors proscribed by the law. The Mosaic law is therefore pedagogic insofar as it gives the deontic commandments necessary to instruct the one who cannot yet reason this way how to live in conformity with right reason.

Moses and Right Reason

In making the suggestion that the gnostic's way of acting in accordance with the Mosaic law is not best understood as involving the application of rules, I might be taken as offering a rather strange proposal. On the face of it, it would appear that there could hardly be anything other than a deontic interpretation of the Mosaic law. With its straight-forward rules such as "Do not kill," and "Do not steal," how could one plausibly interpret the Mosaic law as anything else? And indeed, as we look at the discussion of the law in Clement's *Protrepticus* 10, we do find the Mosaic law appropriated in such a way as to emphasize the deontic nature of the laws;

So let the Athenian follow the laws of Solon, and the Argive those of Phoroneus, and the Spartan those of Lycurgus: but if you enroll yourself as one of God's people, your fatherland will be heaven, and God will be your lawgiver. And what are the laws? "You shall not murder, you shall not commit adultery, you shall not corrupt boys, you shall not steal, you shall not commit false witness, you shall love the Lord your God" [cf. Ex 20:13–16]. And there are also complements of these, laws of reason and holy laws inscribed in human hearts themselves; "you shall love you neighbor as yourself" [Mt 22:39, Mk 12:31, Lk 10:27], "to the one you hits you on your cheek, offer the other" [Lk 6:29], "you shall not lust, for by lust alone do you commit adultery" [Mt 5:28].[26]

Here, the content of the Decalogue is described as complementary to the commandments of Jesus. In the intertextual connections Clement draws here to illuminate the claim that the law of Moses is preparatory for the coming of the Word, we find the suggestion that to live according to the law of true Christianity is, in fact, a matter of obeying deontic rules that mirror the laws set out in Exodus. The moral instruction of the *Paedagogus* likewise implies that being a Christian involves living in accordance with a set of rules, as we

---

26. Clement, *Prot.* 10.108–9.

find the second and third book devoted to instructing the reader in the sorts of behaviors the Christian will avoid.

But it is important to remember that the *Protrepticus* and the *Paedagogus* are not intended for those who are advanced in their Christianity, but for those who are still at an early stage of instruction. There are, however, two distinct, though related, aims to this instruction: the Mosaic laws are intended not only to set out moral precepts to help one live a pious life, but also to prepare the one who obeys them for an understanding of the Word through whom God the Father governs the universe. As Clement says in the *Paedagogus*, "The law was given through Moses, not by Moses, but by the Logos, and through Moses his servant. And on this account it was transitory."[27] If the Mosaic law is transitory, however, how are the commandments of Jesus understood to be their complements? We here find an apparent tension in Clement's thought between the claim, on the one hand, that the Mosaic law has an enduring significance for Christians and, on the other hand, that it is in some way surpassed or superseded by Christ. I propose that it is possible to resolve this apparent tension by considering Clement's exegesis of the Mosaic law against the background of Stoic ideas on rules and the law of reason.

The idea that Moses, in giving the law, demonstrated himself to be the one who reasons rightly about God is evident from the brief discussion of Moses's life at the end of *Stromateis* 1. In book 1, Moses is portrayed as the ideal statesman and ruler who, by perceiving the reality identified with the Logos of God, is able to dispense the law to those he governs. Moses can do so only because he has achieved the capacity for right reasoning, as a consequence of the fact that he has contemplated the Logos.[28]

Law is not the things legislated (just as sight is not the things seen), nor is it every judgment (for wicked judgment is not law), but law is excellent judgment, and excellent judgment is truth, and truth is the discovery and attainment of truth. "He who is has sent me," says Moses [Ex 3:14]. Some, following this excellent judgment, say that the law is right reason [λόγον ὀρθὸν; cf. *Strom.* 2.18.4, 2.19.2–4.], prescribing those things which ought to be done, and proscribing the things which should not.[29]

27. Clement, *Paed.* 1.60.1–2.
28. Cf. ps.-Plato, *Minos*, 319e–321c.
29. Clement, *Strom.* 1.166.4–5.

Observe here both the Stoic language of ὀρθὸς λόγος and the Chrysippean formulation of law recorded in both Marcianus and Philo.[30] Here, Moses, as lawgiver, is described as an imitator of the Divine Craftsman, who provides a law for human beings. In book 1, however, Clement does not discuss the content of the Decalogue. In order to understand how the idea of right reasoning is connected to the actual commandments of Moses, we must turn to Clement's exegesis of the Decalogue in *Stromateis* 6.16, where we find Clement offering an allegorical reading of selected commandments, which, I will suggest, is informed by the idea that the gnostic acts rightly not primarily by acting according to a set of rules, but as a consequence of acting from a certain moral perspective.

Allegorical Exegesis and the Decalogue

In his discussion of the Decalogue, Clement claims that there are two levels on which one might interpret the scriptures, as is revealed in the two tablets upon which the commandments are rewritten: "And perhaps the two tables themselves may be the prophecy of the two covenants. So they were renewed mystically, when ignorance together with sin exceeded all bounds. The commandments are written twofold, it seems, for two spirits, the ruling and the ruled, since "'the flesh lusts against the spirit and the spirit against the flesh' [Gal 5:17]."[31] The person who lives in accordance with both of these will be the person who dominates the carnal spirit, as he says in reference to the tenth commandment:

So the commandment, "You shall not lust" [Ex 20:17] says that you shall not be a slave to the fleshly spirit, but you shall rule over it, for "the flesh lusts against the spirit" [Gal 5:17] and rises up to commit disorder against nature, and the spirit rules "against the flesh" so that the conduct of the person will be according to nature [κατὰ φύσιν].[32]

The idea of living in accordance with nature recalls the Stoic idea of law and right reason. We might therefore take Clement's division here as suggesting that the person who lives according to the spiritual interpretation of scripture is the one who, like Moses himself, lives according to an understanding

30. Philo, *De Jos.* 29.3
31. Clement, *Strom.* 6.133.5–134.1.
32. Ibid., 6.136.2–3.

of the rational principles through which God orders the cosmos; and indeed, this is what we find in Clement's allegorical interpretation of the individual commandments, where he fleshes out the two different levels of scripture. After his exegesis of the first, second, and fourth commandments, which more literally relate to the nature of God, Clement turns to the commandment to obey one's father and mother (Ex 20:12). On the literal level, the commandment means simply to honor one's biological mother and father. On the spiritual level, however, Clement claims that the Father here refers to God, while the Mother here refers to divine knowledge and wisdom:

And next, the fifth is the commandment concerning the honor of father and mother, and it proclaims those who know him sons and gods. And it clearly says that God is Father and Lord. So the creator of all is Lord and Father, and the mother is not, as some say, the Being from which we came, nor, as others teach, the church, but the divine knowledge and wisdom, as Solomon says, calling wisdom "the mother of the just," [Ps 81:6] and it is desirable for its own sake. And everything good and holy is known from the Father, through the Son.[33]

On the face of it, this might seem like a quite arbitrary interpretation of the text. Yet here, divine knowledge is given a quite specific meaning that illuminates what Clement thinks is implied by the concept of a divine law. In particular, Clement's analysis of the different commandments emphasize God's role as the providential creator of the cosmos. Recall the discussion we saw in book 1, where the providential ruler of the cosmos is described specifically as a lawgiver. The very fact that God gives a law implies that God takes concern for the well-ordered governance of the cosmos and the human beings who live it, as a good lawgiver would; God accomplishes this governance through his Son, the Logos. We here find Clement, in book 6, returning to the idea of God as a lawgiver that was discussed in book 1. Acceptance of the Mosaic law as a divinely given and therefore binding law, before anything else, depends upon one's acceptance of the particular theological claims about the nature of God's providence, claims that Clement takes as constitutive of true Christianity.

That Clement's allegorical interpretation of the Mosaic law involves an understanding of God specifically as a providential ruler—an interpretation of the supreme God that was, as I have already noted, far from uncontested during this period of Christianity—is again evident in his exegesis of

33. Ibid., 6.146.1–2.

the commandment against murder (Ex 20:13), where Clement interprets this commandment as a prohibition against destruction of the true doctrine, specifically as a prohibition of the teaching that the world is not ruled by the supreme God.

> Next follows the commandment about murder. And murder is forcible removal. The one wishing to remove the true doctrine [λόγον] concerning God and his eternity, so that he might admit falsity, saying that everything is not governed by Providence, or that the cosmos is uncreated, or any other thing against true teaching, is most abominable.[34]

In understanding the commandment as a prohibition against false teaching about God, Clement takes it specifically as a prohibition against claiming that the supreme God does not govern creation or that the universe had a beginning. On the allegorical interpretation provided here, the divine law forbids one to advance a theological position that would negate the law's own divinity by denying the governance of the cosmos to God. In the exegesis of the commandment against adultery (Ex 20:14), we find an injunction not to abandon true knowledge,[35] and in his discussion of the commandment against stealing (Ex 20:15), we find a prohibition against robbing God of his status as creator by declaring the stars to have governance over the cosmos.[36] Denying God's creation by suggesting that the stars have domain over the universe is tantamount to theft, and thus yet another exhortation to understand God as the ultimate creator and governor of the universe.[37] In these interpretations of the various commandments, a whole host of religious competitors—including astrologers, Platonists who denied the temporal creation of the world, and those Christians like Marcion and Valentinus who rejected the idea of the supreme God as creator—might be imagined as all guilty of the same crime of denying God's cosmic governance.

There are, moreover, substantive ethical consequences to understanding God as governor and lawgiver, consequences that are illuminated by a comparison to the Stoic position that the sage lives according to the cosmic reasoning that structures the universe. In his exegesis of the tenth command-

34. Ibid., 6.147.2.
35. Ibid., 6.146.3–147.1.
36. Ibid., 6.147.3–148.1.
37. On early Christian attitudes toward astrology, see Tim Hegedus, *Early Christianity and Ancient Astrology* (New York: Peter Lang, 2007).

ment, Clement argues that the prohibition against coveting is, on the spiritual level of the text, an exhortation to understand that external objects are created by God for a benevolent purpose, and therefore are not to be desired or avoided in themselves;

And the tenth is the commandment concerning all desires. So just as he who desires inappropriate things is censured, in the same way one is not permitted to desire false things, nor to think that of those things that exist in creation, the animate things have power from themselves, and the inanimate things help or hurt at all. Should someone say that the antidote is not able to heal or hemlock kill, he is unknowingly deceived. For none of these operates without the one making use of the plant and the drug, just as the ax does not operate without the one cutting, nor the saw without the one sawing. And as they do not operate according to themselves, but they have certain physical qualities, which complete their own work with the activity of the craftsman, thus also by the universal providence of God, through the secondary causes, is the active power passed over in succession to individuals.[38]

If one acknowledges that God governs all things, externals have no value in themselves. Clement here adopts the idea, found both in Stoicism and in strands of Platonism,[39] that those things that are external to our virtue cannot, strictly speaking, be thought of as "goods," for he argues that a commitment to the idea that God exercises providence through the Logos means that one will correctly value external objects, not in themselves, but in the way in which they are used by that providence.[40] The one who lives according to the law by reasoning rightly about the nature of God and the implications of that nature for human moral life will cease to have the problematic desires that lead to immoral action. For Clement, we correctly value potential objects of desire when we consider their value to us from the point of view that the sensible world is ultimately governed by the Logos of God for the benefit of human beings, a perspective that is analogous to the Stoic cosmic point of view discussed above, and that informs the Stoic sage's right reason.

To be sure, Clement's allegorical exegesis provides yet another set of rules, yet each of these rules exhorts one to adopt the view that the universe is governed by the highest God. If we are to make sense of Clement's claim that the law is preliminary, in whatever qualified sense (given the entirety of what he

38. Clement, *Strom.* 6.148.4–6.
39. Inwood, "Ancient Goods."
40. Cf. Clement, *Strom.* 4.19.2.

says about the law), I suggest that we might take these allegorical interpretations as a description of the gnostic's behavior rather than as an account of an additional set of rules with which the gnostic reasons. The person who understands the spiritual sense of the Mosaic law is therefore the one who will grasp the rationale behind the literal sense. If one sufficiently apprehends, cognitively and conatively, that what is outside us does not have intrinsic value, one will have no motivation to engage in adultery, steal, or murder. While the one who is in the process of coming to know God follows the Mosaic law by way of obeying certain laws, the rationale behind these laws is made clear only after one has the correct understanding about God's relationship to the cosmos, a governing relationship, which is established by the very law that gives these rules. Rather than diminishing the moral significance of the law in favor of the "higher," spiritual reading, the spiritual reading illuminates the content of the moral sense. The literal content of the commandments that make up the Mosaic law—not to kill, steal, commit adultery, and so forth—are commandments that the person who has properly adopted the correct theological perspective will obey as a matter of course, not from a way of moral rule-following. On this interpretation, the one who fully understands the theological and cosmological principles implicit in the very notion of a divine law will understand the rational basis for the prescriptions and proscriptions contained in the Decalogue. By reasoning from a perspective that fully grasps the implications of the providence God exercises through the Logos, it becomes possible to value correctly the external objects that might otherwise lead us to commit acts of theft, murder, fornication, and so forth. The normative force of the Mosaic law for the gnostic is derivative from the theological perspective the gnostic adopts.

This is not to deny that the Mosaic laws are exceptionless; unlike the Stoic prohibition against suicide, which can be violated by the sage, for Clement there will never be a reason to violate any of the commandments, even for the gnostic.[41] But the difference between Clement's gnostic and the Christian learner, with respect to the sort of moral reasoning the two engage in, is similar in kind to the difference between the Stoic sage and the non-sage, in a way

---

41. I think Clement's exegetical approach does, in various ways, raise concerns about the displacement of the literal text, as discussed in Boyarin, "By Way of Apology"; but I leave these issues for another time.

that has important implications for Clement's understanding of the status of the Mosaic law as propaedeutic. As in Stoicism, the kind of moral reasoning the gnostic engages in is different in kind from that of the learner. While the learner who has not yet acquired this cosmic perspective must obey the letter of the law, the gnostic understands the theological principles upon which that law is based, and reasons accordingly. On the interpretation I have provided here, Moses himself, as a gnostic and someone who acts according to ὀρθὸς λόγος, would not have acted by applying the deontic principles such as "do not commit adultery" or "do not steal" laid out in his law, although his actions would have been in accordance with such laws. Rather, he acted from an understanding of the ethical implications of the providence of the Logos. His law takes the form that it does insofar as it is his responsibility to instruct those who have not yet achieved the contemplative knowledge that he himself grasps.[42]

Here, I have suggested that considering Clement's exegesis of the Mosaic law through the lens of Stoic discussion about moral reasoning helps us not only to understand the logic behind Clement's interpretation, but also illuminates how Clement can claim that the Mosaic law is, in some sense, preparatory to the revelation given by the Logos in the Incarnation, while at the same time maintaining that the law has an ongoing status as revealed scripture. This distinguishes Clement's exegesis from, say, the interpretation of the Mosaic law given in the Epistle to the Hebrews, or that put forth by Ptolemy, who, in the *Epistle to Flora*, argues that the law that is completed by the Savior figure is the law laid down by the merely just, rather than supreme, God. Stoic ideas about the relationship between rule-following and right reason help illuminate how the idea that Moses engages in ὀρθὸς λόγος provides a lens through which Clement can reconcile the two testaments, at a period during which the status of the Hebrew scriptures in Christianity was a seriously contested question. In doing so, he provides a theory of the Mosaic law that, for all its supercessionism, complicates facile distinctions about the dualism between the "universal" and the "particular" in early Christianity, though further elaboration on these issues will have to wait for another time. What I hope to have

42. See Kovacs, "Divine Pedagogy," and Kathleen Gibbons, "Moses, Statesman and Philosopher: The Philosophical Background of the Ideal of Assimilating to God and the Methodology of Clement of Alexandria's Stromateis 1," *Vigiliae Christianae*, 69 (2015): 157–85; and "Moses, Statesman, and Philosopher," in *The Moral Psychology of Clement of Alexandria* (New York: Routledge, 2017), 49–68.

made plausible here is that an appreciation of how Clement used the concept of right reason in defending the idea that the supreme God is the providential creator and governor of the cosmos not only illuminates the origins of natural law in early Christian philosophy, but also helps to illustrate the significance of conceptualizations of Judaism in early Christian debates about self-definition.

8. EUSEBIUS'S MOSES

Hebrew, Jew, and Christian

Moses is a central figure in Eusebius's most important books. Several of the roles Eusebius assigns to him are familiar from earlier authors, but the ensemble is something new. Moses is for him a hinge figure for reckoning time, a theologian, a philosopher of civilization, a legislator, a liberator, and a type of Christ, perhaps the most important in all the Old Testament. In an apologetic scheme unique to Eusebius, Moses is at once Hebrew, Jew, and Christian. Scholarship in recent years has given a good deal of attention to Eusebius's Moses, most of it focused on specific works by Eusebius or on selected aspects of the topic. My paper will treat it comprehensively. Despite the risk of superficiality, a synoptic presentation may have special value for a volume on "the Christian Moses," since Eusebius gave more diversified attention to Moses than any other early Christian writer.

I will consider Eusebius's Moses under four headings: axial figure, philosopher, legislator, and liberator. The main sources are the following works, in the order in which they seem to have been written: the *Chronicle*; the *Ecclesiastical History* (hereafter *HE*), especially books 1 and 9; the *Preparation for the Gospel* (hereafter *PE*) and its fraternal twin the *Demonstration of the Gospel* (hereafter *DE*); and the *Life of Constantine* (hereafter *VC*). Current scholarship believes the first four to have been written within a fairly tight time frame, between the last few years of the third century (before Constantine's final victory in the West in 312) and the period after 320 (allowing for later editions of the *Chronicle* and the *Ecclesiastical History* to have achieved their final forms in or immediately after 325). The *Life of Constantine*, though presumably the last of Eusebius's works (it was begun after Constantine's death in 337 and left unfinished when Eusebius himself died two years later), presents Constantine as a new Moses whose triumph removes any doubts about God's action in ancient times; but the emphasis is already to be found in book 9 of the *Ecclesiastical History*,[1] which celebrates the battle of the Milvian Bridge as a repetition of the death of Pharaoh and his army.

Moses in Eusebius's Chronicle: The Axial Figure

Eusebius's preoccupation with Moses shows up first in his *Chronicle*, the first edition of which its most recent student, Richard Burgess, dates to late 311.[2] The *Chronicle* is a two-part universal history. The first part, usually called the *Chronography*, consists of a mass of historical materials, such as king lists and excerpts from national histories written in Greek.[3] It begins with the Chaldeans, then covers the Assyrians, the Medes, the Persians, the Lydians, the Hebrews, and the Egyptians; then the Greeks, subdivided into several regions and cities (Athenians, Argives, Sicyonians, Lacedaimonians, Corinthians, Thessalians, and Macedonians), and finally ends with Roman history—fifteen nations and city-states in all.[4] The *Chronography* provid-

1. *HE* 9.9.4–8. The standard edition of Eusebius's works, used here, is *Eusebius Werke*, ed. Ivar Heikel et al., 9 volumes in 11, in the series Griechische Christliche Schriftsteller (hereafter GCS) (Leipzig: J. C. Hinrichs, 1902–1975), with several reprints and revisions (more recently Berlin: Akademie Verlag). The text of *HE*, ed. Eduard Schwartz (Rufinus's Latin continuation ed. Theodore Mommsen), *Eusebius Werke* 2.1–3, GCS 9 (Leipzig: J. C. Hinrichs, 1903, 1908, 1909; new edition with revisions by Friedhelm Winkelmann, Berlin: Akademie Verlag, 1999). Individual volumes, and English translations, will be identified where necessary in the notes below.

2. Richard W. Burgess, *Studies in Eusebian and Post-Eusebian Chronography* (Stuttgart: Steiner, 1999), 21–109, at 66. For his argument on behalf of a 311 date, see Richard W. Burgess, "The Dates and Editions of Eusebius's *Chronici canones* and *Historia ecclesiastica*," *Journal of Theological Studies* 48 (1997): 471–504. The date has conventionally been set earlier, in or around 303.

3. The *Chronography* survives in an Armenian version of the *Chronicle*. See the critical edition, with German translation, by Josef Karst, ed., *Die Chronik des Eusebius aus dem Armenischen übersetzt, mit textkritischem Kommentar*, in *Eusebius Werke* 5, GCS 20 (Leipzig: J. C. Hinrichs, 1911), 1–155.

4. For Eusebius's tally of nations, see Rudolf Helm, ed., *Die Chronik des Hieronymus*, in *Eusebius Werke* 7.1, 2nd ed., GCS 47 (Berlin: Akademie Verlag, 1956), 279.16–19. Besides the works of Richard Burgess cited in note 1, above, I have consulted Timothy D. Barnes, *Constantine and Eusebius* (Cambridge, Mass.: Harvard University Press, 2006), 111–20; Jean Sirinelli, *Les vues historiques d'Eusèbe de*

ed the source material from which Eusebius constructed the second part, the
Chronological Canons, a tabular chronology of world history that enabled a
reader to identify, via its synchronizations, events that were taking place at the
same time in different parts of the Mediterranean and Middle Eastern worlds.
Opinion differs as to the degree to which the *Chronicle* should be called
scholarship or apologetics. Burgess calls it "a testament to Eusebius's genius,"
while recognizing that he intended it to serve important apologetic aims.[5] In
trying to coordinate systematically and comprehensively the chronology of
every nation in the *oikoumenê*, Eusebius, says Jean Sirinelli, was bringing about
"a kind of revolution in the domain of chronography."[6] In effecting this revolution, Eusebius wore two faces: he was both polemicist and historian.[7] Although much of the Greek original is now lost, we have Jerome's Latin translation of the *Chronological Canons* and his continuation of it up to his own time
(378), and an Armenian translation that goes back perhaps to the sixth century and that preserves the structure of the whole work, but with omissions.[8]

   A main purpose of the *Chronicle* was to demonstrate the antiquity of "the
Hebrews," and thereby to help acquit Christians of the accusation that they
were mistaken to follow a "barbarian" philosophy. Appeals to the antiquity
of one's own national grouping were common fare in the ancient world. Jewish apologists engaged in such efforts in the Hellenistic and Roman periods,

---

Césarée durant la période prénicéenne (Dakar: Université de Dakar, 1961), 31–99; William Adler, "The
Chronicle of Eusebius and Its Legacy," in *Eusebius, Christianity, and Judaism*, ed. Harry W. Attridge and
Gohei Hata (Detroit, Mich.: Wayne State University Press, 1992), 467–91; Anthony Grafton and Megan
Williams, *Christianity and the Transformation of the Book: Origen, Eusebius, and the Library of Caesarea*
(Cambridge, Mass.: Belknap Press of Harvard University Press, 2006), 133–77; and Alden A. Mossham-
mer, *The* Chronicle *of Eusebius and Greek Chronographic Tradition* (Lewisburg, Penn.: Bucknell University Press, 1979), 22–83, an essential guide to the complicated history of efforts by modern scholars to re-
construct Eusebius's book.

   5. Burgess, *Studies*, 66–90, at 73. Barnes emphasizes the purely scholarly character of Eusebius's
achievement (*Constantine and Eusebius*, 113). In a recent article, William Adler describes Eusebius's
Chronicle as a work in which his devotion to originality and scholarly integrity is at war with his apologetic interests, with the former ultimately having the upper hand: "What we find instead are multiply-
ing problems and ambiguities. Eusebius relegates whole swaths of the past to the unknown or indeter-
minate." Adler, "Eusebius' Critique of Africanus," in *Julius Africanus and die christliche Weltchronik*, ed.
Martin Wallraff, Texte und Untersuchungen 157 (Berlin: Walter de Gruyter, 2006), 147–57, at 156.

   6. Sirinelli, *Les vues historiques*, 37.

   7. Sirinelli, *Les vues historiques*, 58–59, 98.

   8. See Helm's edition of Jerome's translation and continuation of the *Chronicle* (see note 3, above), and
Karst's edition of the Armenian version (see note 2, above). Helm's edition incorporates material from the
Armenian edition in the notes, and also Greek fragments and citations from later sources (pp. 279–455).

and Eusebius's Christian predecessors had happily hijacked their arguments. The dating of Moses played a central role in the demonstration.[9] (Burgess has pointed out that a keen interest in Moses is a noteworthy parallel between the *Chronicle* and the *Life of Constantine*.)[10] Eusebius says so explicitly in another of his early works, the *Prophetic Selections*: "Prior to the present project, please be aware that [in a previous book] we have established the antiquity of Moses and the prophets after him by composing chronological tables [*Chronikoi ... Kanones*, which is his title for the work; see also in *PE* 10.9.11], and setting alongside them a summary of every type of history of both Greeks and barbarians."[11] In his preface to the *Canons*, he puts special emphasis on the antiquity of Moses, "a Hebrew by race, the first of all the prophets to hand down in writing the oracles and divine prophecies about Christ our savior."[12] The problem of the date of Moses was thus the key to his whole chronological project.[13]

In a section of the *PE* devoted to the antiquity of Moses, Eusebius reproduced (so commentators believe) the substance of what he had already written in the *Canons*:[14] "Now it would be well to examine their chronology, I mean the dates at which Moses and the prophets after him flourished;[15] since this would be one of the most conclusive evidences for the argument before us, that before dealing with the learned men among the several nations we should first decide about their antiquity."[16]

Eusebius knew that the consensus view of his Christian and also his Jewish predecessors placed Moses at the time of Inachos, legendary king of Argos, and therefore as much as 700 years before the Trojan War.[17] This dating he rejected. Declaring that he intended to take "a newer [*kainoteran*] approach" to

9. For discussions of Eusebius's dating of Moses, see especially Sirinelli, *Les vues historiques*, 52–59, 497–515; see also Adler, "The *Chronicle* of Eusebius," 470–72, and Adler, "Eusebius' Critique of Africanus," 150–54.

10. Burgess, *Studies*, 73n10; also Burgess, "Dates and Editions," 488–89.

11. Eusebius, *Eclogae propheticae* 1.1, ed. Thomas Gaisford (Oxford, 1842), 1.27–2.2 (my translation).

12. Eusebius, *Chronicle* Pref. 7.11–13, cited and translated by Burgess, "Dates and Editions," 503–4; see the 3rd edition of Rudolf Helm's 1913 text, *Eusebius Werke* 7.1 (Berlin: Akademie Verlag, 1984).

13. Sirinelli, *Les vues historiques*, 53–54, 59, 512.

14. Cf. *PE* 10.9.

15. "Moses and the prophets after him" is a formulaic phrase for Eusebius; see also the passage just quoted from *Eclogae propheticae* 1.1.

16. *PE* 10.8.18, trans. E. H. Gifford (Oxford: Oxford University Press, 1903); see also *PE* 10.9.1–11. Sirinelli comments that it is no accident that the only time the *Chronicle* is mentioned by name in the *PE* is in connection with its discussion of the date of Moses (*Les vues historiques*, 54).

17. The preface to the *Canons* names Clement, Julius Africanus, and Tatian, along with the Jewish

the antiquity of Moses, Eusebius made his starting point the Incarnation. Using data marshaled in the *Chronological Canons*, he counted backward from the time of Augustus, because of "the acknowledged agreement in time between the Roman emperor Augustus and the birth of our Savior."[18] According to Eusebius's calculations in the *Canons*, Moses actually lived 350 years before the capture of Troy.[19] That made Moses the contemporary of Cecrops, the mythical king of Athens, whom the Greeks credited with being the first to call on Zeus as a god ("he not having been previously so named," comments Eusebius drily), and also the first to found an altar at Athens and set up an image of Athena.[20] Eusebius recognized that this reduced roughly by half the years by which Moses antedated the fall of Troy. But Moses still came before virtually all of the Greeks' recorded history, and long before their earliest writers, Homer and Hesiod. Eusebius could also afford to be at ease with this revised dating because Porphyry, his *bête noire*, had placed Moses much further back—at least 800 years before Troy fell—an estimate that freed Eusebius from any fear of being out-flanked by his formidable pagan opponent and allowed him to comment that Porphyry's erroneous dating would bizarrely make Moses earlier than Abraham himself.[21]

Moses in the Preparation for the Gospel: The Philosopher

Eusebius wants to put Moses as far back as possible in time relative to Greek history partly in order to credit Moses with civilizational arts that the Greeks simply copied. That is a major theme in the *Preparation for the Gos-*

---

writers Josephus and Justus (*Chronicle* 7.11–17, ed. Helm, 279.3–8). Origen too adopted the dating of Moses to the reign of Inachos (*Against Celsus*, 4.11).

18. Eusebius draws special attention to the synchronization provided by the rededication of the rebuilt temple in the second year of the reign of the Persian king Darius, which was also the first year of the sixty-fifth Olympiad (*PE* 10.9.2–5; *Chronicle* 10.7–18, ed. Helm, 280.5–17). Commentators agree that this was a crucial reference point in Eusebius's calculations, en route to fixing the antiquity of Moses (Mosshammer: "his Archimedean *dos moi pou stô*," Chronicle *of Eusebius*, 36; cf. Sirinelli, *Les vues historiques*, 77–80).

19. *Chronicle* 10.2–4, ed. Helm, 279.34–280.2. The figure of 350 comes from the preface. In the *Canons* itself, Eusebius says the time between Cecrops and the capture of Troy was 375 years (*Chronicle* 61b.11–13, ed. Helm, 310.45–46), when Moses was thirty-five years old.

20. *PE* 10.9.8, 19.

21. See Sirinelli's discussion, *Les vues historiques*, 512–15.

pel, Eusebius's great apologetic work directed against the classical tradition, written sometime between about 314 and 318, and followed immediately by an equally long work against Judaism, the *Demonstration of the Gospel*. Eusebius argues that the Greeks first got their religious practices from older traditions to the east, and then the other civilizational arts,[22] above all philosophy, in all of its branches: "all the celebrated learning and philosophy of the Greeks, both their elementary studies and their grand systems of logical science have been collected by them from barbarians, so that none of them may any longer lay blame upon us, because we have preferred the religion and philosophy of the barbarians to their grand doctrines."[23] The "all-wise" (*pansophos*) Moses anticipated Plato's tripartite division of philosophy into ethics, dialectics, and natural philosophy, though he did so in the form of a historical narrative:

The all-wise Moses was the first human being who, having transmitted in writing the lives of the Hebrew friends of God who had preceded him, used a historical narrative to teach a way of life both political and practical. From that starting point he produced a universal teaching which posited God as the cause of the universe, and which described the creation of the cosmos and of the human race. Then in his account, he proceeded from the universal to the particular, using the memory of the men of old to urge his disciples toward zeal for their virtue and piety.[24]

Eusebius devotes many pages to arguing that the Platonic tradition in particular was guilty of intellectual property theft from Moses's teachings on God and the creation of the world. Books 11, 12, and half of 13 are filled with long quotations from Plato himself and from the Platonic tradition which show, through the placement in time and the affinity of ideas, that influence moved from east to west, from Moses to Plato. It's in book 11 that Eusebius quotes the famous assertion attributed to the Middle Platonist philosopher Numenius, "For what is Plato but Moses speaking Attic Greek?"[25] Also in book 11, Euse-

---

22. His survey includes even highly practical arts; see the extract from Clement of Alexandria at *PE* 10.6.1–14. Citations of the Greek text of *PE* are from Édouard des Places, Guy Schroeder, and Geneviève Favrelle, eds., *Eusèbe de Césarée, La préparation évangelique*, Sources Chrétiennes 215, 292, 369 (Paris: Éditions du Cerf, 1975–1991), which represents some advances on Karl Mras's GCS volumes—both 1954–1956 and 1982–1983, *Eusebius Werke* 8.1 and 2.

23. *PE* 10.3.26 (trans. Gifford).

24. Ibid. 11.4.4–5. A fuller account of Moses's teaching, though without direct reference to Plato, is found earlier, in *PE* 7.8–12, where the "hierophant" Moses (*PE* 7.10.14) is portrayed as using a "more dogmatic and more didactic" (*PE* 7.11.1) exposition, under the inspiration of the Holy Spirit, to teach theology, rather than syllogisms and arguments.

25. *PE* 11.10.14.

bius tries to show that the "I am who am" (*egô eimi ho ôn* in the LXX) of Exodus 3:14 is the source of Plato's doctrine of true being: citing Exodus 3:14, he claims that not just the idea but the very expression and formula of "the Hebrews" are evident in Plato's classic statement in the *Timaeus* (27d), "What is that which always is and has no becoming? And what on the other hand is always becoming but never truly is?"[26] In general, Eusebius wants to credit Moses for everything that was right and true in Plato's teaching about the divine, about humanity, and about the universe—everything, that is, but the errors: "Everything that he [Plato] has said rightly is in agreement with what was taught by Moses, but whatever he believed that disagreed with Moses and the prophets lacked a rational foundation."[27]

Moses Platonicus (or *Plato Mosaicus*) is probably the feature of Eusebius's appropriation of Moses that is best known and the most studied, but also, I suspect, the one in which he is the least original and the most dependent on the work of others. (Though I would like to know if Eusebius's etymological demonstration of the Semitic origin of the Greek alphabet, at *PE* 10.5 and 11.6.33–35, is original with him; to make his argument work, he substitutes "Syrian" for "Phoenician"—from the story of Cadmus—and then equates "Syrian" with "Hebrew".) The sections of the *Preparation* that deal most directly with my topic actually bear not on the Greeks but on the Jews themselves. In books 7 and 8, Eusebius speaks at length about the difference, as he sees it, between "Hebrews" and "Jews." This, as has long been recognized, is a fundamental apologetic theme of his, and one that is very much his own. With that, however, I must turn to my next topic, Moses as lawgiver.

Moses in the *Demonstration of the Gospel*: The Lawgiver

The *Demonstration of the Gospel* was composed approximately between 318 and 323 in twenty books, of which only ten and a fraction survive.[28] It

26. *PE* 11.9.4.

27. *PE* 11.28.19 (trans. Gifford). Eusebius does not take up Platonic teaching which he regards as erroneous until *PE* 13.14, continuing to the end of book 13.

28. On the *Demonstration*, see Sébastien Morlet, *La "Démonstration évangélique" d'Eusèbe de Césarée: étude sur l'apologétique chrétienne à l'époque de Constantin* (Paris: Institut d'Études Augustiniennes, 2009). Citations of the Greek text of *DE* are from Ivar Heikel, ed., *Die Demonstratio evangelica*, in

stands in the long tradition of Christian biblical proof-texting against the Jews, of which tradition it is the fullest example. It consists of Old Testament texts arranged thematically, with interpretive glosses of varying length. Though directed mainly at the Jews,[29] the *Demonstration* was intended to prove to pagan critics as well that Christianity was not apostate Judaism but the republication of the pure ethical monotheism of the pre-Mosaic friends of God.[30] Eusebius had already announced this, his most distinctive apologetic theme, in the introduction to the *Ecclesiastical History*,[31] and had developed it further, in his distinction between "Hebrews" and "Jews," in the middle of the *Preparation of the Gospel* (books 7 and 8). But it appears front and center in book 1 of the *Demonstration*, and, since Moses is the pivotal person in the transition from Hebrews to Jews, this book is central to Eusebius's appropriation of Moses.

In *DE* 3.2 Eusebius presents an elaborate comparison of Moses and Jesus. It begins with a quotation of Moses's prophecy in Deuteronomy 18:18 that a prophet like himself would arise. How much like himself, Eusebius's typology shows in great detail (see table 8-1).

The comparisons—seventeen in all—tend to minimize the differences between Moses and Jesus, which basically come down to two: first, the message of Jesus is to all nations, whereas Moses's teaching is only for the Jews (and not even for all of them, since the Mosaic law could be completely fulfilled only by those in proximity to Jerusalem);[32] and second, Jesus's words and deeds are in some way or other accomplished with greater power (*kreittoni ... dynamei*)[33] or for a greater end. But the thrust of the typology is really toward a strict parallelism of past and present. There is far more similarity between Moses and Jesus than there is difference. The concern here is mostly with continuity.[34] It would be interesting to know how much Eusebius's approach owes to a lost

---

Eusebius Werke 6, GCS 23 (Leipzig: J. C. Hinrichs, 1913). Translation (slightly adapted throughout this paper) by W. J. Ferrar, *The Proof of the Gospel, Being the* Demonstratio Evangelica *of Eusebius of Cæsarea*, 2 vols. (London: S.P.C.K., 1920).

29. *DE* 1.1.16.

30. *DE* 1.2 and 1.7.18–19.

31. *HE* 1.4.

32. *DE* 3.2.1.

33. *DE* 3.2.11 (ed. Heikel, 98.8).

34. Although the third book of the *DE* is devoted especially to the career of the Word in his earthly sojourn, so that should be taken into account as well.

Moses was first to turn the Jews away from idolatry, to teach them monotheism, and as lawgiver to establish their way of life and polity for them alone.	Jesus did the same as teacher, though more powerfully, and as lawgiver established a "new" way of life and polity for all the nations.
Moses further taught about the origin of the universe and the immortality of the soul to the people of the Jews. "He is therefore rightly called the first and only legislator of piety for the Jews, but Jesus [the same] for all the nations."	Jesus was the first to do so in a more fittingly divine way for the rest of the nations.
Again (*palin*), Moses performed miracles as part of his proclamation.	So too in the same way did Christ.
Again, Moses brought the Jewish people from slavery in Egypt to freedom.	Jesus the Christ brought the whole human race from slavery to Egyptian idolatry into freedom.
Again, Moses proclaimed a holy land and a godly and most blessed way of life to those who kept the law.	Jesus the Christ said blessed are the meek, for they will inherit a much better land and a truly godly way of life, not in Judaea, but in a kingdom in heaven.
Moses fasted forty days and nights.	In the same way did the Christ fast for forty days when he was led by the devil into the desert.
Again, Moses provided food for the people in the desert.	In the same way so did our Lord and savior.
Again, Moses led the people in their path through the sea.	In the same way but more divinely Jesus the Christ of God walked on water and made Peter go to him.
Again, Moses subdued the sea with a powerful south wind.	In the same way but more powerfully did our savior calm the wind and the sea.
Again, when Moses came down from the mountain, his face shone with glory.	In the same way but more excellently did our savior lead his disciples up a mountain and he was transformed, his face shining like the sun.
Again, Moses cleansed a leper.	In the same way but with greater power, the Christ of God cleansed a man of his leprosy.
Again, Moses said the law was written by the finger of God on tablets of stone.	In the same way Jesus the Christ of God said, "If by the finger of God I cast out demons…"
In addition, Moses renamed Nave as Jesus (LXX).	In the same way the savior renamed Simon as Peter.
Again, Moses appointed seventy men from the elders of Israel to be leaders of the people.	In the same way the savior appointed seventy disciples and sent them off two by two.
Again, Moses sent twelve men to look over the land.	In the same way our savior sent out twelve apostles to overlook all the nations.
Again, Moses gave as the law not to kill, commit adultery, steal, or bear false witness.	Our savior extended the law, not only against killing but even against being angry (similarly for adultery and lust), and not only forbade stealing but ordered giving of property to the needy, and forbade swearing at all.
They say that no one knew the death of Moses or the place of his burial.	Nor did anyone witness our savior's change into his divinity after his being restored to life.

work by the third century Christian writer Ammonius, *On the Harmony* (*Peri symphônias*) *of Moses and Jesus*, which must have worked along similar lines.[35] Eusebius mentions Ammonius's book in the *Ecclesiastical History*,[36] in connection with his response to Porphyry's critique of Origen's allegorical reading of the Hebrew scriptures. Here too the intention is to see Moses not as an allegorical cipher but as a predecessor whose work Jesus continues rather than erases.

The continuity theme had been announced already in book 1:

And now having lived in all ways according to the Law of Moses, he made use of his apostles as ministers of the new legislation, on the one hand teaching them that they must not consider the Law of Moses either foreign or hostile to their own religion, on the other hand as being the author and introducer of a legislation new and salutary for all men, so that he did not in any way break Moses' enactments, but rather crowned them, and was their fulfillment, and then passed on to the institution of the Gospel law. Hear him as he says, "I have not come to destroy the law but to fulfill it" (Matt 5:17). For if he had been a transgressor of the Law of Moses, he would rightly have been considered to have canceled it and given a contrary law: and if he had been wicked and a law-breaker, he could not have been believed to be the Christ. And if he had canceled Moses' Law, he could never have been considered to be the one foretold by Moses and the prophets. For he would have had to embark on a new law, in order to escape the penalty of breaking the old.[37]

The second text we will consider, *DE* 1.8, comes immediately after this passage from book 1, but at first sight it subverts the continuity theme.[38] Here too we have a typological comparison of Jesus and Moses, in which Moses is once again a lawgiver, as is Jesus. But this time we seem to be dealing with contrast rather than with continuity. The contrast has to do both with the form in which the law is given (written vs. oral), and with the substance of the law itself, since Jesus's law consists of "perfect commandments." But Eusebius immediately complicates the picture by telling us that Jesus's followers, with his consent, "accommodated" the perfect commandments to the people to whom

35. It is wrongly attributed to Origen in the *VC*. See *Eusebius, Life of Constantine*, introduction, translation, and commentary by Averil Cameron and Stuart G. Hall (Oxford: Clarendon Press, 1999), 193.

36. *HE* 6.19.10.

37. *DE* 1.7.1–2.

38. My comments here are adapted from my article "Hebrews, Jews, and Christians: Eusebius of Caesarea on the Biblical Basis of the Two States of the Christian Life," in *In Dominico Eloquio—In Lordly Eloquence: Essays on Patristic Exegesis in Honor of Robert Louis Wilken*, ed. Paul Blowers et al. (Grand Rapids, Mich.: Eerdmans, 2002), 172–84.

they delivered them. The perfect commandments of the perfect teacher were suitable, Eusebius says, only for those who had risen above nature. For those—and they were in the majority—who had not reached that level but were stuck in the muck of the passions and in need of healing, to them the followers of Jesus handed down a mitigated form of the commandments, which is all they were capable of accepting. (Eusebius further complicates, or subverts, his typology by saying that these accommodated commandments themselves were both in written and in unwritten form, but that is an aspect I cannot pursue here.)

The distinction between a perfect morality for an ascetical elite and an accommodated morality for the masses takes up the rest of the comparison. The elite disavow marriage, offspring, property, and money, in order to devote themselves to contemplation and to spiritual intercession for the rest of humanity. Their way of life is above nature (*hyperphysê*) and beyond ordinary human society (*politeias*). As Eusebius portrays them, they are a quasi-monastic corporation who nevertheless should not be identified strictly with the clergy.[39] Those unable to attain to this level have a separate way of life that is "subordinate and more human" (*hypobebêkôs anthrôpinôteros*),[40] in that they are permitted to marry, bear children, serve in government and in the military (for just wars), and engage in farming, trade, and public affairs.

There are thus, Eusebius says frankly, two distinct ways of life in Christianity, one superior and the other inferior though permitted. Years ago, Henri-Irenée Marrou singled out this text as the first instance in Christian literature of a permanent double standard in the Christian community. It cannot be a coincidence that Eusebius composed these words not long after Constantine's victory at the Milvian Bridge, and even closer to the Council of Arles, convened at Constantine's order in August 314, the third canon of which appears to excommunicate Christian soldiers who resign from their army commissions during times of peace.

But what about Moses, and how can Eusebius introduce such a strongly-framed contrast typology immediately after telling readers that Jesus' teaching is in fundamental continuity with Moses's? To answer that question, we need

---

39. That the ascetical elite are not, in Eusebius's mind, identical with the clergy is clear from the discussion that follows this passage, in *DE* 1.9–10.

40. *DE* 1.8.3 (ed. Heikel, 39.28).

to look at the pivotal role Moses plays in Eusebius's distinction between "Hebrews" and "Jews." Though "a Hebrew of the Hebrews,"[41] Moses is the one who first introduces the legal system—Eusebius likes to call it a *politeuma* (constitution)—with its priesthood, sacrificial cult, ritual and dietary laws, and liturgies, as a means to wean the people from the vicious habits they had contracted during their sojourn in Egypt. It was a "lower and less perfect way of life to children of Abraham, who were too weak to follow in the footsteps of their forefathers."[42] The law was to lead them back to God, a "first step [*bathmos*] of holiness at the threshold and entrance to the temple of the more perfect."[43] Here is how Eusebius describes Moses's work in effecting this transition:

> You can define the difference between "Hebrews" and "Jews" this way: the latter take their name from Judah, the tribe from which the Jewish monarchy eventually arose, whereas the former are named after Eber [cf. Gn 10:21, 24–25], who was an ancestor of Abraham. As for their type of religion, Moses was the first to establish a legislation for the Jews: he passed down a day for the Sabbath, and the greatest possible observance of it, as a reminder of the study of the scriptures; the distinction between animals that could be eaten and those that could not; the calendar of religious feasts; certain other purifications of the body; and long periods to be understood more spiritually according to their symbolic meaning. The Hebrews were prior to Moses in time, and were therefore not bound by the entire Mosaic legislation. They practiced a free and unconstrained religion, and were marked by a life according to nature. Their extraordinary freedom from passion meant they had no need of laws to rule them, but possessed a true knowledge of doctrines about God.[44]

What is more, Moses built a planned obsolescence into this system, for a time when it was no longer needed. Knowing (as a prophet) that Hadrian would eventually banish the Jews from Jerusalem, he framed the law so that it couldn't be practiced in its fullness apart from proximity to Jerusalem.[45]

The historical dialectic of Hebrew and Jew served Eusebius not just as a way to devalue Judaism while permitting Christianity an end-run around it. He insists that the Mosaic law had a real if provisional validity, and that is why Jesus had to obey it. More interesting, the two-stage model *itself* is incorporated into Christianity. Just as Moses fulfilled God's plan by creating a religion

41. *PE* 7.7.1.
42. *DE* 1.6.31.
43. *DE* 1.6.32.
44. *PE* 7.6.2–4, my translation.
45. *DE* 1.6.37–39.

suitable for those who were in need of therapy, so Jesus and his followers have imitated his work by implementing a Christian version of a dual standard. In Eusebius's view, the majority of mediocre Christians practice a "secondary stage of piety" (*deuteros eusebeias ... bathmos*),[46] just like the one Moses legislated for the Jews (*deuteron ... eusebeias ... bathmon*).[47] The *Demonstration of the Gospel* 1.8 thus expresses a complex typology that sublates two distinct stages of salvation history into a unity, in that the earlier system lives on, transformed, in the later. This is still supersessionism, to be sure, but put to novel uses that have no precedent in earlier Christian literature, and that preserve or mimic in a comprehensive way basic elements from Christianity's Jewish origins.

A further reflection of how badly Eusebius wanted to see the Christian community of his day anticipated by Moses is found in the use that he makes of excerpts from Josephus and especially from Philo in book 8 of the *Preparation for the Gospel*. Having dealt with the pre-Mosaic "Hebrews" in book 7, in book 8 Eusebius says he intends to discuss the polity (*politeian*)[48] that came into being in the time of Moses. Eusebius quotes Josephus's account of the Mosaic polity: "Some peoples have entrusted the supreme political power to monarchies, others to oligarchies, yet others to the masses. Our lawgiver, however, was attracted by none of these forms of polity, but gave to his constitution [*politeuma*] the form of what—if a forced expression be permitted—may be termed a *theocracy*, placing all sovereignty and authority in the hands of God. To him he persuaded all to look, as the author of all blessings."[49] Josephus justifies his choice of words on the grounds that Moses made religion preeminent in his polity: "For he did not make religion part of virtue, but other things parts of religion".[50] And to ensure that the laws and the constitution could never be changed, Moses put the administration of chief affairs in the hands of the priests as a collective, and of government over the priests in common in the hands of the High Priest.[51] Although I can't prove it, I wonder

46. *DE* 1.8.4.
47. *PE* 8.1.1.
48. *PE* 8.1.1. Also referred to in *PE* 8.6.10 as "the *politeia* established for the nation of the Jews according to the laws of Moses." The chapter heading for book 8 reads: "On the Godly Polity [*politeuma*] according to Moses."
49. From *Against Apion* 2.165–66 (trans. Thackeray), as quoted in *PE* 8.8.3.
50. Josephus's work is quoted in *PE* 8.8.7.
51. The quotation continues in *PE* 8.8.19.

whether Eusebius's quotation of this long excerpt about Moses and his "theocracy" is an endorsement of priestly governance more generally.

The citations from Philo are quite different. After excerpts from Aristeas and Aristobulus on the allegorical meaning of the Mosaic laws, Eusebius reminds his readers about the division of the Jewish people into two categories:

> It would be next in order to indicate the following point, that the whole Jewish nation is divided into two sections. And while the lawgiver meant to lead the masses on gently by the precepts of the laws as enjoined according to the literal sense, the other class, consisting of those who had acquired a habit of virtue, he meant to exempt from this sense, and required them to give attention to a philosophy of a diviner kind that exceeded the grasp of the many, and to contemplation of the things signified in the meaning of the laws.[52]

Two excerpts follow in the *Preparation for the Gospel*, both dealing with the Essenes. The first comes from a partially extant work of Philo's called the *Apology for the Jews*.[53] It is immediately followed by another from Philo's *That Every Good Man is Free*.[54] Eusebius naturally admired the communal and contemplative way of life that Philo attributes to the Essenes: they devote themselves to the service of God but not by animal sacrifices; they own property in common and donate the profits of their labor to the common fund; they are industrious and self-supporting; they renounce violence and the instruments of war; they treat each other as equals and do not own slaves; and they repudiate marriage and embrace continence. Their way of life recalls the Christian *ascetical* elite that embrace the perfect commandments of Christ.

But note where Eusebius has put Philo's account of them: in the section of the *Preparation* that deals with the Jews, not the Hebrews. And so they, too, are part of the Mosaic *politeia*, not the pre-Mosaic friends of God. No doubt Eusebius admires them in particular because, unlike the pre-Mosaic Hebrews, who were married, produced offspring in abundance (or tried to), and accumulated wealth, the Essenes practice a renunciatory way of life. So the "Jew-

---

52. *PE* 8.10.18 (trans. Gifford).

53. *PE* 8.11. Uncertainty attaches to the provenance of this fragment and its relation to the earlier fragment of Philo's *Hypothetica* quoted in *PE* 8.6–7, which is marked by a rather diffident interpretation of Moses that emphasizes the severity of his laws; see the puzzlement of Philo's editor, F. H. Colson, in *Philo*, 10 vols. plus two supplements, Loeb Classical Library (Cambridge, Mass.: Harvard University Press, 1967), 9:408–9.

54. *PE* 8.12.

ish" stage established by Moses is even closer to the Christian *politeia*, in that it too has room for a higher and a lower way.

Moses and Constantine: The Liberator

Eusebius's use of Moses as a model for Constantine has received much attention in recent years.[55] His first connection of Moses with Constantine is found in the account of the battle of the Milvian Bridge in the *Ecclesiastical History*, in which the drowning of Maxentius's soldiers in the Tiber is portrayed as another Exodus, replete with quotations from Exodus 15.[56] Those to whom God had granted victory could at least in deeds if not in actual words sing a victory song like those of old who were led by Moses, "the great servant [*therapôn*] of God":[57] "they sank like lead ... horse and rider he has thrown into the sea" (Ex 15:10–11). It happened, says Eusebius, "just as the divine oracles had predicted,"[58] thereby creating an Exodus political typology that was going to have a long future in Christianity (and outside it as well).[59]

---

55. Moses and Exodus as models receive considerable attention in the introduction and notes to *Eusebius, Life of Constantine*, Cameron and Hall, 34–39, 185–86, 192–99, 202–11, 215–16, 223, 246, and 265. See also Anna Wilson, "Biographical Models: the Constantinian Period and Beyond," in *Constantine: History, Historiography, and Legend*, ed. Samuel N. C. Lieu and Dominic Montserrat (London: Routledge, 1998), 107–35 (see esp. 112–21 on Moses as model). Claudia Rapp, "Imperial Ideology in the Making: Eusebius of Caesarea on Constantine as 'Bishop,'" *Journal of Theological Studies* 49 (1998): 685–95, also notes the importance of the Moses comparison in understanding what Eusebius was up to in his description of Constantine as a kind of universal bishop. See also Marilena Amerise, "Costantino il 'Nuovo Mosè,'" *Salesianum* 67, no. 4 (2005): 671–700; Michael Stuart Williams, *Authorized Lives in Early Christian Biography: Between Eusebius and Augustine* (Cambridge: Cambridge University Press, 2008), the first chapter of which deals with Moses in the *Life of Constantine* (see review of Charles Stang in *Journal of Early Christian Studies* 19 [2011]: 475–76); Sabrina Inowlocki, "Eusebius's Appropriation of Moses in an Apologetic Context," in *Moses in Biblical and Extra-biblical Traditions*, ed. Axel Graupner and Michael Wolter, *Zeitschrift für die alttestamentliche Wissenschaft* Supplements 372 (Berlin: de Gruyter, 2007), 241–55; and Finn Damgaard, "Revisiting Eusebius' Use of the Figure of Moses in the *Vita Constantini*," in *Eusebius of Caesarea: Tradition and Innovations*, ed. Aaron P. Johnson and Jeremy Schott (Cambridge, Mass.: Harvard University Press/Center for Hellenic Studies Press, 2013), 115–32.

56. *HE* 9.9.2–9.

57. *HE* 9.9.7–8.

58. *HE* 9.9.7.

59. Eusebius says that many considered the Exodus event to have been a myth—"*phêmê ... palaia, mythou schêmati tois pollois paradedomenê*" (*VC* 1.12.2, ed. Friedhelm Winkelmann, *Eusebius Werke* 1 [21.14–15], GCS 9, 2nd ed. [Berlin: Akademie Verlag, 1991])—the actuality of which Constantine's victory had now confirmed, since it was an event that all could see with their own eyes. This is an inversion of the normal rhetorical thrust of typology, in which the past precedent confirms and validates the present. In this case, the verification and legitimation seem to operate reciprocally.

Eusebius was so satisfied with the Exodus parallel that he excerpted it wholesale a quarter of a century later when he composed the *Life of Constantine*, begun (though there is debate about the exact date) after the emperor's death in May 337 and apparently left incomplete at the time of Eusebius's own death two years later.[60] The new book's highly rhetorical character was well suited to squeezing the most out of the Moses comparison. The *Life* doesn't conform completely either to the traditional genre of a funerary panegyric or to that of a biography, and looks more like a hybrid of both.[61] The *synkrisis* or "comparison" that was a standard feature of encomia could also lend itself to the portrayal of character in a biography, and that seems to be the case in the *Life of Constantine*, in which "the running *synkrisis* with Moses is fundamental to [its] organization."[62]

The definition of its genre isn't the only controverted feature of the *Life*. There is intense debate about its purposes, its apologetic *Tendenz* in tension with its historical reliability, and even the validity of its political theology. At least we're no longer debating whether the *Life* is really *by* Eusebius.[63] The parts of the *Life* that are most relevant to the discussion of Moses are book 1, especially *VC* 1.12, 19–21, 27–32, and 37–38, and the first part of book 2, dealing with Constantine's war with Licinius. The *Life* begins by comparing Constantine very favorably to victorious kings of the past, such as Cyrus and Alexander.[64] But then Eusebius abruptly drops the secular comparisons and explains that he is going to omit great deeds of victory in war and peacetime governance

60. *VC* 1.37–38 = *HE* 9.9.2–8. See the apparatus in Friedhelm Winkelmann, ed., *Über das Leben des Kaisers Konstantin*, in *Eusebius Werke* 1.1, 2nd rev. ed., GCS (Berlin: Akademie Verlag, 1991), 34–35. The new version makes the identification with Moses even more explicit, though, when Eusebius writes that after his victory, Constantine gave thanks to God, "the timely giver of his victory, in the same way as that great servant [*therapôn*]" (*VC* 39.1).

61. On the question of genre, see the summary in Cameron and Hall, *Eusebius, Life of Constantine*, 27–34. The editors finally opt for a hybrid assessment that recognizes elements alike of imperial panegyric (the *basilikos logos*), narrative history or biography, and even incipient hagiography. A similar synoptic approach ("a hybrid ... and deliberately conceived as such from the start") is taken by Wilson, "Biographical Models," 107–19, esp. 113–16. A similar conclusion is reached by Friedhelm Winkelmann, ed., *Leben des Kaisers Konstantin*, xlix–lvii.

62. Wilson, "Biographical Models," 116. Wilson comments on how the examination of *ethos* in a favorable biography and the presentation of an individual as an ideal character in panegyric lead easily to a convergence of the genres—see her citations to Menander (126n1).

63. Cameron and Hall, *Eusebius, Life of Constantine*, 49; Winkelmann, *Leben des Kaisers Konstantin*, lvi–lviii.

64. *VC* 1.7–9.

and to "write down only what pertains to a life dear to God."[65] Then he gives us a narrative of Constantine's early years as a virtual hostage in the court of Diocletian and his escape to join his father in Britain.[66] That account begins with a reference to the story of Moses's upbringing in the house of Pharaoh. Eusebius tells how God, "who is gracious to the oppressed," caused Moses, "who would liberate the Hebrews from enslavement to their enemies," to be raised in the palace and family of the tyrant who ruled them. Just so with Constantine, who, "like that very servant [*therapôn*] of God," lived uncorrupted at the hearth of the tyrants who had made war with God and oppressed his church.[67]

Eusebius makes use of Exodus in a host of ways, though the direct parallels cease in book 2 with the defeat of Constantine's former imperial ally Licinius, "whose heart God hardened," Eusebius says, explaining how Licinius turned from friend into enemy. In case readers failed to see that Licinius, like Maxentius before him, had also become Pharaoh, Eusebius quotes Exodus 9:12 to make the point.[68] Eusebius borrows from Exodus again when his narrative of Constantine's career parallels the three periods of forty years each into which Exodus divided the career of Moses, a structural parallel first identified by Marguerite Harl: first, Moses's birth and upbringing in the Egyptian court; second, his leadership of the people out of Egypt; and third, his giving of the law, building of the tabernacle, and overthrowing of idolatry.[69] Among many other such details from Exodus, one of the best is Eusebius's account of the origin, construction, and use of the *labarum*, Constantine's battle standard. The inspiration for the *labarum* is alleged to come from the dream Constantine had before the battle with Maxentius;[70] the dream and the vision of the cross in the sun were Constantine's equivalent of the heavenly sign given to Moses in the burning bush.[71] The design and construction of the *labarum* are

---

65. *VC* 1.11.1.

66. In his new book, Barnes firmly rejects this feature of Eusebius's narrative as a propaganda invention of Constantine himself to distance himself from the court of the persecutors. See Timothy Barnes, *Constantine: Dynasty, Religion and Power in the Later Roman Empire* (Chichester, U.K.: Wiley-Blackwell, 2011), 2–4, 54–56.

67. *VC* 1.12.1–2.

68. *VC* 2.11.2 (ed. Winkelmann, 53.10–11).

69. Cameron and Hall, *Eusebius, Life of Constantine*, 193, and Wilson, "Biographical Models," 124, citing M. Harl, "Les trois quarantaines de Moïse," *Revue des études grecques* 80 (1967): 407–12.

70. *VC* 1.31.

71. List of references taken with acknowledgement from Cameron and Hall, *Eusebius, Life of Constantine*, 38–39, and from Wilson, "Biographical Models," passim.

described in such a way as to evoke the making of the Ark of the Covenant (Ex 25–28),[72] which accompanies the Israelites on their travels. On the march, its position at the head of the army recalls the role of the pillar of cloud and the column of flame in the escape of the people from Egypt.[73] Its miraculous powers recall the staff of Moses (cf. Ex 4:1–5 and 14:16).[74] Eusebius illustrates those powers with stories that he claims Constantine had told him personally. A bodyguard of fifty soldiers, the emperor said, had been organized to carry and protect the *labarum*, and the *labarum* in turn protected them; in one episode, a soldier who panicked in battle and dropped the standard was killed immediately by an enemy javelin; the man who picked it up became a magnet for more spears, which all stuck harmlessly in the pole of the *labarum*.[75] Thus it is evident that Moses and the Exodus story have left their mark on *The Life of Constantine*; and Constantine, as he is depicted in *VC* and *HE*, is drawn in the shape of the liberator of the Hebrew people.

Conclusion

To summarize the results of our survey: we've looked at four different roles that Eusebius assigns to Moses, who for him is a "Hebrew of the Hebrews" and therefore also a Christian, in fact if not in name, to quote a formula that Eusebius had adopted already in book 1 of the *Ecclesiastical History*.[76] But Moses is also the founder (constitutional language seems to fit here) of the *politeia* of Judaism, which in turn is the foundation on which Christianity is built, as a recapitulation of the whole prior history of God's dealings with the human race. Moses is a hinge on which that history turns, the philosopher of monotheism and of the creation of the world, a founder of civilization, the lawgiver of the Jewish *politeia*, the prophet and foreshadower of the Christian polity, and, finally, the liberator and freedom fighter on behalf of the oppressed.

As noted in the beginning of my paper, some of these roles are not original to Eusebius and were more or less natural responses to the apologetic sit-

---

72. *VC* 1.29–31.
73. This detail is emphasized by Wilson, "Biographical Models," 117.
74. *VC* 2.6–9.2.
75. *VC* 2.8.2–9.3.
76. *HE* 1.4.6–7.

uation in which educated Christians found themselves. Other roles, however, if not unique to him, are at least highly characteristic and grow out of the new situation created by the emergence of a victorious emperor with a keen interest in the Christian religion. Two features of the new situation underlie his casting of roles for Moses especially in the *Demonstration of the Gospel* and the *Life of Constantine*. One is the changing shape of the Christian community, now faced with new opportunities for growth and expansion, opportunities that would put unprecedented stress on Christianity's high expectations of human moral performance. The churches, of course, had for a long time been coping with less than total commitment on the part of the faithful. The problem was now going to take on another dimension altogether. Eusebius recognized the unavoidability of some type of permanent double standard, and his construal of Moses as the pivot between the "Hebrews" and the "Jews" offered an exegetical and apologetic rationale for that.

The other feature was the fact of a Christian emperor and the incorporation into the Christian community of the sword, the legitimate use of which had long been accepted in principle as a corollary of Romans 13, but not hitherto as exercised by Christians themselves. The Exodus story was an apt typological vehicle for interpreting what came to pass as a result of the events of October 312. I've suggested in the past, only half facetiously, that Eusebius was the first liberation theologian. At that juncture in Christianity's history, the figure of Moses offered obvious attractions. What would be interesting to know is whether later royal and imperial theologians found Moses equally useful. I should think that actual Israelite kings were more appropriate—Christian Davids and Christian Solomons, but not Christian Moseses. For Eusebius, though, Moses spoke with special power and fittingness to the need for a biblical legitimation both of the changes in the Christian community, and of the new fact of a Christian emperor.[77] As a final thought, I would like to ask how viable Eusebius's portrayals of Moses were likely to be in the future. They were functional for a fairly brief window in time, when the playing field between Christians and Jews was still somewhat level. As relative arrivistes, Christians were still in need of Mosaic legitimation. But the situation

---

77. For an interesting comparison, consider how Philo construed Moses's kingly attributes in his adaptation of the Hellenistic ideal of the king as "living law": see John W. Martens, *One God, One Law: Philo of Alexandria on the Mosaic and Greco-Roman Law* (Leiden: Brill, 2003), 90–95.

was changing, and changing fast—in discussion afterwards, Daniel Boyarin suggested perhaps fifty years, which seems about right, for that would take us into the reign of Theodosius I. After that point, Christians would feel freer to distance themselves from their origin, whether "Hebrew" or "Jewish," and the existence of a double moral standard would seem so self-evidently right that Eusebius's clever defense would become redundant, if not a little uncomfortable, as a reminder of a time when things were otherwise and Christianity did not have the unquestioned upper hand.

Ellen Muehlberger

9. THE ASCETIC LEADER
IN GREGORY OF NYSSA'S
LIFE OF MOSES

Among the biblical exempla that early Christians utilized for pedagogical and moral lessons, none save Abraham received quite as much attention as did Moses. His career, as recounted in Exodus, Leviticus, and Numbers, reflected a combination of courage, inventiveness, and perseverance that ancient authors often sought to evoke in their audiences. The virtues of that life were first retold by Philo of Alexandria, whose *Life of Moses* converted the narrative of Moses's journey out of Egypt and through the wilderness into a work of classical biography.[1] As was the case with many of Philo's works, his *Life of Moses* was read and preserved by later Christian communities; its influence is visible in the diverse ways that Christian writers have created later depictions of Moses. The works in this volume speak to that diversity, but they are just a beginning. For example, Gregory of Nyssa, the Cappadocian writer and bishop whose career spanned the second half of the fourth century, knew Philo's *Life* and took its form of retold biblical narrative to create his own, distinctive *Life of Moses*. It offered its audience a mechanism by which to transfer the virtues of Moses's various actions to their own daily struggles. That mechanism was underdetermined, so that the transfer of the courage Moses showed in the

1. Philo, *Life of Moses*, trans. F. H. Colson, in *Philo*, vol.6, *On Abraham, On Joseph, On Moses*, Loeb Classical Library (Cambridge, Mass.: Harvard University Press, 1935).

presence of Pharaoh and his army, or of the perseverance Moses drew upon to lead the distractible Israelites through the wilderness, into a viable pattern to be adopted in the life of the reader was a loose process. Moses's inspired example was seemingly open to any who are willing to pursue a deeper knowledge of God. It is for this reason that Gregory's *Life of Moses* is a popular modern work: there are no fewer than three translations into English currently available, and the most frequently cited of those translations emphasizes the versatility of the pattern Moses strikes, introducing the text in a way that makes it directly applicable to any modern Christian reader.[2]

The highly adjustable correspondence between the pattern of Moses and the enactment of that pattern in a reader's life is in fact loose by design. The ancient author of the *Life of Moses* did not simply value mimesis for its own sake, but rather tried to engage the reader in an active pedagogical process, by which the figure of Moses could be converted into practical directions for facing new and different challenges. This is in part because the *Life of Moses* was composed in response to a request from a less experienced Christian for "some direction regarding the perfect life."[3] Gregory responded to this request as a teacher would, offering both an example of the pursuit of the perfect life and a repeated warning that adopting the example would require painstaking, long work on the part of the reader. He suggested that the imitation of exemplary figures from the biblical past was certainly possible, and even desirable, because the very "reason why the custom of these lofty people has been narrated so carefully is in order to provide a direction to the life that leads to the good by way of the imitation of these early doers of good."[4] The question, however, of precisely what details of a life like Moses's a reader should imitate remained obscure because of the distance between Moses's environment and the reader's own. No contemporary person could in fact stare down the Pharaoh or

2. Abraham J. Malherbe and Everett Ferguson, *Gregory of Nyssa: The Life of Moses*, Classics of Western Spirituality (New York: Paulist Press, 1978); see also the preface by John Meyendorff.

3. Gregory of Nyssa, *Life of Moses* prologue 2, ed. H. Musurillo, in *Gregorii Nysseni: De vita Moysis*, Gregorii Nysseni Opera 7.1 (Leiden: Brill, 1964), 2.8–9. Throughout this essay, I will give the book and chapter numbers as established by Jean Daniélou in his edition and French translation, *Grégoire de Nysse, La Vie de Moïse*, Sources Chrétiennes, 1 (Paris: Éditions du Cerf, 1955), 1–135. Revised editions appeared in 1968 and 2000, with different pagination. Daniélou's divisions of the text have governed the most popular English translation; but I have made my own translations from the best critical edition, that of Musurillo, cited above.

4. Gregory of Nyssa, *Life of Moses* prologue 13 (ed. Musurillo, *De vita Moysis*, 6.5–8).

chastise the Israelites gathered at the base of Sinai for their idolatry, as Moses had, so what could episodes like these mean for a reader who wanted to imitate them? The difficulty of translating the pattern into action was, in fact, a spur to greater knowledge, because making use of such exempla required, as Gregory wrote, "a subtle use of one's intelligence and piercing vision" at the same time.[5] In truth, all of this hedging about the trouble of imitation was not aimed at putting the reader off—just the opposite. The talk of the mechanism of imitation's difficulty worked in concert with the claims that imitation of Moses was the best way to accomplish the perfect life, to encourage the reader to pay extremely close attention not just to Moses, but also to his (the reader's) own interpretative practices. Getting the student to scrutinize the pattern of Moses and to work out precisely how to apply its lessons is the central goal of the *Life of Moses*.

This essay engages in a different, but related, task. Instead of reading the *Life of Moses* as its author indicated, with an eye to understanding how to draw lessons about one's life from the details of Moses's example, I will scrutinize the *Life* with an eye to figuring out one of its most enticing puzzles: the location in which and social situation for which it was written. To whom did Gregory direct this text, and who was optimally suited to follow its guidance? In the first part of the essay, I will trace the current scholarly understanding of the context of the *Life of Moses*, rehearsing the foundation on which scholars have come to the conclusion that it is a work of Gregory's late career and a treatise meant to introduce a mystical tradition to the ascetics gathered in the community founded by Gregory's late brother, Basil of Caesarea. In so doing, I will call attention to the problematic nature of this understanding, both the thinness of its social location and the portions of the text that do not yield to its claims. In the second part of the essay, I will suggest an alternate context for the *Life*, based on the assumptions the text holds about the social and pedagogical priorities of the person to whom its lessons are directed. I argue that the person whom the text enjoins to imitate Moses was most likely an ascetic leader, and that the problems of life as a leader of a religious community are the central problems Gregory sought to address with his example of Moses. I explore prior identifications of the *Life of Moses* as a text about the role of bishops, and I suggest that, based on the detailed theological and anthropological assump-

5. Gregory of Nyssa, *Life of Moses* prologue 14 (ed. Musurillo, *De vita Moysis*, 6.20–21).

tions expressed in Gregory's advice, it is likely that the ideal leader addressed by Gregory was not a bishop, but an ascetic leader conversant with one particular style of asceticism extant in late ancient Christianity. At the end of the essay, I will suggest how this novel context for the *Life of Moses* not only can change our understanding of Gregory and his use of Moses's career as an exemplar for one particular kind of Christian life, but also can add evidence to the ongoing conversation among scholars about the use of Scripture in late antiquity.

The Current Understanding of the Context of the *Life of Moses*

The biographical details of Gregory of Nyssa's own life have themselves been an important foundation for the current scholarly consensus regarding the purpose and environment for which the *Life of Moses* was written. Gregory was born in Cappadocia in 335 C.E. to a family whose members included several Christians later famous for their practice and their theological brilliance.[6] Though Gregory wrote many pieces of literature, including homilies, philosophical and educational treatises, and biographies, his most well-known works were written on account of relationships he held with those famous family members. Gregory made many theological interventions, but his theology of the Trinity in the work defending his brother Basil *Against Eunomius* is chief among them; Gregory wrote often in praise of education, but his *Treatise on the Soul and the Resurrection*, an imagined dialogue including his sister Macrina, is the most widely read. Consequently, the portrait we have of Gregory's development as a theologian and a writer is built around his biography and the biographies of those around him, family as well as friends. And that is standard practice in early Christian studies: we often approach the early Christian period by parsing the field author by author, then parsing each author's output by arranging his texts in the flow of his life, ideas, and relationships. There are three or four works, however, that do not have any clear location in Gregory's life or any clear, direct relationship to other works of Gregory's, though they have a relationship among themselves. The *Life of Moses*, which is often grouped with two other mystical treatments of scriptural

6. For an extended overview of Gregory's life and works, see Anthony Meredith, SJ, *Gregory of Nyssa*, The Early Church Fathers (London: Routledge, 1999), 1–26.

themes, the *Homilies on the Song of Songs* and the *Treatise on the Inscriptions of the Psalms*, speaks of a path of Christian progress, a perpetual stretching out toward a good that does not exist as a fixed end, but retreats as it is approached.[7] In the case of the *Life of Moses*, the highest part of this stretching takes place in darkness, signified in Moses's career by the darkness he encountered when he met God on Sinai. These formulations are distinctive; for that and for their lack of clear reference to known points in Gregory's biography, they do not square easily with other works more securely dated to well-documented eras in Gregory's life.

As a result, scholars of Gregory have posited a "mystical period" in Gregory's writing for these texts, the situational details of which explain the uniqueness of the ideas espoused in them when they are compared to Gregory's other writings. That period is assigned to the years assumed to be Gregory's last, between his last dateable work, a funeral oration given in or around 386 C.E., and his presumed death in the mid-390s C.E.. Though it is an elegant explanation of the mystery of these texts (not to mention the mystery of the end of Gregory's life, about which we know nothing), the notion of Gregory's "mystical period" is based on a slim foundation, the constructed nature of which has been obscured as scholars of Gregory repeat the notion in their introductory surveys of Gregory's work. The existence of this "mystical period" depends on three interlocking assertions. The first is that the three texts I have mentioned form a group, equally important and similar in theme and aim, a fair though not incontrovertible claim.[8] The second is the mention of the author's "gray hair" in the prologue to the *Life of Moses*, which is taken literally in order to assign this work, and the two others, to Gregory's old age.[9] In order to hold that assumption, a scholar must disregard both Gregory's earlier references to his "gray hair" (see, for example, its use in *Against Eunomius*) as well as the fact that other writers in Gregory's environment feel comfortable refer-

---

7. For the doctrine of *epektasis*, see Lucas Francisco Mateo-Seco, "Epektasis," in *The Brill Dictionary of Gregory of Nyssa*, ed. Lucas Francisco Mateo-Seco and Giulio Maspero, trans. Seth Cherney (Leiden: Brill, 2010), 263–68.

8. See the way that scholars interested in mysticism focus now on the *Songs* homilies and often leave *Life of Moses* to be mentioned only in passing; for an example, look at Sarah Coakley's treatment in the introduction to *Re-thinking Gregory of Nyssa* (London: Blackwell, 2003), 1–14.

9. Gregory of Nyssa, *Life of Moses* prologue 2 (ed. Musurillo, *De vita Moysis*, 2.13). See the reconstruction of Jean Daniélou, *Platonisme et théologie mystique: Essai sur la doctrine spirituelle de saint Grégoire de Nysse* (Paris: Aubier, 1944).

ring to their own "gray hair" as early as their early thirties.[10] The third assertion that supports the existence of a "mystical period" at the end of Gregory's life is even stranger: scholars assume these works were written at the end of Gregory's life because that is when he finally became a widower and, unencumbered, could indulge the mystical thoughts he had previously suppressed on account of the commitment it took to maintain a relationship with his spouse.[11] Questionable assertions, but the chronology they support—created by one influential scholar, Jean Daniélou, and later upheld by the premier editor of Gregory's work, Werner Jaeger—has long been understood as a fact of Gregory's life, such that all current editions of the *Life of Moses*, the *Songs* homilies, and any works associated with them are assigned to this late, mystical period in Gregory's life.[12]

The field of early Christian studies, however, has expanded since the scholarship that established this date for the *Life of Moses* appeared, adding new knowledge about the diversity of early Christian thought; new awareness of the tropes of self-presentation used by Christian writers; and new caution about imparting psychological motivations to authors whose cultural contexts are quite different from our own. Instead of seeking the context of a piece of writing in its author's biography, many scholars now mine the details of the surviving texts *themselves* to try to establish a thicker account of the social contexts in which and for which they were written. Such historical and intellectual investigation has unearthed the local frameworks for many ideas voiced by Gregory, even such heady theological concepts as the infinity of the divine and the love between God and the church.[13] This approach has the benefit of

10. See, for example, Gregory of Nazianzus's wide-ranging use, as in the twelve instances noted by Bradley Storin, "The Letters of Gregory of Nazianzus: Discourse and Community in Late Antique Epistolary Culture" (Ph.D. diss., Indiana University, 2012), 204n181.

11. For his arguments about Gregory's wife, Theosebeia, and Gregory's turn to mysticism as a result of his having free time and freedom after her death, see Daniélou, "Le mariage de Grégoire de Nysse et la chronologie de sa vie," *Revue des Études Augustiniennes* 2 (1956): 71–78, where he concludes, "In 385, Gregory lost Theosebeia. From that point on, the monastic ideal, which had been only an instance of nostalgia for the previous fifteen years, finally lay open to him."

12. See Jaeger's reconstruction in *Two Rediscovered Works of Ancient Christian Literature: Gregory of Nyssa and Macarius*, Harvard Institute for Classical Studies (Leiden: Brill, 1954), 115–42, especially 118–22.

13. On divine infinity, see Mark Weedman, "The Polemical Context of Gregory of Nyssa's Doctrine of Divine Infinity," *Journal of Early Christian Studies* 18 (2010): 81–104; on the purpose of the *Songs* homilies being the advancement of doctrine, rather than a generic mysticism, see Coakley's introduction to *Re-thinking Gregory of Nyssa*, 1–14.

expansiveness: it is not tied to any person, or to any particular theory about the motivations or intentions of human beings, and, in a time when historians are ever reminded of the tenuous nature of our identification of authors of texts from the past, it does not require us to be absolutely certain of the author's identity in order to make claims about the text.[14]

I want to impress upon the reader the limits of our current estimation of the *Life of Moses* because I think that the text itself offers far richer evidence about its composition and use than do psychologizing assumptions about Gregory's life path or taking literally a creative element in Gregory's elaborate self-fashioning. In the next section, I will consider the *Life of Moses* afresh, looking at the text as if it had just been discovered for the first time and needed to be located, not even necessarily among Gregory's works and in the time frame of Gregory's career, but at the least among the various theological and anthropological positions held by writers represented in the full range of existing late ancient Christian texts.

The Advice of the *Life of Moses* as a Clue to Its Context

To read the *Life of Moses* from start to finish is to recognize its pedagogical nature. Though the work is a retelling of Moses's career, it is influenced throughout by the hand of an author intent on guiding his reader to draw very specific lessons from Moses's example. There are direct instructions to the reader in the prologue, as I have mentioned, that alert him to the work of interpretation he will be required to do. In addition to these instructions, the author tells the story of Moses no fewer than four times in the text; each of these retellings serves an educational purpose. The first third of the treatise after the prologue is tagged a "history" of Moses. It retells the biblical story with one recurring adjustment, repeatedly pointing the reader to the hand of a "divine power" acting in events in Moses's life, keeping watch over Moses and

14. See the warnings of Anthony Grafton, *Forgers and Critics: Creativity and Duplicity in Western Scholarship* (Princeton, N.J.: Princeton University Press, 1990), where he suggests a significant portion of identified medieval documents were not written by their "authors." Though this perspective has not been extended to the late ancient world, scholars would be wise to acknowledge that late antiquity, like the Middle Ages, was replete with textual critics and the idea that a text held a certain kind of authority—conditions that lead to insecure associations between authors and texts. This is not even to raise the issues of pseudonymity and intertextuality.

arranging situations to his benefit.[15] A second retelling constitutes the second book of the *Life*: this time, the moments in Moses's life are explicitly interpreted at length for the reader as the narrative progresses. A third recap (*Life of Moses* 2.227–30) and a fourth (*Life of Moses* 2.305–14) summarize Moses's career in the middle and at the end of the book. The complex nest of tellings and retellings frames Moses's life and guides the reader to draw the best possible conclusions from Moses's actions. Thus the multiple tellings are hints about the social situation of the author, his educational aim in sharing the Moses story, and the social situation he assumes for the readers who will take his lessons.

The text of the *Life of Moses* has often been interpreted as a guide to mystical progress for any Christian, but its details suggest that the ideal reader will in fact apply its lessons to his leadership of a group of people. Scholars have focused on the *Life*'s description of Moses's meeting with God on Sinai and have built on its three-fold pattern of illumination, entry into the cloud surrounding the mountain, and the eventual darkness that descends when Moses encounters God, as a pattern of mystical experience that could be enacted by a Christian.[16] Moses's experience on Sinai is a climactic moment in his life, to be sure, but the *Life of Moses* presents that experience rather briefly in comparison with Moses's overall trajectory of experience journeying from Egypt to Canaan. Moses's time alone with God is actually but a minute fraction of the text's recounting of his life; much, much more of Moses's time, according to the *Life*, is spent freeing, then managing the Israelites. He is called to lead them out of Egypt, through the Red Sea, through the wilderness, away from idolatry, and finally to Canaan. If Moses's experience on Sinai is important, it is for the "freedom" and "boldness" it granted him, which allowed him to then lead others to the same freedom. For the reader, the lessons about leading the Israelites are given greater weight, for examples regarding how to lead one's own "Israelites" are by far the largest part of the text.

The specific advice offered by the *Life of Moses* about how to lead these "Israelites" can help identify the social situation of both the leader who imitates Moses and those he leads. Problems related to life in community are the topic of many of the *Life*'s interpretations of scenes between Moses and

15. Gregory of Nyssa, *Life of Moses* 1.16–77.
16. See especially Daniélou, *Platonisme et théologie mystique*.

the Israelites. For example, the instance of the manna from heaven becomes a moment to emphasize the equality of all persons among the Israelites and to showcase the futility of hoarding food.[17] A second example addresses group discipline: when he returned from the mountain and found the Israelites engaged in idolatry, Moses allowed some Levites to attack and to kill the idolaters and those around them. This, the *Life of Moses* suggests, offers a lesson to those who need to require the corporeal punishment of those under their care, whether singly or as a group.

The discourse here aids us in another way: When they all decided *en masse* to act badly, and the whole encampment became as one in their evil-doing, they were whipped, first one then another, indiscriminately. For when someone is caught up in a group being tracked down for evil deeds and is tortured by blows to this or that part of his body, he knows, as he endures the whipping, that the pain he experiences in various parts of his body will spread to the whole. In the same way, a group of people who decide together to engage in evil are punished as a whole. For when [they see] parts of the group being whipped, they realize that the whipping is being directed at all of them. So, when some comparable evil is enacted by many, it is not always the many that suffer the wrath of God, but only some. It is appropriate to think that the correction [in this case] is done for the love of humanity: not all are struck, but all are brought to consider turning away from evil by the blows inflicted on some.[18]

If one were to draw a lesson from Moses's life in this regard, it is that the leader needs to chastise those he leads, sometimes corporately, sometimes the part for the whole. Both of these vignettes, the manna and the punishment, speak to a leader who deals with issues like the equitable sharing of resources and the discipline of a corporate body. There are many contexts to which this could apply in late ancient culture—discipline was the backbone of ancient schooling, the army, and emergent Christian congregations—but the monastic context is most salient among them.

It is on this basis that others have suggested that the *Life of Moses* was written in order to develop for Basil's growing ascetic community a mystical perspective that it previously had lacked. Yet there were many different types of ascetic communities in late ancient Christianity, and the particular guidance that the *Life of Moses* offers does not coincide with what we know of Basil's community. This is especially clear in the terms in which the *Life of Moses*

17. Gregory of Nyssa, *Life of Moses* 2.141–43.
18. Gregory of Nyssa, *Life of Moses* 2.205–6 (ed. Musurillo, *De vita Moysis*, 104.19–105.8).

couches the inevitable struggle of maintaining the discipline of an ascetic life. A collection of interpretations of the plagues that God brought on Egypt, for instance, reveal the author's assumption that the leader who imitates Moses will have to both convince his Israelites that they want freedom and also prepare them for it by the execution of some rather harsh actions. Moses, when he "sought to lead those of his nature to a free life," needed to show them the alternative, so in order to "induce a desire" for that life of freedom, he acted as God instructed him, bringing about the plagues that struck Egypt (see Exodus 7:1–12:30). By these disasters, he could teach the Israelites the necessity of utterly destroying the "first genesis of evil," by which he means the firstborn children among the Egyptians. Elsewhere in the treatise, Gregory identified Egyptians with evil thoughts, or demons, and here too, he reads the Egyptian firstborn children as the first among the passions: lust and anger.[19] To fight off such "Egyptians" there are special practices. If we "want to grasp more keenly the message of this story," Gregory wrote, we should understand that "when the destroyer has been found inside, we do not cast him out through concentration, but instead we fashion a chief guard by using the law against him gaining entrance to us."[20] To some students of ancient Christianity, this kind of defense against the dominant passions—anger, lust, gluttony, and the like—by means of the law will sound familiar. Evagrius of Pontus proposed such a practice against passions in his treatise *Talking Back*, where he offered a different passage of Scripture to be used as a talisman against each of various situations in which an ascetic might be tempted by a passion.

The prospect of Evagrian-style advice appearing in a treatise of Gregory's may seem far-fetched, but the anthropological assumptions of the treatise, too, are detailed and resonant with the way human constitutions are described in Evagrius's work. Immediately following the section of the *Life* I have just described, in which Moses stands as an example of the leader who kills off the firstborn of evil, namely lust and anger, Gregory provides a framework in which to understand the action of such passions on the human being. Three parts of the human—the rational, the desiring, and the passionate parts—need to remain in the proper hierarchy for the Christian to be safe

19. Gregory of Nyssa, *Life of Moses* 2.93.
20. Gregory of Nyssa, *Life of Moses* 2.95 (ed. Musurillo, *De vita Moysis*, 62.5–7). This and the following several lines of *VM* appear to be only slightly paraphrased versions of a fragment of a commentary on Exodus by Origen; cf. PG 12:285.15–20.

from attack. If they happen to fall out of order, with the desiring or passionate part taking the fore, then there is a chance that the "destroyer will be able
to steal into the person" and disrupt his calm.[21] The mechanism by which the
"destroyer" slips in to the person's interior is rather specific, being directly tied
to the thoughts (λογισμοί) a person holds, which are the "parents of virtue."[22]
So, if one allows only "temperate and careful" thoughts, then all is well, but
the allowance of more lax or even wicked thoughts causes ruin.[23] The author
of the *Life of Moses* feels so strongly about the importance of thoughts as the
index of an individual's state that he equates them with wicked people who
must be killed.

According to the *Life*, if one wishes to be a "friend of God," as Moses is,
then one has to be willing to attack and kill even those who are closest to him,
whether brother, stranger, or friend.[24] Gregory wrote, "Regarding progress,
we think when we look to the contemplation that every person who looks
to God and the law is purified by the slaughter of those who are evilly familiar with him.... We think these are the thoughts that share our nature, whose
life is death to us, but whose death brings about our life."[25] To control these
thoughts—to "slaughter," so to speak, those that are resident, but evil—was
not simply a matter of exercising one's will or keeping the attention away from
such thoughts. Instead, the author suggested that thoughts must be controlled
at their source: the passions. Anger, lust, and greed all accomplish the perver-
sion of the thoughts, but the audience of the *Life of Moses* should keep watch
for one particular entity that this author includes among the passions: "Of all
the existing passions that contend against the thoughts of human beings, none
of them is more capable against us than pleasure."[26] "Pleasure," the *Life of Moses* warns, "reveals human beings to be wild beasts," conquering those who cannot be conquered by other means.[27] Thus, the wise leader who wishes to imitate Moses must already understand that the passions, especially pleasure, can

21. Gregory of Nyssa, *Life of Moses* 2.98; cf. 2.123. This, too, echoes the same passage in Origen's Exodus fragments.
22. Gregory of Nyssa, *Life of Moses* 2.4 (ed. Musurillo, *De vita Moysis*, 37.17–18).
23. Gregory of Nyssa, *Life of Moses* 2.7 (ed. Musurillo, *De vita Moysis*, 35.9–10); cf. Athanasius, *Life
of Antony* 55.
24. Gregory of Nyssa, *Life of Moses* 2.207 (ed. Musurillo, *De vita Moysis*, 105.13–14).
25. Gregory of Nyssa, *Life of Moses* 2.208 (ed. Musurillo, *De vita Moysis*, 105.18–20; 106.1–3).
26. Gregory of Nyssa, *Life of Moses* 2.301 (ed. Musurillo, *De vita Moysis*, 136.20–137.2).
27. Gregory of Nyssa, *Life of Moses* 2.302 (ed. Musurillo, *De vita Moysis*, 137.13–14).

influence the thoughts negatively and thus derail the advancement he seeks to produce among his own "Israelites."

What is more, the advice given to the ascetic leader in the *Life of Moses* anticipates the fluctuations in the progress of those he leads, as well as their eventual independence. The ascetic journey is difficult, just as the Israelites' journey was difficult. Many of the leader's group will be frightened off by attacks of the adversary, which begin the moment they start their program, just as Pharaoh attacked the Israelites immediately upon their departure from Egypt. Of those who choose the journey, some will gain fortitude by fighting the adversary and his temptations, but others who are weak will be "struck down" by those encounters, and even regret their decision to follow the leader. Those who imitate Moses's leadership should expect some of their charges to complain: "They say quite openly that they would rather have remained deaf to the call of freedom than have had these things happen to them for freedom's sake."[28] This is an essential time for the leader to give support, because some of the beaten and broken Israelites who would otherwise be liable to quit can be buoyed up by the promise of reinforcements. The *Life of Moses* says it is the duty of Moses, "or someone like him who leads the people like he does," to reassure frightened novices and to "fend off their fear with the sign of the hope of a divine ally, in order to embolden their fallen minds."[29]

Elsewhere I have argued that this passage and others like it in the *Life of Moses* point to a tradition that developed in certain Egyptian academic and ascetic circles: that of expecting the assistance of a companion angel, whose presence would help the ascetic attain the "sweetness" of the discipline to which he submitted.[30] That tradition, as it developed, emphasized that each individual ascetic was responsible for his own progress. Such individual responsibility is a central theme that the advice given to the leader who imitates Moses also repeats. The exercise of choice is a part of human nature, the *Life of Moses* holds, and the status of any particular human being is directly related to the choices exerted by that person.[31] Thus, when an individual is lifted or falls in

---

28. Gregory of Nyssa, *Life of Moses* 2.57 (ed. Musurillo, *De vita Moysis*, 49.20–23).

29. Gregory of Nyssa, *Life of Moses* 2.117 (ed. Musurillo, *De vita Moysis*, 69.11–14).

30. E. Muehlberger, *Angels in Late Ancient Christianity* (New York: Oxford, 2013), 133–45; see also *Life of Moses* 2.132, 193, 285, 316, which all speak of the sweetness of the path undertaken by those who are following the leader who imitates Moses, a trope common to the letters of ascetics Antony and Ammonas.

31. Gregory of Nyssa, *Life of Moses* 2.80–81. As an example, even the plagues that happened to the

his pursuit of the perfect life, that change is the result of his own choice, not a determination by any other power.[32] The importance of self-direction and se-lection extends to all areas of life, including the use of texts: the author of the *Life of Moses* even warns that different readers will inevitably draw different lessons from Moses's actions.[33] Taken together, these lessons for a leader sug-gest already that such a leader has a group of people to lead as Moses did the Israelites. What is more, the specific details of the guidance about how to lead those "Israelites" resonates with the anthropological perspectives preserved in a distinct set of ascetic networks, those associated with Evagrius of Pontus.

Why the *Life of Moses*'s Imagined Leader Is Not a Bishop

The specific instructions in the *Life of Moses* to the leader who imitates Moses point us, I have argued, toward a social context in which that leader is responsible for the progress of a group of people. For some, this context is specifically the situation of a bishop, and thus the *Life of Moses* is an extension of Gregory's thoughts about being a bishop, that is, the urban and authorita-tive leader and patron for a group of lay Christians. From this perspective, the *Life of Moses* coheres with Gregory's earlier eulogy for his brother Basil, de-livered in 381 C.E. (*In Basilium fratrem*). There, Gregory offers an extended formal comparison (*synkrisis*) between Basil's acts of leadership and those of Moses. Marguerite Harl has argued that the elegy is Gregory's "plea for epis-copal authority," and Andrea Sterk later agreed, saying that this speech is the clearest possible statement of Gregory's "theology of the episcopate."[34] If Basil, and thus Moses, represents the ideal bishop in this elegy, both scholars hold, then Moses as presented in the *Life of Moses* is another portrait of the same set

---

Egyptians, often interpreted as the result of the hardness of heart that Pharaoh exhibited, are in this text the result of the Egyptians' own "choices" (τοῖς προαιρέσι). Gregory of Nyssa, *Life of Moses* 2.86 (ed. Mu-surillo, *De vita Moysis*, 58.24).

32. Gregory of Nyssa, *Life of Moses* 2.74–76.

33. Gregory of Nyssa, *Life of Moses* 2.305.

34. Marguerite Harl, "Moïse figure de l'évêque dans l'Eloge de Basile de Grégoire de Nysse (381): Un plaidoyer pour l'autorité épiscopale," in *The Biographical Works of Gregory of Nyssa: Proceedings of the Fifth International Colloquium on Gregory of Nyssa*, ed. Andreas Spira and Christoph Klock (Cambridge, Mass.: Philadelphia Patristic Foundation, 1984), 71–119; Andrea Sterk, *Renouncing the World Yet Leading the Church: The Monk-Bishop in Late Antiquity* (Cambridge, Mass.: Harvard University Press, 2004), es-pecially the chapter "Gregory of Nyssa: On Basil, Moses, and Episcopal Office," 95–119.

of ideas. Thus Harl can say that "without a doubt" the events reported in the *Life of Moses* "prefigure the functions of the bishop."[35] Her interpretation of the various mentions of sight, eyes, and vision in the *Life* connects, with effort, at length to these tropes in the ongoing spiritual work of bishops: they are the ones who open the eyes of and provide illumination to their congregations.[36] Sterk, for her part, argues that the *Life of Moses* provides "a similar vision of the making of a Christian bishop" to what was laid out in Gregory's eulogy for Basil.[37] For the fact that the *Life of Moses* ends with "the patriarch, the friend of God, successfully interceding on behalf of the people" is a sign that it is a work about the episcopate. She summarizes: "Indeed, it is the image of Moses that perhaps best embodies Gregory's vision of episcopal leadership."[38] Both of these scholars make a solid case: the *Life of Moses* can be, and over time has been, read as a guide to the spiritual leadership a bishop can provide to a group of people, his own "Israelites."

Of course, in the *Life of Moses*, the role assumed for the leader who imitates Moses changes over time as a result of the changing status of those he leads as they make progress. According to the *Life of Moses*, the leader who wishes to follow Moses's example needs to understand that he is a goad, a source of encouragement and hope to his charges, but he does not always remain an authority figure for them in a traditional sense. This is most clear in a passage in which Gregory taught, by recounting the states in the journey of the Israelites, the progress the leader can expect from the Christians he will guide.

Do you see the sequence of the story? When the human being is weak, having been distressed by the wicked tyrant, he does not fend off the enemy on his own, because he is not able. But there is another who defends the weak ones, who strikes the warmonger with blow after blow. When the human being is freed from servitude to those who rule him and when he is made sweet by the wood, and when he rests from the fight in the place of the palms, and understands the mystery of the rock and partakes of the heavenly food, then he no longer fends off the warmonger by the hand of another. Instead, because he has gone beyond the age of a child and has grasped the height of youth, he wrestles opponents on his own. No longer does he use Moses, the servant of God, as a general, but God himself, whose servant Moses has become.[39]

35. Harl, "Moïse figure de l'évêque," 84.
36. Ibid., 85.
37. Sterk, *Renouncing the World Yet Leading the Church*, 100.
38. Ibid., 116–17.
39. Gregory of Nyssa, *Life of Moses* 2.148 (ed. Musurillo, *De vita Moysis*, 80.13–26).

Gregory clarifies precisely what he means by "God": as Joshua is the successor to Moses, so too, Jesus, whose name is a homonym for Joshua's, is the successor to the leader who imitates Moses. That leader should see this as a natural transition; as he led his own "Israelites" out of "Egypt," the events of the journey itself would harden them into people capable of fighting the enemy on their own. Thus the leader should strive to release his direct authority over his charges, training them to the point that they are able to be led by God directly. This is, to be sure, a much different theory of leadership than the ideas about the episcopate presented in Gregory's oration for his brother.

Additionally, both Harl and Sterk have also noted other divergences between Gregory's use of the figure of Moses in his elegy for Basil and the way Moses is presented in the *Life of Moses*. First, there is a difference in emphasis: in the elegy for Basil, Moses is in fact only one of a number of biblical patriarchs to which Basil is compared, whereas the *Life of Moses* focuses solely on Moses.[40] Second, the *Life of Moses* includes one biblical figure that the earlier texts avoid, namely Aaron. In the biblical account, Aaron is a troubling figure: he is Moses's brother and assistant, but also chief among the Israelite idolaters. For that reason, Harl explains, Gregory did not include Aaron in the speech for Basil, though Aaron plays a large role in the *Life of Moses* and in other contemporary works, like the *Apostolic Constitutions*.[41] Third, Sterk notes a difference in the "genre and style" between the two works. In the case of the speech for Basil, she argues that because Gregory regularly returned to "Basil's role and functions as bishop," the speech as a whole was about that office. "Gregory's purpose to portray him as a model of episcopal authority," she writes, "is fundamental to the entire encomium."[42] But the *Life of Moses*, Sterk notes, does not make the same explicit connections to the office of bishop that the oration does because it "is not much concerned with historical circumstances."[43] Even so, Sterk works hard to match the complaints in the *Life* about those who misuse or misunderstand power to the "personal experience" Gregory must have had of the abuses of other bishops he knew, though the references to such problems in the *Life of Moses* are so vague that they could

40. Harl, "Moïse figure de l'évêque," 79–80. See her description of the *Epitaph for Meletius*, which also uses multiple biblical *comparanda* and was written the same year as the elegy for Basil.
41. Harl, "Moïse figure de l'évêque," 82–83.
42. Sterk, *Renouncing the World Yet Leading the Church*, 105.
43. Ibid., 111.

describe almost any situation in which different people vie for authority.[44] The differences between the presentation of Moses in the elegy for Basil and in the *Life of Moses*, the fact that one is clearly linked to episcopal office and the other is more abstract, even ascetic in tone, does not trouble Sterk. In fact, the opposite: she uses these divergences to argue that Gregory was offering a different portrait of the ideal for bishops than previously had been advanced, a hybrid model that resulted from "the intersection of [Gregory's] ascetic and episcopal ideals."[45]

These are, of course, strong and well-supported readings of the *Life*. It is entirely possible that Harl and Sterk are correct, that the oration for Basil is an earlier version of the ideas about episcopal leadership and authority that came to full fruition in the *Life of Moses*. And yet, the option I have offered here is at least as strong, and perhaps stronger, because it acknowledges rather than apologizes for the large number of differences between Gregory's theory of the episcopate expressed in the elegy for Basil and the idea of leadership presented by the *Life of Moses*. What is more, it accounts for the coherence between the specific lessons of the *Life*—the management of thoughts and passions, the presence of "Egyptian" demons, and the Aaronic companion guide—and the world of ideas presented by ascetic literature of a certain stripe.[46]

Conclusion: Looking Again at Moses's Life as Scripture

If the elements I have presented in this essay are convincing, then there are several results we should consider when we think about the *Life of Moses*. The first is the possibility that the *Life* was not written to express ideas about a general path of mysticism, episcopal office, or the community of ascetics founded by Basil. The ideas it assumes to be common among its readers point in a different direction, resounding with ideas extant in the letters and treatises written by ascetics in Egypt, Evagrius of Pontus among them. If this is the case, how did these ideas come to appear in the *Life*? One option is that Gregory's allegiance to Origen's teachings is sufficient basis for the assumptions

44. Ibid., 111.
45. Ibid., 101.
46. I could add to these the way that Moses seeks to have no identifiable grave and possesses a luminous body, both characteristics of Antony in Athanasius's *Life of Antony*.

about human beings and their progress expressed in the *Life*; this option is less than convincing, however, because the *Life*'s version of Christian progress is more detailed than Origen's teachings. Its ideas were certainly influenced by Origen, but they represent a likely later, more ramified understanding of the human person in his or her pursuit of advancement. A second option is that Gregory, like Athanasius of Alexandria before him, utilized several existing sources about the character at the center of the holy biography he created; he wove these sources and their ideas together into a larger, composite document.[47] A third possibility is that Gregory himself continued to have contact with these kinds of ideas as they developed and become more specific in the workshop of Evagrian-style asceticism.[48] The fourth and most radical option to consider is that the *Life of Moses* has been attributed to Gregory, but may have been the work of another author. Even the most conservative of these options, however—that in which we continue to attribute this text to Gregory as a monograph—has radical consequences, because it forces us to acknowledge for Gregory the viability of ideas about human beings and human progress that have previously been associated only with Egyptian ascetic contexts.

Having chosen any one of these options, we also need to consider how, in the *Life of Moses*, the use of Moses as a pattern contributes to our evolving understanding of the use of Scripture in Christian late antiquity. Guy G. Stroumsa has written extensively about the emergence of certain scriptural practices within ascetic communities, arguing that "a new culture of the book was born" in the monastic environment of late antiquity. As he indicates, monks read Scripture directly and learned many works of Scripture by heart.[49] If the *Life of Moses* is indeed a set of guidelines for an ascetic leader, based on the

47. We have already seen above that one part of the *Life of Moses* has borrowed from Origen's *Commentary on Exodus*. Additionally, there are two later texts that reflect passages from the *Life of Moses*, albeit in a different order than the accepted text of the *Life*: the papyrus text discussed by Hugo Landwehr in "Griechische Handscriften aus Fayyum," *Philologus* 44 (1885): 1–29; and Pseudo-Caesarius's *Questions and Answers*, discussed by Rudolf Riedinger in "Neue Quellen zu den Erotapokriseis des Pseudo-Kaisarios," *Jahrbuch der Österreichischen Byzantinistik* 19 (1970): 153–84, especially the tables on 168–73. These texts have traditionally been understood as later parts of anthologies or selections from the *Life* itself, but, when they are juxtaposed with Origen's text and the close reminiscence of Origen in 2.95–98 (Origen's being clearly the earlier work), they point to an interesting possibility: that the *Life of Moses* as we have it is not a monograph, but a patchwork pulled together from multiple existing traditions.

48. I argue this position in my book, *Angels in Late Ancient Christianity*, especially chapter 4, "Crossing Over," 119–47.

49. Guy G. Stroumsa, "The Scriptural Movement of Late Antiquity and Christian Monasticism," *Journal of Early Christian Studies* 16 (2008): 68, 70–71.

example of Moses, it is crucial to recognize that that example is only loosely related to the texts of Exodus, Leviticus, and Numbers. The *Life of Moses* is
not a commentary on the scriptural account of Moses's life; in fact, if there is
a central text that the *Life of Moses* interprets it is the "history" that forms the
first one-third of the work. The *Life* even offers an explanation for the utili-
tarian cast of its kind of interpretation: though Moses's life is important, authoritative, and necessary to interpret, anything not useful from the story can
be skipped over "as something unintelligible and unprofitable for our goal."[50]
This is, of course, the implicit way that Scripture was often treated in the
theological work of the fourth century—as a wellspring of interesting narrative situations, divine speech, and descriptive words and phrases, the difficult
sections of which could be passed over or not mentioned. But to adopt this
approach in the narration of a life of a character whose career is abundantly
represented in Scripture and whose figure looms large in subsequent Christian
literature shifts that approach into a new genre: no longer just the practice un-
derlying the writing of theology, this kind of reading can also inform biography. Such a shift also suggests a much wider use of Scripture, and texts related
to Scripture, as teaching materials in ascetic communities than many scholars
have yet recognized. As a teaching text, aimed at the eager leader of an ascetic
community, the *Life of Moses* has much to teach us about early Christian culture and thought.

50. Gregory of Nyssa, *Life of Moses* 2.50 (ed. Musurillo, *De vita Moysis*, 47.18–19).

Ann Conway-Jones

10. MOSES ASCENDS TO HEAVEN

Gregory of Nyssa's Tabernacle Imagery
in Life of Moses *2.170–201*

Gregory of Nyssa's depiction of Moses ascending Mount Sinai in *Life of Moses* is often seen as an allegory of the soul on its journey into the darkness of divine incomprehensibility. However, according to Exodus, once within the darkness of Mount Sinai, Moses is shown the pattern [תבנית; παράδειγμα] of the tabernacle [משכן; σκηνή] which the Israelites are to build.[1] In his quest to find the *dianoia*, the deeper meaning, of Exodus, Gregory does not ignore this. Whereas the "radiant darkness,"[2] the focus of much scholarly attention, takes up three paragraphs of *Life of Moses* (2.162–64), the tabernacle vision occupies thirty-two (2.170–201). Gregory uses it to set out a theological mini-manifesto, exploring the divinity of Christ, the Incarnation, the use of divine names, the angelic world, the church's worship, and virtuous living. In my PhD thesis, I investigate Gregory's use of tabernacle imagery.[3] I show that although he

I would like to thank the Arts and Humanities Research Council (AHRC) for funding my PhD research, on which this paper is based.

1. Ex 25:9.

2. *Vit. Moys.* 2.163. Unless indicated otherwise, translations of *Life of Moses* are my own. The paragraph numbers are those found in Jean Daniélou, *Grégoire de Nysse: La Vie de Moïse, ou Traité de la perfection en matière de vertu*, Sources Chrétiennes 1 (Paris: Éditions du Cerf, 2000).

3. Ann Conway-Jones, "Not Made with Hands: Gregory of Nyssa's Doctrine of the Celestial Tabernacle in Its Jewish and Christian Contexts" (PhD thesis, University of Manchester, 2012). Now published as *Gregory of Nyssa's Tabernacle Imagery in its Jewish and Christian Contexts* (Oxford: Oxford University Press, 2014).

builds upon the work of his Alexandrian predecessors, Philo, Clement and Origen, his fourth-century theological context forces him into very different interpretations. I also compare and contrast Gregory's work with a range of heavenly ascent texts,[4] both Jewish and Christian,[5] from the Hellenistic and Late Antique periods. This was designed as a heuristic exercise: I do not argue that Gregory was influenced by any of these texts in particular. But I do suggest that his use of the heavenly ascent paradigm should be taken seriously, and that by investigating the wide variety of ways in which that paradigm could be exploited we see more easily the choices Gregory made, whether consciously or unconsciously. Comparisons with texts Gregory could not possibly have known: *Songs of the Sabbath Sacrifice*, the Hekhalot literature, and the Babylonian Talmud, turn out to be the most illuminating.

The pattern, or model, of the tabernacle viewed by Moses came to be understood as the heavenly tabernacle or temple, as can be seen from Wisdom 9:8: "Thou hast given command to build a temple on thy holy mountain, and an altar in the city of thy habitation, a copy of the holy tent [μίμημα σκηνῆς ἁγίας] which thou didst prepare from the beginning."[6] The whole argument of Hebrews 8–10 depends on there being a greater and more-perfect tabernacle, a heavenly sanctuary, "set up not by man but by the Lord."[7] This sanctuary "not made with hands" could also take on an eschatological signifi-

---

4. For an introduction to heavenly ascent texts, see Martha Himmelfarb, *Ascent to Heaven in Jewish and Christian Apocalypses* (Oxford: Oxford University Press, 1993).

5. Boyarin has questioned the use of the terms "Judaism" and "Christianity," arguing that "there is no nontheological or nonanachronistic way at all to distinguish Christianity from Judaism until institutions are in place that make and enforce this distinction, and even then, we know precious little about what the nonelite and nonchattering classes were thinking or doing." Daniel Boyarin, "Rethinking Jewish Christianity: An Argument for Dismantling a Dubious Category (to Which Is Appended a Correction of My *Border Lines*)," *Jewish Quarterly Review* 99, no. 1 (2009), 28. Heavenly ascent texts provide prime examples of the inadequacy of the labels "Jewish" and "Christian." For example, *2 Enoch* has been designated a Jewish pseudepigraphon dating from the first century C.E.—see Andrei A. Orlov, *The Enoch-Metatron Tradition*, Texts and Studies in Ancient Judaism 107 (Tübingen: Mohr Siebeck, 2005), 9—yet it was preserved by Christians, and is now studied thanks to medieval Slavonic manuscripts. Frankfurter has suggested that texts such as Revelation, *Ascension of Isaiah*, and *Testaments of the Twelve Patriarchs* might be "the work of *continuous* communities of halakhically-observant Jewish groups—perhaps of a sectarian nature—that incorporated Jesus into their cosmologies and liturgies while retaining an essentially Jewish, or even *priestly*, self-definition." David Frankfurter, "Beyond 'Jewish Christianity': Continuing Religious Sub-Cultures of the Second and Third Centuries and Their Documents," in *The Ways That Never Parted: Jews and Christians in Late Antiquity and the Early Middle Ages*, ed. Adam H. Becker and Annette Yoshiko Reed (Minneapolis, Minn.: Fortress, 2007), 134–35.

6. Quotations of the Bible are taken from the RSV.

7. Heb 8:2.

cance, as the dwelling pre-prepared by God for the end of time. The saying attributed to Jesus in Mark 14:58—"I will destroy this temple that is made with
hands, and in three days I will build another, not made with hands"—heralds
a new age. Heaven and its temple were seen as existing "in a different dimension," whether of space or time, in "a realm where different physical laws apply, where things can happen that defy the laws operating in this world."[8] In
heavenly ascent texts, starting with *1 Enoch* 14, privileged human beings are
described as ascending to God's extra-terrestrial sanctuary, in order to catch
a glimpse of the divine glory on the *merkavah* throne in the heavenly holy
of holies. The paradoxes of the heavenly temple are conveyed with vivid details, in language that draws upon Ezekiel 1. In *1 Enoch* 14, for example, the
outer wall of the temple is built of hailstones surrounded by tongues of fire;[9]
and the second house is "greater than the former one,"[10] despite seemingly being contained within it. In *Songs of the Sabbath Sacrifice*, a liturgical invocation of angelic worship found at Qumran, the architectural elements of the
heavenly temple become animated and join in the praise: "With these let all
fo[undations of …] holies praise, the uplifting pillars of the supremely lofty
abode, and all the corners of its structure. Sin[g-praise]."[11]

The later Hekhalot literature refers to a series of palaces (*hekhalot*)
through which the adept must journey. The sixth palace "looked as if a hundred thousand thousand myriads of myriads of waves of the sea were billowing
in it, yet there was not a single drop of water in it but only, of brilliant air, the
pure marble stones with which the palace was paved, the brilliance of the appearance of which was more terrible than water."[12] For writers in the Alexandrian tradition, steeped in Platonism, the heavenly tabernacle plan became the
kosmos noētos, its furniture representing the immaterial and invisible Forms believed to be the archetypes of the material world.

8. Philip S. Alexander, "The Dualism of Heaven and Earth in Early Jewish Literature and Its Implications," in *Light against Darkness: Dualism in Ancient Mediterranean Religion and the Contemporary
World*, ed. Armin Lange et al. (Göttingen: Vandenhoeck & Ruprecht, 2011), 170.

9. *1 En.* 14.9.

10. *1 En.* 14.15; trans. George W. E. Nickelsburg and James Van der Kam, *1 Enoch: A New Translation* (Minneapolis, Minn.: Fortress, 2004), 35.

11. *Song* 7.12 (4Q403 1 i 41, 4Q405 6 2); trans. James H. Charlesworth and Carol A. Newsom, *Angelic Liturgy: Songs of the Sabbath Sacrifice*, The Dead Sea Scrolls: Hebrew, Aramaic, and Greek Texts
with English Translations 4B (Tübingen: Mohr Siebeck, 1999), 163.

12. *Hekhalot Zutarti* §408; trans. Christopher Rowland and Christopher R. A. Morray-Jones, *The
Mystery of God: Early Jewish Mysticism and the New Testament*, CRINT 12 (Leiden: Brill, 2009), 292.

Where does Christ fit into the heavenly world? Christian writers put forward a variety of possibilities. Mark's Gospel draws on Daniel 7:13–14 as it envisages the Son of man sitting at the right hand of Power, and coming with the clouds of heaven.[13] Hebrews pictures Christ as the high priest in the heavenly tabernacle.[14] In *Ascension of Isaiah* the climax of the prophet's journey is a Trinitarian vision: the Lord Christ and the Holy Spirit on either side of the Great Glory.[15] Origen seems to be drawing on a similar tradition when he interprets both the seraphim of Isaiah's vision and the cherubim of the holy of holies as Christ and the Holy Spirit.[16] Clement, meanwhile, in his exploration of temple symbolism, sees Christ as represented by the seven-branched candlestick.[17] Gregory cannot draw on any of these traditions, because in his theological context Christ is not an intermediary between the transcendent God and the material world, but fully divine. Since he cannot talk of Christ as the high priest, or as symbolized by one element of tabernacle furniture, he puts forward a new interpretation, in which the tabernacle as a whole represents Christ:

> We say that Moses was educated beforehand by a type in the mystery of the tabernacle which encloses everything. This would be Christ, "the power of God and the wisdom of God" [1 Cor 1:24], which in its own nature is not made by hands, yet allows itself to be physically fashioned when this tabernacle needs to be pitched among us, so that, in a certain way, the same is both unfashioned and fashioned: uncreated in pre-existence, but becoming created in accordance with this material composition.[18]

The vision of the tabernacle not made with hands seen by Moses in the darkness of Mount Sinai symbolizes the preexistent Christ, and the earthly tabernacle built by the Israelites prefigures the Incarnation.

As Gregory puts forward this interpretation of the tabernacle as a type of Christ, or, in other words, as a suitable name for Christ, he leans heavily on Colossians 1:15–19 and John 1, themselves developments of Jewish wisdom traditions. The purpose of the earthly tabernacle built by the people of Israel was to provide a dwelling place for the glory of God:

---

13. Mk 14:62.

14. Heb 8:1–2.

15. *Ascen. Isa.* 9.27–42.

16. See Origen, *Princ.* 1.3.4, and *Comm. Rom.* 3.8.5. The Jewish-Christian exegetical tradition drawn upon by *Ascension of Isaiah* and Origen is discussed in Darrell D. Hannah, "Isaiah's Vision in the Ascension of Isaiah and the Early Church," *Journal of Theological Studies* 50, no. 1 (1999): 80–101.

17. *Strom.* 5.35.1.

18. *Vit. Moys.* 2.174.

Then the cloud covered the tent of meeting, and the glory of the Lord filled the tabernacle.[19]

John 1:14–16 reworks the key concepts of that verse—glory, filling, and tabernacle:

And the Word became flesh and tabernacled [ἐσκήνωσεν] among us, full [πλήρης] of grace and truth; we have beheld his glory [δόξαν], glory as of the only Son from the Father.... And from his fullness [ἐκ τοῦ πληρώματος] have we all received, grace upon grace.[20]

Colossians 1:19 also refers to fullness:

For in him all the fullness [πᾶν τὸ πλήρωμα] was pleased to dwell...

In 2:9 this seems to be commented upon and clarified:

For in [Christ] the whole fullness of deity dwells bodily...[21]

Gregory relates these references to the tabernacle:

For the power ... in whom "dwells the whole fullness of divinity" [Col 2:9], ... enclosing everything within himself, is rightly called "tabernacle."[22]

He is taking "fullness" (πλήρωμα) as linked to the verb "to fill" (πλήθω) in Exodus 40:34. Christ, like the tabernacle, is filled with the fullness and glory of God. Three times Gregory repeats variations on the phrase "who encloses [περιέχων] everything within himself."[23] This phrase alludes to Colossians 1:16–17—"in him all things were created ... and in him all things hold together." Christ is "the power which encloses all existence [ἡ περιεκτικὴ τῶν ὄντων δύναμις]" and "the common shelter of all."[24] But the phrase "who encloses everything within himself" is also an echo of an expression used by Philo to designate God's transcendence: "enclosing, not enclosed [περιέχων, οὐ περιεχόμενος]."[25] For Gregory, this is a statement of divine infinity. As he says when commenting on Moses's request to see God in Exodus 33:18,

19. וכבוד יהוה מלא את־המשכן; καὶ δόξης κυρίου ἐπλήσθη ἡ σκηνή. Ex 40:34, cf. 1 Kgs 8:10–11.
20. RSV amended.
21. Commentators on Colossians debate the meaning of "bodily" (σωματικῶς), given the present tense of "dwells" (κατοικεῖ). Rowland suggests that it refers to Christ's glorious heavenly body. Rowland and Morray-Jones, *The Mystery of God*, 161.
22. *Vit. Moys.* 2.177.
23. *Vit. Moys.* 2.174, 175, 177.
24. *Vit. Moys.* 2.177.
25. See, for example, *Leg.* 1.44.

[Moses] learns from what was said that the Divine is by its very nature infinite.... Since what is encompassed [περιεχομένου] is certainly less than what encompasses [περιέχοντος], it would follow that the stronger prevails. Therefore, he who encloses the Divine by any boundary makes out that the Good is ruled over by its opposite. But that is out of the question. Therefore, no consideration will be given to anything enclosing infinite nature.[26]

So Gregory presents us with the paradoxical picture of the heavenly Christ as an infinite tent. But the heavenly world always has been paradoxical. And the paradoxes continue at the Incarnation, when Christ consents to be confined within a temporary human body, just as the glory of God had filled the holy of holies of the earthly tabernacle.

According to Colossians 1:16, "in (Christ) all things were created, in heaven and on earth, visible and invisible, whether thrones or dominions or principalities or authorities." Thanks to this verse, in *Life of Moses*, 2.178–82, Moses's vision of the tabernacle not made with hands morphs from being a vision of Christ to being a vision of the angelic world. Whereas Philo interprets the tabernacle furniture cosmologically,[27] and Clement adds Christological glosses,[28] for Gregory it represents the heavenly powers:

The pillars bright with silver and plated with gold, the carrying-poles and rings, and those cherubim, covering the ark with their wings, and all the other elements which the description of the tabernacle's construction contains, if one examines them by looking to things above, are the supercosmic powers [ὑπερκόσμιοι δυνάμεις], which are contemplated in the tabernacle, and which undergird everything in keeping with the divine will.[29]

As Daniélou points out, this personalizes the Platonic world of Forms: "Les objets contenus dans le Tabernacle sont les réalités du monde céleste. Mais ce monde céleste n'est pas le monde des idées impersonnelles, des archétypes, mais celui des anges personnels."[30]

In *1 Enoch* 14 the heavenly temple is constructed out of the primordial elements of fire and water, albeit in impossible combinations. In *Songs of the*

26. *Vit. Moys.* 2.236, 238; trans. Abraham J. Malherbe and Everett Ferguson, *Gregory of Nyssa: The Life of Moses*, Classics of Western Spirituality (New York: Paulist Press, 1978), 115–16.

27. *Mos.* 2.71–135.

28. *Strom.* 5.32–40.

29. *Vit. Moys.* 2.179.

30. "The objects within the Tabernacle are the realities of the heavenly world. This heavenly world, however, is not the world of impersonal ideas, of archetypes, but that of personal angels." Daniélou, *La Vie de Moïse*, 225n2.

Sabbath Sacrifice the celestial edifice appears to be composed of living angelic powers. "All the decorations of the inner room make haste with wondrous psalms," and "the likeness of the living godlike beings is engraved in the vestibules."[31] This conception was presumably arrived at by extending Ezekiel's picture of the angelic *merkavah* to the whole heavenly temple. In *Life of Moses* too the heavenly temple is a spiritual edifice, made up of angelic powers. But Gregory has used Colossians 1:16 to personalize Platonic Forms. When working through the details he is not entirely consistent, partly because he shoehorns in older traditions, such as the association between the mercy-seat and Christ's redemptive action (cf. Romans 3:25), or between the seven lights of the candlestick and the seven characteristics of the Spirit described in the LXX version of Isaiah 11:2–3.

In *Life of Moses* 2.184–88, Gregory turns his attention to the earthly tabernacle, now not as a type of the Incarnation, but of the church. Like Origen before him, he sees its furniture as representing the members of the Christian community, although the two writers differ in their details.[32] In commenting on the tabernacle not made with hands Gregory has mentioned angelic worship:

Hearing "altar" and "incense altar," I understand the adoration by heavenly beings, which is continuously performed in this tabernacle. For he says that not only the tongues of those "on earth" and "under the earth," but also of "heavenly beings," offer praise to the Origin of all things [Phil 3:10–11]. This is the sacrifice pleasing to God, the "fruit of lips" [cf. Heb 13:15], as the apostle says, and the fragrance of prayers.[33]

Now, in the earthly tabernacle, the altars represent earthly worship:

In this tabernacle both a "sacrifice of praise" [Heb 13:15] and an incense of prayer are seen being offered continually at daybreak and at nightfall. Great David also allows us to understand these things, directing the incense of prayer as "a fragrant offering" [Eph 5:2; Phil 4:18] to God and performing the sacrifice by the stretching out of hands [cf. LXX Ps 140:2].[34]

Unlike *Songs of the Sabbath Sacrifice*, where the earthly worshippers address the heavenly ones and encourage them in their praise, Gregory keeps human

---

31. *Song* 7.36 (4Q403 1 ii 13), *Song* 9.14 (4Q405 14–15 i 5); trans. Charlesworth and Newsom, *Angelic Liturgy*, 167, 175.
32. See Origen *Hom. Exod.* 9, 13; *Hom. Num.* 5.3.2.
33. *Vit. Moys.* 2.182.
34. *Vit. Moys.* 2.185.

and angelic worship separate.[35] According to Exodus, Moses ascends Mount Sinai alone; the people stay down below. Gregory sees this as symbolic of arrangements in the church:

The multitude was not capable of hearing the voice from above but relied on Moses to learn by himself the secrets and to teach the people whatever doctrine he might learn through instruction from above. This is also true of the arrangement in the Church: Not all thrust themselves toward the apprehension of the mysteries, but, choosing from among themselves someone who is able to hear things divine, they give ear gratefully to him, considering trustworthy whatever they might hear from someone initiated into the divine mysteries.[36]

Whereas Moses has a vision of the tabernacle not made with hands—of Christ and the angelic world—the rest of the Israelites build the earthly tabernacle as their place of worship. In other words, Gregory uses the paradigm of heavenly ascent only to undercut it—the majority of Christians are not to try and imitate Moses. Their aim is not to ascend to heaven, but to participate in the body of Christ on earth.

Gregory continues the theme of discipleship being lived out on earth in his commentary on the priestly vestments. In heavenly ascent texts the ascending hero is often given new clothes. There is a particularly clear example in *2 Enoch*, in which the transformed Enoch becomes like an angel:

The Lord said to Michael, "Take Enoch, and extract [him] from the earthly clothing. And anoint him with the delightful oil, and put [him] into the clothes of glory." And Michael extracted me from my clothes. He anointed me with the delightful oil.... And I gazed at all of myself, and I had become like one of the glorious ones, and there was no observable difference.[37]

And in the *Testament of Levi*, Levi undergoes a priestly investiture ceremony:

And I saw seven men in white clothing, saying to me:
Arise, put on the robe of the priesthood
and the crown of righteousness
and the breastplate of understanding

35. In other works, he describes a reunion between humanity and the angels at the end of time. See, for example, *Inscr.* 1.9 (Gregorii Nysseni Opera [GNO] 5:66.7–67.9).

36. *Vit. Moys.* 2.160; trans. Malherbe and Ferguson, *The Life of Moses*, 94.

37. *2 En.* 22.8–10; trans. Francis I. Andersen, "2 (Slavonic Apocalypse of) Enoch," in *The Old Testament Pseudepigrapha*, vol. 1, *Apocalyptic Literature and Testaments*, ed. James H. Charlesworth (New York: Doubleday, 1983), 139.

and the garment of truth
and the plate of faith
and the turban of (giving) a sign
and the ephod of prophecy.[38]

Gregory argues that the garments described in Exodus 28 represent "a certain adornment of the soul woven by virtuous pursuits."[39] He does not mention that they were designed for the high priest, calling them simply "the apparel of the priesthood".[40] And in his commentary he implies that the virtue that they represent can be acquired by all. The one high priest has been replaced by the company of the virtuous. He describes the full-length blue robe as an airy tunic, in contrast to the heavy and fleshy garment of life.[41] Christians are to prepare themselves for heaven by living a life of virtue now:

[We] should respin this bodily nature, in order that when we hear the last trumpet, and are found weightless and light in responding to the voice of the one who urges us on, we may be carried on high through the air together with the Lord [cf. 1 Thess 4:17], with no weight dragging us back to earth.[42]

As in other heavenly ascent texts, Gregory uses clothing imagery to signal transformation, but the transformation Gregory seeks is an ethical one.[43]

   Life of Moses is usually described as a mystical work. And mysticism tends to be seen as existing apart from the rough and tumble of ecclesiastical life. So Daniélou's picture of Gregory after 387 C.E.:

Once freed from administrative burdens and the heat of theological controversy, Gregory now turned himself wholly towards the life of the spirit. It was a change which reflected the interior evolution which he had been undergoing. The writings that come from this period reveal an extraordinary originality and mastery of his

---

38. *T. Levi* 8.2–10; trans. H. W. Hollander and M. de Jonge, *The Testaments of the Twelve Patriarchs: A Commentary*, Studia in Veteris Testamenti Pseudepigrapha 8 (Leiden: Brill, 1985), 149.

39. *Vit. Moys.* 2.190.

40. *Vit. Moys.* 2.189.

41. He is drawing upon Philo's cosmological interpretation of the robe as an "an image of the air [ἀέρος ἐκμαγεῖον]" (*Mos.* 2.118).

42. *Vit. Moys.* 2.191.

43. For more details see Ann Conway-Jones, "The Garments of Heaven: Gregory of Nyssa's Interpretation of the Priestly Robe (*Life of Moses* 2,189–191) Seen in the Light of Heavenly Ascent Texts," in *Studia Patristica, Vol. 50—Including Papers Presented at the National Conference on Patristic Studies Held at Cambridge in the Faculty of Divinity under Allen Brent, Thomas Graumann and Judith Lieu in 2009*, ed. Allen Brent and Markus Vinzent (Leuven: Peeters, 2011), 207–15.

subject. We now see him completely in control of a solid spiritual doctrine, as we find it in ... the little treatise, *The Life of Moses*.[44]

Focusing upon Gregory's tabernacle imagery forces a reconsideration of that picture. McGinn writes that "to neglect the Jewish roots of Christian mysticism and to see it, as many have done, as a purely Greek phenomenon is to risk misconstruing an important part of its history." He presents the Jewish apocalypses, alongside the philosophical-religious tradition begun by Plato, as "major components of the background of Christian mysticism."[45] We see that even in *Life of Moses*, a fourth-century work heavily suffused with Platonism, the influence of the apocalypses is still discernible. Gregory works within the paradigm of heavenly ascent: Moses does not just experience the darkness of divine incomprehensibility, he glimpses the mysteries of the celestial world—the tabernacle not made with hands—as do the heroes of heavenly ascent texts. This vision reveals a new name for Christ—"tabernacle"—which encapsulates the paradoxes of both the uncreated and created Only Begotten God. Gregory therefore interweaves into his description of the vision theological themes close to his heart, such as the divinity of Christ and the infinity of God. Mysticism is not separate from theology. And despite his own prologue, in which he puts forth Moses "as our example for life,"[46] Gregory does not present Moses as a model for all. Heavenly ascent traditions were problematic for church leaders, as they could imply that it was possible to bypass ecclesiastical structures and make one's own way to the divine source of authority. In tractate *ḥagigah* 13a–15b of the Babylonian Talmud we see the rabbis struggling with a similar threat in a Jewish context: "the work of the chariot" is presented as a dangerous activity best left to rabbinic experts. Gregory is able to undercut aspirations to ascend to the heavenly tabernacle by exploiting the earthly one. In *To Theophilus, Against the Apollinarians*, he argues that because most people cannot ascend to the heavenly heights, they have been given knowledge of God through the Incarnation:

44. Jean Daniélou's introduction, translated in *From Glory to Glory: Texts from Gregory of Nyssa's Mystical Writings*, ed. Herbert Musurillo (repr., Crestwood, N.Y.: St Vladimir's Seminary Press, 2001), 9–10.

45. Bernard McGinn, *The Foundations of Mysticism: Origins to the Fifth Century* (New York: Crossroad, 1991), 22, see also p. 5.

46. *Vit. Moys.* 1.15; trans. Malherbe and Ferguson, *The Life of Moses*, 33.

If everyone had the ability to come, as Moses did, inside the cloud, where Moses saw what may not be seen, or to be raised above three heavens as Paul was and to be instructed in Paradise about ineffable things that lie above reason, or to be taken up in fire to the ethereal region, as zealous Elijah was, and not to be weighed down by the body's baggage, or to see on the throne of glory, as Ezekiel and Isaiah did, the one who is raised above the Cherubim and glorified by the Seraphim—then surely if all were like this, there would be no need for the appearance of our God in flesh.[47]

In *Life of Moses*, the logic is reversed: given the Incarnation, there is no need to ascend to heaven. Believers become part of the body of Christ by participating in the earthly tabernacle. They don airy garments and become transformed by living lives of virtue. Gregory describes the tabernacle not made with hands as the ultimate limit for the one who is ascending from peak to peak.[48] His Christian Moses sees that heavenly mystery, but it is by no means the end of his journey. He does not rest in "insatiable contemplation face to face," as does the gnostic high priest at the conclusion of Clement's exposition of temple symbolism.[49] He comes down the mountain to face the crisis of the golden calf. Heavenly ascent is but a preparation for leadership.

47. GNO 3:1.123–4; trans. Gary A. Anderson, "Towards a Theology of the Tabernacle and Its Furniture," in *Text, Thought, and Practice in Qumran and Early Christianity: Proceedings of the Ninth International Symposium of the Orion Center for the Study of the Dead Sea Scrolls and Associated Literature, Jointly Sponsored by the Hebrew University Center for the Study of Christianity, 11–13 January, 2004*, ed. Ruth A. Clements and Daniel R. Schwartz, Studies on the Texts of the Desert of Judah 84 (Leiden: Brill, 2009), 187.

48. *Vit. Moys.* 2.167.

49. *Strom.* 5.40.1; trans. Annewies van den Hoek, *Clement of Alexandria and His Use of Philo in the Stromateis: An Early Christian Reshaping of a Jewish Model* (Leiden: Brill, 1988), 141.

Robin M. Jensen

11. MOSES AND THE CHRISTIAN "NEW MOSES" IN EARLY CHRISTIAN FUNERARY ART

The lid of a fourth-century Christian sarcophagus now in the Arles Archeological Museum shows Moses in three-quarters profile, receiving the tablet of the Law from the divine hand (figure 11-1). Although the image is quite damaged, we can see that Moses wears the traditional tunic and *pallium*—as well as the heavy beard—of a philosopher or teacher. He has planted his sandaled left foot firmly on a small flat rock, probably a reference to Mt. Sinai. The tablet he receives bears an inscription that, on first glance, appears to be inscribed with Roman numerals corresponding to the Ten Commandments. However, a closer examination reveals that the bottom of the tablet bears a Christogram instead of the numeral X. This manifest allusion to Christ, placed on the tablets of the Law, is consistent with the way early Christians interpreted the Sinai event, as it was presented to them through catechesis, preaching, liturgy, or visual art. God's giving the Law to Moses was not a discrete incident in the history of Israel, but part of an overall divine plan that would be fulfilled in the coming of Christ and his revelation of a new Law. This extension of Moses's role into the Christian story of salvation is indicative of why Moses became an extraordinarily popular subject for early Christian figurative art.

Moses was far from the only Hebrew Bible character to be represented in early Christian art, but he was one of the most popular. In contrast to most of

Figure 11-1. Moses receiving the law. Detail from a fourth-century sarcophagus,
now in the Musée de l'Arles et de la Provence Antiques. Photo: Author.

those other Old Testament heroes (e.g., Abraham, Noah, or Daniel), whose
appearances are limited to one or—at most—two scenes, surviving images of
Moses show him in as many as five distinct episodes.[1] The earliest examples,
dating to the late third century, show him striking the rock at Horeb to produce a fountain of water for the thirsty Israelites (Ex 2:1–6). Fourth-century
depictions of Moses show him being drawn from the Nile as a baby, removing

1. Jonah and Susanna are exceptions. Jonah appears in a sequence of images, almost always shown
together (thrown overboard and swallowed by the sea creature, regurgitated up, and reclining on dry
land under his gourd vine); Susanna appears in a sequence of scenes that include the judgment of Daniel.

his sandals in response to God's voice, receiving the Law at Sinai, and leading the Israelites through the Red Sea and out of danger from Pharaoh and his army.[2]

The frequency and diversity of these Moses images corresponds to the significance that early Christian preachers and teachers perceived in the biblical narratives, which went well beyond seeing them as purely historical accounts. To early Christian exegetes, these events (e.g., the giving of the Law or the crossing of the Red Sea) pointed to future episodes in Christ's life or prefigured certain Christian sacraments (e.g., baptism). Using methods long applied by Jewish interpreters of the Bible or by classical expositions of Homer or Virgil, Christian commentators on Hebrew scripture discovered typological, symbolic, and prophetic implications beneath the literal or historical sense of those stories. Similarly, visual depictions of these stories were never merely Bible illustrations, strictly tethered to (or limited by) the details of their textual sources. They were imaginative constructions that expanded and elaborated on those narratives and, as such, were exegetical endeavors in their own right.

The selection and visual composition of biblical episodes undoubtedly were influenced by parallel verbal interpretations (or vice versa). Textual and visual interpretation arose in a common culture and advanced the same interpretive agenda. Viewers, like readers or listeners, would have been trained to discern and assign potential meanings to particular figures or scenes. The frequent repetition of certain themes demonstrates their importance, and the abbreviation or elaboration of narrative details creates emphasis. Moreover the ways some stories or images were joined to others reveals a broader programmatic purpose that somehow connected them together.

Based upon this belief that early Christian iconography serves a parallel function to written or verbal forms of exegesis, the following discussion analyzes and contextualizes the three most popular Moses images in Christian iconography in order to discern how Christians understood and represented the figure of Moses. In particular it investigates the visual image of Moses as both an exemplary and prophetic type of the new lawgiver, founder of the

2. The infant Moses scene appears in the Via Latina Catacomb (ca. 325–50), and later on the Brescia casket; Moses before the burning bush appears in both the Domitilla and Via Latina catacombs. Moses scenes also appear in non-funerary art, beginning in the fifth century on the wooden doors of Rome's Basilica of Santa Sabina (ca. 420–30) and a century later on the cycle of nave mosaics in Rome's Basilica of Sta. Maria Maggiore (ca. 535–40).

church, and liberator (from slavery to sin and death rather than from political bondage). It also challenges a common, more politically driven, interpretation of Moses as parallel to the Emperor Constantine.

Receiving the Law

An image of Moses receiving the Law appears regularly on fourth-century sarcophagus reliefs.[3] Like the one discussed above, most present Moses in three-quarters profile, facing left. His left foot is slightly elevated as if he is stepping up on a large boulder, which probably is intended to represent Mt. Sinai (see figure 11-1). His right hand reaches across his torso to grasp the Law, shown either as a tablet or scroll, and being handed to him by God.[4] Although the scene occasionally appears among depictions of other biblical narratives, it most often shows up immediately to the left of a large, central portrait medallion where it is compositionally parallel to a depiction (on the other side of the medallion) of Abraham about to sacrifice his son. God's right and left hands reach out simultaneously, on one side to give Moses the Law and on the other to restrain Abraham from slaying Isaac. The two hands suggest the outstretched arms of an otherwise invisible, divine presence.

The frequent juxtaposition of these two scenes—Moses receiving the Law and Abraham offering his son—begs an explanation. One possibility, that the composition symbolizes Jesus' roles as lawgiver (the new Moses) and sacrificial victim (the new Isaac), is already present in the New Testament, where Jesus is presented as Moses's successor: the one whom the ancient prophets declared would fulfill and complete the Law. For example the prologue to the fourth Gospel declares, "The Law was indeed given through Moses; grace and truth came from Jesus Christ" (Jn 1:17). In a setting that recalls Sinai, Jesus' Sermon on the Mount both affirms the Mosaic Law and amplifies it (e.g., Mt 5:17–48: "You have heard.... but I say..."). Peter explicitly identifies Jesus with Moses's

3. Paintings of the scene also occur in the catacombs; they are found in the Via Latina Catacomb (with the raising of Lazarus), and once in the Catacomb of the Giordani.

4. Moses receives either a scroll or tablets on sarcophagi, but only a scroll in later iconography (e.g., at San Vitale in Ravenna or St. Catherine's in Sinai). The scene of Moses receiving the Law in the Dura Europos Synagogue shows him with the tablets. See the essay by Galit Noga-Banai, "Visual Prototype versus Biblical Text: Moses Receiving the Law in Rome," in *Sarcofagi tardoantichi, paleocristiani e altomedioevali*, ed. Fabrizio Bisconti and Hugo Brandenburg, Monumenta di Antichita Cristiana 18 (series 2), (Vatican City: Pontificio Istituto di Archaeologia Cristiana, 2004), 175–85.

promised one (Acts 3:22, citing Dt 18:15–16), and, in the speech that precipitated his martyrdom, Stephen recounts Moses's story from his birth to the construction of the tabernacle. Stephen concludes that while the Jews had received the Law, they had not kept it; they killed those who foretold the coming of the Righteous One, the one who would fulfill the Law given to Moses on Sinai (Acts 7:20–45).

Several other points of New Testament scripture underscore this Moses-Jesus identity. The Gospel of Matthew asserted that the Holy Family's flight into Egypt and return to Nazareth (Mt 2:13–15, 20–21) fulfilled the messianic prophecy that the son (Israel) will be "called out of Egypt" (cf. Hos 11:1). Jesus' forty days in the wilderness after his baptism corresponds to Moses forty days' fast on Sinai (Ex 34:28). One of Jesus' temptations in that wilderness was to turn stones into bread, an act that would have reproduced the miracle of the manna (Ex 16:13–16), a parallel reinforced by Jesus' quoting a line from Deuteronomy that specifically referred to that event: "man does not live by bread alone" (Dt 8:3). Such passages prompted comparisons and contrast between old and new Law, which were instantiated by the figures of Moses and Christ. A dramatic example of this comes from Eusebius's *Demonstration of the Gospel*, when he compares the "lifeless tablets" of Moses's Law with the "perfect commandments" of the new covenant inaugurated by Jesus.[5]

Yet, while early commentators recognized the clear correspondence of Moses and Jesus, they also acknowledged the identification of Jesus with Moses's successor, Joshua, an identification that arose largely from the equivalence of their names (Jehoshua is Hebrew for the "one who will save," cf. Mt 1:21). Augustine argues that Moses's changing his earthly successor's name from Hoshea (son of Nun) to Joshua was a prophetic act. Augustine explains that Jews who want to be Jews by the spirit rather than the letter (i.e., "true Israelites") will recognize this clear sign: the symbolic Jesus (Joshua) leads the people into the true Promised Land.[6]

Jesus is not only a new Moses, he is also a new Isaac: the miraculously conceived, beloved, only, and obedient son, willingly offering himself for sac-

---

5. Eusebius, *Dem. ev.* 1.8; and see, in this volume, chapter 8, Michael Hollerich, "Eusebius's Moses: Hebrew, Jew, and Christian."

6. Augustine, *Faust.* 16.19–20. Many other early writers make this connection, among them the author of *Ep. Barn.* 12.8; Justin, *Dial.* 75.1–3, 89.1, 113.1–7; Tertullian, *Adv. Jud.* 9, 10; Irenaeus, *Epid.* 40; Eusebius, *Hist.* 1, 3 (see quotation below), and *Dem. ev.* 4.17; Lactantius, *Div. inst.* 4.7.

rifice. Early Christians perceived the parallels. The wood that Isaac carried up Mt. Moriah for the burnt offering foreshadowed the cross that Jesus carried to Calvary. The journey to Moriah took three days; on the third day Isaac was rescued from death (cf. Heb 11:19, also 5:7–8). The ram that redeemed Isaac symbolized the sacrificial lamb; the thicket that entangled the ram signified Christ's crown of thorns. This kind of typological reading was a staple of early Christian teaching, and was so from the earliest days.[7] Paul clearly identified Christ with Isaac (cf. Gal 3:16). John's Gospel alludes to these parallels at several points (e.g., Jn 3:16; 8:56). Such readings influenced Christian iconography. Abraham's binding of Isaac is often paired, in early Christian iconography, with a scene of Jesus before Pilate, arguably as a substitute for depicting the crucifixion itself.[8]

Thus, the visual parallel could refer to the textual tradition of Moses and Isaac as figures or types of Jesus' roles as lawgiver and sacrificial victim, or perhaps could be a way of representing a new relationship between humans and God that incorporated both covenants with Abraham and Moses. In this sense, the iconographic juxtaposition of Moses with Abraham in these compositions might refer to the Pauline teaching on the connection between Law and faith (Rom 4:13; Gal 3:6–18). This could also explain why Moses always appears on the left, and Abraham on the right. Although Abraham appears chronologically earlier than Moses in scripture, Paul's theology asserts that righteousness depends ultimately on having faith (like Abraham) and not only on keeping the Law. In early Christian anti-Jewish polemic, the Law of Moses produces guilt while Abraham's faith elicited divine blessing and affirmed the ancient covenantal promise, a promise that Paul believed was (in Christ) extended beyond Israel to the Gentiles.

Jesus as lawgiver (instead of Moses) appears in another common fourth-century visual motif that shows an ascended Jesus transmitting the "new law" to his holy apostles Peter and Paul (the *traditio legis*). When from Rome, most of these scenes show Jesus passing the scroll to Peter, and Paul making a ges-

---

7. See, for example, *Ep. Barn.* 7.3; Clement of Alexandria, *Paed.* 1.5.23, Melito of Sardis, *Frag.* 9; Irenaeus, *Haer.* 4.5.4. Among the later writers, see John Chrysostom, *Hom. Gen.* 47.24; Augustine, *Civ.* 16.32; Cyril of Alexandria, *Pasch.* 5. On this also see Edward Kessler, *Bound by the Bible: Jews, Christians, and the Sacrifice of Isaac* (Cambridge: Cambridge University Press, 2004).

8. On this subject see Robin M. Jensen, "The Offering of Isaac in Jewish and Christian Tradition: Image and Text," *Biblical Interpretation* 2 (1994): 42–51.

ture of acclamation. Although Peter and Paul are jointly favored, only one receives the actual document, symbolizing his commission. In some images, the
scroll bears the legend *Dominus legem dat* ("the Lord gives the law").[9] These
images transform the roles of lawgiver and law-receiver, however. This scene
makes Peter rather than Jesus into the new Moses (because here Peter receives
the Law, as Moses did on Sinai, from the hand of God).

Although the motif lacks a clear biblical source, some scholars have argued that it refers to Christ's naming of Peter as the "rock of the church" (see
Mt 16:18), an act that arguably gave him apostolic primacy.[10] This *traditio legis* image likely appeared in the apse of Rome's original basilica of St. Peter,
which would have reinforced the Petrine claim to be the founder of the Roman church and even preeminent Christian vicar. This Peter-Moses equation
may have been further reinforced by a cycle of Old Testament scenes on the
basilica's north wall that depicted Peter as a second Moses.[11] In like fashion,
the late fourth-century basilica of St. Paul possessed a parallel cycle depicting Paul as a new Aaron.[12] The conjunction of these ancient brothers with the
"brother apostles" not only emphasized their fraternal relationship but also
indicated their distinct and dual roles.[13] The late fourth-century bishop of
Brescia, Gaudentius, affirmed the harmonious relationship between Peter and
Paul (the *concordia apostolorum*) by explicitly comparing them to Moses and

9. Examples appear in the fifth-century mosaic in the dome of the early Christian baptistery in Na-
ples (San Giovanni in Fonte) and on a gold glass now in the Toledo Museum of Art.

10. For a long time, this was the argument of the Roman School, including Giovanni Battista de
Rossi, Raffaele Garrucci, and Josef Wilpert. It continued in the work of Johannes Kollwitz, "Christus
als Lehrer und die Gesetzesübergabe an Petrus in der konstantinischen Kunst Roms," *Römische Quartalschrift* 44 (1936): 46–66; and Peter Franke, "Traditio legis und Petrus primat: Eine Entgegnung auf
Franz Nikolasch," *Vigiliae Christianae* 26 (1989): 263–71.

11. See Giacomo Grimaldi's enumeration and sketches: *Descrizione della basilica antica di S. Pietro
in Vaticano: Codice Barberini latino 2733*, ed. Reto Niggl (Vatican City: Biblioteca Apostolica Vaticana,
1972), 140; noted in Herbert Kessler, *Old St. Peter's and Church Decoration in Medieval Italy* (Spoleto:
Centro Italiano di Studi sull'Alto Medioevo, 2002), 9, 53, 76–77, 98–99. Also, briefly, Hugo Brandenburg, *Ancient Churches of Rome* (Turnhout: Brepols, 2004), 98.

12. On this see Melania Guj, "La Concordia Apostolorum nell'antica decorazione di San Paolo
fuori le mura," in *Ecclesiae urbis: atti del congresso internazionale di studi sulle chiese di Roma, IV-X secolo*,
vol. 2, ed. Federico Guidobaldi (Vatican City: Pontificio Istituto di Archeologia Cristiana, 2002), 1873–
92. This is illustrated in Angela Donati, *Pietro e Paolo: La storia, il culto, la memoria nei primi secoli* (Milan: Electa, 2000), 135, cat. 56.

13. See Herbert Kessler, "The Meeting of Peter and Paul in Rome: An Emblematic Narrative of
Spiritual Brotherhood," *Dumbarton Oaks Papers* 41 (1987): 265–75, esp. 268; and Janet Huskinson, *Con-
cordia Apostolorum: Christian Propaganda at Rome in the Fourth and Fifth Centuries*, BAR International
Series (Oxford: BAR Publishing, 1982).

Aaron. He claimed that they were brothers in spirit, sharing one mission and teaching.[14]

Striking the Rock

The image of Moses striking the rock with a staff to produce a spring of water for the thirsty Israelites is the only surviving Moses depiction that confidently can be dated to the pre-Constantinian era. It turns up in the Roman catacombs (including those of Priscilla, Domitilla, Peter, and Marcellinus), and on a late third-century sarcophagus (the so-called Jonah sarcophagus, now in the Museo Pio Cristiano). It also appears on at least one gold glass from the fourth century. Most examples of the motif show Moses striking a wall-like rock with his wonder-working staff to produce a gushing fountain. The Jonah sarcophagus also depicts three men leaning into the water to drink. Like Moses's, one of their heads has been restored to match the surviving two.

A somewhat puzzling combination of Moses scenes, dated to the early fourth century, appears in the Catacomb of Callixtus (figure 11-2). On the left, a youthful (beardless) Moses hears God's voice (depicted as a hand reaching down from a cloud). In response he props his left foot on a boulder in order to remove his sandals. The burning bush is not visible.[15] On the right, and within the same frame, a different-looking, bearded Moses figure produces a waterfall from a rock and a single, small person cups his hands to catch some of the water. The divergence in Moses's appearance may have been meant to show him at different ages: a young man when he first heard God's call and a mature man when he led the Israelites across the wilderness.[16]

The staff that the images show Moses using to perform his water miracle at Meribah (in both scripture narrative and visual image) must be the one he wielded, by God's authority and with God's blessing, to turn Nile water to blood or to produce plagues of frogs and gnats. Yet, according to scripture, Moses should not have used it in this particular episode. Although God told Moses to *command* the rock to yield its water (Nm 20:8), Moses instead struck

---

14. Gaudentius, *Serm.* 20.10.

15. The burning bush appears in later iconography—as at St. Catherine's in Sinai and San Vitale in Ravenna—but is not evident here.

16. Suggested by William Tronzo, *The Via Latina Catacomb: Imitation and Discontinuity in Fourth-Century Roman Painting* (University Park: Pennsylvania State University Press, 1986), 62.

Figure 11-2. Moses removing his sandal; Moses/Peter striking the rock. Photo: Watercolor from Josef Wilpert, *Roma sotterranea: le pitture delle catacombe romane* (Rome: Desclée, Lefebvre, 1903), Tav. 237a.

the rock with his staff. As a consequence of his lack of faith (or his disobedience), God barred Moses from entering the Promised Land with his people (Nm 20:12). This might seem like a good reason to avoid the subject in visual art or, alternatively, to make it an anti-Jewish parable, but the earliest Christian references to the story interpret the rock as a figure of Christ, who gave the "ancestors" spiritual drink (1 Cor 10:4).

Moses's staff garnered special notice from some early commentators. Ambrose, citing its transformation into a serpent and then back again into a staff (Ex 4:2), and its ability to part the sea, produce a fountain from a rock, or sweeten the stream of Marah, saw the staff as evidence of sacramental power.[17] Alternatively, Cyril of Jerusalem and Augustine saw Moses's staff as a prophetic figure of Christ's death and resurrection. Following the Gospel of John, they conflated it with the brazen serpent that Moses set up on a pole (Nm 21:8–9, Jn 3:14).[18]

From the middle of the fourth century on, the rock-striking scene was

17. Ambrose, *Myst.* 51.
18. Cyril of Jerusalem, *Cat.* 18.12; Augustine, *Enarrat. Ps.* 73.5.

modified in certain significant ways. The new image was extraordinarily popular. In addition to at least sixty examples in catacomb frescoes, and more than a hundred sarcophagus reliefs, the image also appeared in a variety of other media: ivory, glass, wood, mosaic, and metal.[19] In nearly every one of these later images, the staff-wielding figure has a short, curly beard and bushy hair growing low on his forehead. This is, unmistakably, Peter's physiognomy, not Moses's. As if to eliminate any ambiguity, two gold glasses, now in the Vatican, even identify Peter by name. Here, instead of Jesus as Moses's successor, the iconography suggests that Peter is the new Moses.

In numerous sarcophagus reliefs, the Peter identification is confirmed by adjacent depictions of Peter with his rooster (alluding to his denial of Christ) and of his arrest by two Roman soldiers (figure 11-3). Furthermore, in most of these later examples, the two or three figures that reach up to catch the water are dressed in Roman military garb, with short tunics, capes, and the little woolen or leather *pannonian* caps worn by troops on the eastern frontier. Like Moses, now transformed into Peter, the Israelites have been turned into Roman soldiers.

Art historians have offered several explanations for this iconographic modification of Moses. André Grabar, probably thinking of the Pauline identification of the rock as Christ (1 Cor 10:4), argued that the desert rock was the antitype of the crucified Christ, from whose side poured water and blood, and Peter was the one who "tapped" Christ as a source for Christian salvation.[20] By contrast, Theodore Klauser believed that the scene had little to do with Moses at all. Rather, he thought it alluded to the story of the rich man and Lazarus (Lk 16:19–26). Acknowledging the funereal context of the imagery, Klauser suggested that it depicted Peter providing the rich man some refreshment to ease his suffering in Hades—the *refrigerium interim.*[21] Others, including Giuseppe Marucchi, proposed that the scene depicted Peter baptizing the centurion, Cornelius (Acts 10).[22]

19. This count is approximate, based on a survey of many different catalogues. See Robin M. Jensen, "Moses Imagery in Jewish and Christian Art," in *SBL Seminar Papers,* ed. Eugene H. Lovering Jr. (Atlanta, Ga.: Scholars Press, 1992), 389–418, esp. 395n21.

20. André Grabar, *Christian Iconography: A Study of Its Origins* (Princeton, N.J.: Princeton University Press, 1968), 143.

21. Theodor Klauser, in Julie Märki-Boehringer, *Frühchristliche Sarkophage in Bild und Wort* (Olten: Urs Graf-Verlag, 1966), 50–51.

22. See a summary of opinions in Charles Pietri, "Pierre-Moïse et sa communauté," *Roma Christiana* 1

Figure 11-3. Arrest of Peter; Peter striking the rock. Detail from a fourth-century sarcophagus in the Museo Nazionale, Palazzo Massimo. Photo: Author.

The possibility that the image reflects Christian anti-Jewish attitudes by recalling God's penalizing Moses for his lack of trust (demonstrated when he struck the rock) seems initially plausible.[23] This was the reason that Joshua was given the responsibility for leading his people into the Promised Land and thus was a type of Jesus as Moses's successor. Yet, here the iconography shows Peter and not Joshua (or Jesus) as the new Moses, and it seems as if it would be rather problematic to show Peter performing the same task for which Moses was punished.

Some possible clues to the meaning of this transformation come from the depiction itself. Most, if not all, of the images show Peter performing the miracle with a staff. Like Moses's, Peter's staff is a symbol of God-given authority and reinforces the connections between the two figures. Jesus is the only other character in Christian art who wields such a staff. Jesus uses it when he changes

(1976), 336–40. Pietri here argues that the image, adapted from the Exodus narrative, shows the baptism of the "army" of Christ.

    23. In support of this, see Justin Martyr, *Apol.* 75; Tertullian, *Marc.* 3.16, 4.7, *Jud.* 9–10; Eusebius, *Hist.* 1.3.4, Cyril of Jerusalem, *Cat.* 10.11; Jerome, *Ep.* 53; Augustine, *Faust.* 12.322.

water to wine, multiplies loaves and fish, or raises the dead (e.g., Lazarus or Jairus's daughter). Thus, the staff is a link among the three (Moses, Peter, and Jesus): it signifies God-given power to work miracles.[24] Another revealing detail is the likeness between Peter's two arresting soldiers and the two little figures who receive the water. Apart from their difference in overall stature, they might be the same individuals. Peter is not producing water for the rich man in Hades or baptizing Cornelius, he has created a fountain for his two arresting officers.

Such an event actually is recounted in a sixth-century insertion into the *Acts of Peter*. According to this story, while Peter was in Rome, awaiting execution, he converted his two guards, Proclus and Martinus, and they sought baptism. Since the jail (the Mamertime Prison) lacked water, Peter struck his cell wall with his staff, water gushed out, and the two jailers were baptized.[25]

Although this pseudonymously authored insertion dates too late to be a direct source for the iconography, the legend must have circulated in some prior form (even orally). The iconography itself attests to this. The pairing of Peter's arrest with the scene of two, nearly identical, Roman soldiers receiving water from a rock is clearly an allusion to this jail-cell miracle.

One final aspect of the Petrine tradition may be relevant to understanding this composition. Theoretically, Peter, as its first bishop, was also Rome's first official baptizer. Furthermore, since Peter's name (*Petrus*) means "rock" (Mt 16:18), he is the obvious one entrusted to strike the spiritual rock that Paul identifies as Christ (1 Cor 10:4). Peter thereby delivers "living water" to the people and so, in this sense, is a new Moses. While Moses gives ordinary water to literally thirsty Israelites, Peter gives spiritual water to the new Israelites. And, unlike Moses, Peter does not lose God's favor by doing so.

Despite the popularity of this visual image, early Christian documents seem almost strangely reticent about the rock-striking episode, and rarely associate it with Peter. Tertullian simply includes it on a list of baptismal types and, like Paul, names Christ as the rock. Cyprian elaborates by quoting a parallel Isaiah passage (48:21): "He made water flow for them from the rock;

24. See Lee Jefferson, "The Staff of Jesus in Early Christian Art," *Religion and the Arts* 14 (2010): 221–51.

25. *Ps. -Linus, Martyrium beati Petri apostoli a Lino constriptum 5*. See R. Lipsius and M. Bonnet, eds., *Acta Apostolorum Apocrypha*, vol. 1 (Leipzig: H. Mendelssohn, 1891), 1–22. The connection between the text and the image was originally made by G. Stuhlfauth, *Die apokryphen Petrusgeschichten in der altchristlichen Kunst* (Berlin: de Gruyter, 1925), 50–51. On this document also see Carl O. Nordström, "The Water Miracles of Moses in Jewish Legend and Byzantine Art," *Orientalia Suecana* 7 (1958): 78–109.

he cleft the rock and the water gushed out." Here again, Christ is the rock, split when he was pierced on the cross.[26] Only Basil of Caesarea identifies the rock-striking episode as prefiguring baptism, but he also sees its Eucharistic implications: the people drank from the spiritual rock and ate the bread of angels (see Ps 77:25).[27]

Ambrose likewise sees the water from the rock, along with the manna, as symbolizing the Eucharist. He mentions the miracle of the rock several times in his catechetical lectures and, in each instance, connects it with the water that is mixed with Eucharistic wine. Also following Paul (1 Cor 10:4), Ambrose explains that the "very mobile rock" not only poured forth water but also accompanied his sojourning people. Exhorting his audience also to drink, so that Christ also can accompany them he asks them to:

Consider this mystery. Moses as a prophet touched the rock with his staff, that is, with the word of God; as a priest, he touched the rock and water flowed forth, and the people of God drank. The priest, therefore, touches the chalice, water flows into the chalice, and it "wells up to eternal life," and the people of God who have received his grace drink from it.[28]

Moses thereby becomes the type of a Christian priest. By striking the rock, he gives his people the sacramental water, but here in a chalice rather than a baptismal font.

Crossing the Red Sea

Modern readers probably consider the Red Sea crossing a far more significant event in Moses's life than his rock-striking miracle. Thus, it may seem strange that the Red Sea story does not appear in Christian art before the late fourth century, significantly after the first appearance of the popular rock-striking image. Nevertheless, the Red Sea crossing made up for lost time. While initially it was just one part of a larger composition (figure 11-4), in the 380s and 390s, the subject blossomed into a full-scale battle scene, often cov-

---

26. Tertullian, *Bapt.* 9.3; Cyprian, *Ep.* 63.8.2. Other brief references to this are in Basil of Caesarea, *Bapt.* 2 and Aphraates, *Dem.* 12.8. This concurs with Grabar's argument noted above (note 20).

27. Basil, *Prot. bapt.* 2; see also *Spir.* 32–33.

28. Ambrose, *Sac.* 5.2, trans. E. Yarnold, *The Awe-Inspiring Rites of Initiation*, 2nd ed. (Collegeville, Minn.: Liturgical Press, 1994), 141. See also Ambrose, *Myst.* 48 and 51; and Augustine *Trac. Ev. Jo.* 26.12 and 45.9.

ering the entire front of a sarcophagus or covering three adjacent walls of a hypogeum.[29] Read from left to right, the iconography normally shows Pharaoh's army pursuing the Israelites into the sea. In the center, the waves drown Pharaoh's horses and chariots. The Egyptians are dressed like Roman soldiers (military-style short tunics, *chlamydis*—semicircular capes fastened at one shoulder—boots, crested helmets, and shields). The personification of the sea often appears beneath one of the chariots.

Moses stands on dry land, just to the right of center. He wields his staff to bring water back into the sea. His sister Miriam appears on the far right, carrying her tambourine and leading the procession of delivered Israelites, some of them leading children, some looking back at the destruction.[30] A column, undoubtedly meant to be the pillar of fire (Ex 13–14), rises in the background. Many of the sarcophagus reliefs of this scene show Pharaoh's army emerging from a city gate on the far left and the Israelites entering one on the far right. As the Exodus narrative never mentions gates—in fact sets the story in a wilderness context—this allusion to urban architecture is interesting.

Other early Christian sarcophagus reliefs, borrowing from conventions in contemporary Roman sculpture, frame sections of their compositions with such gates. However, here the scene is active and not static; it depicts both departure and arrival. As such, it has some parallels with contemporary depictions of an imperial *adventus* (the emperor's ceremonial entrance into a city). The image of such an *adventus* appears on Thessalonica's Arch of Galerius, which commemorates that emperor's triumphant return from his Persian campaign. On the left, Galerius, in a horse-drawn chariot and wearing military garb, leaves one city. On the right, we see another city gate and a crowd of cheering citizens to welcome him.

29. The Red Sea sarcophagi were catalogued and studied in detail by Clementina Rizzardi, *I sarcophagi paleocristiani con rappresentazione del passaggio del Mar rosso* (Faenza, 1970). Earlier, Jean Lassus, "Représentations du 'Passage de la Mer Rouge' dans l'art chrétien d'Orient et d'Occident," *Mélanges d'Archéologie et d'Histoire* 46 (1929): 159–81. The sarcophagi are more recently discussed by Thomas Mathews, *The Clash of Gods: A Reinterpretation of Early Christian Art*, 2nd ed. (Princeton, N.J.: Princeton University Press), 75–77; and Jaś Elsner, "'Pharaoh's Army Got Drownded': Some Reflections on Jewish and Roman Genealogies of Early Christian Art," in *Judaism and Christian Art: Aesthetic Anxieties from the Catacombs to Colonialism*, ed. Herbert Kessler and David Nirenberg (Philadelphia: University of Pennsylvania Press, 2011), 10–44.

30. Elsner, "Pharaoh's Army," discusses the depictions of the fleeing Israelites and their children in some detail, noting the similarities with the Roman depictions of children, especially of representations of Aeneas fleeing Troy with Iulus, pp. 19–28.

Figure 11-4. The Red Sea crossing. Detail of relief from a fourth-century
sarcophagus, now in the Church of St. Trophime, Arles. Photo: Author.

Since city gates occasionally appear in early Christian reliefs showing Jesus' entry into Jerusalem, art historians have argued that it should be interpreted as a kind of imperial *adventus*.[31] Interestingly, however, they don't usually make that same association with the Red Sea scene. Rather than a depiction of an *adventus*, scholars have commented on the similarities between the Pharaoh's drowning armies and Maxentius's drowning soldiers on a frieze found on Constantine's triumphal arch. Here we see the emperor on the left watching his enemies tumble off the Milvian Bridge. According to many interpretations, this was a model for the iconography on the Red Sea sarcophagi.[32]

31. See Mathews, *Clash of Gods*, 24–25, for discussion and citations. See also Johannes Deckers, "Constantine the Great and Early Christian Art," in *Picturing the Bible: The Earliest Christian Art*, ed. Jeffrey Spier (New Haven, Conn.: Yale University Press, 2007), 87–109, esp. 105–7.

32. The most influential interpretations are by Ernst Becker, "Konstantin der Grosse der 'neue Moses,' Die Schlacht am Pons Milvius und die Katastrophe am Schilfmeer," *Zeitschrift für Kirchengeschichte* 3 (1910): 161–71; and idem, "Protest gegen den Kaiserkult und die Verherrlichung des Sieges am Pons Milvius in der christlichen Kunst der konstantinischen Zeit," in *Konstantin der Große und seine Zeit*, ed. Franz J. Dölger (Freiburg im Breisgau: Herder, 1913), 155–90. See this influence reflected in Sabine McCormack, *Art and Ceremony in Late Antiquity* (Berkeley: University of California Press, 1981), 37–8; Ross Holloway, *Constantine and Rome* (New Haven, Conn.: Yale University Press, 2004); and Paul

Passages in two of Eusebius's works support this linking of Moses with Constantine. In his *Life of Constantine*, Eusebius notes that his eponymous hero, like Moses, was reared in the palace of an "oppressor." Also, like Moses, Constantine grew up to avenge the injustices levied against his people and to liberate them from their suffering and bondage (*Vit. Const.* 1.12). In his *Ecclesiastical History* (9.9.5–9), Eusebius writes:

[As, for example,] in the days of Moses himself and the ancient and godly race of the Hebrews, "Pharaoh's chariots and his host he cast into the sea, his chosen horsemen, even captains, they were sunk in the Red Sea, the deep covered them." In the same way also Maxentius and the armed soldiers and guards around him "went down into the depths like a stone," when he turned his back before the God-sent power that was with Constantine, and was crossing the river that lay in his path, which he himself had bridged by the joining of boats.... So that suitably, if not in words, at least in deeds, like the followers of the great servant Moses, those who had won the victory by the help of God might in some sort hymn the very same words which were uttered against the wicked tyrant of old, "Let us sing unto the Lord, for gloriously has he triumphed: the horse and his rider thrown into the sea." [33]

Eusebius's presentation of Constantine as a new Moses makes the iconographic identity of the two seem a foregone conclusion.[34] However, Thomas Mathews has rightly pointed out that the sarcophagus and arch friezes differ significantly. While both show a drowning army, nothing else really matches. On Constantine's arch, the emperor stands on the left, flanked by the goddesses Victory and Roma. Except for two trumpeters on the right bank, the enemy troops are strewn across most of the remaining panel. Thus, here Constantine is in the relative position of Pharaoh, not of Moses. Furthermore, no parallel to the unarmed and fleeing Israelites appears on the right, and the Pharaoh figure on the Christian sarcophagus friezes looks more like an emperor than Moses does. Pharaoh wears imperial garb, holds a shield aloft, rides in a chariot, and leads at the head of an army. Finally, Mathews points out that, in any

---

Stephenson, *Constantine: Roman Emperor, Christian Victor* (New York: Overlook, 2010). Interestingly, there is a kind of *adventus* on the arch: the frieze of Constantine leaving Milan on the west side—although only one city gate is visible, the scene is clearly a procession from left to right, showing soldiers, horses, musicians, and image-bearers. Constantine rides in a chariot.

    33. Eusebius, *Hist.* 9.9.5–9, trans. J. E. L. Oulton (slightly updated by the author), Loeb Classical Library, vol. 2, 361–63.

    34. As in Timothy Barnes, *Constantine and Eusebius* (Cambridge, Mass.: Harvard University Press, 2006), 271, where Barnes characterizes Constantine as "God's new Prophet and Lawgiver."

case, the Red Sea sarcophagi are generally dated to the Theodosian era, long after Constantine's victory at the Battle of the Milvian Bridge.[35]

Nevertheless, these battle and triumphant entrance scenes often have been cited as manifesting the imperial influence on post-Constantinian Christian art. While this may be true, positing the influence of imperial motifs on post-Constantinian art does not necessarily mean that they carried the same meaning or message. Common visual vocabulary commonly served a new or different purpose. This victory scene does not depict a mundane military conquest, either from distant or recent history. Rather, the visual allusion to the Red Sea story on a Christian sarcophagus adapts a recognizable scene of defeated human enemies and safe passage in order to symbolize something else: the deceased person's deliverance from sin and death. It's rather like singing "When the Saints Go Marching In" at a modern funeral.

Two fourth-century wall paintings found in Rome's Via Latina Catacomb lend additional support to this interpretation. The two paintings appear on parallel walls of their different burial niches (cubicula C and O) and are noticeably similar. Here Egyptians (dressed as Roman soldiers) ride their horses into the sea while the unarmed and barefoot Israelites stand safely on the other side. The people of Israel wear simple short tunics, while Moses, the exception, wears a long tunic and sandals and holds his wonder-working staff.[36] In cubiculum C, the painting covers three adjacent walls of the chamber and is flanked by depictions of Moses removing his sandals on the left and striking the rock on his right.

These scenes have little in common with imperial iconography. Rather, the compositions emphasize a contrast between the delivered Hebrews, moving toward the Promised Land, and the chaotic fury of stampeding Egyptians, about to be destroyed in the tide. Given the funeral context of these paintings, as well as of the sarcophagus reliefs, they should be interpreted as symbols of deliverance from supernatural enemies, not earthly ones.

This interpretation corresponds with the ways that early Christian exe-

35. Mathews, *Clash of Gods*, 76–77, and 202n44, says that Moses looks more like the philosopher or citizen type than like an emperor.

36. Compare the Israelites' appearance here with that in the frescoes from the synagogue at Dura Europos. Four scenes, which read from right to left, show the Israelites as armed rather than weaponless. See discussion in William Tronzo, *The Via Latina Catacomb*, 42–47. Note, Moses's staff does not appear in the Bible at this point.

getes read the Red Sea narrative. From Paul onward, the Exodus story was explained as prefiguring baptism: "our ancestors were all under the cloud and all passed through the sea, and all were baptized into Moses in the cloud and in the sea" (1 Cor 10:1–2). Taking their cue from this passage, third- and fourth-century theologians elaborated this figure, focusing more on the destruction of Pharaoh and his armies, who represented Satan and the powers of evil. The passage through the water thus symbolizes the baptismal annihilation of sins and arrival in the true Promised Land. Both painting and relief sculpture emphasize drowning and deliverance.

Thus, Moses is a baptizer, not an emperor, and his companions are Christian neophytes, not Roman troops. Long before these sarcophagi were fabricated, Tertullian had articulated the way its symbolism could be understood:

The first [testimony to the use of water as a means of grace] was when the people were liberated from Egypt and, by passing through the water, escaped the Egyptian king's power, the king himself with all his forces having been destroyed by water. How is this figure manifest in the sacrament of baptism? Plainly that, in this age, the Gentiles are (also) liberated through water and have forsaken their original oppressor, the Devil, who is drowned in that water.[37]

Many subsequent writers similarly viewed the drowning Egyptians (especially Pharaoh) as personifying sins obliterated in the font.[38] Origen, for example, compared the neophytes' singing as they process from the baptistery with the Israelites' singing as they enter the Promised Land.[39] A century later, Zeno of Verona echoed this comparison, when he interpreted Miriam as a type of the church; she beats her timbrel and leads the people through the water into the heaven itself.[40]

Gregory of Nyssa's *Life of Moses* allegorizes the Egyptians as various base human passions (covetousness, rapaciousness, conceit, arrogance, malice, de-

37. Tertullian, *Bapt.* 9.1 (CCL 1:284), trans. author. On the Red Sea as baptismal type see Franz J. Dölger, *Der Durchzug durch das Rote Meer als Sinnbild des christlichen Taufe, Antiquité Classique* 2 (1930): 63–69; Jean Daniélou, *The Bible and the Liturgy* (Notre Dame, Ind.: University of Notre Dame Press, 1856), 86–98; Jean Daniélou, *From Shadows to Reality: Studies in the Biblical Typology of the Fathers* (London: Burns and Oates, 1960), 175–201; and Per Lundberg, *La typologie baptismale dans l'ancienne église* (Leipzig: A. Lorentz, 1942), 116–46.

38. Cyprian, *Ep.* 69.15.1–2. See a parallel statement by Jerome, *Ep.* 69.6.

39. Origen, *Hom. Exod.* 5.5.

40. Zeno, *Tract.* 54 (*De Exodo*).

ceit, etc.) that are overcome in baptismal water.[41] Similarly, in his sermon for the Day of Lights (Epiphany), Gregory declares that candidates entering the font symbolically escape Egypt (their burden of sin).[42] Basil of Caesarea reminds the unbaptized that if the Israelites had not gone through the sea, they would not have escaped Pharaoh and entered the Promised Land. He asks how they expect to enter Paradise, unless they enter the water to escape Satan's tyranny.[43]

In his catechetical lectures, Cyril of Jerusalem provides an overall summary of the Exodus story (including the Passover) and explains how it mystically symbolizes both the pre-baptismal rites in which the candidate renounced Satan and the candidate's subsequent plunge into the font:

This moment, you should know, is prefigured in ancient history. When that tyrannous and cruel despot, Pharaoh, was oppressing the noble, free-spirited Hebrew nation, God sent Moses to deliver them from the hard slavery imposed upon them by the Egyptians.... After their liberation, the enemy gave chase, and on seeing the sea part miraculously before them, still continued in hot pursuit, only to be instantaneously overwhelmed and engulfed. Pass, pray, from the old to the new, from the figure to the reality. There Moses was sent by God to Egypt; here Christ was sent from the Father into the world.... There the blood of a lamb was the charm against the destroyer; here, the blood of the unspotted Lamb, Jesus Christ, is appointed your inviolable sanctuary against demons. Pharaoh pursued that people of old right into the sea; this outrageous spirit, the impudent author of all evil, followed you, each one, up to the very verge of the saving streams. That other tyrant is engulfed and drowned in the Red Sea; this one is destroyed in the saving water.[44]

Other than Eusebius, no early Christian exegete makes the emperor, or his military triumphs, parallels with Moses, much less with the destruction of sin or passage into salvation, either through political or spiritual conquests. Considering the documentary evidence, it is nearly impossible to view the im-

---

41. Gregory of Nyssa, *Vit. Mos.* 2.125. Also see Ambrose, *Sac.* 1.20; *Myst.* 12; Didymus, *Trin.* 2.14; Ephrem, *Epip.* 1.6; and Aphraates, *Dem.* 12.8.

42. Gregory of Nyssa, *Diem lum.*

43. Basil of Caesarea, *Prot. bapt.* 2. See also Augustine, *Enarrat. Ps.* 106.3; and *Tract. Ev. Jo.* 45.9, quoted below.

44. Cyril of Jerusalem, *Myst.* 1.1–3, trans. Leo McCauley, *The Works of Saint Cyril of Jerusalem*, vol. 2, Fathers of the Church 64 (Washington, D.C.: The Catholic University of America Press, 1970), 153–54. Compare Basil of Caesarea, *Sanct. Spirit.* 14. For similar use of the blood and the Passover themes see John Chrysostom, *Catechillum.* 3.23–24; Ambrose, *Sac.* 1.12, 20, and 4.18; and *Myst.* 12; and Augustine, *Catech.* 20.34.

age of the Red Sea crossing apart from its sacramental significance. In this instance, Jesus, not Peter, is the new Moses. Augustine sums it up, "The Red Sea
signifies baptism; Moses signifies Christ; the people who passed through the
sea signify believers; the death of the Egyptians signifies the destruction of
sins."[45]

Concluding Considerations

Interpreting the figure of Moses in early Christian art may be illuminated by the various ways exegetes read the Moses stories, but documents are not
decisive, and visual art should be evaluated on its own terms. It is misguided
to make a complete one-to-one equation between verbal and visual exegesis.
One of the important distinctions between written texts and material objects
is the fact that the former were produced for a listening or reading audience of
individuals or groups, within liturgical services or at private devotions. Documents are reproducible and can be widely disseminated and quoted. Art objects, by contrast, are intended to be seen (rather than heard or read) and, even
if portable, are designed for a particular context. They do not explain or elaborate, they simply present their messages. Furthermore, their physical surroundings, which they concretely share with their viewers, condition that message.
For example, catacomb paintings or sarcophagus reliefs are not public monuments, even if their iconography bears some similarity to the decoration on
a triumphal arch or the walls of a major basilica. Thus, it seems unjustified to
assign political meaning to them. Moses's appearance in the fifth-century nave
mosaics of Rome's Basilica of Sta. Maria Maggiore undoubtedly conveyed a
different message, just as it may have in the perhaps earlier but now lost frescoes from St. Peter's. A patron, choosing the decoration for a family tomb,
presumably selected the themes, even if from a preexisting catalogue of con-
ventional types, to create a customized statement of belief.

On many of these personal monuments, Moses appeared, receiving the
Law, striking the rock, or leading the Israelites out of Egypt. In most instances,
he was joined with a whole company of other biblical characters, whose stories
in some way related to his, as chapters in the Christian narrative of salvation.
This narrative, though shared by a community, was also a matter of person-

45. Augustine, *Tract. Ev. Jo.* 45.9 (CCL 36: 392), trans. author.

al conviction and, in the face of death, a statement of hope. By the gift of the new Law, Christians were included in the Promise and, through the baptismal water, delivered from the grip of sin and death. These images represented their passage from old to new, from past to present, and from death to new life.

Thus, early Christian iconography has much—if not everything—in common with early Christian exegesis. Stories were mined, amplified, elaborated, and squeezed as types, figures, allegories, or moral exempla. Literary devices were thereby made into pictorial signs, referring to any or all of their potential meanings through compressed and layered images. They were evocative and referential, not illustrative or literal; complex and suggestive rather than simple or direct. Finally, they were suited to their context and reflected on it. Funerary art was intended to console as well as edify its viewers. It summarized their salvation story and assured them of their place in the Promised Land.

Naomi Koltun-Fromm

12. MOSES AT SINAI

From Aphrahat to Rabbula

Often, when we think of Moses, even in academic circles, somewhere in the back of our brains an image of Charlton Heston as Moses lurks, the narrative running, perhaps silently, muted out of our own frustration, in a constant cinematic loop. Yet the biblical narrative, which forms the basis for this epic movie, is not really all that straightforward, especially concerning Mt. Sinai. According to De Mille, Moses ascends the mountain and then descends, a simple narrative. Yet in the biblical text itself, Moses actually ascends and descends the mountain several times. Critical studies of Scripture inform us that the multiple narratives represent several different retellings of the same event. Moreover, despite the conflicting details, the basic focus remains the same: the various stories equally present an all-important, game-changing audience between the people of Israel and God, in which Moses plays a key role. The convoluted biblical narrative reflects both these various traditions and the heavy editorial hand of our redactor, who probably believed that weaving the versions together into one would boost its longevity. And indeed it has. Nevertheless, for the exegete, the lengthy texts provide ample fodder for new creations and imaginations. As there remains no one biblical narrative of Moses at Sinai, so there can really be no one exegetical Moses either.

In this essay, I introduce Aphrahat, Ephrem, Jacob of Sarug, and the illuminated Rabbula Gospel manuscript as examplars of exegesis in Syriac. Thus, limiting my scope and literary corpus, what I present here resembles not so much an image of Moses in the Syriac tradition, but constructs of Moses as a fungible and multifaceted biblical character and exegetical tool. I focus on Moses at Sinai, as that is the moment captured by both Aphrahat and the Rabbula image. Nonetheless, as the different images and texts come together for me, I find an overall exegetical theme or motif that emanates from Moses at Sinai: a notion of holiness, hiddenness, and revelation.

Rabbula Gospel Manuscript: Moses at Sinai

I begin, chronologically at the end, with an image from the Rabbula manuscript. While I have always thought of this as a large image, because of the size of my digital file, it is really a miniature in the corner of the page, one of six illustrations surrounding a canonical table (see figure 12-1). The schema of the whole page thus presents Eusebius's canonical tables in the middle of an arched structure with columns. In the upper left corner (illustrated here) we find Moses. Aaron is opposite him, on the right. The middle register displays two birds standing breast to breast on a vase on the left of the tables, and a framed image of Zacharias and the angel, on the right. Two deer or gazelles flank the lower ends of the table in the two lower corners. We know precious little about this manuscript, except that the scribe called himself Rabbula, and hailed from somewhere in Mesopotamia (a monastery in Zagba), and finished this Peshitta Gospel manuscript in the year 586 C.E. Scholars assume the miniaturist to be an artist of the same time period. By the middle of the fifteenth century, this manuscript had ended up in Florence, where it remains today.[1]

One recognizes Moses immediately, not only by the label, in Syriac, above his head, but because he clearly receives a tablet from a divine hand descending from the cloud. The words *isra pitgameh*, "ten words," appear inscribed on the tablet. Moses wears a pallium, the Levite stripes of his tunic just showing through, his hands are covered as he reaches for the tablet, he appears as a bearded man with a halo, and he wears no shoes or sandals. The curve of the arch serves to represent the mountain, and Moses appears to be jumping or climbing up to God, hanging perhaps, in mid-air above the ground depicted

---

1. Carlo Cechelli, et al., ed., *The Rabbula Gospels: Facsimile Edition of the Miniatures of the Syriac Manuscript Plut. I, 56 in the Medicaean-Laurentian Library.* (Olten: URS Graf-Verlag, 1959), 9.

Figure 12-1. Moses receiving the Law. Miniature from the Rabbula Gospel,
sixth century. Laurentian Library, Ms. Plut. 1:16, c. 3v, Florence. Reprinted with the permission of
the Ministry for Cultural Heritage and Activities.

beneath him. Yet he looks not at God but perhaps back down the mountain at
the Israelites. Or perhaps, with the turn of his head, he simply avoids the holy-
yet-dangerous divine gaze.

Does this image merely represent or reproduce Moses the Law giver and
receiver? Does it simply render pictorially the text of Exodus 19–20? Or even
32–34? Two details stand out: the hands and the feet. Moses stands, or jumps,
with his feet bare but his hands covered. One can trace the idea of bare feet
back to Exodus 3, where God specifically instructs Moses to take off his shoes

before approaching the burning bush (supposedly on this same mountain top), but nowhere else in the Moses narrative is he so instructed. Nonetheless it is easy to make the association—if in this holy place one has to remove one's shoes, surely in another holy place, or at another time in the same holy place—especially when that holiness is defined by God's very presence. And if one assumes that the burning bush burned so brightly because it was also on Mt. Sinai, again one can easily construct the inference: Mt. Sinai is holy ground—always. But what about the hands? Why are they covered? Because they receive holy words? Early Christians often approach holy objects with hands covered in some liturgical traditions. This practice manifests itself most readily in certain Eucharistic practices, for often such rites require priests to cover their hands. Also in Jewish rabbinic tradition holy texts are said to defile the hands if touched. So clearly Rabbula's Moses has all things awesome (authority) and holy (divinity, divine words and objects), and sacred space (bare feet) covered in this one image.[2]

Although we often think of Moses as a quintessentially "Jewish" figure, he appears quite often in Christian art (see chapter 11, by Robin Jensen, in this volume). I was not able to locate any Syriac images that pre-date this one, though surely they exist. But the images of Moses from St. Catherine's Monastery, which is situated at the foot of Mt. Sinai, provide one close geographical and chronological example. It is of course not surprising to find Moses depicted in a monastery located on the traditional site of Mt. Sinai, as that community absorbed him as a local saint because of the biblical narrative. There, he appears prominently three times in the main chapel of the monastery, first flanking the central Transfiguration scene, with Jesus and Elijah, and then in two separate mosaics on either side. In the register above the Transfiguration, on the left Moses stands at the burning bush, and to the right he receives the tablets at Mt. Sinai. At the bush, Moses looks directly at the divine hand (pointing at him) as he kneels to remove his sandals (figure 12-2); in the other image (not illustrated here) he looks away as his covered hands receive

2. For Christian images see, for instance, Henri Leclercq, "Mains," in the *Dictionnaire d'Archéologie Chrétienne et de Liturgie* 10.1, 1209–12; for the Jewish notion that sacred texts defile the hands, see Martin Goodman, "Sacred Scripture and 'Defiling the Hands,'" *Journal of Theological Studies* 41 (1990): 99–107. Although the rabbis for obscure reasons develop a theory of defiled hands so that, presumably, people would handle the sacred scrolls carefully, there does not seem to be any discussion of covering the hands in order to do so. In the Dura images, the Moses/Ezra figure does not cover his hands while holding the Torah scroll.

Figure 12-2. Moses at the burning bush. Transfiguration mosaics at
St. Catherine's Monastery at Mt. Sinai. Image reproduced through the courtesy of the Michigan-
Princeton-Alexandria Expedition to Mount Sinai.

the tablets from a divine hand; he stands with straight legs and bare feet on the ground.[3]

The wall murals from Dura Europos provide another productive comparison. In this third-century C.E. synagogue, to the right and left of the Torah ark, situated on the western wall, we find four portrait images, several of which most likely represent Moses. In the top right as you face the ark, Moses stands clearly at the burning bush, we can see his shoes to the side. He fac-

3. These two images are similarly paired on a crucifix also found in this monastery—where the receiving Moses closely resembles Rabbula's: bowing or jumping with bare feet on the one arm of the cross; taking off a sandal on the other. It is also sixth-century Palestinian or Syrian in origin. See images at the end of Kurt Weitzman and Ihor Ševčenko, "The Moses Cross at Sinai," *Dumbarton Oaks Papers* 17 (1963): 385–98.

Figure 12-3. Moses at the burning bush. Dura Europos Synagogue wall panels.
Image reproduced with permission from the Yale University Art Gallery,
Dura-Europos Collection.

es his audience (God? the congregation?), gesticulates to them, and appears
to be walking toward them as well (figure 12-3). To the left, on the same level,
is a severely damaged image, in which we can decipher only a pair of bare feet
and some shoes. Could this be Moses reaching up to receive the commandments? This would be a logical image to paint on a synagogue wall. But of
course there exists another possible image of Moses with a Torah *scroll* just below the burning bush image. Although some scholars argue that that image
depicts Ezra, not Moses, I think one can also imagine Moses as the persona
depicted in this knee-down-only image. Thus if three out of the four represent
Moses, the fourth most likely does as well.[4]

4. E. R. Goodenough argues that all four portraits represent Moses, while others disagree. See his

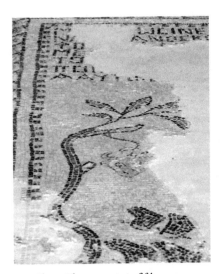

Figure 12-4. Shoes. Floor mosaic in fifth-century synagogue,
Sephoris. Author's image.

Other Jewish images, though of a different century, biblical story, and
geographical location likewise depict bare feet on sacred ground. On the floor
of the fifth-century synagogue in Sephoris, for instance, Abraham and Isaac
walk off to meet their maker, and we can see (in my partial illustration) their
shoes clearly left behind (figure 12-4). If Jewish tradition puts the *Akedah*, the
near-sacrifice of Isaac, on Mt. Moriah and associates Moriah with Mt. Zion
in Jerusalem, these ideas of holy space converge with Sinai—sacred mountain
tops upon which God resides: first at Sinai then in Jerusalem, or Zion.[5]

So where does that leave us? What kind of Moses do we have here? In
some of these artistic traditions, I think Moses finds his shoes again, but in
these Eastern artworks the two images of burning bush and receiving the Law
merge into an icon tradition called the *Theo-optes* (the God-viewer): Moses,
without shoes, jumps over the burning bush to receive the Law, hands covered
of course, staring straight at God all the while. This image can be found in two

discussion in *Jewish Symbols in the Greco-Roman Period*, vol. 9, *Symbolism in the Dura Synagogue* (New
York: Pantheon Books, 1965), 110–23.

    5. See, for instance, 2 Chronicles 3.

twelfth-century icons also at St. Catherine's. Alternatively, in Leo the Great's bible (Carolingian, ninth century) Moses finds his shoes again, maybe because there he must avoid the many burning bushes depicted as covering the mountaintop.[6] Yet here he has also lost his hand coverings, and he receives a scroll! But these later images remain out of this essay's purview.

To return to the Rabbula image—can we place it within some known Syriac tradition? We will look at Aphrahat, Ephrem, and Jacob of Sarug as possible Moses-image-makers, though all the while I will keep in mind Annabel Wharton's warning (made in reference to the Dura Europos images): image does not necessarily descend from text.[7] A quick survey of these authors finds many different representations of Moses within the Syriac textual tradition. Here I present only five:

1. The mystic Moses,
2. Moses, the Law receiver and giver,
3. The unseeing Moses—the veiled Moses,
4. Moses of the Transfiguration,
5. Moses, author of the Genesis narrative.

1. The Mystic Moses

We start with Aphrahat, who presents perhaps the most positive image of Moses, and certainly a very compelling one. Aphrahat flourished in the mid-fourth century in central Persian Mesopotamia. We know little of his biography, and he left only twenty-three homilies; he wrote in a simple Syriac, minimally affected by Greek or even Persian inflection or context. In his *Demonstrations*, Moses appears as leader, lawgiver, and precursor to Jesus. But in one demonstration, Moses stands out on his own as the one fully human biblical character, who nevertheless speaks "mouth to mouth" with God. This is Aphrahat's description of Moses's moment on Sinai:

For if [Moses] was performing the duties of marriage, he would not have been able to perform the duties of the majesty of his Lord. Similarly, Israel was not able to re-

6. Yet it is interesting to note that in the almost-identical painted image of Moses in Charles the Bold's bible (in the Bibliothèque Nationale) Moses has no shoes.
7. Annabel J. Wharton, "Good and Bad Images from the Synagogue of Dura Europos," *Art History* 17 (1994): 8–10.

ceive the holy speech and the living words that the Holy One spoke with Moses on
the mountain until he sanctified the people for three days, and then the Holy One
spoke with him. For he said to Moses, "*Go down to the people and sanctify them for
three days*" [Ex 10:10]. Moses spoke plainly to them in the following way: "*You must
not approach [any] woman*" [19:15]. Then, on the third day, when they had been sanctified for three days, the Holy One revealed himself in a fierce storm, a great glory, a
powerful voice, rolling thunder, a mighty trumpet, continuous brightness, and brilliant flashes of lightning. The mountains shook and the heights were in motion. The
sun and the moon altered their courses. Moses ascended Mount Sinai, entered the
cloud, and received the commandment. Moses saw the glorious splendour; he was terrified and began to shake. Trembling seized him because he had seen the Shekinah of
the Most High, which rests on the mountain, the great power of the throne of God.
When they minister to him, the myriads and thousands hide their faces from his glorious splendour. They hasten and fly with their swift wings; they cry out and sanctify
and exalt his majesty. Watchful, prepared, swift in their courses, lovely, beautiful, desirable, and attractive, they hasten and sanctify and fulfill his commandment, ascending and descending in the air, like swift flashes of lightning.

Moses spoke and God answered him in a voice. Israel stood trembling,
fearful, and quaking that day; they fell on their faces and were unable to endure it. They said to Moses, "*God must not speak with us, or else we will die!*"
[20:19]. O stubborn one, [you] who are troubled by these things and stum-
ble [over them]! If the Israelites, with whom God spoke for only one hour,
were unable to listen to the voice of God until they were sanctified for three
days (even though they did not go up the mountain or enter the fierce cloud),
how could the man Moses, prophet and bright eye of the whole people (who
stood the whole time before God and spoke with him from face to face), have
had conjugal relations? And if God spoke with the Israelites, who were sanctified for only three days, how much more excellent and attractive are those
who sanctify and keep watch and prepare [themselves] and stand before God
all their days? Should God not love them even more, and his Spirit dwell in
them?[8]

For Aphrahat then, Moses at Sinai, gazing in awe at the divine splendor,
represents the ideal image, the ideal moment in history. Whether this literary description depicts true mystical union with the godhead I do not know,
but it certainly comes awfully close, and Aphrahat enthusiastically advises his

8. Aphrahat, *Dem.* 18.4–5, trans. Adam Lehto, *The Demonstrations of Aphrahat, The Persian Sage*
(Piscataway, N.J.: Gorgias Press, 2010), 400–402.

readers to strive for it. Yet, only in a state of *qaddishutha* (sexual renunciation) could Moses have gotten that far, and thus those who wish to emulate him must also renounce their conjugal relations. All that divine awesomeness remains inaccessible to the sexually active.

Thus, Aphrahat's Moses appears doubly holy—holy by virtue of his asceticism (which Aphrahat calls *qaddishutha*, "holiness") and by virtue of his closeness to God. Anyone who speaks mouth to mouth with the divine holiness, let alone enters the cloud, must attain some level of holiness too. Thus, Moses achieves holiness personally and acquires it through divine grace. Does the Rabbula Moses image with bare feet yet covered hands project the same notion of holiness? I am not so sure. He resides beneath the cloud, not in it, and he averts his eyes. This Moses is not (yet?) a mystic, or at least not a successful one.

Raymond Tonneau, who brings together the Syriac Moses traditions from a wider swath of Syriac literature than I was capable of accomplishing, would call Aphrahat's image simply the model of divine service. He also points out that Aphrahat puts Moses at the height of piety, but no higher, for it is his faith that brings him to the miracles.[9] Tonneau's Moses also models perfect charity; Moses fasts better than others too (forty days); he excels at prayer; and of course he is the most accomplished ascetic by far. But I see something deeper in Aphrahat's text here: Moses's asceticism reaches another spiritual level, and thus its results—closeness to God—elevate him to a much higher spiritual plane. Aphrahat's Moses has achieved something awesome and holy, and he urges all true Christians to emulate him. Aphrahat likens Moses to the angels ministering before God.[10] Aphrahat argues that adept Christian mystics can reach those stars—quasi-angelic status—through diligent and dedicated sexual renunciation.

2. Moses the Law Giver/Receiver: Ephrem

Ephrem, Aphrahat's younger yet more prolific colleague, was based in Edessa and later in Nisibis, both cities on the Persian-Roman border, during the

---

9. Raymond M. Tonneau, "Moïse dans la tradition syrienne," in *Moïse, l'homme de l'alliance*, ed. H. Cazelles (Paris: Desclée, 1955), 245–47.

10. Aphrahat also compares Elijah to angels in *Dem.* 6.1.

latter half of the fourth century. Ephrem successfully bridged the Greek-Syriac divide in his education and composition. He wrote much about Moses, but, in contradistinction to Aphrahat, he shied away from elevating him spiritually. In Ephrem's hands, Moses remained the human Law receiver and giver, barely allowed a special relationship with God. Ephrem complimented his capable leadership and his important role as God's messenger, and even in the end allowed that Moses was the first to truly understand God's message. Yet, for Ephrem, Moses was no mystic who achieved spiritual elevation and super-human closeness to God.

At the burning bush, for instance, Ephrem carefully separates Moses from the holiness he encounters there. In his commentary on the book of Exodus, Ephrem explains:

"While Moses was tending the sheep alongside Horeb, he saw an angel in the fire that burned in the bush" [Ex 3:1–2]. Moses went to look at the bush that the fire did not consume, and as he approached, a simple vision of an angel appeared to him. As he came [closer], it was not the angel that [first] appeared to him who addressed him, but God, who later appeared to him by means of an angel in an awesome vision and said to him: *"Do not approach this spot as you would some common place. This is a holy place"* [Ex 3:5] as the place where Jacob slept [was holy] on account of the ladder and the angels who were ascending and descending to guard him [Gen 28:10ff]. And this place [is holy] on account of God who dwells in the fire that burns in the bush. *"Remove your sandals"* [Ex 3:5] and go trample the Egyptians. See, it is thirty years past the time of their picking. Up to this point, Moses proceeded without fear. But when he saw a sight that was more than his eyes [could bear], he hid his face out of fear of looking at God the way he looked at the angel.[11]

In this passage, Ephrem differentiates between Moses's *seeing* an angel in the bush and *hearing* the voice of God that later comes out of the bush. When God spoke to Moses from within the bush, Moses could not take in the full sight—it was indeed too awesome; he heard God, but saw only an angel. In this way, I think Ephrem also regards the physical encounter with sacred space: Moses approaches, comes close to holiness, but is not one with it. Ephrem separates the removal of the sandals—for the sake of the sacred spot on which he stands—from the interaction with God. In the biblical text,

---

11. Ephrem, *Commentary on Exodus*, 3.1, trans. A. Amar, in *St. Ephrem the Syrian: Selected Prose Works*, ed. K. McVey, Fathers of the Church 91 (Washington, D.C.: The Catholic University of America Press, 1994), 231.

Moses must remove his shoes before approaching God. Ephrem mentions the sandal-removing after the encounter and understands it to symbolize how Moses will best the Egyptians (perhaps by changing from shepherd's sandals to military boots).

For Ephrem then, Moses's subsequent interactions with God on Mt. Sinai do not contain the awesome detail or reverence that Aphrahat applies to the moment. Rather matter-of-factly, he reports that Moses ascended the mountain (again) to get the commandments:

In the third month, forty-five days after their departure from Egypt, Moses went up the mountain to God who said to him: *"You have seen for yourselves what I have done to the Egyptians"* [Ex 19:4], that is, the plagues which I inflicted on them on the land and in the sea. I lifted you up, as on eagles' wings, by the cloud guided you, and I brought you to me on this mountain. *"Now, if you hear my voice, you will be more beloved to me than all nations,* because I have chosen you alone for myself from all generations to become a kingdom of priests, and a holy nation for me"* [Ex 19:6, not exact]. Accordingly, some of them [became] kings, some [became] priests, and all of them [were] pure of the uncleanness of the nations.[12]

Here there are no bells and whistles, no thunder and lighting, nor even a cloud descending. Moses simply goes up and receives the commandments. More emphatically, Ephrem reads the biblical language of Israelite distinctiveness as simply history—some Israelites will indeed become kings and priests. Ephrem interweaves the various laws given, and the various times Moses appears to ascend the mountain to receive them into one rambling narrative in which Moses, Joshua and the seventy elders all have encounters or visions of God, which do not seem out of the ordinary or differ much from one another. In short, I do not think Ephrem wishes to make much of Moses's time on Mt. Sinai. Ephrem barely comments on the awesome vision that God granted the seventy elders during their covenantal meal, nor that of the people below. The manuscript unfortunately ends before we get to the second giving of the commandments. Nevertheless, we gain a sense of Ephrem's Moses from other sources, particularly those that focus on the aftermath of the "second giving": Moses's glowing face and the veil he wears to cover his radiance.

---

12. Ephrem, *Commentary on Exodus*, 19.1, trans. Amar and McVey, 257–58.

3. The Seeing and Unseeing Moses and the Veil:
Ephrem and Jacob of Sarug

R. Tonneau notes that in Ephrem's twenty-sixth *madrasha* "contre les Scrutateurs" ("Against the Investigators"), Ephrem problematizes Moses's seeing God face to face.[13] Thinking philosophically, Ephrem claims that God is inscrutable, invisible to the human eye. One cannot know God perfectly, only the parts God chooses to reveal. What Moses saw on the mountain must have been an image or a reflection of God, but not the real thing. As Ephrem divides God's image (the angel) from God's voice for Moses at the burning bush, so he elaborates on this idea in his longer *Homily on our Lord*, in which Moses's veil becomes a metaphor for not seeing God fully.[14] In this section Ephrem argues, not that God cannot be seen—that is, perceived, conceived of or understood fully—but, more in a physical sense, God simply cannot be seen by the naked eye, if one should gaze on him, for frail human eyes would burst. God's glory is simply too bright. So when Moses asked to "see" God in Exodus 33, God allows him a peek, but only from a shielded and protected position (behind a rock and God's hand). Ephrem writes:

This is why Moses saw without seeing: he saw in order to be uplifted, but he did not see so that he would not be harmed. By the fact that he saw, his frailty was uplifted, and by the fact that he did not see, his weakness was not overwhelmed. In the same way, our eyes look at the sun but do not see it. They are aided by what they see, but by what they do not see, they are not harmed. The eye sees so as to be of use; it is not bold, in order to avoid being damaged. And so out of love, God kept Moses from seeing the glory that was too harsh for his eyes.[15]

Therefore Moses gazed but did not completely physically see; yet he gained something, for he now also radiates a glory when he descends the mountain. Thus, in a quasi *imitation of the divine*, Ephrem further notes, Moses too hides some of his radiance from his people because they could not withstand its heat: it was too physically bright for their present state. Therefore on a very literal level, Ephrem understands that neither Moses nor the

13. Tonneau, "Moïse," 255.
14. Aphrahat mentions the veil only once: *Dem* 21.10: "Moses lifted the veil from his face and God spoke with him [Ex 34:34]; Jesus lifted the veil from the faces of the Peoples so that they could hear and receive his teaching [cf. 2 Cor 3:16]," trans. Lehto, 447.
15. Ephrem, *Homily on Our Lord*, 29.3, trans. Amar and McVey, 304.

Israelites could physically stand the intensity of overexposure to God's brilliant glory. Yet elsewhere he construes Moses as figuratively hiding something
else: the spiritual truth. That which he did "see," that is, what he perceived,
learned, understood, and accepted as divine truth on Mt. Sinai, he knows he
cannot reveal to the people, for they will neither understand nor accept it.[16] In
Ephrem's eighth hymn on faith he further elaborates:

> The Veil on Moses' face
> and the stammering of his mouth
> were two covers
> that covered the blind People;
> but to the just You were revealed
> to those who yearned for Your day
> The deniers, to today, are blind, with their eyes covered;
> They stammer and see only dimly,
> Blind to your beauty,
> Muzzled in silence in response to Your teaching.[17]

Ephrem depicts Moses's veil as a double blind. On the one hand, Moses perceives the truth, but conceals it from the people, but on the other hand the
people refuse to see the truth (they "wear" their own veils). Additionally,
the ancient Israelites' willful blindness symbolizes the similar blindness of
Ephrem's "un-orthodox" Christian opponents. Here Jesus is the truth concealed from the people behind Moses's veil. Nevertheless, Moses had to radiate—as proof that he had actually seen God or had been touched by God
somehow. Ephrem proves himself leery of any non-Christian peoples' ability
to believe without physical witnesses. Moses's radiation bears witness to God's
existence. Yet, at the same time, it seems that only true, "orthodox" believers
will be able to perceive the truth that was hidden from the ancient Israelites.
Nevertheless, as Christine Shepardson argues, Ephrem, throughout his writings on Moses, deftly separates him from his people. Moses becomes a model
of *Christian* faith (he saw and understood what the others did not); especially in comparison to the bad and unfaithful behavior of his people. Further on

16. Ephrem, *Commentary on Genesis*, 14.2, trans. E. Mathews, in *St. Ephrem the Syrian: Selected
Prose Works*, ed. K. McVey, Fathers of the Church 91 (Washington, D.C.: The Catholic University of
America Press, 1994), 107. Ephrem notes that Adam and Eve's faces radiated to the animals as well, and
the animals could not look at them either.

17. Ephrem, *Homilies on Faith*, 8.5. Found in Sebastian Brock's introduction to *Jacob of Sarug's
Homily on the Veil on Moses' Face* (Piscataway, N.J.: Gorgias Press, 2009), 6.

in the *Homily on our Lord* he notes that Moses had "interior Christian eyes."[18] The light that radiates out to the people, projects a different truth into Moses' soul. Ephrem presents Moses as one who sees and perceives the truth, who finds true (Christian) faith, as opposed to the people of Israel, who miss it or deny it time and again.

Jacob of Sarug

Jacob of Sarug shares with Ephrem this notion that Moses's veil conceals more than just his face (or faith). For Jacob, Moses at this point in the narrative is a type for prophecy—all prophecy. That is to say, all the biblical prophetic books contain concealed Christian truths, yet they are not necessarily obvious to the casual or, especially, untutored reader. Moses learned this truth on Mt. Sinai, but he concealed it from the people of Israel because he knew they were not yet ready for it.

Jacob of Sarug composed several hundred *memres*, or homilies, many of which have been preserved, yet among these only a few focus on or mention Moses. I think for Jacob, as well as for Ephrem, Moses is more of a tool, less of a personality or biblical character with a life of his own. His purpose in life (or text) is to illuminate Jesus. He is a type for Jesus, yet he is also a type for prophecy, which Jesus fulfills. As Sebastian Brock illustrates through his introduction and commentary on Jacob of Sarug's *Homily on Moses' Veil*, Jacob bases his homily on an earlier one by Ephrem.[19] But these themes of hiddenness are found elsewhere in Ephrem's writing as well. Through allusions to the biblical text and to Ephrem, Jacob builds his own image of Moses. If for Ephrem Moses stands as a barrier between God and the people, both because of the divine glory and for the sake of the divine truth, for Jacob Moses is also a type for prophecy—all of it—and especially for the spiritual truths that are hidden there as well. He writes:

> The prophets were God's "friends" and shared in His mysteries,
> and so He hinted to them in parables concerning His Beloved One.
> He covered up Moses so that the world might learn by that veil
> The way and manner in which prophecy too is veiled.

18. Christine Shepardson, *Anti-Judaism and Christian Orthodoxy: Ephrem's Hymns in Fourth Century Syria* (Washington, D.C.: The Catholic University of America Press, 2008), 90; Ephrem, *Homily on Our Lord* 32.3; trans. Amar and McVey, 308.

19. Brock, introduction to *Jacob of Sarug's Homily on the Veil*, 5–6.

The whole Old Testament is veiled after the fashion of Moses:
in him all the prophetic books are depicted;
within that veil which lies over the Scriptures there sits resplendent Christ as judge
All the prophets veiled every reference to Him in their books
So that He might not be spoken of openly in the presence of outsiders.[20]

For Jacob, Moses on Mt. Sinai perceived God's splendor but also the truth that Jesus represents. Moses radiated this glorious truth that salvation comes through faith in Jesus Christ. Yet, Moses knew his fellow people would not yet be able to understand or accept this. So he willfully concealed it. Thereafter, all other prophets learned from this first prophet that prophecy must be couched in parables, in order to conceal that same truth until the world was ready to hear it. Only when Jesus physically comes to earth can he remove this veil from Moses's face, and from all Scripture, to show to the world that which had been hidden.[21] Toward the end of this homily, Jacob writes concerning Moses's gaze and veil experience:

Moses gazed upon Him, and the skin of his face shone out,
for the brightness of the Son rested upon the personification of prophecy.
This was the reason why that veil was required, so that the Son of God might
    thereby be veiled from onlookers.[22]

Moses, personified here as (female) Prophecy, channels the Son of God's future message, yet the time is not ripe. Only after Jesus' crucifixion can the veil be removed.

4. Transfiguration.

Jacob of Sarug further pushes this typology of Moses/Jesus through his discussion of the New Testament Transfiguration scene. The Gospel Transfiguration narratives clearly represent the image of Moses as a type for Jesus. In these narratives Jesus ascends an unnamed mountain, meets Moses and Elijah there and then "transfigures," that is, he reveals his true divine self to the few witnesses present: Simon Peter, and James and John, the sons of Zebedee. In these narratives, Jesus clearly draws authority from and spiritually transcends

20. Jacob of Sarug, *Homily on the Veil,* 55–63; trans. Brock, 18–19.
21. See Jacob of Sarug, *Homily on the Veil,* 69–84, trans. Brock, 18–20.
22. Jacob of Sarug, *Homily on the Veil,* 303–5, trans. Brock, 44–45.

both Moses and Elijah, biblical characters who had close relationships with God.

While most of Christian tradition places this event on Mt. Tabor in Galilee, it seems to me that the presence of Moses, Elijah, and the divine cloud from which a voice speaks is more reminiscent of Mt. Sinai as a go-to place of divine-human interaction. Both Elijah and Moses encounter God at a desert mountain. And indeed, the Transfiguration mosaic remains central to the architecture in St. Catherine's Monastery at Mt. Sinai. And it is beside that mosaic that we find the two additional images of Moses at the burning bush and receiving the Ten Commandments. Jacob, following the biblical texts, leaves the mountain unnamed (in fact the only mountain mentioned in the homily is Mt. Nebo). Wherever the locale, Jacob emphasizes the divine glory there revealed:

> In Him there was light and it was covered up and they were not aware of it
> and out of Him He sent forth light and they saw His glory and they became
>   amazed [Lk 9:28–32].
> Belonging to Him and in Him there was glory which was hidden from the
>   onlookers.[23]

In this rendition of the Transfiguration scene, Jacob emphasizes that Jesus shone forth with his own light—it was always there, just hidden from the apostles' view. So unlike Moses, who was given light to radiate by an outside source, God, Jesus is that source, Son of God. To push this point Jacob emphasizes the divine glory (which is only mentioned in Luke), not only the light that shines forth. The Gospel texts describe Jesus as becoming white through his inner light shining forth, and this is understood to be the divine glory, and that glory is what rubs off on Moses (a little) and reflects *off* him, but shines *through* Jesus. In order to differentiate Jesus from Moses, Jacob has to make sure that God's glory, which is native also to Jesus, is the source of Jesus' transfiguring brightness. Jesus becomes one with the source, Moses remains just a carrier, a lamp to radiate the glory.

Yet Jacob also plays with the theme of hiddenness: just as Moses must hide the glory that reflects off him, Jesus must hide his own glory until the right moment. Throughout this homily Jacob plays with these Moses-Jesus parallels, yet

---

23. Jacob of Sarug, *Homily on the Transfiguration*, 171–75, trans. T. Kollamparampil, *Jacob of Sarug's Homily on the Transfiguration of Our Lord* (Piscataway, N.J.: Gorgias Press, 2008), 24–25.

always taking from Moses and giving to Jesus. As he noted in the *Homily on the Veil*, it is Jesus that makes Moses shine forth—that is, Moses reflects the glory of Jesus as much as he reflects the glory of the Father—for they are one and the same glory. Moses is exposed to it, but he remains apart from it.

Moreover, at this very important moment in the Gospel narratives Jacob describes Moses as handing over the keys of the kingdom. Moses ascended Sinai to receive the Law—the Law that described both how to live in God's kingdom on earth and how to achieve entry to the kingdom to come—and now Jesus' grace and sacrifice supersedes that Law. Moses must hand over the keys of prophecy to the apostles—for they will spread the gospel.

> The keys of Moses He wished to confer upon John [*Yohanan*] in order to give
>   him at the beginning to write spiritually,
> So that instead of the son of Amram, there entered the son of Zebedee,
> That he also should become a great teacher of the hidden mysteries of the divinity
>   [Mt 4:21; Mk 1:19]
> The authority which was with Elijah he had given to Simon,
> In order to loose and to bind divinely as the steward.
> He joined those of the household of Simon to the household of Moses,
> so as to make the New equal with the Old in his proclamation....
> He gave rest to Moses and set the toil upon John,
> He spared Elijah and brought to Simon to loose and to bind [Mt 16:19].
> He wished to ratify his new covenant,
> And he brought the old servants of His Father to subscribe to it.
> He called the apostles and brought the prophets to treat them as equal,
> So that He might manifest the single teaching of the truth to the whole world.
> He had united the New with the Old so that the world might become conscious
>   of the fact that He is the Lord, both of the latter and the former....
> He had wished to give rest to that Law which was through the hands of Moses,
>   and He summoned him to entrust the truth to Simon, and (then) to depart.[24]

Starting with the allusion to Matthew 16:19, in which Jesus gives the keys of the kingdom of heaven to Simon Peter, Jacob follows through with a whole drawer full of keys that need to change hands to complement Jesus' transfiguration. Moses passes his keys of teaching the divine Law to John, son of Zebedee; Elijah passes his keys of prophetic authority to Simon Peter; and Moses hands over his keys of writing to John. Yet, Simon is the steward of the divine word and somehow this word must replace, or better combine with,

---

24. Jacob of Sarug, *Transfiguration*, 215–37, trans. Kollamparampil, 30–33.

Moses's divine words. In short, it is a meeting of divinely touched minds. Elijah and Moses transmit whatever divinity, authority, teachings, and prophecies they have to Simon Peter and John so that the world can finally understand that what Moses and Elijah earlier taught (the Old) has been absorbed into and transfigured by the New. It is not that the Old and the New are really the same, nor that one simply replaces the other, but rather that the New is the Old in a remarkably better form. Thus for Jacob, the transfiguration scene is not just the moment when Jesus reveals his true nature, but when all the trappings of religion—Law, authority, ritual, and text—are passed from one generation of leaders to the next. Moses remains a central figure here as warden of the "keys" that pass on to Simon and John, yet Jacob notably demotes him. If before he was a type for Jesus, now Jacob pairs him with Simon and John, mere apostles. (See chapter 11, by Robin Jensen, in this volume, concerning the passing of authority from Moses to Simon Peter in the Roman tradition.)

5. Moses as Author of Genesis

Last, but not least, I present one more Moses, also to be found in both Ephrem and Jacob: this is the image of Moses as author of the book of Genesis. In both the opening and the closing passages of his commentary on the book of Genesis, Ephrem claims that Moses wrote the story of creation so that the world would have a written witness to creation and therefore to the Creator. He sums up this idea more poetically in the following hymn:

> In his book Moses
> Described the creation of the natural world
> So that both nature and Scripture
> Might bear witness to the Creator:
> Nature, through man's use of it,
> Scripture, through his reading of it.
> These are the witnesses
> Which reach everywhere,
> They are to be found at all times.
> Present at every hour
> Confuting the unbeliever
> Who defames the Creator.[25]

25. Ephrem, *Hymns on Paradise*, 5.2; trans. Sebastian Brock, in *St. Ephrem the Syrian: Hymns on Paradise* (Crestwood, N.Y.: St. Vladimir's Seminary, 1990), 102–3.

In this hymn, Ephrem suggests that Moses wrote down the creation narrative in order to enlighten the world, bearing witness to the Creator. Telling the story of the Creator's creation verifies the truth of the creation itself and thus the existence of the Creator (albeit through circular reasoning). Ephrem feels compelled to argue for creation and its Creator and against those who might mistakenly believe in an eternally existing world.

Nonetheless, what I find most fascinating here is the insistence that Moses authored the book, especially the creation stories. In his commentary, Ephrem notes that, while the stories were known from the days of Adam, Abraham's descendants forgot them, and thus the Children of Israel in Egypt recollected them not at all. God therefore brings Moses to prove the Egyptians wrong *and* to re-enlighten the Israelites: both with this text and with his miracles.

For Jacob, the very idea of contemplating creation brings him near to spiritual ecstasy. Yet to reach those heights he must first enter through Moses's text. In his *Homily on the First Day of Creation* he enthuses:

> Lo, [my] intellect rides through the heights to rise ever higher,
> that it might go and see, then come back to speak about creation.
> It is by reading Moses, the scribe of truth, that the mind
> Is enriched to speak of the wonder of creation.[26]

In this poem of 520 stanzas—about creation—Jacob mentions Moses twenty-eight times. And Jacob here insists that though the creation is God's alone, the words belong to Moses:

> Moses set it down at the highest point of prophecy,
> and he saw that [God] had come down to bring forth a creation as yet uncreated
> there came that first impetus from the Self-Existent One,
> and the signal went out and made nothing into something
> It was at this point that Moses began to speak:
> "In the beginning God created the heavens and the earth."[27]

And while Jacob is in awe of what Moses must have seen on the mountain, through his reading of Moses, Jacob also espouses and defends a theology of creation from nothing. While he was up on Mt. Sinai, Moses saw everything that God had created, but he declined to record his full vision. His sole pur-

---

26. Jacob of Sarug, *Homily on the Six Days of Creation: The First Day*, 55, trans. E. Mathews, *Jacob of Sarug's Homily on the Six Days of Creation: The First Day* (Piscataway, N.J.: Gorgias Press, 2009), 12.

27. Jacob of Sarug, *First Day of Creation*, 131–35, trans. Mathews, 22–23.

pose, as claimed also by Ephrem, was to reveal God's truth to the world: that there exists a Creator who created this physical world. Thus Moses did not feel inclined to write about angels and other "invisible" yet created things that were also created during the six days of creation. In this way, Jacob can defend a full creation of the visible and the invisible within the six days of creation and present Moses as the first among prophets. The rest of creation is revealed bit by bit through his "descendants": David, Isaiah, Ezekiel, Daniel, and all the prophets. Moses as author is also Moses as prophet—not just of the future, but of the past as well. And yet Jacob repeats the theme of concealment here. As with Moses's veil, the prophets conceal some of the truth because the time is not ripe to reveal it. Ironically, perhaps, Jacob's personal mystical journey, like Aphrahat's, also begins with Moses. While Aphrahat imitates Moses's *qaddishutha* for God, Jacob reads and contemplates Moses's written testimony about God.

Conclusion

So where does this leave us? I have presented five different Moses:

1. the mystical Moses,
2. the divine drudge, lawgiver Moses,
3. the unseeing Moses behind the veil,
4. Moses of the Transfiguration, and
5. Moses the author of the account of creation and the book of Genesis.

Do any of these representations of Moses relate backward (or forward), match, support, illustrate, or illuminate the Rabbula image we started with? In my mind Rabbula's Moses sits somewhere between Aphrahat's and Ephrem's. While not reaching the mystical union that Aphrahat aspires to, he clearly remains well above the rest of the Israelites, participating in God's glory or holiness in some manner, more than I think Ephrem allows him. With covered hands and bared feet he still, for me, reaches toward the divine glory, but his turned-away face perhaps indicates an inability, or resistance to full union (the veil?). He cannot or will not look directly at God. His role as master of concealment perhaps prevents him. Yet Moses successfully presents God's words to the faithful; perhaps, the words themselves should suffice a true mystic, as

Jacob seems to imply. The rabbis of this same period have no trouble painting Moses as larger than life, acknowledging that his ability to speak "mouth to mouth" with God puts him on a higher spiritual plane than any Israelite who came before him or any envious rabbi who came after. But they do not allow him full union with God.[28]

One would suspect, then, that the Syriac tradition keeps Moses one step behind or below Jesus. Moses, though superior to the other Israelites, remains inferior to Jesus. Yet the motifs of hiddenness continue to bring these various depictions together. God cannot be seen by just anyone, only by his selected one (Moses) or by those who self-select through asceticism (Aphrahat), or through assiduous study (Jacob); obviously Moses's veil represents many layers of hiddenness: God's full glory, Jesus' glory, and spiritual truth (Ephrem); Jesus' full glory is hidden until the Transfiguration, but its revelation is not enough until the master of hiding, Moses, bears witness to him and his glory (Jacob). Finally, the Scriptures themselves are veiled and contain deep secrets that Moses purposely hid (for safe keeping, mind you, not in defiance) until they could be revealed by God's ultimate messenger. In the Rabbula image, Moses covers his hands, while God reveals his. What does this mean? Perhaps this ultimate sacred game of hide and seek is the full story: faithful Christians will continue to desire total divine union as a primal religious desire and goal, even as it continues to remain elusive.

28. Naomi Koltun-Fromm, *Hermeneutics of Holiness* (New York: Oxford, 2010), chapter 7, on rabbinic holiness.

Paula Fredriksen

13. AGAINST THE MANICHAEAN MOSES

Augustine on Moses and Scripture

Antiquity had no category corresponding to what we think of as "religion." Relations between heaven and earth were commonly configured along ethnic lines. Divinities and humans both living and dead clustered into family groups, and these groups themselves commonly clustered around cities.[1] Protocols for maintaining good relations with one's gods were thought of as inherited, passed from generation to generation: *paradosis patrikōn, mos maiorum, hoi patria nomoi,* "ancestral custom." In anthropological terms, this meant that cult was an ethnic designation, and that ethnicity *eo ipso* was a cult designation.

---

1. Apollos, in Acts 18.24, is described as "of the *genos* of Alexandria." See the general discussion of such divine-human ethnic clusterings in P. Fredriksen, *Augustine and the Jews* (New Haven, Conn.: Yale University Press, 2010), 6–15; on their practical application within the world of ancient politics, C. P. Jones, *Kinship Diplomacy in the Ancient World* (Cambridge, Mass.: Harvard University Press, 1999); cf. its Jewish refraction in the Spartan-Judean *suggeneia* of 1 Macc 12:21 and Josephus, *Antiquities* 1.24–41, discussion in E. Gruen, "Jewish Perspectives on Greek Culture and Ethnicity," *Ancient Perceptions of Greek Ethnicity,* ed. I. Malkin (Cambridge, Mass.: Harvard University Press, 2001), 347–73; see too D. Miller, "Ethnicity Comes of Age: An Overview of Twentieth-Century Terms for *Ioudaios,*" *Currents in Biblical Research* 10, no. 2 (2012): 293–311. Gentile Christians ultimately would avail themselves no less of this idea that "religious" groups form kinship groups: Clement speaks of "the one *genos* of the saved people," *Miscellanies* 6.42.2; Polycarp, of the "*genos* of the righteous," *Martyrdom of Polycarp,* 14.1; on which the fundamental study is by D. Buell, *Why This New Race? Ethnic Reasoning in Early Christianity* (New York: Columbia University Press, 2005).

This ethnic configuration of heaven and earth had theological imp
tions. First (and like their humans), many ancient gods were also ethnic. Second, all gods existed, their existence attested by their people, their cult, their
city, their sancta. Different groups might argue for the relative importance or
power of one god or another (an issue that could be settled by war); philosophers might systematize relations between divinities; particular cities might
promote particular cults. But the existence of all gods was a fact of life presumed both by pagans and by those ancient groups whom we habitually designate "monotheists," namely, Jews and Christians.[2]

Hellenistic Jews, inhabiting the Graeco-Roman city, lived at close quarters with other gods. They made their peace with these foreign deities, generally demurring from public cult but finding other ways to show them respect.
The Bible itself, in its Greek voice, advised, "Do not revile the gods" (Ex 22:28
LXX).[3] All of these ancient deities, pagan or Jewish, could be brought into
relative position with each other by appeal to a common (and originally pagan) conceptualization, the idea that divinity was organized along a gradient.
Lower gods were *daimones*, "demons." Demonic deities tended to be local, involved in the material cosmos, and partial to blood sacrifices.[4] (For these reasons, some Gentiles—pagan and, later, Christian—identified the Jews' god as
a demon.) Jews returned the favor: "The gods of the nations are *daimones*,"
sang the Psalmist in Greek (Ps 95:5 LXX; cf. 1 Cor 10:20).[5]

Curiously, and despite their confidence in their god's ethnic loyalties,

2. On the inappropriateness of the unqualified use of the word "monotheist" to describe either Judaism or ancient Christianity, see Paula Fredriksen, "Mandatory Retirement: Ideas in the Study of Christian Origins Whose Time Has Come to Go," *Studies in Religion/Sciences Religieuses* 36 (2006): 231–46.

3. The Hebrew beneath the Greek had commanded "Do not revile the Lord." On this interesting
Hellenistic adaptation of this verse in Exodus, P. van der Horst, "'Thou Shalt Not Revile the Gods': The
LXX Translation of Exodus 22.28 (27), Its Background and Influence," *Studia Philonica* 5 (1993): 1–8.

4. On the daemonic organization of divinity, M. Kahlos, *Debate and Dialogue: Christian and Pagan Cultures, c. 360–430* (Aldershot: Ashgate, 2007); H. Chadwick, "Oracles of the End in the Conflict of Paganism and Christianity in the Fourth Century," in *Mémorial André-Jean Festugière: Antiquité
païenne et chrétienne*, ed. E. Lucchesi and H. D. Saffrey (Geneva: Patrick Cramer, 1984), 125–29; J. Rives,
"The Theology of Animal Sacrifice in the Ancient Greek World," in *Ancient Mediterranean Sacrifice*, ed.
J. Knust and Z. Várhelyi (New York: Oxford University Press, 2011), 187–202.

5. Christians developed the theme further, associating daemonic pagan gods with the fallen angels and their offspring of Gn 6:1–4 as developed in *1 Enoch* 1–35, e.g., Justin, *2 Apology* 5, on which see
Annette Y. Reed, "The Trickery of the Fallen Angels and the Demonic Mimesis of the Divine," *Journal
of Early Christian Studies* 12 (2004): 141–71; cf. too Augustine's comment on gods as demons, *de civ.
Dei* 9.23.

Jews also insisted that theirs was *the* universal deity, the supreme or highest god. Such a position stood in tension with the canons of philosophical
paideia, according to which the highest god was radically transcendent, eth-
nically nonspecific, utterly incorporeal, and certainly above any involvement
in matter, change, and time. Educated Hellenistic Jews, confronting their own
sacred texts with such criteria of ultimate sanctity in mind, squared this circle by developing allegorical interpretations, rewriting biblical texts through
commentary. And finally, two very ancient peculiarities of Jewish tradition—
its aniconism, and its cultic specificity limiting sacrifice in principle to Jerusalem—further facilitated Yahweh's Hellenistic makeover. The prayer-houses of
diaspora communities held neither cultic statues nor altars. These facts combined to persuade even so unsympathetic an outsider as Tacitus: on the basis
of the Jews' aniconism and non-sacrifice, he concluded that they worshiped
sola mente, thereby paying homage, he said, to the high god (*History* 5.4).

I review this cultic and theological terrain in order to place in context a
late Latin Manichaean interpretation of Moses, and Augustine's response to
it. Manichaeism had come out of Persia in the late third century, and its original theology can be understood as a creative Christian refraction of Zoroastri-
an dualism. But as they travelled west, Manichaean missionaries encountered
other Christian communities and absorbed aspects of their teachings. Para-
mount among these were elements drawn ultimately from Marcion and from
various catholic traditions *contra Iudaeos*.[6] What concerns us here is the way
that the fourth-century North African Latin Manichaean tradition mobilized
this Western theological amalgam to construct its polemical portrait of Moses. (That Manichaean tradition is most famously displayed in the *Capitula* of
Faustus, Manichaean bishop of Milevis in Numidia, now in modern Algeria;
but the *Capitula* survive only in Augustine's rejoinder, his *contra Faustum*.)[7]

In the early second century, in keeping with antiquity's commonsense association of particular divinities with particular ethnicities, Marcion had distinguished between the Jewish god (the active, ethnic deity presented in Jew-

6. I. Gardner and S. Lieu, *Manichaean Texts from the Roman Empire* (Cambridge: Cambridge University Press, 2004) provides an excellent one-volume introduction to Western Manichaeism. On the
Marcionite exegetical legacy, M. Tardieu, "Principes de l'exégèse manichaéenne du Nouveau Testament,"
Les Règles de l'Interprétation, ed. M. Tardieu (Paris: Éditions du Cerf, 1987), 123–28; on the Manichees'
absorption of catholic traditions *contra Iudaeos*, Fredriksen, *Augustine and the Jews*, 213–89.

7. August. *contra Faustum*, ed. J. Zycha, CSEL 25 (Vienna: Tempsky, 1891). All English translations
of this text are my own.

ish scriptures) and the highest god. The Jewish god, who presided over the Jewish people and who dwelt in Judea, was the source of Jewish law. The highest god, by contrast, a transcendent non-ethnic deity associated with pure spirit, goodness, light, and love, said Marcion, was the father of Jesus Christ. Marcion made his case exegetically, contrasting Law and Gospel, counterposing passages from the LXX to others drawn from the ten letters of his Pauline corpus and his version of Luke's gospel (the *Antitheses*). Instantiating this theology textually, Marcion also urged that Christians relinquish the Jewish scriptures to the Jews, putting in their place a specifically, and heavily Pauline, Christian canon, a "new" testament.[8]

Some hundred and thirty years later, Mani, like Paul, presented himself to his community as "the apostle of Jesus Christ." Unlike Paul, Mani self-consciously wrote new scriptures, a five-book canon for his mission church. Marcion had had to evolve a theory of interpolations to conform his new testament's texts to his theology. He went through Paul's letters and the gospel, "purging" them of "later" Judaizing additions, thereby (in his view) restoring the texts to their original non- or post-Jewish message. Standing on their own scriptures, by contrast, Western Manichees could be equally critical of the New Testament as well as the Old: both, in their view, were "too Jewish." Far from dismissing these texts on that account, however, Western Manichees developed a highly sophisticated critical biblical exegesis that bolstered their theological points of principle. This close critical reading, in many ways a legacy from Marcion, was one of the Manichees' most effective missionary techniques among less exotic Mediterranean Christians.[9]

But Manichaean theology was mapped onto a cosmos different from Marcion's. Marcion's Graeco-Roman universe was hierarchically organized, with immaterial spirit superior to the flesh or matter that was its contrast: redemption, like the high god to which the saved soul ascended, was purely spir-

<hr/>

8. On Marcion's theology and the place of the Judaean god within it, P. Fredriksen, *Sin: The Early History of an Idea* (Princeton, N.J.: Princeton University Press, 2012), 62–79; on the ways that Marcion's reading of Paul undergirds his theology, J. Marshall, "Misunderstanding the New Paul: Marcion's Transformaton of the *Sonderzeit* Paul," *Journal for Early Christian Studies* 20, no.1 (2012): 1–29; see too J. Lieu, "'As Much My Apostle as Christ Is Mine': The Dispute over Paul between Tertullian and Marcion," *Early Christianity* 1 (2010): 41–59.

9. On the similarities and differences between Marcion's and Mani's respective readings of NT texts, especially the Pauline letters, Tardieu, "Exégèse manichaéene," 142–44.

itual.[10] The Jewish god, in this scheme, as an ethnic, cosmogonic deity, was ipso facto but neutrally "lower," as was *demiourgos* to *ho theos*. Manichaeans, by contrast, besides being materialist, were true dualists. Their universe was organized around two independent and eternally opposed principles, Good and Evil, whose material interpenetration defined the world's moral condition. Particles of light, trapped in Evil's kingdom, could be liberated and returned to their proper place only through the purificatory practices of the Manichaean elect.[11] Like Marcion, the Manichees identified the principle of goodness with the highest god, the father of Jesus Christ. Unlike Marcion, however, they identified the good god's *opponent*, the ruler of darkness, with the demonic god of the Jews. More than merely subordinate, the Jewish god in their system was actually evil.[12]

Faustus wrote his *Capitula* in the mid-380s. Organized around a selection of talking points, themselves catholic challenges to Manichaeism, Faustus intended his handbook as an aid to missionaries to help them engage and persuade North African catholic Christians (August. *c. Faustum* 1.2). The *Capitula* well communicates the constitutive anti-Judaism of late Latin Manichaeism. Throughout, Faustus bound together a close reading of the catholic double canon and the normative theology that distinguished between the high god and the demiurgic god with a more global indictment of Jewish fleshliness.[13] Faustus's close reading of scripture drew much from Marcion. His distinction between non-ethnic high god and ethnic lower god stemmed ultimately from Greco-Roman paideia. And his indictment of Jewish fleshliness especially echoed catholic traditions *contra Iudaeos,* on display in such texts as Justin's *Trypho* and Tertullian's *contra Marcionem.*[14]

These two earlier writers had indicted the Jews as a way to save the OT and its god for their church: if the Law seemed offensive, carnal, and religious-

10. Marcion's reading of 1 Cor 15:50—"Flesh and blood cannot inherit the kingdom of God"—was much more straightforward than Tertullian's, given the latter's commitment to the resurrection of the flesh: adv. Marc. 5.10 passim; 12.6; 14.4.

11. Jason BeDuhn provides an excellent introduction to these rituals of purification in *The Manichaean Body in Discipline and Ritual* (Baltimore, Md.: Johns Hopkins University Press, 2000).

12. Cf. Marcion's more neutral theology, Marshall, "Misunderstanding the New Paul," 12–18.

13. "By their censures of the catholic faith, *and chiefly by their destructive criticism of the Old Testament,*" Augustine observed, "the Manichees affect the unlearned," *de util. cred.* 2.4.

14. See, for instance, Justin, *Dialogue* 19–23, on Israel and the Golden Calf; similarly Tertullian, *adv. Marc.* 4.31.4ff.; Fredriksen, *Augustine and the Jews,* 223–40; and Fredriksen, *Sin,* 85–89.

ly wrong, the fault lay not with the god who gave the Law but with the people to whom he gave it. It was *their* carnality that had called forth such laws.[15] Faustus appropriated the argument, though not its goal, combining his negative criticisms of scripture and of the (lower, demonic) god of the Jews with a baroque iteration of catholic charges of Jewish turpitude, and a blanket rejection of Judaism itself. Or, as he succinctly stated his position, "We [Manichees] are enemies … of Judaism" (August. *c. Faust.* 22.2).

Faustus brings all of his criticisms together around the figure of Moses.[16] Moses is multiply indicted—as a terrible sinner, as the author of a bad book and giver of bad laws to a bad people, as a purveyor of a flawed god and of flawed ideas about God, and as a blasphemer against Christ and his church. Such a man, with such ideas, Faustus urges, can hardly have prophesied Christ. Faustus mobilized these arguments in order to sever any connection between the two testaments, undermining catholic confidence in the double canon. If Moses's books refer solely to the Jews, and to the powerless Jewish god long ago defeated by Rome, why should the church, like an unfaithful wife, intercept writings from this lord, who was different from and lower than her true spouse (*c. Faust.* 15.1)? And if these Jewish books cannot serve to foretell Christ, then what possible relevance to the (true) Christian could they have?

Augustine disputed Faustus's arguments in the thirty-three books of his *c. Faustum.* Only five of these are taken up with Faustus's attacks on the New Testament. Assorted criticisms of monotheism (pagan, Christian, and Jewish) take up a further four books; arguments against the Incarnation, another nine. But fully fourteen books—by far the greatest concentration of Faustus's arguments, and thus of Augustine's efforts—are given over to the assault on the Old Testament: its absurd and repugnant laws, its fleshly promises, the deeply flawed character of its god and its heroes.[17] Faustus also makes a commonsense "ethnic" argument: since most of the church is made up of Gentiles, and

15. This pattern of heresiological works' deploying the most virulent rhetoric *adversus Iudaeos* was first noted by D. Efroymson, "The Patristic Connection," in *Anti-Semitism and the Foundations of Christianity*, ed. A. Davies (New York: Paulist Press, 1979): 98–117.

16. Rightly noted by Alban Massie: "Moïse est celui que Faustus critique le plus … il reflétait la malignité du Dieu dont il se voulait le prophète," *Peuple Prophétique et Nation Témoin: Le peuple juif dans le* Contra Faustum manichaeum *de saint Augustin* (Paris: Institut des Études Augustiniennes, 2011), 178–79.

17. These are books 4, 6, 8, 9, 10, 12, 13, 14, 15, 16, 22, 25, 32, and 33.

the Law—which Gentiles don't observe in any case—is for the Jews, then the Jewish books should be left to them, too.[18]

It is his construction of Moses that serves Faustus as the rhetorical fulcrum by means of which he leverages these arguments of his broader polemic. Faustus opens his frontal attack on Moses in book 14. "If you ask why we do not believe in Moses," he begins, "it is on account of our love and reverence for Christ." Moses's blasphemies against things human and divine are bad enough, Faustus continues, but worse is "the awful curse he has pronounced upon Christ the Son of God, who for our salvation hung on a tree.... His words are, 'Cursed is everyone who hangs on a tree.'"[19]

Faustus gets a lot of mileage out of this one line, stretching its implications in four different directions. First, he says, Moses must have cursed Christ either intentionally or unintentionally. If intentionally, then he blasphemed; if unintentionally, then he was no prophet. Second, Moses's curse also repudiates the sufferings of Peter, Andrew, and other apostolic martyrs thought to have died by crucifixion: How can he have been a true prophet if he denounces men such as these? Third, Moses's curse is nonsensical: how could he not distinguish between those who are rightly hanged (like criminals), and those (like Christ, or like Peter) who were hanged wrongly? "Perhaps," Faustus speculates, "Moses was in the habit of cursing every good thing," and he brings up, specifically, Dt 25:5–10: "Cursed is everyone who does not raise up seed in Israel." This curse not only targets all those vowed to chastity, but also the chaste Jesus himself. "Moses hurls his curses against Christ, against light, against chastity, against everything divine." Some holy man! Some prophet!

Book 16 of the *c. Faustum* develops these themes further. There Faustus points to those New Testament verses in which Jesus seems to assert the Jewish scriptures' witness to himself, for instance, at John 5:46: "Moses wrote of me, and if you believed Moses, you would also believe me" (16.1). "I am quite willing to believe that Moses, though so much the opposite of Christ, may seem to have written of him," Faustus continues. "Why may we not take the prophecies of Christ from a religion whose rites we condemn as useless?"—the approach to the Old Testament and the Law that Faustus had elsewhere

18. See, for instance, August. *c. Faust.* 6.1, 9.1, 13.1.
19. Dt 21:23/Gal 3:10; August. *c. Faust.* 14.1.

identified as hypocritical, inconsistent, and catholic.[20] "We do not hate the unclean spirits less because they confessed plainly and openly that Jesus was the Son of God. If any similar testimony is found in Moses, I will accept it. But I will not on this account be subjected to Moses' law, which to my mind is pure paganism" (16.1; we will see shortly why Faustus says this).

But *does* Jesus declare that Moses wrote about him? That is the question. Faustus points out that Jesus, when arguing with the Jews, refers to the Torah as "*your* Law." Jesus did not actually quote Moses in this passage, nor did he claim to, or the Jews would have challenged him. Their silence, Faustus concludes, proves that [the historical] "Jesus never made such a statement" (*c. Faust.* 16.2). Here we see the polemical benefit of Faustus's critical reading of the NT texts. Marcion, as we have noted, in theory would have regarded such a statement as a Judaizing interpolation: excising it would restore the text to its putative original state. Faustus, on the other hand, sees the entire gospel text as produced by *nescio quibus … semi-Iudaeis,* "obscure half-Jews." The entirety of the text was suspect, "discordant and diverse" (33.3). For Manichees, the NT was not "scripture," but something closer to apocrypha. Its claims that Moses witnessed to Christ, therefore, were *not* to be taken on faith.

So much for NT verses that speak of prophecies in the OT. What about those passages in the OT that catholics take to point ahead to the NT? "What about that passage that you often quote," says Faustus, "where Moses' god says to him, 'I will raise up from among them a prophet like you'" (Dt 28:66; *c. Faust.* 16.4)? Jews see immediately that this does not refer to Christ; Christians should see that even more clearly. Not only was Christ not a prophet: he was not at all like Moses, nor Moses like him. Moses was merely human; Christ was God. Moses was a sinner; Christ was sinless. Moses was born in the ordinary human way; "according to you, Christ was born of a virgin; according to me, he was not born at all." (Manichaean Christology was Docetic.) Moses offended his god, and so died upon a mountain; Christ died voluntarily, and God was well pleased with him. Christ could not be less like Moses. Clearly, then, this Deuteronomic verse can have nothing to do with him.

---

20. "I reject circumcision as disgusting; so do you.… I reject sacrifice as idolatry; so do you.… Both of us regard Passover and Sukkot as useless and needless.… both of us despise and deride the various laws against mixing types of cloth, or species of animals.… You cannot blame me for rejecting the Old Testament, because you reject it as much as I do.… You deceitfully praise with your lips what you hate in your heart. I'm just not deceitful, that's all." August. *c. Faust.* 6.1; see too 18.1.

Finally, Moses gave (absurd) laws about Sabbath, circumcision, food, and sacrifices, which Faustus frequently characterizes as "disgusting." Of all of these, the most self-evidently inculpating were the laws concerning blood offerings. Pure paganism, charged Faustus: "I reject blood sacrifices as idolatry; and so do you" (c. Faust. 6.1). Here Faustus echoes a long catholic tradition whose North African Latin roots trace back to Tertullian, who in turn drew on Justin. For all of these Christians, blood sacrifices were intrinsically bound up with wrong religion, the worship of idols, taught to humanity by the fallen angels of Genesis 6 and their demonic offspring.[21] Why then would God have mandated such cult to Israel? Because Jews were themselves prone to idol worship, as they demonstrated in the notorious incident of the Golden Calf.[22] God accordingly gave Israel the laws of sacrifice, permitting them to imitate this form of pagan worship as long as it was focused on him alone,[23] on the principle, evidently, that "worshiping the right god in the wrong way is better than worshiping the wrong god altogether."[24]

For the catholic contra Iudaeos tradition, in other words, though the god who had been worshiped in this way was the "Christian" god, the practice of blood offerings was itself purely pagan. Given that Faustus thought that the god who gave these laws and who was worshiped through these offerings was not the father of Christ, his position was more consistent. Not only were these practices pagan; so too were Moses's laws, and (for that matter) Moses's god.

But the Jews were so attached to these fleshly laws, continued Faustus, that they rejected Jesus, because he preached against them (c. Faust. 16.6). Contemporary catholic Christians, Faustus notes, completely (and rightly) disregard Moses's laws. Why then don't they acknowledge forthrightly what they otherwise presuppose, namely, that Jesus himself opposed and rejected Moses's laws as well? Thus, Faustus concludes, the verse in the fourth Gospel is again proven false: "If you believed Moses, you would have believed me also, because Moses wrote of me" (Jn 5:46). But Moses never wrote of Jesus. And,

---

21. Justin, *Second Apology* 5.

22. The claim had been prepared by Stephen's speech in Acts 7:35–53, where Luke, through reference to the Calf and through his careful use of phrases like "made with human hands," returns to a sense that the sin of idolatry is ethnic, no longer the "pagan" sin *par excellence*, it becomes the "Jewish" sin *par excellence*; see Fredriksen, *Sin*, 82–87.

23. Justin, *Dialogue with Trypho*, 22.

24. D. Ullucci, "Contesting the Meaning of Animal Sacrifice," in Knust and Várhelyi, *Ancient Mediterranean Sacrifice*, 57–74, at 68.

in light of how opposed their teachings are, how could anyone believe in both of them in any case? (16.7) By believing in Christ, the Christian ipso facto *dis*believes in Moses. Catholics should thus stop referring to the Ten Commandments together with the rest of the "disgusting precepts about circumcision and sacrifice," Faustus opines: to refer to all these as "the Law" is unconscionably imprecise (22.2). Let "Law" stand just for the Ten Commandments, which sit in a befouled context, the Jews' books.

The Jewish *laws* are bad enough; but Moses's god is even worse:

These books ... portray a god so ignorant of the future that he gave Adam a command without knowing that he would break it.... Envy made him fear that a human being might eat of the tree of life and live forever. Later, he was greedy for blood and fat from all kinds of sacrifices, and jealous if these were offered to anyone other than himself. At times his enemies infuriated him, at other times, his friends. Sometimes he destroyed thousands of men over little; at other times, over nothing. And he threatened to come with a sword and to spare no one, whether the righteous or the wicked. (August. *c. Faust.* 22.4)

Clearly, a deity so morally defective had nothing to do with God the Father. This deity is god only to the Jews. They and their god have in fact set their sign upon one another. "This is for purposes of mutual recognition," suggests Faustus. Their god gave the Jews "the disgusting mark of circumcision, so that in whatever land or among whatever people they might find themselves, they can be recognized as his. And they call him the god of their fathers, so that, wherever he might be, among whatever crowd of gods, he knows he's addressed when he hears 'the god of Abraham, Isaac and Jacob'" (25.1). This ethnic, lower god, of course, cannot be the divine father of Christ.

Moses's deity, meanwhile, is well matched by Moses's heroes:

We [Manichees] are not the ones who wrote that Abraham, enflamed by his frantic craving for children, did not fully trust God's promise that Sara his wife would conceive. And then—even more shamefully, for he did so with his wife's knowledge—he rolled around with a mistress. And later—in fact, on two different occasions—he marketed his own marriage, out of avarice and greed selling Sara into prostitution to two different kings, ... claiming duplicitously that his wife was his own sister, because she was very beautiful. And what about Lot, ... who lay with his own two daughters? ... And Isaac who, imitating his father, passed off his wife Rebecca as his sister, so that he could shamefully benefit from her? ... And Jacob, Isaac's son, who had four wives and who rutted around like a goat among them? ... And Judah, his son, who slept with Tamar, his own daughter-in-law? (August. *c. Faust.* 22.4)

But what would you expect? Just look at the author of these tales, Faustus urges. Moses himself committed murder. He was a thief. He commanded cruelties and performed them himself. This is Faustus's quick summation of Moses's killing the Egyptian (Ex 2:12), of his despoiling the Egyptians before leaving the country (Ex 12:35–36), and of his various demands that Israelites kill other Israelites or butcher others in battle (Ex 17:9). To a fourth-century Christian mendicant ascetic, as well as to his late Latin catholic audience, this is clearly not the profile of a holy man. Savage in war, sexually undisciplined ("not content with one wife," *c. Faust.* 22.5), of impure and defiled mind (since to the pure all things are pure, whereas so many of Moses's laws concerned impurity, (*c. Faust.* 31.1; cf. Ti 1:15–16)—Moses, concluded Faustus, Moses's laws, Moses's people, Moses's god, and Moses's book are (rightly) all of a piece. How can catholics countenance such things? No wonder they pick and choose what little they can use of Moses's text, and disregard the rest (*c. Faust.* 32.1). "You sip so daintily from the Old Testament that your lips are scarcely wet!" (32.7).

Of all his enormous literary production—some five million words *in toto*—Augustine referred to three works in particular as *magna opera*, "huge efforts." One, begun when he was in his thirties and not finished until he was in his seventies, was his handbook on biblical interpretation, the *de doctrina Christiana* (1.1). The second, in twenty-two books, was his *City of God* (*magnum opus et arduum*, Praefatio). The third, in thirty-three books, was his *contra Faustum* (see his *Retractationes* 2.7.1). These last two treatises had been long, difficult slogs against a lot of rhetorical headwind; and many of Augustine's signature arguments about history, about the importance of historical context for interpreting the Bible, and about moral intention distinguishing the seemingly similar actions of various agents, on prominent display in *de civitate Dei*, are rehearsed and indeed perfected in his response to Faustus's challenge. By calling into question the status of the Old Testament vis-à-vis Christian revelation, Faustus had also called into question fundamental catholic teachings—about creation, about Incarnation, and about bodily redemption. In defending the OT, Augustine was defending (as he saw it) Christianity. And to defend catholic Christianity, Augustine first of all had to mount an apology for Moses.

One example of how he does this is by affirming Faustus's reading but reversing his interpretation. For example, Faustus had insisted that, in penning Deuteronomy 21:23, Moses had in effect cursed Christ. Augustine undermines Faustus's point by vigorously concurring. In so doing, he makes Moses's curse into a defense of the Incarnation: only an enfleshed and truly human Christ could assume the curse of death on behalf of humanity, thus bringing humanity to eternal life. (The argument goes on for eleven columns in the PL: I condense it here—*c. Faust.* 14.2–12.) Augustine's point is that Moses indeed curses Christ; and that in so "cursing" Christ, Moses witnessed to catholic Christology.

What about Moses's other curse, which supposedly indexed his hostility to continence and virginity? On this point, Augustine deploys his idea, developed at length in his prior treatise the *de doctrina Christiana* (3.10.15–12.20), that behaviors are specific to historical periods. Thus, he now says against Faustus, in the period before the coming of Christ, "the continuation of the people was a civil duty" (*c. Faust.* 14.13). In the present (that is, in c. 399 C.E.) things are different; but that implies no culpability for those who were sexually active earlier. Moses's exhortation to Israel to produce children thus indicates no principled hostility to continence: the one ethic was appropriate to the earlier period, the other, to the period after Christ. Or, as Augustine says elsewhere in this treatise, the differences between Moses's teaching and the church's teaching is not one of doctrine, but "of the times" (*tempora*; 16.28).

What about the many differences between Moses's character and that of Christ? Complaining about "the string of showy antitheses with which you try to ornament your dull discourse," Augustine proceeds to defend Moses, arguing further that precise episodes in Moses's life prefigure typologically episodes in the life of Christ (*c. Faust.* 16.15–16). If Faustus can show how Moses and Christ are unlike, Augustine can (and does) turn the exercise around and show how they are like (16.18). Through this appeal to typology, Augustine demonstrates that the entire OT—not just the first five books, but the whole of the law, the prophets, and the writings—"speak everywhere of Christ [*Christum igitur sonant haec omnia*]" (22.94).

What about Jesus' supposed hostility to Moses, his teaching and acting specifically against Moses's laws? Here Augustine debuts a "historical Jesus" quite different from that figure constructed, only a few years prior, in *de doctrina Christiana*. There, Augustine had insisted that Jesus had angered his

Jewish contemporaries because he treated the Torah with flagrant disregard.[25] Now, against Faustus, he urges that Jesus had not only kept the Law, but that he did so more fully and faithfully than had these other Jews. In fact, the issue between Jesus and his contemporaries was not that they had adhered to Moses's Law, but that they had not. "Christ did not break any of God's commandments, but found fault with those who did so" (*c. Faust.* 16.24). The Jews did not believe in Christ *not* because of their supposed attachment to the Law, but, on the contrary, because they were not attached to the Law. They did not fulfill even the plain precepts of Moses (16.32; cf. Mt 23:23–24). So scrupulously did Jesus keep the Law, by comparison, that he was careful to honor it even in death. This was why Jesus died by Friday afternoon, putting down his fleshly body well before Shabbat came in, resting in the tomb all of Shabbat, and not rising again in the flesh until after Shabbat was out (16.29). Augustine's point: how "pagan" could Moses's laws have been, how directed toward a wrong god, if Christ himself had gone to such pains to keep them?

What then about the shocking character of Moses's god, and of Moses's heroes? Particularly in book 22—with ninety-eight chapters, the longest in the *c. Faustum*—Augustine defends Moses's presentation. He deflects Faustus's descriptions of the biblical god by constructing a rhetorical pagan who makes the same ostensibly embarrassing observations about Christ in the New Testament. Again and again, Augustine demonstrates how Faustus's descriptions of God could be drawn, also, from NT scenes with Christ—*if* one were to read in the intellectually flat-footed way that Faustus does. Moses's god seems astonished? Does that make Christ, too, astonished when he says of the centurion, "Truly, I have not found such great faith in Israel"? Clearly not. "Thus an irreligious pagan might bring the same reproaches against Christ in the gospel that Faustus brings against God in the Old Testament" (*c. Faust.* 22.14, which goes on for two columns to show how Christ might be seen as fearful, timid, greedy for blood, and so on).

What about the "pure paganism" of Moses's blood sacrifices? Here Augustine has to argue not only against Faustus, but also against some two centuries of catholic tradition that had made the same case. Typological coherence provides the bulwark of Augustine's defense: an attack on blood sacrifice is an attack against Christian salvation, wrought through the crucifixion of the

---

25. August. *de doc. Chr.* 3.6.10.

(necessarily incarnate) Christ. "Faustus reproaches God in reference to those animal sacrifices which prefigured the sacrifice of blood-shedding by which we were redeemed" (*c. Faust.* 22.14). "These sacrifices typified what we now rejoice in, *for we can be purified only by blood, and we can be reconciled to God only by blood.* The fulfillment of these types is in Christ.... Whatever kind of sacrifice you name, I will show you that it prophesies Christ" (18.6). "God, using certain types, prefigured the true sacrifice" (22.21).

Justin and Tertullian had argued similarly, also saying that the true meaning of the sacrifices was that they typologically prefigured Christ. But theirs had been an either-or approach: since the sacrifices' true meaning was Christ, the Jews had been wrong to actually make blood offerings. Augustine, however, and uniquely in the patristic literature known to me, insists that the Jews had been *right* to sacrifice. That way they enacted in historical time the *actuality* of Christ's sacrifice, which to work could be accomplished only by a truly incarnate savior.[26] Thinking semiotically, Augustine urges further that "material symbolic acts," *corporalia sacramenta*, are a kind of visible speech, *verba visibilia* (*c. Faust.* 19.15). Actions, like verbs, have "tenses," a temporal aspect.[27] The blood sacrifices of the Jews, the sacrifice of Christ, and the sacrifice of the Eucharist thus vary according to their symbolic actions, their visible *verba*; but they are all temporal phases of the *same* Law, and all articulate the *same* mystery. For this reason, he concludes, the whole Jewish people, whether they understood the symbolism of the sacrifices (as Moses did) or not, had been a great prophet, prefiguring in deed as well as in word the (catholic) redemption in Christ (4.2; 13.15; 22.24).

But, Faustus—or Tertullian, for that matter—could object that typology does not address the fundamental problem with this mode of worship, namely its demonic origins. Augustine here turns this long tradition, too, on its head. It

26. Fredriksen, *Augustine and the Jews*, 246–59; see also 314–19.

27. "With spoken language, the form of the verb changes in terms of the letters and syllables according to its tense: 'done' indicates past action, 'to be done' indicates future action. Why then, likewise, should those symbols which declare the death and resurrection of Christ not differ from those older symbols which only predicted these things? We perceive a difference in the sound and in the form of words if they indicate past or future: 'has suffered' and 'about to suffer,' 'has risen' and 'about to rise.' So too with material symbolic acts, a form of visible speech which, though sacred, is also changeable and transitory. For while God is eternal, the water of baptism—in fact, every corporeal aspect of rite—is transitory. And the very word 'God,' which must be pronounced in the consecration, is only a sound that passes away in a moment. The actions and sounds pass away ... but the spiritual gift that they communicate is eternal," August. *c. Faust.* 19.15.

is true, he says, that demons taught blood sacrifices to pagans. But this was because they knew that God intended such worship for Israel. In other words, Jews did not imitate pagans when they made blood offerings; rather, pagans, because of this demonic instruction, were imitating Israel (*c. Faust.* 22.17–18). And furthermore, he insists, arguing "historically" from the case of Abel, it is further clear that blood offerings had always pleased God (22.17). Deceitful demonic mediation therefore cannot undermine sacrifice's rightful and holy function, namely, to foretell redemption through the blood of the truly incarnate Christ.

What then of the unfortunate sex lives of Moses, and of so many of the men whom Moses wrote about? Augustine labors long over the details of Faustus's critique, arguing for example that Abraham did not *exactly* lie when he called Sarah his sister, he just withheld information, not adding that she was also his wife (*c. Faust.* 22.31–37). Lot's behavior with his daughters proves a little more difficult to domesticate for the defense. On this point, Augustine comments that he "defends sacred scripture, not man's sins": "In the story of Lot's daughters, the action is related, not commended" (22.45). What about Jacob and his four wives? "A plurality of wives was no crime when it was custom" (22.47). But still: all that sexual activity? Augustine responds that while the patriarchs did have sex, because of their extraordinary discipline of mind, they didn't particularly enjoy it.[28] Their appetites controlled, their activity was strictly determined and constrained by their desire to have children, the sole legitimate end of marital intercourse.

Had Faustus been less corrupted by the "shocking tenets of his sect"— which held that intercourse was permissible as long as it did *not* eventuate in procreation—then he, too, would have seen scripture's obvious meaning in this regard (*c. Faust.* 22.50). From this point, Augustine embarks on another long typological analysis of the meaning of Jacob's four wives (22.51–59, seven columns), finally dismissing Faustus's observations as shabby tactics, an effort to discredit the Incarnation by bringing reproach on Christ's fleshly ancestors. As for the unelevating story of Judah's behavior with his daughter-in-law Tamar, the episode typified the future good of salvation. (It takes Augustine four columns to tease this *tupos* out of the story: I condense.)

---

28. "The holy patriarchs in their conjugal intercourse were actuated *not* by the love of pleasure, but by their intelligent desire for the continuance of their family. Thus the number ... of wives does not make the patriarchs licentious," August. *c. Faust.* 22.48; see further Fredriksen, *Augustine and the Jews*, 335–37.

So much for sex: what about murder? This criticism touches not only on what Moses wrote, but also on how Moses himself had acted. "This great and good man should not be judged by Faustus's malicious representations of him, but from what God says of him," instructs Augustine. "We love and admire his servant Moses, and to the best of our power we imitate him, falling far short of his merits, even though we have killed no Egyptian, nor plundered anyone, nor carried on any war ... which in the latter case was commanded by God" (c. Faust. 22.69). Moses's killing the Egyptian, like Paul's persecuting the church, and like Peter's cutting the ear off the chief priest's servant, was a mark of zealous commitment. God works with such zeal, and in such leaders it bodes well for the future (22.70). Besides, when he did execute wars at God's command, Moses demonstrated not ferocity, but obedience (22.74). For the rest of this passage, Augustine sketches his ideas on just war, both its motivations and its conduct (22.74–77). Besides, Christ in the New Testament, like God in the Old Testament, likewise counsels his followers to arm themselves (22.77): "It is therefore mere mindless calumny to charge Moses with making war" (22.78). As for the slaughter of only some of those who had worshiped the Calf, those people were killed according to the "secret judgment" of God's inscrutable will: Moses obeyed, and God had his reasons for choosing the particular victims of the slaughter (22.79).

Augustine's main point throughout book 22 is a hermeneutic one: "In foretelling good, it does not matter whether the type is itself good or bad." "The merit or demerit of the [narrative] agents is not important, as long as the action and the thing signified truly correspond" (c. Faust. 22.83). Thus, Tamar is a stand-in for the church, gathered from the corruption of Gentile superstition (22.89); Moses's killing the Egyptian is a type of Christ slaying the devil (22.90); the incident with the Calf becomes, astonishingly, a prediction of the salvation of the Gentiles by the apostles and the church (22.92–94).[29] True, then, scripture contains many difficult passages, and a parade of flawed heroes. This is its strength. The proofs that the episodes of the Old Testament prophesied events in the life of Christ and his church is, Augustine concludes, "irresistibly strong."[30] The Old Testament has *everything* to do with

---

29. Fredriksen, *Augustine and the Jews*, 248–49. Even for the genre, Augustine's associations are baroque.

30. August. *c. Faust.* 22.96.

the New Testament. Moses cannot have more clearly spoken of (the catholic) Christ. And Faustus cannot have been more wrong.

There are so many moving parts to Augustine's prolix rejoinder to Faustus's *Capitula* that it is easy to become enmeshed in all the gears. If however we hold on to the basic idea that in antiquity cult was an ethnic designation, and ethnicity a cult designation, that gods and humans in antiquity formed kinship groups, we might better see how many of these parts fit together, particularly as concerns the figure of Moses.

The dipoles of Faustus's theology determined much of his anti-Judaism. This lower, fleshy cosmos was evil; any involvement in its organization was *eo ipso* evil as well. Thus the moral valence of the Jews' god slipped into an entirely negative register: what for Valentinus or Marcion had been merely a demiurgic deity became for Latin Manichaeism an actively evil one.

Faustus expressed this theology in an *ethnic* key in two ways. First, he defined as "Christian" only those who knew the true identity of God the Father: by his lights, the Manichees alone. *Everyone* else—pagans, Jews, and other sorts of Christians—believed that there was only one sole high principle. In effect, this broke humanity into only two *gentes*: the Manichees, and everybody else. Jews and Christians, Faustus held, were *also* pagans, because they worshiped a false god (20.3–4). "In fact, only two truly distinct groups exist: you gentiles, and we Manichees." People are identified with and by the gods they worship.

Second, and availing himself of normative Christian traditions *contra Iudaeos*, Faustus reviled the Jewish law and the Jewish people as intrinsically, hopelessly, helplessly carnal. This fleshliness was on full display in the books of Moses, with all their getting and begetting and fleshly feasting and sacrificing. And it was particularly broadcast morally by the people who kept Moses's laws in their villainy toward Christ, whom Moses had cursed. Again, gods run in the blood. Let this awful god, Faustus urged, stay with his awful people. Having pried the Old Testament loose from Christian canon, Faustus could then work on the unseemly Jewishness of the New. By the time he (or the missionary following his instruction) was finished, the catholic listener would be ready to begin to learn of Mani's revelations—the sole access to the true Christ, and the true God the Father.

The carnal, morally obtuse Moses served as Faustus's rhetorical whipping-boy for all these points. Moses was the unquestioned author (or medium) of Jewish law. His books were inimical to true Christianity; those loyal to them were the enemies of Christ. Moses's unquestionable ethnicity and the ethnicity of his laws made Faustus's points for him. Moses served in this sense as the *pars pro toto* of fleshly Israel.

Augustine, pushed by Faustus, had to focus particularly on Moses as well. Thus he insists that Moses was a faithful prophet, and that the books he assembled teemed with figures who typologically announce the coming of Christ—specifically, of Christ *in the flesh*. But the Christ whom Moses thus announced, Augustine insisted, was more than just truly incarnate. He was also truly Jewish, a halachically observant Christ who lived the Law, who kept the Sabbaths and the feast days of his people, a Christ who was circumcised on the eighth day and who sacrificed in the Temple.[31] And even after the resurrection, his disciples, and Paul the apostle, continued to live according to the Law as well. No reason not to: they too were Jews.[32]

Moses's law does not just lead to the gospel: the Law *is* the Gospel, the message of atonement, of forgiveness for sin and salvation from sin, in two different historical modalities. The historical articulation varied according to its *tempora;* but the Word was always the same. "The *same* Law that was given to Moses became grace and truth in Jesus Christ" (*c. Faust.* 22.6, recalling the Gospel of John 1:17). Accordingly, "the Apostle himself… when praising and commending Israel's privileges, specifically mentions the giving of the Law. If the Law had been bad, the Apostle would not have praised the Jews for having it" (12.3, a reference to Romans 9:4).

Finally, Augustine charges, Faustus exaggerated the Jews' hostility to Christ, too. "Many Jews have believed in the Gospel," he observes, "… and many Jews will eventually believe as well" (*c. Faust.* 22.89). And even those Jews who do not believe, now or later, nonetheless continue and will always continue to serve their vital and prophetic function as witnesses to the church (16.21). Even if they do not know Christ, Jews—unlike Manichaeans—know the true god. For this reason, Augustine counters, Christians and Jews stand

31. He had been aided in framing these arguments by his prior debate with Jerome, August. *Ep.* 82; Fredriksen, *Augustine and the Jews*, 236–40; see too, Fredriksen, "Augustine on Jesus the Jew," Saint Augustine Lecture 2010, *Augustinian Studies* 42, no. 1 (2011): 1–20, at 16–18.

32. Points worked out again against Jerome, August. *Ep.* 40.

united in one religious community. "If we divide all those who have a religion into those who worship the one God and those who worship many gods, by this distinction … the Manichees belong with the pagans, and we belong with the Jews" (20.10). This of course is one of the "ethnic" arguments that Faustus himself had made: that by holding onto the Jews' books, and by worshiping the Jews' god, catholics were essentially Jews. Augustine argues with this sort of ethnic reasoning by way of agreement. By defending the idea of Jewishness, he was able to assert, minus any opprobrium, the same thing.

For Augustine no less than for Faustus, then, Moses stands as the *pars pro toto* of Israel. For this reason, Augustine does *not* use Moses as a type or a figure of Christ.[33] Rather, Moses, like his people, is a faithful prophet; he, like them, is a true witness; he, like them, is the church's faithful servant. Augustine's Moses is thus a subordinate figure; but he is one whose Jewish ethnicity (thus, Jewish "religiousness") Augustine—both like and unlike Faustus—vigorously insisted upon. Gods, customs, and peoples cluster together. This is how and why Augustine, in defending catholic Christianity against the charges brought by Faustus, not only defends Moses but also, in so doing, likewise defends Jews and Judaism.[34]

33. As Massie notes, "L'évêque d'Hippone ne voit pas en Moïse une figure du Christ—une telle correspondance est rarement faite par Augustin.… La figure de Moïse est celle d'un serviteur fidèle, le *famulus*, symbole des Juifs constituent la première communauté chrétienne. Moïse joue le rôle du peuple juif," *Peuple Prophétique*, 370–71.

34. Though compare Massie's important qualification of this view, ibid., 540.

Lee Blackburn

14. MOSES THE METONYM

*Cyril of Alexandria on the Law's
Self-Critique*

Two of the least-studied texts by Cyril of Alexandria are his exegetical
works on the Pentateuch: the *De Adoratione et Cultu*, which is likely his first
literary opus, and its subsequent companion piece, the *Glaphyra*.[1] Like most
of Cyril's exegetical works, the *De Adoratione et Cultu* and the *Glaphyra* tend
to be eclipsed by the long shadow of his later anti-Nestorian writings.[2] However, for those interested in the Christian construction of Judaism in late antiquity, as well as for specialists in patristic exegesis, these texts merit close and
sustained attention. The present paper is primarily concerned with the *De Adoratione et Cultu*, although it will occasionally have recourse to the *Glaphyra*.[3]

1. The handful of works in the past century that have treated the *De Adoratione et Cultu* in detail
include Alexander Kerrigan, *St. Cyril of Alexandria: Interpreter of the Old Testament* (Rome: Pontificio Istituto Biblico, 1952); Sebastian Schurig, *Die Theologie des Kreuzes beim frühen Cyrill von Alexandria, dargestellt an seiner Schrift "De adoratione et cultu in spiritu et veritate"* (Tübingen: Mohr Siebeck,
2005); Robert Wilken, *Judaism and the Early Christian Mind: A Study of Cyril of Alexandria's Exegesis
and Theology* (New Haven, Conn.: Yale University Press, 1971). Wilken's study is most directly relevant
to the topic of this essay, but treats only the first book of the *De Adoratione et Cultu*. Neither Kerrigan
nor Schurig focuses on Cyril's use of Old Testament exegesis in his polemics against Judaism. The *Glaphyra* has received even less attention from scholars; it is mined by Kerrigan and Schurig but mostly ig-
nored by Wilken.

2. For a helpful overview of Cyril's conflict with Nestorius, in both its political and theological dimensions, see John McGuckin, *Saint Cyril of Alexandria and the Christological Controversy: Its History,
Theology, and Texts* (Crestwood, N.Y.: St. Vladimir's Seminary Press, 2004).

3. Neither text is available in a critical edition; Jean Aubert produced the last major edition of *De*

The *De Adoratione et Cultu*, though predominantly exegetical in substance, is not a straightforward biblical commentary. For one, Cyril wrote it in
the form of a dialogue between himself and a presumably fictional Palladius.
Second, he eschews a linear approach to the biblical text, preferring instead to
arrange the order of texts thematically. Indeed, the entire work is framed as a
response to a question that Palladius poses in the opening pages of the work:
what is the Christian to make of the law of Moses? Is it still in any way authoritative, and, if so, how? According to Cyril, the law is in fact normative for
Christians, with the crucial proviso that it be interpreted spiritually, that is to
say, in the light of Christ.[4]

However, in the roughly five hundred pages that follow Cyril does not
merely treat the law as a figural anticipation of the Christian way of life. He also
finds in the Pentateuch a bevy of images that obliquely disclose the law's man-
ifold and grave soteriological deficiencies, thus ascribing to the law not only a
prospective thrust, but also a self-referential and self-critical quality. Put blunt-
ly, in Cyril's hands the law becomes its own harshest critic. The law, in Cyril's
rendering, testifies to its own multiple failings, including its inability to bestow
true knowledge and vision of God, intimate access to God, and sanctification.
I will limit the scope of this paper to Cyril's presentation of the figure of Moses
himself as a cipher of the law's shortcomings. In the final section of this essay, I
will speculate on what propelled Cyril to construe Moses in this way.

As we turn to Cyril's rendering of Moses as a metonym of the law, it is
well to note that Cyril is not unremittingly negative toward the law of Moses.
In fact, on at least one occasion he discerns in Moses himself an image of the
law's monotheistic pedagogy, which was of course salutary for the Israelites.
According to Cyril, Jethro's entrance into Moses's tent, as described in Exodus
18:1–9, and his immediately subsequent avowal of faith in the God of Israel,
is a parable of the law's efficacy in inculcating authentic monotheistic faith.[5]
But Cyril does not leave it at that. He goes on to ponder the import of the fact
that after his confession of faith Jethro, along with Aaron and the Israelite elders, ate bread in the presence of the Lord (Ex 18:12). For Cyril, Aaron here

---

Adoratione et Cultu and the *Glaphyra* in 1638. The texts found in Migne (PG 68–69) are reprints of Aubert's editions. Neither text, either in part or in whole, has been translated into a modern language. The
translations offered throughout this paper are my own.

4. PG 68:140a.

5. PG 68:281a–284a.

functions as a type of Christ, who alone grants access to the presence of God; conversely, Moses's conspicuous absence from the eating party witnesses to the law's impotence to grant such access.[6] In this way, Cyril's commendation of the pedagogy of the Mosaic law is tempered by his assertion of one of the law's most telling defects.

Indeed, Cyril's explication of Jethro's bread-eating with Aaron and the elders is much more characteristic of his overall treatment of the law in general and Moses in particular than is his interpretation of Jethro's dwelling in Moses's tent. And this passage in the *De Adoratione et Cultu* is hardly unique in its presentation of Moses as a symbol of the law's inability to overcome human estrangement from the divine presence. For instance, Cyril construes Moses similarly in his exegesis of Exodus 40:33–38, in which a cloud covers the completed tabernacle and fills it with the glory of God.[7] The salient detail for Cyril is that Moses was unable to enter the tent of witness, which, so says Cyril, signifies the church of the Gentiles.[8] For Cyril, Moses's exclusion from the tabernacle represents the fact that Israel, because it "was not able to bear the rays of divine light" and did not understand the mystery of Christ, could not enjoy close access to God. Of course, it is precisely the Israelites who were under the auspices of the law of Moses who could not attain intimacy with God. Once again, then, Moses metonymically illustrates the law's failure to furnish its adherents with access to the divine presence.

Another target of Cyril's theological critique of the law is its epistemic limitations. For one, the law's limited geographical scope ensured its minimal impact. On several occasions, Moses symbolically underscores the law's modest circulation. For instance, Moses's slowness of tongue signifies that the law is "weak-voiced," inasmuch as it was heard by the Israelites alone.[9] Likewise, in the *Glaphyra*, Cyril contrasts Moses's faltering voice with the trumpet blast heard in the camp when God descended on Sinai. While Moses's feeble

6. Cyril usually, but not always, treats Aaron as a type of Christ. See PG 69:596a, in which Cyril takes Aaron to be a figure of Jewish chauvinism. Conversely, on rare occasions Cyril does not regard Moses as a metonym of the law, as in his interpretation of Exodus 29:10–34, wherein he claims that Moses serves as a type of God (PG 68:761b).

7. PG 68:692c–693a.

8. Books 9 and 10 of the *De Adoratione et Cultu* contain Cyril's most concentrated reflections on the ways in which the tabernacle prefigures the church.

9. PG 68:252a.

voice signifies that the knowledge of the law did not extend beyond Judea, the trumpet represents Christ, whose voice echoes throughout the whole world.[10]

But for Cyril, more serious than the law's provinciality is its impotence to communicate adequately saving knowledge of God or, put differently, the full vision of God's glory. Indeed, it is this limitation of the Mosaic law that prevented it from vouchsafing to its observers intimate access to God. In Cyril's treatment, the law's inadequacy as a conduit of the contemplative knowledge of God finds figural confirmation in the averting of Moses's face from the burning bush. According to Cyril, Moses's downcast face signifies "the infirmity of mind of those who were led by the pedagogy of the law … a mind that was unable to turn its face toward God, and neither was it possible for it to see his glory."[11] This interpretation of Moses's countenance comes on the heels of, and complements, Cyril's construal of the burning bush itself as an icon of the failure of the law to illumine the Israelites' minds; the fact that the heat of the fire did not consume the leaves is for Cyril a symbol of how the Israelites' minds were not penetrated by the light of the law.[12] For Cyril, then, the law is not without its luminosity, but its light can benefit only those on the near side of Christ's resurrection; if not opened by the hermeneutical key of Christ, the law is a lockbox whose spiritual treasures are inaccessible.[13]

According to Cyril, the story of the burning bush not only highlights the law's incapacity to impart saving knowledge of God, but also its inability to effect sanctification. Indeed, throughout the works at hand, one of Cyril's most insistent and trenchant criticisms of the law is that it lacked the intrinsic power to sanctify, and hence could neither purge the moral impurity of its devotees nor deliver them from death. It must be borne in mind that for Cyril, the crux of salvation history is that postlapsarian human beings are no longer able to cultivate the life of virtue and to dedicate the fruits of that life to God; to put the matter in Cyril's idiom, they were no longer capable of spiritual worship. Therefore to maintain, as Cyril frequently does, that the law lacks the capacity

---

10. PG 69:505d. A similar but not identical interpretation of the trumpets heard on Sinai can be found in Gregory of Nyssa, *Mos.* 2.158–59 (Sources Chrétiennes 1:206–8).

11. PG 68:236c–237a.

12. PG 68:232d.

13. Cyril makes this point in his interpretation of Lev 19:23–25 (PG 68:585b–588b). Cyril takes the fact that the fruit of the trees of the land will not be edible until the fifth year as an intimation that the law was not a source of spiritual nourishment until the coming of Christ, who first made the spiritual contemplation of the law possible.

to sanctify and hence to enable spiritual worship is to expose the gravest conceivable defect in the law's constitution. God's command for Moses to remove his shoes, which Cyril takes as a type of the law, serves for Cyril as one of a host of figural intimations in the Pentateuch of the law's sanctificatory deficit. Cyril maintains that this command signifies that the way of life prescribed by the law was not one of "complete blamelessness [ἀμώμητος παντελῶς]," and that it was "not yet pure [οὔπω καθαρὰν]," inasmuch as it still retained a remnant of the mortality and corruption, signified by the leather of Moses's shoes, that humans inherited from Adam.[14] Cyril thus infers from this episode that "the law did not release us from corruption and mortality and all those things that concern impurity," but that only "faith in Christ and the most perfect purification [ἡ τελειοτάτη κάθαρσις] of the evangelical way of life" can so liberate us.[15] Conversely, the discalced Moses is an icon of the Christian who, with her feet freed from this world, draws near (ἐγγίζειν) to God by walking in the path of life in Christ.[16]

Cyril frequently adduces Moses as an image of the law's intrinsic powerlessness to sanctify and to deliver from mortality. For example, in the *Glaphyra*, Cyril juxtaposes (a) Moses's ineffectual request, before Pharaoh, to lead the Israelites out into the wilderness with (b) the efficacy of the tenth plague, and concludes: "it is impossible for death to be abolished through Moses or the law. But the precious blood of Christ is sufficient for its destruction, and it releases those who have been sanctified from corruption."[17] Cyril cites several other episodes from the life of Moses as further demonstration of the law's shortcomings. Once again, Cyril wrings significance from Moses's lack of oratorical prowess; his lack of qualifications to be Israel's spokesperson represents "the shabbiness [μικροπρεπὲς] of the way of life prescribed by the law"; and a shabby way of life can hardly be a holy way of life.[18] Cyril also espies figural import in Moses's fear, which manifests itself in several episodes. For example, Moses's indecisiveness about returning to Egypt from the land of the Midianites symbolizes the "divided" (μεμερισμένης) nature of the way of life required by the law, a way of life that does not demand its adherents to dedicate all

14. PG 68:236a–b.
15. Ibid.
16. PG 68:236c.
17. PG 69:420a.
18. PG 68:253b.

things to God, but rather allows them to oscillate between human and divine things.[19] In like manner, Moses's flight from Egypt in fear for his life figuratively discloses that the law was unable to liberate Israel from the slavery of the fear of death.[20] For Cyril, then, on several occasions Moses figuratively enacts the law's failure to deliver the Israelites from the moral impurity that rendered them slaves to death and the fear thereof.

As already indicated, Cyril's figural rendering of Moses is but one tactic he deploys in his broader strategy of presenting the law itself, understood as both the aggregate of precepts found in the Pentateuch and the narratives pertaining to their promulgation, as an encoded exposé of the law's own imperfections. No Greek exegete prior to Cyril either so insistently presented the law as a herald of its own soteriological limitations or so frequently construed Moses as emblematic of the salvific inadequacy of the law that bears his name. A survey of some of the most important pre-Cyrillian Greek Christian expatiations on the law—including *The Epistle of Barnabas*; Justin Martyr's *Dialogue with Trypho*; Melito of Sardis's *On the Pascha*; Clement of Alexandria's *Stromateis*; Origen's sermons on Exodus, Leviticus, and Numbers; and Gregory of Nyssa's *Life of Moses*—indicate that the vast majority of Cyril's anti-Jewish figural readings of Pentateuchal passages were original to him. The audacity and novelty of Cyril's treatment of the law in general and Moses in particular impels one to inquire into the factors that may have prompted Cyril to undertake it.

At this point, we must return to the beginning of the *De Adoratione et Cultu*, where Cyril frames the entire work. His interlocutor Palladius is perplexed about how to reconcile Matthew 5:17–18, in which Jesus appears to vindicate the letter of the law, with Jesus' promotion of spiritual worship in John 4:21, whence the title of Cyril's work is taken. We know from Cyril's later work *Contra Julianum* that Julian the Apostate was fond of citing Matthew 5:17–18 in order to take Christians to task for not observing the Mosaic law. For Julian, the Christians' disregard for the law belies their own claims to be "Israelites" who obey and honor Moses and the prophets. According to Julian, in order to justify their non-observance of the law, Christians must take refuge in the sophistry of Paul, whose views change "as the polyp changes its colors

---

19. PG 68:256a.
20. PG 68:256b.

to match the rocks."[21] In fact, Julian declares, Christians side with Paul even when he flatly contradicts the Old Testament, as he does in Romans 10:4, where he declares that Christ is the end of the law. "Where," Julian asks, "does God announce to the Hebrews a second law besides what was established?"[22]

So what does Julian's polemic against Christianity have to do with Cyril's hermeneutical handling of Moses in the texts at hand? Clearly, Julian's *Against the Galileans* was a text that haunted Cyril, as the voluminous *Contra Julianum*, written over half a century after Julian's death, attests. Although the *De Adoratione et Cultu* was probably written about twenty years before *Contra Julianum*, it is certainly possible that Cyril had been exposed, directly or indirectly, to Julian's writings by the time of the former text's composition.[23] If so, then Cyril may have rendered Moses as he did at least partly for apologetic effect. Backlit by Julian's contention that Christianity disdains the actual words of the Old Testament and hides behind the capricious assertions of Paul, Cyril's presentation of Moses as a symbol of the law's inadequacies, and indeed the law itself as a cryptogram of its own deficiencies, becomes more intelligible. Through the interpretations described in this paper, and in many more besides, Cyril suggests not that the Pauline account (inclusive of the Epistle to the Hebrews) of the law's soteriological shortcomings represents a Christian travesty of the Pentateuch, but rather that the Pauline account finds ample figural corroboration in the law in general and in the life of Moses in particular. Cyril implies that by symbolically enacting the defects of the law, no less an authority than Moses himself justifies its non-observance once a superior covenant has appeared.

It is worth noting in conclusion that Julian's brief against Christianity

21. Julian, *Against the Galilaeans*, 106b, trans. Wilmer C. Wright, *Julian*, vol. 3, Loeb Classical Library 157 (Cambridge, Mass.: Harvard University Press, 1923), 342.

22. Julian, *Against the Galilaeans*, 319e–320b, trans. Wright, LCL, 408–10.

23. The *Contra Julianum* was written sometime after 433. It is impossible to date the *De Adoratione et Cultu* or the *Glaphyra* with precision. Most scholars—with the exceptions of Noël Charlier, "Le Thesaurus de Trinitate de S. Cyrille d'Alexandrie: Questions de critique littéraire," *Revue d'Histoire Ecclésiastique* 45 (1950): 25–81; and Lois Farag, *St. Cyril of Alexandria, a New Testament Exegete: His Commentary on the Gospel of John* (Piscataway, N.J.: Gorgias Press, 2007), 60–67—believe that the *De Adoratione et Cultu* was Cyril's first written work, but there is no consensus regarding whether he wrote it before or after his installation as patriarch. Schurig, *Theologie des Kreuzes*, 29–34, makes a cogent case for dating it sometime between 412 and 418. It is clear that Cyril wrote the *Glaphyra* after the *De Adoratione et Cultu*, since in the former text Cyril sometimes refers back to the latter. In any case, it is beyond reasonable doubt that the *terminus ad quem* of both works is 428, when the Nestorian controversy, to which neither text refers or alludes, erupted.

took on additional bite in view of the abiding presence of actual Jewish communities in the Roman world. Indeed, Julian himself adverts to these law-observant Jews and cites them as further damning evidence of the brittleness of the Christian position on the law; if the Jews have managed to keep the law, albeit to a necessarily limited extent given the destruction of the Temple, then the Christians have no excuse for their delinquency. It is worth recalling at this juncture that Cyril himself, in the early years of his patriarchate, around the time he composed the *De Adoratione et Cultu* and the *Glaphyra*, was acutely aware of and unremittingly antagonistic toward the Jews in his Alexandrian milieu. In fact, in the early years of his episcopate he was involved in a violent altercation with Alexandrian Jewry, one that apparently eventuated in the expulsion of (at least some of) the Jews from the city and the sequestration of their synagogues by Christians.[24] What is more, Cyril's early festal letters provide indirect evidence of tension between the Christian and Jewish communities in the Egyptian capital; although anti-Jewish rhetoric is a hallmark of Cyril's corpus as a whole, it is found in a concentration and intensity in his early festal letters that would not be matched by subsequent ones.[25] John McGuckin has even speculated that behind Cyril's vehement denunciations of Jewish observances in these letters stands the phenomenon of ecumenical "leakage," that is to say, Christians participating in some way in Jewish festivals.[26] Even if McGuckin's hypothesis is unwarranted, Cyril's polemics against Judaism in his two works on the Pentateuch and his early festal letters can be fully explained

24. Our main historical source for this incident is Socrates Scholasticus, *HE* 7.13.14 (GCS, neue Folge 1:357–60). His narrative is retold with a few minor variations in the seventh-century *Chronicle* of John of Nikiu, 84.90–99. An English translation can be found in R. H. Charles, *The Chronicle of John, Coptic Bishop of Nikiu* (Amsterdam: APA-Philo Press, 1916). According to Socrates, Cyril expelled the entire Jewish community from Alexandria. Recent scholars agree that while such a claim is likely hyperbole, there is no cogent reason to discount the main lines of Socrates's narrative. See David J. Cassel, "Cyril of Alexandria and the Science of the Grammarians: A Study in the Setting, Purpose, and Emphasis in Cyril's Commentary on Isaiah" (PhD diss., University of Virginia, 1992), 15–18; McGuckin, *Saint Cyril of Alexandria*, 12; Wilken, *Judaism and the Early Christian Mind*, 57.

25. See especially *Hom. pasch.* 1.5–6 (SC 372:170–74); 2.1 (SC 372:192); 4.4–6 (SC 372:258–68); 6.6–11 (SC 372:364–92). An English translation of the first twelve of Cyril's festal letters can be found in *St. Cyril of Alexandria: Festal Letters 1–12*, ed. John J. O'Keefe and trans. Philip R. Amidon, SJ. (Washington, D.C.: The Catholic University of America Press, 2009).

26. McGuckin, "St. Cyril of Alexandria: Bishop and Pastor," in *The Theology of St. Cyril of Alexandria: A Critical Appreciation*, ed. Thomas G. Weinandy and Daniel A. Keating (London: T&T Clark, 2003), 226.

only with reference to the socio-religious conflict between Jews and Christians during his first decade as patriarch of Alexandria.

Connections between Cyril's exegesis and his episcopal militancy should be made cautiously, but it stands to reason that the socio-religious conflict between Jews and Christians in Alexandria in the early fifth century provided an additional spur to Cyril's construal of Moses as a witness to the law's soteriological defects and hence its obsolescence upon the advent of Christ. To be sure, anti-Jewish rhetoric is ubiquitous in early Christian literature, and some scholars, following Adolf von Harnack's lead, have contended that such polemics are rarely caused by socio-political factors, but rather are almost always deployed because of the utility of Judaism as a heuristic foil for Christianity.[27] Nevertheless, the temporal conjunction of Cyril's particularly hostile relations with his Jewish counterparts and his remarkably extensive and apparently original exegetical case against Judaism, of which his treatment of Moses as a symbol of the law's salvific failings is but one facet, suggest that the anti-Jewish interpretations found in the *De Adoratione et Cultu* and the *Glaphryra* ought not to be explained in exclusively theological terms. Indeed, it is not improbable that Cyril's clashes with Alexandrian Jewry would generate as a desideratum of an exegetico-theological discrediting of Judaism that could underwrite the Alexandrian church's adversarial posture toward the synagogue. By embedding in (or from Cyril's perspective, extracting from) the Mosaic law itself a critique of its literal observance *post Christum*, Cyril gainsays the legitimacy and coherence of Judaism in his own day in a manner maximally neuralgic to Jews. If, as Cyril suggests, Moses can be enlisted for Paul, then Julian got it backwards; it is Cyril's Jewish contemporaries, not the Christians, whom Moses puts in the dock.

27. See Miriam Taylor, *Anti-Judaism and Early Christian Identity: A Critique of the Scholarly Consensus* (Leiden: Brill, 1995).

Michael Müller

15. BETWEEN INDIVIDUAL
AND PROTOTYPE

Moses in Late Antique Latin Christian Epic

In late antiquity, starting in Constantine's days, the (sub)genre of biblical epic emerged, and it was to stay around for a long time. Biblical motifs have, for various reasons, been used mostly by Christian authors, including numerous writers of high medieval literature, Milton, Vida, Klopstock, and, if you like, even Philip Pullman in very modern days.[1]

The poems written in late antiquity, on which this paper focuses, have had a lot of impact. Iuvencus, who wrote under Constantine, made the match between pagan epic and the Christian faith; the most prolific of his successors, Sedulius, caught the attention of Luther, who translated his hymns

I am grateful for advice from Lauren Schwartzman, Christoph Schubert, Kelly Shannon, and Christina Zimmermann.

1. A very good introduction to Iuvencus, Sedulius, and Arator is Roger P. H. Green, *Latin Epics of the New Testament: Juvencus, Sedulius, Arator* (Oxford: Oxford University Press, 2006); challenging but seminal is Reinhart Herzog, *Die Bibelepik der lateinischen Spätantike: Formgeschichte einer erbaulichen Gattung I* (Munich: Fink, 1975). Wolfgang Kirsch, *Die Lateinische Versepik des 4. Jahrhunderts* (Berlin: Akademie Verlag, 1989), takes a different view of the development of genres. On the paraphrastic techniques employed, see Michael Roberts, *Biblical Epic and Rhetorical Paraphrase in Late Antiquity* (Liverpool, U.K.: Cairns, 1985). For some very different approaches see Daniel Deerberg, *Der Sturz des Judas. Kommentar (5, 1–163) und Studien zur poetischen Erbauung bei Sedulius* (Münster: Aschendorff, 2011), following Herzog and deeming "Erbaulichkeit" the foremost aim of biblical epic; and Karl-Olav Sandnes, *The Gospel "According to Homer and Virgil": Cento and Canon* (Leiden: Brill, 2011), who places it in the schooling tradition.

Hostis Herodes Impie and *A Solis Ortus Cardine*, which was later adapted by Bach. After Cyprianus Gallus, the second poet who concentrated on the Old Testament was Alcimus Avitus. He was the first poet-theologian to introduce the figure of Lucifer, which inspired John Milton. All the texts these poets use as their sources have four facts in common that are very important for the discussion in this volume.

First, though they have several different sources and aims, they all draw from pagan epic to serve the aesthetic needs and expectations of their readership. Second, as time goes on, they become increasingly theological works, including contemporary exegesis, first subtly, later more overtly. Third, they also serve pastoral needs, drawing from homilies and being suitable to be read both in private and in public, in schools and by individuals attempting to deal with the biblical texts.[2] Last, they or their sources feature Moses. This paper will examine the role this most important figure of Judaism can play in decidedly Christian texts, and how the story of one particular people is adapted to serve the needs of a now worldwide religion. These texts will show how Moses was treated not only in early exegesis, but also in literary reception of the Old Testament.

The first two poets, Iuvencus and Cyprianus Gallus, are less overtly theologians and thus have a bit less to offer than Sedulius, Arator, and Avitus. They began a development in this direction, though, and traces of later features of biblical epic can be seen in their works, especially in the focus on Moses in Old Testament epic. Thus I will take a brief look at both of them before turning to their successors.

Iuvencus, the first Christian epicist, whose poem is praised by Jerome and the Pseudogelasian decree *De Libris Recipiendis*,[3] stuck very close to his model, chiefly the Gospel according to Matthew. Thus he does not yield much with respect to Moses. For him, Moses is not an important character. Moses's writings and laws necessarily lead up to Christ, as it says in John 5:45–47: "'But do not think I will accuse you before the Father. Your accuser is Moses, on whom your hopes are set. If you believed Moses, you would believe me, for he wrote about me. But since you do not believe what he wrote, how are you going to believe what I say?'"[4]

---

2. See note 2.

3. See Hier. *De vir. ill.* 84, and *Ep.* 70.5. See also M. A. Norton, "Prosopography of Juvencus," in *Leaders of Iberian Christianity*, ed. J. M. F. Maricq (Boston: St Paul's, 1962), 114–20.

4. Translations of scripture are taken from the 2011 edition of the New International Version.

The first poet to treat the Old Testament was (Pseudo-)Cyprianus Gallus, about whom we know nothing at all. He rendered the Enneateuch (of which only the first seven books, i.e., his rendition of the Heptateuch, remains) mostly in hexameters, the songs in Exodus 15 and Deuteronomy 32 in lyric meters. Cyprianus, like Iuvencus, stuck to his model texts very closely, more noticeably lacking imagination or maybe the bravery to adapt rather than paraphrase. Still, his depiction of Moses has some remarkable features.

In the first chapters of Exodus, Moses is introduced as a keeper of peace. After he has slain the Egyptian overseer in Exodus 2, he sees two of his fellow Hebrews fighting and offers his help (Ex 2:13f.). Moses's intervention is described as helping the weaker part and reintroducing peace.[5] "The one he rebuked then shouts at him: 'Why do you hold your head so high, as if you held the scepter of a high lord or as if written laws roared with you as their keeper?'"[6]

A very common feature of biblical epic is irony, which becomes clear in these words. A fifth-century reader, of course, knows that the episode is taken from what he thinks of as Moses's very own writings. Moses's claim to authority, which the Hebrew in this passage denies, is thus justified ironically. Furthermore, the importance of sacred laws for securing peace is stated.

Shortly afterward (Ex 2:16f.), Moses encounters women who want to lead their sheep to a well, but who are kept from doing so: "Suddenly shepherds dispelled the weak band, the fearful sex. Those who did not dare to stay or to raise their hands, Moses defended...."[7]

Again, the difference in power between Moses's protégées and their enemies is noticeable, and the poet makes a point of highlighting the prophet's

---

Iuvencus renders these verses, *Evangel. Quatt.* 2.687–91, "Nec uos arguerim coram genitore, sed illic / accusator erit, quem spes modo uestra celebrat, / Moyses, quem fidei nullo seruastis honore. / eius enim scriptis uester si crederet error, / crederet et nobis, Moysi quem scripta frequentant." ("I will not accuse you before your creator, but he will be your accuser there; Moses, whom alone your hope rests upon, but whom you have not honoured by being faithful. If now you sinners believed his writings, you would also believe me, whom Moses's writings mention so often.") Iuvencus is edited by J. Huemer, CSEL 24 (Vienna: Tempsky, 1891). All translations of this and other ancient sources are, unless otherwise indicated, my own.

5. Cypr. Gall. *Ex.* 86, ed. R. Peiper, CSEL 32 (Vienna: Tempsky, 1891): "Infirmamque iuvat partem pacemque reducit."

6. Cypr. Gall. *Ex.* 90f.: "celsa cervice tumes, ceu principis alti / sceptra regas scriptaeque fremant, te praesule, leges?"

7. Cypr. Gall. *Ex.* 102–5a: "Infirmam sed forte manum sexumque paventem / pastores trusere procul; quas sistere contra / nequaquam audentes promptasve opponere palmas / vindicat ... Moses...."

good deed in protecting the weak. Still, Moses is not easily excited, but stays humble in all situations, as we know from Numbers 12:3, when Moses hears the people of Israel grumbling: "The eager prophet, meeker than all, heard of this, and with innocent mind, silently, refused to be angry."[8]

Another very common feature of biblical epic is "psychologization": the epic has a much stronger focus on emotions than is present in the biblical model. This emphasis takes place here: Moses, who is called meek in Numbers 12:3, also has a soft heart, and is not prone to anger at all. These are the qualities that make him the right leader for the people of Israel, as God goes on to say in the following verses, which declare that Moses is the only living man who can see the Lord face to face.[9]

Moses's first encounter with Pharaoh (Ex 7) provides an example of why and how Moses, this time together with his brother Aaron, is made the leader and the one who speaks up for the people of Israel. After God commands Aaron to be his brother's prophet,[10] Moses's miraculous age is proclaimed along with his qualities.[11] He is called a *pius vates*, and his life is explicitly peaceful. Still, he is a mere human. Shortly before he dies at the end of Deuteronomy, Moses passes on his inheritance to Joshua, clearly classifying his task and the final song he sings and teaches in Deuteronomy 32: "So that the Judean throng could throw over the altars of the false Gods, he wrote the lyrics to a melodic hymn."[12] In the model, no connection has been made between the song of Moses and the events to come, nor is there any explicit order to Joshua to destroy altars of false gods. Joshua's task there is to lead the people of Israel on, just as Moses had done.

Moses has fulfilled his task in leading the people of Israel out of Egypt and in giving them all the necessary tools: a law to fulfil, securing peace, and an inspirational song commemorating God's deeds. Finally, he himself, rather than the Lord, inaugurates a military commander as his successor. Several

---

8. Cypr. Gall. *Num.* 276f.: "Sedulus haec vates et cunctis mitior audit / innocua cum mente silens seque abdicat irae."

9. Cypr. Gall. *Num.* 278–98. Jerome (*Ep.* 129) even calls him a type for Christ in respect to this trait.

10. Cypr. Gall. *Num.* 278–98.

11. Cypr. Gall. *Ex.* 263f.: "iamque pius vates bis quadraginta per annos / pacificam vitam mortali in carne terebat." ("By then the pious prophet had lived a peaceful life in his mortal flesh for eighty years.")

12. Cypr. Gall. *Dtn.* 150f.: "Utque libet Iudaea manus subverteret aras / mentitosque deos, hymno dat verba melodo."

of his individual features have been (subtly) highlighted, thus making him an ideal leader, and at the same time a model for all Christian leaders to come.[13]

About Sedulius, again we know virtually nothing, but his impact was immense.[14] His *Carmen Paschale*, consisting of five books, treats the Gospel narrative in books 2 to 5. His first book, however, begins with a few select episodes from the Old Testament. The poet also tells us why he initially turns to this first part of the canon. He says he lacks the words to show that God is indeed almighty, and so the author has to turn to a greater authority. This authority, the testimonies of the patriarchs, is never to be neglected or abolished. It carries more weight (as Paul says in 1 Cor 13) than brass instruments.[15] So, the Old Testament, while it may not offer actual salvation from a Christian perspective, is very useful for this first step of evangelization and catechesis, that is, for teaching monotheism. Sedulius continues by noting that truth can be found in the Old Testament, for example in Exodus: Just as God showed the Israelites dry ground underneath the pernicious waters of the Red Sea, he shows the Christians how to find the means of salvation beneath the pernicious effects of following the Old Testament law. Starting from what Paul says in 1 Cor 10:2–4, Sedulius elaborates: "The blue waters of the divided sea stood open.... Nature changed its way, and right through the sea the people already experienced a primitive baptism. Their leader was Christ, for scripture announces loudly: 'The voice of God reaches over many waters.' This voice then

13. According to Ambrose, *Expos. in Ps. 118*, 5.5, he is a type for Jesus and all other leaders (*imperator*).

14. On the sparse available information, see Carl P. E. Springer, *The Gospel as Epic in Late Antiquity: The "Paschale Carmen" of Sedulius* (Leiden: Brill, 1988) and Green, *Latin Epics of the New Testament*, 135–43.

15. Sedul. *Carm. Pasch.* 1.92–102, ed. V. Panagl, CSEL 10 (Vienna: Tempsky, 2007): "Cunctaque divinis parebunt tempora dictis / indicio est antiqua fides et cana priorum / testis origo patrum, nullisque abolenda per aevum / temporibus constant virtutum signa tuarum. / ex quibus audaci perstringere pauca relatu / vix animis conmitto meis, silvamque patentem / ingrediens aliquos nitor contingere ramos. / nam centum licet ora movens vox ferrea clamet, / centenosque sonos humanum pectus anhelet, / cuncta quis expediet, quorum nec lucida caeli / sidera nec bibulae numeris aequantur harenae?" ("All times will obey the divine commands. The old faith is proof of this and the grey origin of the old forefathers bears witness to this, and the sighs of your virtue remain fast forever, and no time can abolish them. I commit my soul to sing a few of these in audacious recital, and I make an effort to enter the open forest and touch some of its branches. For if a brazen voice, moving a hundred mouths, shouted out aloud and if human lungs gave breath for a hundred songs, who could relate it all, to which neither heaven's lucid stars nor the thirsty sands are equal in number?") The thought that the Old Testament is the primary source to prove the existence and power of God can also be found in Hilary of Poitiers, *Comm. in Ps.* 51.19; 65.10; 134.18 and 25.

is the Word, and Christ is present as the Word, who, governing the harmonious testaments of the twofold law, opened the old abyss, so that [his] doctrine could follow and enter the plain field."[16] Paul's conception of the crossing of the sea as a baptism is commonplace, but Sedulius introduces another parallel by recalling Psalm 29:3 ("The voice of the Lord is over the waters, the God of glory thunders, the Lord thunders over the mighty waters") and Exodus 14:21 ("The Lord drove the sea back with a strong east wind").[17] Sedulius interprets this wind as the voice of God over the waters and thus as a symbol for "the Word of God," which according to John's Gospel will become the incarnate Logos, Christ himself. Thus he makes Christ the means by which both Testaments are written and the people are led through the pernicious waters of the Red Sea. Moses does not appear at all in the poem, not even in the account of the burning bush.[18] It is clear that Moses performed the miracle of parting the waters in Exodus 14 not by his own authority, but as an instrument of God.[19] From Sedulius's Christian perspective, the person who conveys salvation cannot be Moses, but must be Christ.

The same exegetical point is made in the following episode. In Exodus 17 the people of Israel grumble because of their thirst. Moses is then told by the Lord to strike a rock, from which water flows. Sedulius again completely omits him: "[The host of the Israelites] suddenly drew water from dry rocks, and from barren stone liquid flowed, and infertile marble poured out new drink. In these three things he is already giving his sacred gifts: Christ is the bread, Christ the rock, Christ in the waters."[20] The bread, of course, is the

16. Sedul. *Carm. Pasch.* 1.136, 141–47: "Peruia diuisi patuerunt caerula ponti … / Mutauit natura uiam, mediumque per aequor / ingrediens populus rude iam baptisma gerebat, / cui dux Christus erat, clamat nam lectio: multas / vox Domini super extat aquas; uox denique uerbum est. / Verbum Christus adest, geminae qui consona legis / testamenta regens ueterem patefecit abyssum, / ut doctrina sequens planis incederet aruis."

17. The influence of Genesis 1:2 is also possible, but the parallel with the Psalm quoted above is far more striking.

18. Sedul., *Carm. Pasch.* 1.127–31: "Ignibus innocuis flagrans apparuit olim / non ardens ardere rubus, nec iuncta calori / materies alimenta dabat, nec torrida vivens / sensit damna frutex, sed amici fomitis aestu / frondea blanditae lambebant robora flammae." ("Now a thorn bush seemed to be burning without burning, alight with flames that did not harm it; neither did its wood give fuel to the heat, nor did the living bush feel its fiery end, but the flames gently licked the foliage and wood of their friend, the tinder.")

19. Ambrose of Milan, *De spiritu sancto* 4.21, and *Exp. in Ps.12*, 45.2, also make this very clear.

20. Sedul. *Carm. Pasch.* 1.152–59: "Subitas arente metallo / hausit aquas, sterilique latex de rupe

manna that was found in the desert shortly before. In Sedulius's version there is nobody who opens the rock; the only persons mentioned are the thirsty throng of the Israelites, who find seemingly unsolicited water. So, the Lord does not save his people through his "tool" Moses, but the rock itself brings forth the saving water. There is, then, a multitude of references to be found in this passage: Christ as bread is an obvious reference to the Eucharist, Christ as the cleft rock hints at John 19:34, when blood and water flow out from his body. Christ's being in the waters is a double reference. It also hints at John 19:34, but in addition it refers back to the explanation of Exodus several lines earlier. While the water was pernicious to some, it made it possible for others to be baptized through the power of Christ. The reference to the Eucharist goes back to Origen, who says: "Moses shows him [the reader] the rock which is Christ and leads him to it that he may drink from it and quench his thirst. But this rock will not give water unless it has been struck, but when it has been struck it brings forth streams."[21] References to baptism can be found later, for instance in Chrysostom's and Clement of Alexandria's writings.[22] Thus this episode, which in its original form aims at showing the saving power of the Lord, is turned into a symbol for baptism, and, more importantly, a foreshadowing of the Eucharist; another particularly Christian way of conveying salvation. For Sedulius, there is no use for Moses.

After quickly recounting some Old Testament episodes, Sedulius again gives a short account of why he has done so. He speaks of the "select miracles of the old law" by which is shown "what God the Father has done, together with the Holy Spirit and joined by God the Son's virtue."[23] The use of the word "law" is striking at first. Sedulius did not mention any of the Jewish laws, and even omitted the person who is usually credited with codifying them. Thus we have to take *lex* as a general term for "the Old Testament." Iuvencus

---

manavit, / et ieiuna novum vomuerunt marmora potum. / His igitur iam sacra tribus dans munera rebus, / Christus erat panis, Christus petra, Christus in undis."

21. Orig. *Hom. in Ex. XI*, 2, translation taken from Joel C. Elowsky, *Ancient Christian Commentary on Scripture, New Testament IVb, John 11–21* (Downers Grove: InterVarsity Press, 2007), 327f. Several later parallels are to be found in Elowsky's book.

22. See Elowsky, *Ancient Christian Commentary*.

23. Sedul. *Carm. Pasch.* 1.291–93: "Digesta … veteris miracula legis / … Sancti coniuncto Spiritus actu / quae genitor socia Nati virtute peregit." Sedulius repeats this point at 294–96: "per digesta rudis necnon miracula legis / dicemus, Sancti coniuncto Spiritus actu / quae natus socia Patris virtute peregit." There is also evidence for Jewish usage of the term "law" in this way.

had already used the word in this way. Moreover, the "law" has been detached from the people of Israel and incorporated into Sedulius's contemporary theological discourse, here the defense of the doctrine of the Trinity. In his rendering of the New Testament Sedulius is, with respect to Moses, surprisingly incoherent. After eliminating the prophet entirely from the Old Testament, he calls him *typicus Moses verusque propheta*,[24] when he recounts Matthew 14:13–21, the feeding of the five thousand. It is unsurprising that Moses, who fed the people with manna (or was God's tool in doing so) should be called *typicus... verusque propheta*, but it *is* surprising that Sedulius did not mention this before. Still, calling Moses a type for Christ helps explain why Moses has been (mostly) eliminated: to make room for Christ, the true head of the true Israel,[25] whom Moses's only role is to foreshadow.

For another hundred years there were no examples of biblical epic until Arator turned to the Acts. He relies quite a lot on Augustine's theology, and he is more overtly theological than Iuvencus and Cyprianus, but less so than Sedulius, compared to whom his strategy is one of close paraphrase.[26] His poem also refers to the Old Testament in several places, and we can see that, from the firth to the sixth century, theology has hardly changed with respect to Moses, the validity of the Jewish laws, and the meaning of Old Testament events. Arator's poem contains a little "instruction manual" on how to understand the Old Testament, illustrated by an example from the wedding at Cana in John 2: "He often spoke of the three teachings of the Church: it *sounds* like an historical, moral, and typical book. So did the six pots contain twenty gallons (three metretes) each, which were red with new wine, by the old law."[27]

Arator provides an allegorical reading of an important New Testament episode (Acts 9:32–35) that depicts the Jewish law and thus partly also Moses, its author, very negatively: "This the period of eight years of feebleness makes

24. Sedul. *Carm. Pasch.* 3.208: "The type and true prophet Moses."

25. Michael Mazzega, *Sedulius, Carmen paschale, Buch III* (Basel: Schwabe, 1996), 194f. Moses occurs only once more in a New Testament episode in Sedulius—*Carm. Pasch.* 3.285–290—when he appears during the transfiguration (Mt 17:1–13 par). He carries the epithet *clarus*, but has no other remarkable features or function.

26. On Arator's theology, see Johannes Schwind, *Arator-Studien* (Göttingen: Vandenhoeck & Ruprecht, 1990). Arator's technique has been called the perfect mix between paraphrase (like Iuvencus) and exegesis (like Sedulius). On this, see Deerberg, *Der Sturz des Judas*, 423, with further literature.

27. Arator, *De Actibus Apostolorum* 2.890–93, ed. A. P. McKinlay, CSEL 72 (Vienna: Tempsky, 1951): "ui canit Ecclesiae tria dogmata saepius edit / historicum, morale sonans, typicumque volumen. / Sic etenim ternas capiunt sex vasa metretas, / quae veteri de Lege novo rubuere liquore.")

known: for that amount of time, all power has justly left the weak limbs, lying down under the old law; indeed, those whose child is wounded on the eighth day always carry dangerous wounds. From this Christ healed the harsh wounds and solidified them after long danger for their flesh in running water.... From there wounds creep up, from here they are dissolved, there a law oppresses with punishments, here medicine purges in the water."[28] This episode is full of anti-Jewish polemics, of which I pick out the most important ones.

First, the paralyzed man's condition came about because he is still under the ancient law.[29] That he had been paralyzed for eight years now allows number symbolism: on the eighth day, Jews traditionally circumcise their children. This is deemed a corporeal and spiritual defacement, an unnecessary wound, which binds these children to the harmful old laws. The way out of this is, of course, baptism. This exegesis cannot be paralleled anywhere, for two reasons. First, there is hardly any systematic exegesis of the Acts in the early Church.[30] Second, the five hallways around the pool are interpreted as the five books of Moses.[31] Their "victims," locked in, have no chance of freeing themselves, but they need Jesus. After Jesus' coming, however, he can free those who are under the law of sin—again, Pauline theology (see Rom 3–7)—by leading them to baptism. There is nothing positive to be said about the law. Still, before ending this episode, Arator makes one very important turn, freeing him from possible allegations of Marcionism. It is the Mosaic law that needs to be abolished, not the entirety of the Old Testament scriptures. These are, by Peter,

28. Arator, *Act.* 1.771–79, 783–85: "Octo quod annorum languoris proditur aetas, / iure per hoc tempus membris defecit ademptis / antiqua sub Lege iacens; iugulantia quippe / vulnera semper habent quorum fit saucius infans / octavo veniente die; sanavit ab illa / parte gravem lacerumque diu discrimine carnis / in liquidis solidavit aquis ... / hinc vulnera serpunt / hinc ablata ruunt; ibi subdit regula poenis, / hic purgat medicina vadis...."
29. Arator, *Act.* 2.775.
30. See Schwind, *Arator-Studien*, 120.
31. Arator, *Act.* 1.789–98: "Heu, nullas praestabat aquas. Piscina ligata / porticibus Iudaea fuit; namque atria quinque / ad sua claustra tenet per quinque volumina Moysi / legis adepta modum, cuius circumdata gyro / debilis aeternum vidit sine munere Iesum / in libris aegrota suis; hinc eripit unum, / cui veniens peccata tulit. Quam rite figuram / mundus ubique gerit; quem postquam sabbata solvens / impulit ad fontem, superavit gratia legem. / Petrus ad Ecclesiam revocat documenta Magistri." ("Oh, it offered no water! The pool of the Jews was surrounded by colonnades, for it has five courts for its barriers, has adopted the constraint of the law through the five books of Moses. It [the pool], weak, encircled by the ring of the law, sees now, in its books, without merit, the eternal Jesus. From there he freed one, whose sins he took away when he came. The world duly enjoys this figure everywhere: Grace surpassed the law, after it has led the world and led it to the source, solving the Sabbath. Peter calls the scripture of his Master back to the Church.")

"called back to the Church," which is the only body that can justly interpret them.[32] Moses is thus responsible for having created a law that is, if handled improperly, harmful, but which might still convey parts of salvation. He is, after all, called "the Teacher."[33] Therefore, not Moses but the Jews have to take the blame.[34] This does not tell us anything about his personality, but about the effects of his deeds. The last point to be made about Arator is his treatment of the Exodus as an exemplary baptism, which openly draws, again, from 1 Corinthians 10. But Arator not only mentions this theological commonplace, but also notes that Christ, the rock, from which later water shall arise, follows Israel through the Red Sea,[35] as Paul teaches in 1 Corinthians 10:4. Moses is the leader of the people of Israel, but he is far from being sufficient. Still, in Moses's laws and deeds, Christ shines through, or would shine through, if only the Jewish religion did not hide the true faith. One typical Christian paradox is noticeable: Even though Moses is "the Teacher," his teachings are misinterpreted by those who primarily follow his law, that is, the Jews. The writings attributed to him are therefore far from being pointless, but they need to be interpreted by the Church. He is clearly not depicted as a model for any contemporary Christian authority or even as Christ himself, but as a symbol for all things pre-Christian and Jewish: good soil for Christians, yet deformed by the Jews. This had been a commonplace ever since the Gospels themselves, and Arator highlights it.

Even though Alcimus Avitus probably wrote several years earlier than

32. Arator, *Act.* 1.796–98.

33. I capitalize "the Teacher," following McKinlay's practice.

34. My translation of lines 791f. is not beyond doubt. I refer *Moysi* to *volumina*, *legis* to *modum*, thus separating the writings of Moses from the law's constraint. It is also grammatically possible to refer both *Moysi* and *legis* to *modum* ("the constraint of the law of Moses"), but I argue against this. Albeit a contrast between *atria quinque—quinque volumina* (without *Moysi*) would suffice and make a sensible point, referring only the last word of line 790, *Moysi*, to *modum* would be a strange enjambment. Furthermore, line 798 is explicitly positive about Moses's writings and criticizes only their interpretation: thus speaking of the constraint of *Moses's* law (rather than a more abstract law) does not seem sensible to me. Referring both *Moysi* and *legis* to *volumina* ("the five books of the law of Moses") is also grammatically possible, but pointless, since *modum* would, without an explaining genitive, be very vague.

35. Arator, *Act.* 2.83b–87: "Nec epistola cessat / haec iterare docens: 'Patres baptismate nostri / in Rubro fulsere Freto sub nomine Moysi / per legem cum petra simul sequeretur euntes; / nam petra Christus erat. Quid adhuc, gens dura, requiris?'" ("Neither does his epistle cease from teaching this over and over again: 'Our forefathers shone from baptism in the Red Sea under the name of Moses by his law, when a rock followed the walking crowd at the same time; for this rock was Christ. What now, obstinate race, do you require?'")

Arator, he should be treated last. He was bishop of Vienne, in what is now France, from 494 to 518, and he was a relative of Sidonius Apollinaris and the emperor Avitus. In his works, he adapted several Old Testament stories, such as the Creation, Original Sin, and the Deluge, and, most importantly for this paper, the Exodus.

At the beginning of his poem *De transitu maris rubri* (*Carmina* 5), Avitus, like Sedulius, tells us why he wants to tell such a story at all. First, such a splendid story needs to be told in high style, but by saying that this is not his first aim, he is employing a *topos* of humility.[36] Second, he wishes to kindle belief in his readers, something that Sedulius also wanted to do, by referring to certain Old Testament episodes: "And if someone cannot give thanks in words, he has no small virtue in simply believing in the deeds."[37] Furthermore, this belief is classified as something distinctly Christian, as foreshadowing baptism and the entirety of salvation: "The work's beauty was great enough at the level of the story it told but still greater in the figurative sense, for within its fecund shell it conceived and brought forth life itself."[38] The following examples from Avitus's poem show that Moses serves as what Arweiler has called a "Streiter Gottes,"[39] a (both spiritual and physical) "warrior of God," but also as a prototypical high priest, in the same sense in which Christ is the One High Priest. The first major deed of Moses is the "battle" against Pharaoh's magicians,[40] during which the prophet makes his adversaries look even more like fools than they do in the Bible. Pharaoh himself, even though he is black, becomes white with shock,[41] but does not want to admit defeat so easily. He calls upon his magicians to prove that they also can make their staffs trans-

---

36. Avit. *Carm.* 5.6–7, ed. R. Peiper, MGH, auctores antiquissimi 6, 2 (Berlin: Weidmann, 1883): "Sed non ut dignum tanti praeconia facti / eloquium captent." All translations of Avitus, unless otherwise indicated, are taken from George W. Shea, *The Poems of Alcimus Ecdicius Avitus* (Tempe, Ariz.: Nabu, 1997).

37. Avit. *Carm.* 5.9f.: "Quod si quis nequeat verbis persolvere grates, / non minimum virtutis habet vel credere gestis."

38. Avit. *Carm.* 5.17–19: "Pulchrior exuperat praemissae forma salutis / historiis quae magna satis maiorque figuris / conceptam gravido peperit de tegmine vitam."

39. Alexander Arweiler, *Die Imitation antiker und spätantiker Literatur in der Dichtung De spiritalis historiae gestis des Alcimus Avitus, mit einem Kommentar zu Avit. carm. 4,429–540 und 5,526–703* (Berlin: De Gruyter, 1999), 144.

40. Avit. *Carm.* 5.65–97.

41. Avit. *Carm* 5.75f.: "conterritus haesit / aeternumque niger tunc palluit ore tyrannus." ("The tyrant sat still, transfixed by terror and, although he had always been black, turned pale.")

form into snakes, but they can only come up with images and petty tricks,[42] not standing a chance against Moses's actual (rather than imaginary) powers.[43] This is an episode very suitable for an epic rendition of a biblical text, and it tells us a bit about the Christian perception of Moses: in the New Testament his victory over Pharaoh's magicians is mentioned only in 2 Timothy 3:8, and it comes up very rarely in exegesis.[44] Aaron is completely eliminated from the story. Unlike in Exodus 7, it is not Aaron's staff but that of Moses that is important here. Still, there is more to be discovered on the lexical level. When Aaron and Moses step before the Pharaoh, they are called "elect prophets," with Moses being the leader, *primus*.[45] The meaning of *vates* is ambiguous. Both "prophet" and "priest" are possible, and we can assume that Avitus had that double meaning in mind: "prophet" because that is a generic title for Moses, "priest" because of the role he was to play within this poem and typologically; I shall return to this below. The performance of magic then starts with Moses being called the "law-giving hero."[46] For the next twenty-five lines he does not appear in person, until, referred to again by his actual name, he closes the "spectacle of virtue."[47] Avitus then adds a short closing remark: "Need I say more? It became the staff it had been and with it the holy man made more

---

42. Avit. *Carm.* 5.86–90: "armant quisque suas noto phantasmate virgas / dant iactae vanas species anguesque putati / illusos terrent oculos fallente figura. / Nec longum tumuere magi." ("Each armed himself with the wand his own familiar demon had enchanted. When they were thrown down, the wands gave the illusion of snakes, which, although imaginary, took in and terrified the eyes of the onlookers with their deceptive appearance. The magicians, however, did not swell with pride for long.")

43. Avit. *Carm.* 5.90f.: "consumitur omne, / quod fecisse rati Fictos namque arte dracones / primus adhuc mordax absorbit ore cerastas." ("Everything they thought they had accomplished was quickly devoured, for the first snake, still eager to unleash its fangs, swallowed with its viper's mouth those that had been formed by the magicians' art.")

44. Jerome calls it a victory of truth against lies (*Ep.* 121.11).

45. Avit. *Carm.* 5.40f.: "ilicet electi vates mandata ferebant / depromit regi cum primus talia Moyses." ("The chosen priests at once began to carry out God's commands, as Moses, their leader, addressed these words to the king.")

46. Avit. *Carm.* 5.63f.: "virgam forte manu gestabat legifer heros." ("Now it happened that Moses, the patriarch and lawgiver, was holding a staff in his hand.") Moses is again called *legifer* in Avit. *Carm.* 5.372, when he is also portrayed as the leader of the Israelite army, a minor aspect, which I shall pass over in this paper. On the many aspects of the battle between the Israelites (and God) and the Egyptians, see Arweiler *Die Imitation*. The meaning of "law" has been mentioned above (see the section on Sedulius) and will be quickly examined again, on Avitus in particular, below.

47. Avit. *Carm.* 5.92f.: "Postquam virtutis clausit spectacula Moyses / victorisque tenens caudam tellure levavit...." ("Then, after Moses put an end to this show of power by taking hold of the victor by the tail and lifting it from the ground....")

portents appear as time passed."[48] The poet includes two major announce-
ments in these lines. First, Moses's staff is going to be the tool by which more
"signs"—implying that they point to New Testament events—are going to be
shown. Second, Moses is going to act as *sacerdos*: priest.

That this is an important role can be illustrated first with the institution of Passover. Moses is praying with all his heart, joined by his brother, until God finally hears them and teaches them about a sacred rite containing
a "mystic victim."[49] The people of Israel are still kept in Egypt, even though
nine of the ten plagues have already struck. Moses, assisted by his brother, is
then the one who prays urgently and intently—we get another look at his psychological situation—on behalf of his people and is rewarded with an answer
by the Lord, who institutes the Passover rites. Just like the entirety of the Exodus, Passover also has its counterpart in the New Testament, since the *victima*, the Passover Lamb, is *mystica*, pointing to something else in a spiritual way. The rite, of course, is festal in both ways, both the original Passover,
and the Christian adaptation of it in the Eucharist. This Passover-Eucharist
is, as Avitus informs us in the next lines, an everlasting law (thus Moses is, as
has been stated above, a "law-giving hero")—and an everlasting rite.[50] When
the Lord has finished giving Moses his instructions, the narrator addresses the
reader directly. The reader shall understand that he himself still does figuratively what was commanded to Moses by the Lord himself: since the body and
blood of Christ are nothing other than what the body and blood of the Passover Lamb foreshadowed, Christians stand in this tradition whenever they
either make the sign of the cross or celebrate and partake in the Eucharist.[51]

48. Avit. *Carm.* 5.96f.: "Quid multis? Fit virga prior, qua deinde sacerdos / plurima succiduo mon-
stravit tempore signa."

49. Avit. *Carm.* 5.217-21: "Moyses interea lacrimas, ieiunia, vota / continuat precibusque frequens
ac pervigil instat, / maioris natu fultus solamine fratris. / Instruit hos sacris simul informatque creator /
mystica sollemnem quo pandat victima ritum." ("In the meantime, Moses was steadfast, weeping, fasting
and making vows to God. With prayer after prayer, he carried out his vigil, supported by the solace his
elder brother gave. And the Creator instructed them in holy observances, teaching them so that a mystic
victim might reveal a sacred rite.")

50. Avit. *Carm.* 5.231f.: "Vos modo perpetuos sacrorum discite mores / cultibus et propriis mansu-
ra lege tenete." ("As for you, your only task is to learn rituals that will survive forever and to abide by your
own observances under an enduring law.")

51. Avit. *Carm.* 5.247-51, 254-57: "Sic nos, Christe tuum salvet super omnia signum / frontibus
impositum; sic sanguis denique sanctus, / tunc praemonstrati dudum qui funditur agni, / oribus infusus
postes lustrasse tuorum / ... credatur.... / Tu cognosce tuam salvanda in plebe figuram, / ut, quocumque
loco mitis mactabitur agnus / atque cibo sanctum porrexerit hostia corpus, / rite sacrum celebrent vitae
promissa sequentes." ("As Your sign, Christ, when it is placed on our foreheads, is our best salvation, so

These words are the words of the narrator, not those of Moses or the Lord. Moses, however, is called *rector* right after this passage, thus being made the first person to, at least mystically, celebrate and codify the Eucharist.[52] While the equation of Passover and the Eucharist is commonplace, Avitus considerably highlights Moses's role. There is one more clear reference to this. Manna and the water that came forth from the stricken rock are signs that God will always feed his people (see my remarks on Sedulius above). First of all, since the manna came down from heaven (consider also the reference to the bread of heaven, in John 6) it foreshadows Christ's descent from heaven, being born of the Virgin. Thus, God presents himself as a meal on earthly altars.[53] Now what does this have to do with Moses? As part of the same sign, there is need of a high priest, namely Moses, who has to strike a rock to make water come forth.[54] He becomes part of this process, both real (in the desert) and mystical, of feeding the chosen people (foreshadowing the Eucharist) and he thus plays the part that Christ himself shall later play as the One High Priest at the Last Supper, or that any priest shall play when he is acting as *alter Christus*.

One of the qualities highlighted is the prophets' sanctity.[55] When the people of Israel grumble (yet again), Moses and Aaron, the holy leaders, heed

---

let the holy blood shed by the pre-ordained lamb and poured into our mouths now be believed to have cleansed the portals of Your people.... Understand, reader, this figure, living among a people marked for salvation. Henceforth in whatever place the gentle Lamb is sacrificed and the Victim provides its holy body as food, let those who abide by His promises of life fittingly perform their own holy ceremony.")

52. Avit. *Carm.* 5.260: "finierat rector leges et foedera festi / paschalis mandare viris." ("The divine Teacher had finished giving the laws and covenants of the paschal holiday to the men of the nation.")

53. Avit. *Carm.* 5.456–61: "Dum sacrum populo victum candentia manna / ferrent et caeli frugem terrena viderent. / Per quam sublimis praediceret ante figura / edendum ex utero purum sine semine corpus / quo caperet pascenda salus de sede superna / inlabente deo sanctis altaribus escas." ("Shining manna would provide holy food for your people, and earth's realm would behold the bread of Heaven. So a sublime figure would foreshadow that a pure body would one day be born of a womb untouched by human seed and that from it a meal of salvation would claim nourishment from Heaven itself, as God made His descent to our holy altars.") Ambrose, *Ep.* 15.42.7 sees a connection between making a rock bring forth water and a virgin's giving birth—both could be called impossible, but are not so for God.

54. Avit. *Carm.* 5.462f.: "Hoc signo summus percussa rupe sacerdos / protulit irriguos populis sitientibus haustos." ("And as part of this sign, the high priest also struck a rock and produced a watery draught for the thirsting people.")

55. Avit. *Carm.* 5.556f., 568, 575f.: "Tum sancti coepere duces promissa referre / solarique metum fletusque abstergere dictis.... / 'quin magis erectas firma spe tollite mentes.' ... / Talibus intenti vates deiecta levabant / corda virum, sancta sedantes voce timorem." ("Then the holy leaders began to recall what had been promised and with these words soothed their fears and wiped away the people's tears.... 'Rather, with an unwavering hope, lift up your spirits and keep them high....' With words like these their diligent priests lifted up the dejected hearts of the people and calmed their fears with their holy voices.")

their cries and bring them solace.[56] They call the people to show strong faith and trust in God and succeed in calming them.[57] Moses and Aaron are explicitly called *vates* again, prophet-priests, and they do as any good spiritual leader would do: They call the people back to faith and expel all fears.[58] They do so even more by speaking with holy voices—twice in just twenty lines the poet refers to them or their actions as holy.

Besides the Eucharist, the other sacrament foreshadowed in the Exodus and partly acknowledged by Moses is, again, baptism. Avitus refers to Moses's song after the actual crossing of the Red Sea in Exodus 15: "The renowned leader described this remarkable event in that hymn of celebration which is now recited throughout the world, when guilt is purged and washed away by baptism, and the waters that bring life-giving cleansing produce new offspring to replace the guilty men of old whom Eve bore."[59] Moses's song, the song of the renowned leader, has gained value not only for the people of Israel, but for all those baptized. The water of baptism then, foretold by the water of the Red Sea, not only destroys the Egyptians, but also replaces the former human race with a new one. These are "figures which the holy prophet explained in his five volumes."[60] The story the poet has just told does not have meaning for the Jews, or at least not for them alone, but now for the true Israel, to which the *pius vates* figuratively referred in his five books. The same can be said for the songs of Moses, who thus finds his place in the new, "true" Christian tradition. Just as the Exodus thus foreshadows baptism, Moses as prophet and leader, the one put in charge by the Lord, foreshadows later figures who brought and bring baptism about.

To summarize: In New Testament epics, Moses is very rarely depicted, which is partly because he does not occur in the respective model texts very often (Iuvencus and Arator), partly for theological reasons (Sedulius). There is a stronger focus on God's omnipotence in Sedulius's work than on individ-

---

56. Avit. *Carm.* 5.556f.

57. Avit. *Carm.* 5.568.

58. On the contrast between the faith of the prophets and the people's lack thereof, see Arweiler, *Die Imitation*, 144.

59. Avit. *Carm.* 5.704–6: "Inclitus egregium sollemni carmine doctor / describit factum, toto quod psallitur orbe, / cum purgata sacris deletur culpa fluentis / emittitque novam parientis lympha lavacri / prolem post veteres, quos edidit Eva, reatus." Translation from Shea, *The Poems of Avitus*, shortened and slightly altered.

60. Avit. *Carm.* 5.718f.: "Figurae / quas pius explicuit per quinque volumina vates."

uals in the Old Testament. Salvation is bestowed by God not through Moses, but through Christ. To avoid a seemingly competitive situation between Moses and Christ as the one particular mediator of salvation, Moses is eliminated. This is a treatment he suffers nowhere else in the exegetical tradition of the early Church. While most authors view typological readings as more important than the figure of Moses himself, such a radical silence about him is not attested. This is a major argument for seeing biblical epic and Christian poetry in general as relevant theological writings. For Iuvencus and Arator, Moses is the misunderstood lawgiver of old. This is a typical example of anti-Jewish polemic, which begins in the New Testament itself. In the poems that treat only events from the Old Testament, Moses is not eliminated, but is used for Christian purposes. First, for Cyprianus Gallus, Moses is clearly not a conveyor of salvation in his own right: his role is primarily that of a leader of the people, their mediator to God, and a peacemaker, being an excellent individual, a model for later leaders, and the one who figuratively showed and pointed to Christian salvation. God does not need or "use" him as often in the epic as he does in the model texts, because if God needs a medium to communicate salvation, this role falls to another person of the Holy Trinity. That Avitus was, first of all, a theologian in the Augustinian tradition is quite clear; his first poems draw heavily from *De Genesi ad litteram*. But the later poems, *De diluvio mundi* and *De transitu maris rubri*, treating topics on which Augustine did not write in *De Genesi ad litteram*, feature noticeable traces of the poet's own theology, his own view of Moses.[61] The prophet is a holy man, possessing a holy voice, who fears God and who is by his many actions—foreshadowing the two major sacraments—a model for all who have a leading role in society or the Church. At times, he is explicitly an ideal high priest. Moses in Christian epic is, finally, an individual depicted very positively who is an important part of many a prototype.

61. On Avitus as a theologian in the Augustinian tradition, and as one in his own right, see Ian N. Wood, "Avitus of Vienne, the Augustinian Poet," in *Society and Culture in Late Antique Gaul: Revisiting the Sources*, ed. Ralph W. Mathisen and Danuta Shanzer (Aldershot: Ashgate, 2001), 263–77.

Vadim Prozorov

16. DISCIPLINE AND MERCY

Moses as a Pattern for Good Rulers in the Works
of Pope Gregory the Great

In the late 570s and 580s the future pope Gregory the Great, at that time
the papal ambassador to Constantinople, delivered an extensive moral and ecclesiological exposition of the Book of Job to a very narrow circle of monks,
who were accompanying him to the imperial capital. Later, in the mid-590s,
during his pontificate, he revised these *Morals on the Book of Job*, usually called
the *Moralia*. In the middle ages, the interpretations and ideas suggested by the
pope in this work became available and appealing to a wider audience through
various important medieval texts.[1] One of his interpretations involves Moses,
who sporadically appears in the Gregorian exegesis and introduces the idea of
the unity of mercy and justice exhibited by the good ruler.

Moses emerges as King of Israel in an episode from book 20 of the *Mora-*
lia.[2] This excerpt was later included in Gratian's influential *Decretum*, the
twelfth-century collection of Church law and the oldest part of the *Corpus*
iuris canonici.[3] Here Gregory the Great explains the concluding phrase from

---

1. René Wasselynck, *L'Influence des "Moralia in Job" de S. Grégoire le Grand sur la théologie morale*
entre le VII et le XII* siècle*, 3 vols. (doctoral thesis, Université de Lille, 1956).

2. Gregory the Great, *Moralia in Iob*, 20.5.14, ed. Marc Adriaen, Corpus Christianorum, ser. lat.
(CCSL) 143A (Turnhout: Brepols, 1979), 1012–14 (hereafter cited as Gregory the Great, *Moralia*).

3. Gratian, *Decretum*, D. 45, c. 9, in *Decretum Magistri Gratiani*, ed. Emil Friedberg, *Corpus Iuris*
Canonici 1 (Leipzig: Bernhard Tauchnitz, 1879), cols. 163–64.

"Job's speech of remembrance" in a dispute with God when Blessed Job recollects his past prosperity and achievements as those of an ideal ruler.[4] He concludes his speech with the following words: "And when I sat as a king with an army standing round, nevertheless I was the comforter of mourners."[5] On the basis of this quotation, the pope develops a discourse on the principal attributes of a good ruler, or *rector bonus*, as Gregory names him. He speaks of mercy and disciplinary justice.

The exegesis starts with the allegorical reading of Job's saying.[6] The pope suggests that in such a king one should see Christ, who dwells in the heart and "rules the clamouring motions of the minds in our thinking." Christ harnesses extreme states of mind, and he is present there surrounded either by diverse thoughts, which are not necessarily elevated, or by a "host of virtues,"[7] depending on the quality of the mind. Besides, the king with an army allegorically signifies the Church, represented by the order of doctors or teachers or preachers (they are interchangeable), who in the corporate union "preside like a king,"[8] and the army of believers equipped with good works, who are always ready to fight against temptations. The mission of the Church in this case is to comfort mourners and to assure believers of the edifying interaction of the strictness of God's judgment and "gentleness of His pity."[9] For the first time

4. Norman C. Habel, *The Book of Job* (Philadelphia: The Westminster Press, 1985), 402.

5. Job 29:25: "Cumque sederem quasi rex, circumstante exercitu, eram tamen maerentium consolator." Here, and in the following pages, I use, with some minor adjustments, the English translation of the *Moralia* in Gregory the Great, *Morals on the Book of Job*, trans. James Bliss, ed. Charles Marriott (Oxford: John Henry Parker, 1845), available online at http://www.lectionarycentral.com/GregoryMoraliaIndex.html.

6. Gregory the Great, *Moralia*, 20.5.12, ed. Adriaen, 1010: "Quasi rex Dominus sedet in corde, quia circumstrepentes regit animorum motus in nostra cogitatione. In mente quippe quam inhabitat, dum torpentia excitat, inquieta frenat, frigida accendit, accensa moderatur, emollit rigida, fluxa restringit; ex ipsa hac diuersitate cogitationum quasi quidam illum exercitus circumstat. Siue certe quasi rex sedet circumstante exercitu, quia praesidentem illum mentibus electorum circumstat turba uirtutum.... Ea uero quae de sanctae Ecclesiae capite diximus, nil obstat si ad uocem quoque eiusdem Ecclesiae referamus. In ea quippe ordo doctorum quasi rex praesidet, quem fidelium suorum turba circumstat. Quae scilicet multitudo fidelium recte quoque exercitus dicitur, quia in procinctu bonorum operum indesinenter cotidie contra temptationum bella praeparatur. Corda quoque maerentium sancta Ecclesia consolatur, dum praesentis peregrinationis aerumna afflictas mentes electorum pensat, et has aeternae patriae promissione laetificat. Considerat etiam quod cogitationes fidelium diuino sint timore percussae; et quos de Deo conspicit districta audisse ut timeant, agit quoque quatenus et mansuetudinem pietatis eius audiant ut praesumant."

7. Gregory the Great, *Moralia*, 20.5.12, ed. Adriaen, 1010, line 10: "turba virtutum."

8. Gregory the Great, *Moralia*, 20.5.12, ed. Adriaen, 101, line 16: "quasi rex praesidet."

9. Gregory the Great, *Moralia*, 20.5.12, ed. Adriaen, 1010, lines 25–26: "mansuetudinem pietatis eius."

in this context, Gregory raises the problem of tension between God's mercy and justice, together with the idea of their complementarity.

With these words about God's concern for man, Gregory the Great moves on to the historical exposition of Job's phrase, "And when I sat as a king with an army standing round, nevertheless I was the comforter of mourners."[10] He underlines that it refers to the good rulers (*boni rectores*), who need to combine the "authority of ruling and loving-kindness of consoling."[11] His exegesis begins with Luke's parable of a good Samaritan.[12] Here wine and oil applied to the wounds of a half-alive man taken to an inn symbolize, respectively, disciplinary justice, designated by Gregory as the cleaning "biting of strictness," and mercy, in Gregory's words, the soothing "tenderness of pity."[13] His interpretation is similar to the one suggested by Caesarius of Arles in the sermon on this parable. It runs: "By the fact that 'He poured on oil and wine,' we understand mercy in the oil and justice in the wine."[14]

Further, the Gregorian exposition proceeds to the description of the Ark of the Covenant in the Epistle to the Hebrews[15] and represents the rod and the manna contained in the Ark as the symbols of, respectively, the strictness of justice ("the rod of severity") and the kindness of mercy ("the manna of sweetness").[16] This strictness and kindness are to be displayed toward his sub-

10. Gregory the Great, *Moralia*, 20.5.12, ed. Adriaen, 1010, lines 20–21: "corda quoque maerentium … consolatur."

11. Gregory the Great, *Moralia*, 20.5.14, ed. Adriaen, 1012, lines 74–76: "sciendum nobis est quod ualde aedificare lectorem etiam iuxta historiam potest, si perpendat quomodo bonis rectoribus mixta sit et regendi auctoritas, et benignitas consolandi."

12. Lk 10:33–34.

13. Gregory the Great, *Moralia*, 20.5.14, ed. Adriaen, 1012, lines 84–92: "uinum adhibetur et oleum, ut per uinum mordeantur uulnera, per oleum foueantur, quatenus unusquisque qui sanandis uulneribus praeest, in uino morsum districtionis adhibeat, in oleo mollitiem pietatis; per uinum mundentur putrida, per oleum sananda foueantur. Miscenda est ergo lenitas cum seueritate, faciendum quoddam ex utraque temperamentum, ut neque multa asperitate exulcerentur subditi, neque nimia benignitate soluantur."

14. Caesarius of Arles, *Sermones*, 161, ed. Germain Morin, CCSL 104 (Turnhout: Brepols, 1953), 662: "quod autem infudit in eum oleum et vinum, in oleo misericordia intellegitur, in vino iustitia." English translation in Caesarius of Arles, *Sermons*, trans. Mary Magdeleine Mueller (Washington, D.C.: The Catholic University of America Press, 1964), 2:377. At least two sermons ascribed to Caesarius have been reattributed to a later period on the ground of the influence of Gregory the Great's texts on them. See Caesarius of Arles, *Sermons*, trans. Mary Magdeleine Mueller (Washington, D.C.: The Catholic University of America Press, 1973), 3:3.

15. Heb 9:3–4 (Vulgata): "post velamentum autem secundum tabernaculum quod dicitur sancta sanctorum aureum habens turibulum et arcam testamenti circumtectam ex omni parte auro in qua urna aurea habens manna et virga Aaron quae fronduerat et tabulae testamenti."

16. Gregory the Great, *Moralia*, 20.5.14, ed. Adriaen, 1012, lines 92–95: "Hoc nimirum illa

jects by a good ruler. His knowledge and understanding of Holy Scripture are the necessary prerequisite for properly balancing them in a way that is profitable and edifying for the people. Finally, Gregory resorts to David's words in a psalm, "Thy rod and Thy staff they comforted me,"[17] and offers the traditional interpretation that can be found, for example, in Cassiodorus's *Explanation of the Psalms*.[18] According to it, the comforting staff, which, like God's mercy, sustains the faithful, and the rod of discipline, which, like God's judgment, severely strikes the wicked, interact and lead the Christians to ultimate consolation.[19]

The methodology of balancing these oppositions for the sake of the souls and restoring order in the Christian community is very important in the thought of Gregory the Great. It creates this "grammar of reconciliation and complementarity" construed by Carole Straw as an overall pattern of the Gregorian way of thinking.[20] In our case, the pope describes how this balancing mechanism works, when he writes: "So then let there be love, that does not enervate, let there be vigour, that does not irritate, let there be zeal, that does not rage excessively, let there be loving-kindness that does not spare more than may be expedient."[21] In the pope's view, a good ruler (*rector bonus*) must avoid the extremes and provide the interaction of justice, discipline, and mercy for

---

tabernaculi arca significat, in qua cum tabulis uirga simul, et manna est, quia cum scripturae sacrae scientia in boni rectoris pectore, si est uirga districtionis, sit et manna dulcedinis."

17. Ps 22:4 (Vulgata): "virga tua et baculus tuus ipsa me consolata sunt."

18. Cassiodorus, *Expositio Psalmorum I–LXX*, 22.4, ed. Marc Adriaen, CCSL 97 (Turnhout: Brepols, 1958), 212, lines 109–29: "Virga enim pertinet ad iustitiam et fortitudinem Domini Saluatoris, sicut in alio psalmo dicit: Virga aequitatis, uirga regni tui. Baculus ad adiutorium humanum respicit, ... Baculum quippe non est dubium consolari, qui ad opem ferendam humanae imbecillitati semper assumitur. De uirga quid dicemus, quae percutit, affligit, et uitia nostra iudiciaria seueritate castigat? Consolatur plane et ipsa fideles, quando eos ad uiam domini adhibita emendatione perducit." English translation in Cassiodorus, *Explanation of the Psalms*, trans. Patrick Gerard Walsh, ACW 51 (Mahwah, N.J.: Paulist Press, 1990), 1:238: "The 'rod' denotes the justice and strength of the Lord Savior. As he says in another psalm, 'The scepter of your kingdom is the rod of justice' [Ps 44:7]. 'Staff' indicates a support for men.... There is no doubt that the staff consoles, for it is always used to aid human weakness, but what shall we say of the rod, which strikes, beats, and corrects our vices through the Judge's severity? Obviously this too consoles the faithful when it brings improvement and leads men to the Lord's path."

19. Gregory the Great, *Moralia*, 20.5.14, ed. Adriaen, 1012, lines 97–99: "Virga enim percutimur et baculo sustentamur. Si ergo est districtio uirgae quae feriat, sit et consolatio baculi quae sustentet."

20. Carole Straw, *Gregory the Great: Perfection in Imperfection* (Berkeley: University of California Press, 1988).

21. Gregory the Great, *Moralia*, 20.5.14, ed. Adriaen, 1012, lines 99–101: "Sit itaque amor sed non emolliens; sit uigor sed non exasperans; sit zelus, sed non immodate saeuiens; sit pietas sed non plus quam expediat parcens."

the common advantage. This strategy brings about stability. Gregory regards equity as a balanced combination of justice and mercy reconciling their extreme manifestations. For him this is the universal principle that governs the Christian world.

In this context of Gregory the Great's exposition, Moses appears as a biblical example of an ideal ruler. In patristic tradition Augustine, in passing, calls him "prince and good ruler [*princeps et rector bonus*]" in the tract *Against the Letter of Parmenian*, Donatist bishop of Carthage (361–391/92).[22] This Gregorian Moses confirms his goodness while he demonstrates the reciprocity of mercy and severity in action. The pope refers to the golden calf incident, which occurs at the moment of the covenant between God and Israel at Sinai,[23] and shows how Moses acts as the leader of the people of Israel, its ruler (*rector*) "loving pitifully and raging severely."[24] When God accuses the idolaters of "an almost unpardonable offence,"[25] and threatens to destroy this "stiff-necked people,"[26] Moses steps forward as the advocate before God, as the intercessor, as "a bar to the impetus of God's indignation."[27] Moses speaks in defense of the Israelites. Moreover, he is ready to sacrifice himself for them, when he says to God: "Either forgive them this sin; or if not, blot me out of Thy book which Thou hast written."[28] And God listened to him and pardoned the transgressions of those who violated their loyalty to the God of Moses and broke the laws just given at Sinai.[29]

Meanwhile, when Moses returns to the camp, inflamed with the "zeal of righteousness" against the vices of his people, in seeking to restore order, he commands the Levites, who did not worship the calf, to "go in and out from

22. Augustine, *Contra epistolam Parmeniani* 2.8, in *Scripta contra donatistas* 1, ed. Michael Petschenig, CSEL 51 (Vienna: F. Tempsky; Leipzig: G. Freytag, 1908), 53, available online at https://archive.org/details/CSEL51/page/n45. See also Augustin d'Hippone, *Contra epistolam Parmeniani*, trans. Guy Finaert, in *Traités anti-Donatistes* 1, Bibliothèque Augustinienne 28 (Paris: Desclée de Brouwer, 1963), 270.

23. Ex 32

24. Gregory the Great, *Moralia*, 20.5.14, ed. Adriaen, 1012–13: "Intueri libet in Moysi pectore misericordiam cum seueritate sociatam. Videamus amantem pie, et districte saeuientem."

25. Gregory the Great, *Moralia*, 20.5.14, ed. Adriaen, 1013, lines 104–5: "paene inveniabilem … offensam."

26. Ex 32:9.

27. Gregory the Great, *Moralia*, 20.5.14, ed. Adriaen, 1013, lines 109–12: "ille semel et iterum pro populo cui praeerat obicem se ad impetum Dei irascentis opponens, ait: 'Aut dimitte eis hanc noxam; aut si non facis, dele me de libro tuo quem scripsisti.'"

28. Ex 32:31–32.

29. Ex 20.

gate to gate throughout the camp, and slay every man his brother, and every man his companion, and every man his neighbour."[30] As a result, about twenty-three thousand men were killed.[31] Gregory concludes that Moses saves all by killing a number of culprits. In this important episode, Moses reveals in himself loving-kindness in persistent intercession before God and exhibits in public the severity of his discipline toward the perpetrators, spared by God but not by himself, who is commissioned with "the sword of judgment."[32] A similar representation of Moses is found in Ephrem the Syrian's *Commentary on Exodus*, where the exegete writes: "At the top [of the mountain] stood the intercessor, and at the bottom of the mountain, the avenger. Faced with justice … mercy. And in the camp [stood] one who was anxious to discipline … the command of God."[33] However, nothing is known of Gregory's acquaintance with Ephrem's works.

Gregory the Great draws a parallel between Christ, who ideally performs mercy and justice, and Moses, who exhibited mercy and justice in the golden calf episode and "blended both in governing the people, so that neither should discipline be lacking to mercy, nor mercy to discipline."[34] The pope calls Moses "both ways a *strong* ambassador, both ways an *admirable* mediator."[35] This designation of someone mediating between God and man and advocating

30. Gregory the Great, *Moralia*, 20.5.14, 1013, lines 118–20: "Ite et redite de porta usque ad portam per medium castrorum et occidat unusquisque fratrem et amicum et proximum suum."

31. Ex 32:27–28.

32. Gregory the Great, *Moralia*, 20.5.14, ed. Adriaen, 1013, lines 122–27: "Ecce qui uitam omnium etiam cum sua morte petiit, paucorum uitam gladio exstinxit. Intus arsit ignibus amoris, foris accensus est zelo seueritatis. Tanta fuit pietas, ut se pro illis coram Domino morti offerre non dubitaret; tanta seueritas ut eos quos diuinitus feriri timuerat, ipse iudicii gladio feriret."

33. *Sancti Ephraem Syri in Genesim et Exodum Commentarii*, ed. Raymond M. Tonneau, Corpus Scriptorum Christianorum Orientalium (CSCO) 152, Scriptores Syri 71 (Louvain: Éditeur Imprimerie Orientaliste [Durbecq], 1955), 155; English translation in Ephrem the Syrian, *Commentary on Exodus*, 32.8, trans. Edward G. Mathews Jr., and Joseph P. Amar, in *Selected Prose Works*, ed. Kathleen McVey (Washington, D.C.: The Catholic University of America Press, 1994), 265. The text of the *Commentary*, preserved in two Syriac manuscripts, is broken in this section and there are some lacunae. The reading of the passage has been suggested by Alison Salvesen: On the mountain Moses was an intercessor, but below he was an avenger; confronted with God's justice, he thought mercy, but in the camp he became a zealot who carried out chastisement. See *The Exodus Commentary of St. Ephrem: A Fourth Century Syriac Commentary on the Book of Exodus*, trans. Alison Salvesen (Piscataway, N.J.: Gorgias Press, 1995), 58.

34. Gregory the Great, *Moralia*, 20.5.14, ed. Adriaen, 1013, lines 136–38: "In regimine ergo populi utrumque Moyses miscuit, ut nec disciplina deesset misericordiae, nec misericordia disciplinae."

35. Gregory the Great, *Moralia*, 20.5.14, ed. Adriaen, 1013 lines 129–30: "Vtroque legatus fortis, utrobique mediator admirabilis."

on behalf of humankind refers again to the figure of Jesus Christ. Elsewhere the exegete commonly applies to Christ the title of mediator.[36] This certainly rests on the text of the Epistle to Timothy, where Christ is called the "Mediator between God and men."[37] In the Gregorian exposition, Moses is typified as Christ: judge, advocate, mediator, versatile ruler, kind and severe, who "pleaded the cause of the people before God by prayers and the cause of God before the people with swords."[38] What is more, through Moses and, perhaps, the quasi-royal figure of the Blessed Job, who is also considered a good leader of his community and a divinely appointed mediator,[39] Gregory the Great obviously associates any good ruler with Christ. But who are Gregorian rulers, or *rectores*?

Gregory the Great often leaves us in doubt whether this title applies only to spiritual pastors and ministers or is also applicable to any bearer of authority. Even his famous *Pastoral Care* (*Regula pastoralis*), in which this term is ubiquitously used, can be viewed as a manual not only for ecclesiastics but also for princes. In his studies of this question, Robert Markus has demonstrated that, in some cases, the pope could mean by *rector* any powerful person in charge of either a secular or an ecclesiastical office.[40] Gregory regards these officers as "analogous," and they are often mentioned in his works under various titles: *rector, praepositus, praelatus, is qui praeest.*[41]

It is not a mere coincidence that in early medieval Europe the *Pastoral Care* was easily adapted as a manual for princes. Its translator into Old En-

---

36. See Carole Straw, "The Mediator of God and Man," chapter 7 in *Gregory the Great*, 147–61.
37. 1 Tm 2:5.
38. Gregory the Great, *Moralia*, 20.5.14, ed. Adriaen, 1013: "causam populi apud Deum precibus, causam Dei apud populum gladiis allegauit. Intus amans, diuinae irae supplicando obstitit; foris saeuiens, culpam feriendo consumpsit. Succurrit citius omnibus, ostensa morte paucorum."
39. Stuart Lasine, *Knowing Kings: Knowledge, Power, and Narcissism in the Hebrew Bible* (Atlanta, Ga.: Society of Biblical Literature, 2001), 35, 184.
40. Robert A. Markus, "Gregory the Great's *Rector* and His Genesis," in *Grégoire le Grand: Colloques internationaux, Chantilly 15–19 septembre 1982*, ed. Jacques Fontaine et al. (Paris: Éditions du Centre National de la Recherche Scientifique, 1986), 137–46; Markus, "*Gregory the Great on Kings*: Rulers and Preachers in the Commentary on I Kings," in *The Church and Sovereignty: Essays in Honour of Michael Wilks*, ed. Diana Wood, Studies in Church History, Subsidia 9 (Oxford: Blackwell, 1991), 7–21; reprinted in Markus, *Sacred and Secular: Studies on Augustine and Latin Christianity* (Aldershot: Variorum, 1994), paper 8.
41. Markus, "Gregory the Great's *Rector*," 143. See also Carole Straw, "Gregory's Politics: Theory and Practice," in *Gregorio Magno e il suo tempo: XIX Incontro di studiosi dell'antichità cristiana in collaborazione con l'École Française de Rome, Roma 9–12 Maggio 1990*, Studia Ephemeridis Augustinianum 33 (Rome: Institutum Patristicum "Augustinianum," 1991), 1:47–63.

glish, the Anglo-Saxon king Alfred, is represented in his *Life*, written in 893 by the royal chronicler Asser, as an exemplary king, as a good "ruler of all the Christians of the island of Britain" according to the principles outlined by Gregory the Great in his pastoral handbook.[42] Additionally, in the prologue to his *Law Code* Alfred "seeks *to unite mercy with justice* so as to bring their unity into the life of his people" and to appropriate the biblical concept of mercy for the benefit of the Anglo-Saxon administrative and legal system.[43] In the earliest English royal *Ordo*, promulgated in the ninth century, the third mission of the king is to "enjoin equity and mercy in all judgements, that the clement and merciful God may therefore grant us his mercy."[44]

Undoubtedly, in book 2 of the *Pastoral Care*, Alfred encountered the idea of the unification of mercy and justice in the practice of a good ruler. Here, in book 2, Gregory has come back to this subject, which he had already expounded in the *Moralia*. The pope even uses the same examples of wine and oil applied to the wounds of the alien by the Samaritan, and the rod and manna kept in the Ark. He repeats his formula of reciprocity quoted above and concludes his discourse by restating that "while justice and clemency are blended in supreme rule, he who is at the head [of the people] will soothe the hearts of his subjects even when he inspires fear, and yet in soothing them, constrain them to reverential awe."[45]

Another earlier case of Gregory's possible influence on barbarian law can be found in Spain. The *Law of the Visigoths* (*Lex Visigothorum*), or the *Book of the Judges* (*Liber Iudiciorum*), promulgated by King Recceswinth in 654, is almost devoid of any notion of mercy. However, the laws, attributed to King

42. David Pratt, *The Political Thought of King Alfred the Great* (Cambridge: Cambridge University Press, 2007), 135–51, 193–209.

43. Michael Treschow, "The Prologue to Alfred's Law Code: Instruction in the Spirit of Mercy," *Florilegium* 13 (1994): 87, 89, 102, 106.

44. Pratt, *Political Thought*, 76. Janet L. Nelson, "The Earliest Surviving Royal *Ordo*: Some Liturgical and Historical Aspects," in *Politics and Ritual in Early Medieval Europe* (London: Hambledon Press, 1986), 358: "Tertium est ut in omnibus iudiciis aequitatem et misericordiam praecipiat ut per hoc nobis indulgeat misericordiam suam clemens et misericors deus." Janet Nelson tentatively dates this *Ordo* to before 856.

45. Gregory the Great, *Regula pastoralis*, 2.6, PL 77, col. 38C: "ut dum se in arce regiminis justitia clementiaque permiscet, is qui praeest corda subditorum et terrendo demulceat, et tamen ad terroris reverentiam demulcendo constringat." English translation in Gregory the Great, *Pastoral Care*, trans. Henry Davies, ACW 11 (Westminster, Md.: Newman, 1950), 67 (translation slightly altered). See also *Grégoire le Grand, Règle pastorale*, ed. Bruno Judic and Floribert Rommel, trans. Charles Morel, Sources Chrétiennes (SC) 381 (Paris: Éditions du Cerf, 1992), 214.

Chindaswinth (642–53) and his successors in the *Liber Iudiciorum* sporadically use it. In particular, Chindaswinth's law under the title "Concerning the exercise of moderation in judicial decisions, and the avoiding of oppression" orders judges "to moderate, in some degree, the severity of the law towards the persons defeated [in court] and especially those who are oppressed by poverty; for if the authority of the law were enforced to the utmost in every instance, there would be no opportunity for the clemency of mercy."[46] And another law "on observing the practice of mercy by the princes" stipulates that "whenever a supplication is made to us on behalf of those who have been implicated in any crime in our cases, we give the opportunity to submit the appeal, and, by our power, continue to absolve from blame delinquents for the sake of pious pity."[47] These laws are closely connected with canon 2 of the Eighth Council of Toledo, held under Chindaswinth's son Recceswinth in 653.[48] They mirror the intricate relationship between the royal power and the elite in mid-seventh-century Visigothic Spain.[49] The council introduced a significant change in the royal attitude toward political opponents and conspirators,[50] and prescribed that rulers be merciful in inflicting the punishments against them and refrain from employing the death penalty.[51] The compilers of the council's *acta* were well acquainted with pope Gregory I's *Moralia* and

46. *Leges Visigothorum*, 12.1.1, ed. Karl Zeumer, MGH Leges nationum Germanicarum 1 (Hanover: Hahnsche Buchhandlung, 1902), 406 (hereafter cited as *Leges Visigothorum*): "Obtestamur itaque iudices omnes cunctosque … conmonemus ad investigandam quidem rei veritatem in causis omnibus sollerter existere et absque personarum acceptione negotiorum omnium contentiones examinare, circa victas tamen personas ac presertim paupertate depressas severitatem legis aliquantulum temperare. Nam si in totum iudicii proprietas adtenditur, misericordie procul dubio mansuetudo deseritur." I use, with slight alterations, the English translation in *The Visigothic Code (Forum Judicum)*, trans. and ed. Samuel Parsons Scott (Boston: Boston Book Company, 1910), 359–60, available online at http://libro.uca.edu/vcode/visigoths.htm.

47. *Leges Visigothorum*, 6.1.7, 256: "De servanda principibus pietate parcendi. Quotienscumque nobis pro his, qui in causis nostris aliquo crimine inplicati sunt, subplicatur, et suggerendi tribuimus aditum et pia miseratione delinquentibus culpas omittere nostre potestati servamus."

48. Karl Zeumer, "Geschichte der westgotischen Gesetzgebung II.," *Neues Archiv der Gesellschaft für ältere deutsche Geschichtskunde* 24 (1899): 66.

49. Rachel L. Stocking, *Bishops, Councils, and Consensus in the Visigothic Kingdom, 589–633* (Ann Arbor, Mich.: University of Michigan Press, 2000), 1–4, 186. See also Roger Collins, *Visigothic Spain, 409–711* (Oxford: Blackwell, 2004), 81–91.

50. On the previous unmerciful attitude towards the opposition see *Leges Visigothorum*, 2.1.8, 53–57.

51. *Concilios Hispanos: Segunda Parte*, ed. Gonzalo Martínez Díez and Félix Rodríguez, Colección Canónica Hispana 5 (Madrid: Consejo Superior de Investigaciones Científicas, Instituto Enrique Flórez, 1992), 392–410.

quoted it in the same canon 2.[52] Thus, the royal power and the Church revived the decision of 633, when the Fourth Council of Toledo, led by the devoted reader of Gregorian works Isidore of Seville, instructed the king to extend mercy to those who were sentenced to death.[53] In its turn, it was done in
the spirit of Pope Gregory's appeal to Visigothic King Reccared to temper his
government with moderation in relation to his subjects.[54] This papal letter was
included in the *Collectio Hispana*, a collection of canons composed probably
in the seventh century, ascribed to Isidore of Seville, and widely spread across
early medieval Europe.[55]

Kings Chindeswinth and Recceswinth and the fathers of the Eighth Council of Toledo in 653 could also have been influenced by Gregory the Great's
scholar-bishop Taio of Zaragoza, a disciple of Braulio of Zaragoza, Isidore of
Seville's friend and his successor to the bishopric. According to the *Chronicle of
754*, Chindeswinth dispatched Taio to Rome to search for Gregory the Great's
Moralia in the papal archive.[56] The prelate executed this commission successfully and later, on the eve of the Eighth Council of Toledo, compiled *Five Books
of Sentences*—thematically arranged extracts from the *Moralia*. The chapter
"On secular princes," which, together with the chapter "On good princes," consists of the relevant Gregorian discourses, refers to Job's saying from Job 29:25,
emphasizing that Blessed Job exercised his princely authority "with immense
dignity, as well as with immense kindness."[57]

52. Ibid., 410.

53. Ibid., 248–260. In this context canon 75 called the king "to rule the people with justice and piety," thus echoing Isidore of Seville's formula in his *Etymologies* (9.3.5): "the royal virtues are these two especially: justice and piety." Jamie Wood, *The Politics of Identity in Visigothic Spain: Religion and Power in
the Histories of Isidore of Seville* (Leiden: Brill, 2012), 141, 143.

54. Gregory the Great, *Registrum Epistularum Libri VIII–XIV*, 9.229, ed. Dag Norberg, CCSL
140A (Turnhout: Brepols, 1982), 809: "Ipsa quoque regni gubernacula erga subiectos magno sunt mod-
eramine temperanda." On the papal letter in the *Collectio Hispana* see Detlev Jasper and Horst Fuhrmann, *Papal Letters in the Early Middle Ages* (Washington, D.C.: The Catholic University of America
Press, 2001), 73.

55. On this canonical collection, see Lotte Kéry, *Canonical Collections of the Early Middle Ages, ca.
400–1140: A Bibliographical Guide to the Manuscripts and Literature* (Washington, D.C.: The Catholic
University of America Press, 1999), 60–80.

56. *Continuatio Hispana a. DCCLIV*, ed. Theodor Mommsen, MGH Auctores antiquissimi 11,
Chronica Minora 2 (Berlin: Weidmann, 1894), 341–43.

57. Taio of Zaragoza, *Sententiarum libri V*, in *España Sagrada* (Madrid: la Emprenta de Don
Antonio de Sancha, 1776), 31:510; PL 80, col. 964C: "Beatus Job principatus honore perfunctus, quan-
tae celsitudinis quantaeque fuerit benignitatis, insinuat dicens: 'Principes cessabant loqui, digitum

The exposition of the golden calf incident in the *Moralia* is textually tied to the phrase from the Book of Job, which refers to the leadership of Job in his community as if he were a king.[58] And further, quite in accordance with the tradition of representing Moses as a sovereign of Israel,[59] Gregory reiterates and highlights that Moses is not only a spiritual leader, standing above his people, but their ruler: he is in charge of his compatriots, he is set over them, he rules them, he is their true king. The pope inserted the episode of Moses's rage, from *Exodus*, in the text of the *Pastoral Care*.[60] However, in this pastoral handbook he interprets it allegorically in the context of the struggle against vices and temptations and never mentions the edifying significance of Moses's behavior in the camp (as it is formulated in the *Moralia*) in respect to ecclesiastical *rectores*, preachers and teachers. These facts suggest that the Gregorian explanation of the attributes of good rulership in the *Moralia* might be addressed to a wider audience than the ecclesiastical circles for whom Gregory primarily intended his *Pastoral Care*. And later usage of the *Moralia* to some extent confirms this hypothesis.

It is also not a coincidence that, as we have seen in the case of Alfred the Great, early medieval political theory borrowed the Gregorian imagery, which comprised the complementary opposition of the "vigour and discipline of governance [*vigor ac disciplina regiminis*]" and the "ministration of piety [*ministerium pietatis*],"[61] and often used it to characterize the imperial and royal functions in later periods. The text on Moses from the *Moralia* was included in the Carolingian *Collection of Diverse Sayings Which Offer Advice on State Affairs*,[62] attributed either to Bishop Jonas of Orléans (c. 780–841/3),

---

superponebant ori suo' [Job 29:9]. Et iterum: 'Cumque sederem, quasi rex circumstante exercitu, eram tamen moerentium consolator' [Job 29:25]."

58. On Job's royalty in Job 29, see Bruce V. Malchow, "A Royal Prototype in Job 29," in *The Psalms and Other Studies on the Old Testament*, ed. Jack C. Knight and Lawrence A. Sinclair (Nashotah, Wisc.: Nashotah House Seminary, 1990), 178–84; Lasine, *Knowing Kings*, 178n1; Mark Wade Hamilton, "In the Shadow of Leviathan: Kingship in the Book of Job," *Restoration Quarterly* 45 (2003): 34, 38–39, 43–45.

59. Wayne A. Meeks, *The Prophet-King: Moses Traditions and the Johannine Christology* (Leiden: Brill, 1967); John Lierman, *The New Testament Moses: Christian Perceptions of Moses and Israel in the Setting of Jewish Religion* (Tübingen: Mohr Siebeck, 2004), 79–123, 273–75.

60. Gregory the Great, *Regula pastoralis*, 3.25, PL 77, cols. 97C–98A; *Grégoire le Grand, Règle pastorale*, ed. Bruno Judic and Floribert Rommel, trans. Charles Morel, SC 382 (Paris: Éditions du Cerf, 1992), 434–36.

61. See note 65.

62. Gerhard Laehr, "Ein karolingischer Konzilsbrief und der Fürstenspiegel Hincmars von Reims," *Neues Archiv der Gesellschaft für ältere deutsche Geschichtskunde* 50 (1935): 125–26.

a confidant of Emperor Louis the Pious and author of the "mirror for princes" treatise *The Royal Institution*, addressed to King Pippin of Aquitaine,[63] or to Archbishop Hincmar of Rheims (c. 806–882), a political adviser of Emperor Charles the Bald and author of the tract *The Person of the King and Royal Ministry*. In this work, Hincmar also employed Gregory's exegesis to elaborate Carolingian royal ideology and epitomized it in chapter 32 of *The Person of the King and Royal Ministry*, entitled "Let a good king have the rod of severity and the manna of sweetness."[64] This perception of Gregory the Great's interpretation developed a peculiar medieval view of the royal staff as a symbol of the unity of the strictness of judgment, disciplinary justice, restraint, and mercy. It is mirrored, for example, in the medieval ritual of French royal coronation. During this ceremony the king of France received the staff with the words: "Receive the rod of authority and equity, by which you may learn to comfort the pious and strike the reprobate with terror, teach the right path to the straying, and extend a hand to those who have fallen back; and with it you shall scatter the proud and raise up the humble." Thanks to Gregory the Great, the image of Moses, the king who united "vigour and discipline of governance" and the "ministration of piety," inspired monarchs and medieval political thinkers to shape a model of medieval European kingship.[65]

63. Chapter 4 of *De institutione regia* argues that "the king must rule with justice and equity, procure peace and concord among his subjects," and refers to Job 29:25, without mentioning Gregory's exposition. Jonas of Orléans. *De institutione regia* 4, PL 106, cols. 290D–2B (translation my own).

64. Hincmar of Rheims, *De regis persona et regio ministerio* 32, PL 106, cols. 855D–6B: "Quod boni regis sit et virga districtionis, et manna dulcedinis" (translation my own). Hincmar also opens his most famous treatise on virtues and vices, based mostly on Gregory the Great's *Moralia* and *Homilies on the Gospel*, with Gregory's already mentioned letter to King Reccared instructing the king on, among other topics, tempering his government. See Hincmar of Rheims, *De cavendis vitiis et virtutibus exercendis*, ed. Doris Nachtmann, MGH Quellen zur Geistesgeschichte des Mittelalters 16 (Munich: MGH, 1998), 118.

65. "Last Capetian Ordo, ca. 1250–1270," in *"Ordines Coronationis Franciae": Texts and "Ordines" for the Coronation of Frankish and French Kings and Queens in the Middle Ages*, ed. Richard A. Jackson (Philadelphia: University of Pennsylvania Press, 2000), 2:400: "Accipe virgam virtutis atque equitatis qua intelligas mulcere pios et terrere reprobos, errantibus viam doce lapsisque manum porrige, disperdasque superbos et releues humiles." See also the twelfth-century *Ordines* from Southern France (or possibly Venice) in *Die Ordines für die Weihe und Krönung des Kaisers und der Kaiserin (Ordines Coronationis Imperialis)*, ed. Reinhard Elze, Fontes iuris Germanici antiqui in usum scholarum ex MGH separatim editi 9 (Hannover: Hahnsche Buchhandlung, 1960), 27, 30. All translations here are my own.

John C. Reeves

17. MOSES AT THE MARGINS
OF SPACE AND TIME

It might strike some as paradoxical to frame the scriptural character of Moses within the discourse of marginality. After all, the figure of Moses occupies center stage in every sustained articulation of a Jewish religiosity, and it likewise plays the prominent roles of prototype and foil in the sibling communities of Christianity and Islam. The name of Moses, for example, appears 136 times in the Qur'ān, and when we take into account the qur'ānic stories that feature aspects of his prophetic career and the passages that allude to his reputed sayings and doings, it becomes clear that Moses is by far the most important pre-Islamic forebear to the Muslim Prophet.[1] An analogous scrutiny of a concordance or standard lexicon of the New Testament and the early literature associated with the Jesus-movement uncovers a similar fixation with the figure of Moses and its centrality for a wide variety of burgeoning Christian discourse.

There are nevertheless some aspects to the character of Moses as it evolves from antiquity into the High Middle Ages that permit an exploration of Moses as a liminal figure. The starting point for my exposition will be the curious

1. Cornelia Schöck, "Moses," in *Encyclopaedia of the Qur'ān*, ed. Jane Dammen McAuliffe (Leiden: Brill, 2001–06), 3:419–26. Subsequent citations from the different volumes of this valuable resource will employ the siglum *EncQur*. Unless otherwise noted, all abbreviations for primary and secondary sources in this chapter will follow the scheme established in *The SBL Handbook of Style for Ancient Near Eastern, Biblical, and Early Christian Studies*, ed. Patrick H. Alexander et al. (Peabody, Mass.: Hendrickson, 1999). All translations of primary sources are the author's, unless otherwise indicated.

passage, which occurs at the end of the Pentateuch, that describes the departure of Moses from life in this world. We read therein: "And Moses, the servant of the Lord, died there in the land of Moab at the command of (עַל פִּי) the
Lord. He buried him in the valley in the land of Moab opposite Beth-Pe'or, yet
no one knows his burial place up to this day" (Dt 34:5–6). Now this, as many
others have remarked, is a very peculiar sequence of statements. Verse 6 is especially perplexing. While on the one hand we seem to have an explicit declaration as to where one might find the tomb of Moses if one were to make search
for it, on the other we are immediately informed that its location is an enig-
ma. This contextual oddity has been aptly labeled "oxymoronic" by the Israeli
folklorist Rella Kushelevsky in her magisterial exploration of the folklore that
surrounds the "death of Moses."[2] The dense narrative turbulence churned
up by this "oxymoron" obscures the actual fate of the Israelite leader, allowing for the possibility that he may have a further role to play in the history of
his community. And there are indeed some suggestive hints in both scriptural
and parascriptural sources that the figure of Moses continues to loom large in
end-time scenarios constructed among various Jewish, Christian, and Muslim
communities during the first millennium of the Common Era.

In the present paper, the following themes will be explored. First, we will
rapidly survey a well-known series of literary statements that indicate there
was widespread uncertainty about the actual fate of Moses as it was depicted in the biblical book of Deuteronomy. These amplifications tend to fluc-
tuate, as a number of scholars have noted, between the poles of "death" and
"occultation."[3] I will next call your attention to a small number of curious
pronouncements that posit an eschatological role for Moses, either freshly resurrected or divinely restored from heaven to earth, during the turbulent sequence of events that mark the arrival of the End of Days. Finally, in light of
the importance of the figure of Moses to a biblically rooted religious trium-
phalism, I want to briefly rehearse certain roles that both material and communal "Moses-surrogates" play within apocalyptic traditions preserved by
Jewish, Christian, and Muslim tradents.

2. Rella Kushelevsky, *Moses and the Angel of Death* (New York: Peter Lang, 1995), xx, and *passim*.
3. See especially the groundbreaking essay of Samuel E. Loewenstamm, "The Death of Moses," in
Studies on the Testament of Abraham, ed. George W. E. Nickelsburg Jr. (Missoula, Mont.: Scholars Press,
1976), 185–217. He suggests that an older "mythological" tale about the final ascent of Moses was gradually but not entirely successfully supplanted by a "rational" account that narrated his death and burial.

Between the Poles of Death and Occultation

Given the effusive accolades heaped upon Moses by certain strata of the Hebrew Bible, it is not all that surprising that some expositors of Israelite epic lore might resist the notion that this "servant of the Lord [עבד י״י/ אלהים]"[4] might have been subject to the same forces of organic entropy that afflict, weaken, and eventually effect the demise of other corporeal beings. His unique status among Israelite worthies is underscored at the end of Deuteronomy 34: "Never again did a prophet like Moses arise among Israel, one with whom the Lord had face to face intimacy, or one who controlled all the signs and marvels [with] which the Lord dispatched him to perform in the land of Egypt against Pharaoh and against his servants and against his land" (vv. 10–11). Other classic pentateuchal sources sound a similar tone. We learn that when Moses would commune with God in the Tent of Meeting, "God would speak with Moses face to face [פנים אל פנים], just like a person would speak to their friend" (Ex 33:11). When Aaron and Miriam protest the seemingly tyrannical authority wielded by Moses over the wilderness generation, the Deity takes up his defense: "I speak with him articulately [פה אל פה] and visually [ומ־ ראה] ... he gazes at the form of the Lord" (Nm 12:8), a characterization uttered in pointed contrast to the coded dreamlike ways by which other mediators of divine guidance receive their instructions. A parallel theme about the uniqueness of the dialogical relationship enjoyed by God and Moses is sounded in the Qur'ān, where one listing of a series of messengers and certain revelatory writings is juxtaposed alongside the terse declaration "but God spoke directly to Moses" (Q 4:164). This very same mark of distinction reappears in another *sūra* where God is represented as saying to Moses: "Moses, <u>I have raised you above other people</u> by [giving you] My messages <u>and speaking to you</u>" (Q 7:144). Later tradition will in fact articulate this distinction of Moses from other prophets with a special honorific; namely, Moses as the *Kalīm Allāh*, or "interlocutor with God."[5]

One might also point to the quasi-mythological materialization of the horned Moses on earth after his lengthy sojourn with God and successful re-

---

4. Jos 1:13, 15; 8:31, 33; 11:12; 12:6; 13:8; 14:7; 18:7; 22:2, 4, 5; 2 Kgs 18:12; Dn 9:11; Neh 10:30; 1 Chr 6:34; 2 Chr 1:3; 24:6, 9. Cf. also Ex 14:31; Nm 12:7–8.

5. On the distinction of Moses from other prophets, see Schöck, "Moses," 424. On Moses as "interlocutor," see Uri Rubin, "Prophets and Prophethood," *EncQur* 4:292.

trieval of the heavenly tablets of the Law (Ex 34:27–35),[6] a physical mutation
that is akin to the apotheosis of Enoch in parascriptural lore. This blurring of
the boundaries between the natural and the supernatural presages the sorts of
attributes awarded to or claimed by Moses in later midrashic portraits such as
can be found in *Deuteronomy Rabbah*, where angels fear to provoke him and
he is portrayed as boasting "I have more power than any other person born
into this world!"[7] There is, in other words, a powerful impetus, stemming already from portions of the biblical text, for treating Moses as somehow more
than human, as someone who shares in the metaphysical dimensions of existence, as an entity who has truly morphed into a *theios anēr* (איש האלהים).[8]

Here one might note the interesting testimony that is supplied by the so-
called Animal Apocalypse, a coherent symbolic dream vision narrating the
course of Israel's epic history from creation to the early days of the Hasmonean
rebellion; the vision is now preserved among that network of traditional tales
to which modern scholars have accorded the title of *1 Enoch* (85:1–90:42).
Therein the human actors in history are coded as various species of animals,
such as bulls, cows, rams, goats, asses, camels, and so on, whereas angelic
agents are represented as stars (if behaving wickedly) or as humans (if behaving correctly). Of particular interest for our purposes are two passages where
animal characters playing the roles of the Flood-hero and Moses are declared
by the visionary to have achieved human form.[9] According to Devorah Dimant, nothing sinister should be read into these two narrative turns, since
such a body was required in order to construct the ark and the tabernacle respectively.[10] Yet one should remain cautious about over-rationalizing what are
at root mythological expressions, especially when it is recalled that the boon
of immortality and sequestration from human society are the normal rewards
granted the Mesopotamian flood-hero, who is certainly the prototype for his

6. Cf. *Pesiq. RabKah.*, *nispaḥ* 1: "[he was] a man at the time he ascended to the heavenly height; [he was] a god at the time he came back down [to us] below." Bernard Mandelbaum, ed., *Pesiqta de Rav Kahana*, 2nd ed., 2 vols. (New York: Jewish Theological Seminary, 1987), 443.6–7. Note also *Deut. Rab.* 11.4: "R. Abin said: his lower half was human and his upper half was divine!" All citations from *Deuteronomy Rabbah* rely upon the common printed edition (Vilna: Romm, 1878).

7. *Deut. Rab.* 11.10 (ed. Vilna): יש בי כח מכל באי העולם.

8. See Dt 33:1; Jos 14:6; Ps 90:1; Ezr 3:2; 1 Chr 23:14; 2 Chr 30:16.

9. *1 En.* 89:1–9, 36–38. A portion of 89:36 survives in Aramaic in 4Q204 frag. 4 line 10, where we read: "that [sh]e[ep] was transformed and became a human being [אתהפך והוא אנוש], and he built...."

10. Devorah Dimant, "Noah in Early Jewish Literature," in *Biblical Figures Outside the Bible*, ed. Michael E. Stone and Theodore A. Bergren (Harrisburg, Pa.: Trinity Press International, 1998), 134n57.

Israelite counterpart. Even though these motifs are now absent from the pentateuchal redactor's portrait of Noah, both are arguably present within the penumbra of parascriptural lore that surrounds the members of the flood generation, and particularly the figure of Enoch, who may once have functioned as the flood-hero in a no-longer-extant version of this legend. Be that as it may, the analogous "transformation" from beast to man that is credited to Moses in the Animal Apocalypse is fraught with a similar significance, suggesting that he—like the flood-hero—achieved a more-than-mortal status by his piety and obedience. Yet the text of the vision goes on to say that the "leader who had become human withdrew from them and fell asleep" (89:38), which suggests that despite his seeming angelification Moses was still subject to the cold fingers of Death. Thus the Animal Apocalypse exemplifies the same marginal tension that we have already observed in Deuteronomy 34 between a terrestrial entombment and a bodily removal from human society.

Other Hellenistic and Roman era sources mirror this same tension. In his rewriting of Deuteronomy 34 that figures in his *Antiquities*, Josephus has Moses suddenly vanish "into a ravine" before the astonished eyes of Eleazar and Joshua while being enveloped by a cloud. This first-century apologist and historian goes on to declare that Moses explicitly wrote in Deuteronomy that he had died in order to dissuade future generations from asserting that he had actually been taken up into the divine world.[11] Philo makes a similar statement about Moses dictating "while still alive the story of his own death, telling before the end how the end would come, telling how he was buried with none present ... [and] how also he was not laid to rest in the tomb of his forefathers but was given a monument of special dignity which no mortal man has ever seen."[12] Yet in another place Philo also has what Daniel Falk rightly characterizes as an "extraordinary" claim that Moses was essentially a part of the Deity and made his return to the divine realm once his mission on earth was concluded.[13] However, a different note is sounded within the *Liber antiquitatum biblicarum* of Pseudo-Philo, a likely late Second Temple–era col-

11. Josephus, *Ant.* 4.326; cf. 3.96.

12. Philo, *Mos.* 2.291. Translation is adapted from Philo, *Moses*, trans. F. H. Colson, Loeb Classical Library (Cambridge, Mass.: Harvard University Press, 1935), 6:595.

13. Philo, *Sacr.* 8–10; Daniel K. Falk, "Moses," in *The Eerdmans Dictionary of Early Judaism*, ed. John J. Collins and Daniel C. Harlow (Grand Rapids, Mich.: Eerdmans, 2010), 969. See also the careful discussion in Wayne A. Meeks, *The Prophet-King: Moses Traditions and the Johannine Christology*, NTSuppl 14 (Leiden: Brill, 1967), 103–6.

lection of biblically allied legends originally authored in Hebrew. After a final dialogue between God and Moses wherein God promises that Moses will finally experience life in the Promised Land after his present demise and future resurrection, God is said to have "buried him [Moses] with His own hands on a high place and in the light of all the world" (19.16), a statement that accents the visible and even public nature of his final disposition and that stands in marked contrast to the veiling cloud invoked by Josephus.[14] Similarly the roughly contemporary *Assumption* or *Testament of Moses* has its hero early on inform his attendant Joshua: "Therefore I shall speak plainly to you. The years of my life have come to an end and in the presence of the entire community I am going to sleep with my fathers" (1.15).[15] Later the same author has Moses issue a computational prediction whose starting point begins "from my death" (10.12), and then he portrays Joshua as delineating the size of Moses's tomb to be equivalent to that of the material universe: "your sepulcher is from the rising to the setting of the sun, and from the south to the limits of the north, the whole world is your sepulcher" (11.8).[16] The well-nigh cosmic dimensions of his final resting place provide perhaps the ultimate retort to those who claim they cannot locate his tomb among the caverns of Moab and therefore conclude he must have been supernaturally removed from human society. When the spot of concealment is coincident with material reality itself, there is little point in authorizing a search for it.

The graphically material nature of Moses's death and interment finds strong accentuation in the targumic versions of the Pentateuch. According to *Targum Onkelos* Deuteronomy 33:21, the trans-Jordanian territory allotted to the tribe of Gad was "the best, for within his share is buried Moses, the great scribe of Israel."[17] The Palestinian targumim to the same verse expand this notice further by calling attention to the early tradition that the "grave of Moses" was one of those anomalous items—like Balaam's ass and the well of Miriam—that God brought into existence at the close of the creation week. They portray his burial place as a sumptuous one that is "inlaid with precious stones

---

14. Yet this visibility is oddly contradicted by *L.A.B.* 19.12: "But neither angel nor man will know your tomb in which you are to be buried until I visit the world." Translations are those of Daniel J. Harrington, "Pseudo-Philo (First Century A.D.)," in *The Old Testament Pseudepigrapha*, ed. James H. Charlesworth (Garden City, N.Y.: Doubleday, 1985), 2:328.

15. Translation is that of John Priest, "Testament of Moses (First Century A.D.)," in *OTP* 1:927.

16. Ibid., 1:933.

17. Based on *t. Soṭah* 4.8.

and pearls," a fitting final resting place for the one who performed the commands of the Lord and taught his ordinances to the people of Israel. An even more emphatic registration of the bodily death of Moses is found in the Geniza Aramaic acrostic poem that accompanies Deuteronomy 34 in a manuscript now housed in the Bodleian Library at Oxford University and published by Michael Klein.[18] Therein Moses refuses to accept God's decree that he, like all of his ancestors, must also experience death. He journeys to the Tomb of the Patriarchs in Hebron, rouses Adam from his "sleep," and castigates the Protoplast for bringing death into the world by his disobedience in Eden. Adam protests however that the blame is misplaced: since the Torah, which narrates the fateful story, preexists Creation itself by two thousand years, there is nothing that the Protoplast could have done to alter this script. "Accept for yourself, O Moses, the cup of death! My name had already been inscribed for death, so why do you rebuke me?!?"[19] A reluctant Moses is thus forced to acknowledge and to acquiesce to the eternally predetermined nature of his own demise.

Recurrent doubts about the physical death and burial of Moses are registered in a wide range of rabbinic works. The halakhic midrash *Sifre* incorporates within its discussion of Deuteronomy 34:5 the following dissident opinion: "There are some who say that Moses did not die, but rather that he abides and performs service in the supernal realm."[20] The same tradition about his survival is repeated in the Bavli in a slightly amplified form, where the hermeneutical reasoning that supports that conclusion is presented, and an interesting anecdote is recounted about how the Roman government once dispatched an army squadron to the hill country of Moab in order to locate and (presumably) to loot or vandalize the tomb of Moses.[21] When they would ascend to a height, they could see it down below them, but once they would descend to that spot, it then appeared to be above them. Even dividing themselves into two search parties in order to simultaneously canvass and coordinate their movements did not achieve their aim, for the tomb although visible to both

18. Oxford Bodleian Ms. Heb. e 25, fol. 64r. See Michael L. Klein, *Genizah Manuscripts of Palestinian Targum to the Pentateuch* (Cincinnati, Ohio: Hebrew Union College Press, 1986), 1:362–63.

19. Adapted from the translation of Klein, *Genizah Manuscripts*, 1:362.

20. *Sifre* Deut §357, in *Sifre Devarim*, ed. Louis Finkelstein (repr., New York: Jewish Theological Seminary, 1969), 428.

21. B. *Soṭah* 13b–14a. Parallel narratives about this expedition can be found in *Sifre* Deut §357 (ed. Finkelstein, 429); also *Midrash Leqaḥ Tov*, ed. Salomon Buber (Vilna: Romm, 1884), 5:134–35.

groups remained stubbornly out of their reach. This tale about the futile imperial attempt to expropriate and subjugate the tomb of the Jewish lawgiver neatly reinforces the point made earlier in the Latin *Assumption of Moses* about its actual cosmic scope, perhaps providing another way of articulating the futility of petty attempts to tie it down to one single plot of real estate. And as the late midrash *Leqaḥ Tov* points out, the tomb's unknown location also discourages misguided devotees from erecting a shrine and engaging in questionable religious practices on the premises.[22]

Efforts to read the disappearance of Moses from human society in terms of a quasi-permanent ascent or temporary occultation were sometimes aided by other verses of scripture wherein Moses is linguistically represented as "going up" to a higher locale in order to converse with God or perform some other task that required an uncluttered view of his spatial or temporal surroundings. An excellent example of this particular trajectory is provided by a Yemenite midrash. Its exegesis of Genesis 5:24 ("and he was no more, because God took him") proceeds as follows: "A *baraita*. Three ascended and [now] perform service in the heavenly heights, and they are Enoch, Moses, and Elijah. [Why] Enoch? Because scripture states, 'for God took him' [Gn 5:24]. [Why] Moses? Because scripture states, 'and Moses made ascent [ויעל] from the plains of Moab ... and no one knows his place of burial' [Dt 34:1–6]. [Why] Elijah? Because scripture states, 'and Elijah ascended in a heavenly storm-wind' [2 Kgs 2:11]."[23] Other passages that couple inflected forms of the verb "ascend" with the subject "Moses" occur in Exodus chapters 19 and 24. But perhaps the most intriguing use of the combination of the motifs of the supposed "death of Moses" and his actual "ascent to heaven" occurs among the chains of traditions that surround the demise of another foundational prophet who seemed to have viewed the narrative *vita* of Moses as archetypal for his own career.

A *ḥadīth* traced through Ibn Shihāb al-Zuhrī to the prominent Compan-

22. *Midr. Leqaḥ Tov* (ed. Buber), 5:135.3–4: "Why did the tomb of Moses remain unknown? (It remained so) in order that Israel would not go and found a temple there and make sacrifices and offerings there, and so that the gentile nations would not pollute his grave with their images and (other) abominable practices!" A similar explanation for God's deliberate concealment of the tomb of Moses is provided by the thirteenth-century Syriac compilation of biblical legendry known as *The Book of the Bee*; see *The Book of the Bee*, ed. Ernest A. Wallis Budge (Oxford: Clarendon, 1886), 70.14–16 (text); 65 (translation).

23. *Midrash ha-Gadol 'al ḥamishah ḥumshey Torah: Sefer Bereshit*, ed. Mordecai Margalioth (Jerusalem: Mosad ha-Rav Kook, 1947), 132.8–11.

ion Abū Hurayra (d. 679) that is found in multiple sources relates that when Muḥammad died, 'Umar b. al-Khaṭṭāb, one of the most important leaders of the early Muslim community, rose up in the mosque and said: "Some of the *munāfiqūn* [hypocrites]²⁴ claim that the Messenger of God is dead. I swear to you by God that the Messenger of God is not dead! Rather, he has gone to his Lord, just like Moses b. 'Imrān went and was absent from his people for forty [days and] nights.²⁵ Moses came back after it had been said that he had died. I swear to you by God that the Messenger of God will come back to us [just like Moses came back]!"²⁶ The scriptural point of reference to which 'Umar makes appeal is of course the famous story of communal perfidy found in Exodus 32, where the forty-day absence of Moses while he procured the first pair of tablets of the Law is interpreted by a vocal cohort of the people of Israel as his willful abandonment of them to their fate: "for this Moses, the man who brought us up out of the land of Egypt, we have no idea what has become of him" (Ex 32:1). They prevail upon Aaron to fashion them a "god"; namely, the infamous golden calf, to take the place of their erstwhile leader. But Moses of course eventually returns and punishes the people for their faithlessness. 'Umar constructs a powerful correspondence between the situation of the Israelites in the wilderness and that of the Muslim community of believers in his own day, both of whom have seemingly lost their leaders prior to the ultimate fulfillment of their respective missions. Those not sufficiently committed to the cause of divine truth—like the *erev rav* or "mixed multitude" (cf. Ex 12:38) of the wilderness generation—endanger the welfare of the rest of the community. The tradition goes on to relate that 'Umar's outburst about the occultation of Muḥammad causes quite a stir among those present in the mosque. It is only after the physical intervention of Abū Bakr, the Companion who would become Muḥammad's successor, and his verbal refutation of 'Umar's prophet-

---

24. On this pejorative term, see Camilla P. Adang, "Hypocrites and Hypocrisy," *EncQur* 2:468–72; also Paul Lawrence Rose, "Muhammad, the Jews and the Constitution of Medina: Retrieving the Historical Kernel," *Der Islam* 86 (2011): 1–29, esp. 14–16.

25. See Q 2:51.

26. Abū Ja'far Muḥammad b. Jarīr al-ṭabarī, *Ta'rīkh al-rusul wa'l-mulūk*, vol. 1, bk. 4, ed. M. J. de Goeje et al. (Leiden: Brill, 1890), 1815.14–1816.2. The passage in brackets is added from the slightly variant version of this *ḥadīth* that is found in the *Sīra* of Ibn Hishām. See also Ibn Sa'd, *al-ṭabaqāt al-kubrā*, vol. 2, bk. 2, ed. E. Sachau et al. (Leiden: Brill, 1912), 53.12–17; 53.19–21; 55.21–56.4; Saïd Amir Arjomand, "Islamic Apocalypticism in the Classical Period," in *The Encyclopedia of Apocalypticism*, ed. Bernard McGinn, John J. Collins, and Stephen J. Stein (New York: Continuum, 1998), 2:247.

ic assimilation with a timely quotation from scripture ("Muḥammad is only an apostle, and the apostles prior to him have passed away" [Q 3:144], with its implication that messengers are expendable, but only God is not subject to death), that the people accept the reality of Muḥammad's death.[27] 'Umar then ruefully confesses his error and admits that "the Messenger of God indeed is dead!"[28]

Moreover the *ṭabaqāt* of Ibn Sa'd relates some other traditions that point toward a reading of Muḥammad's destiny as a renewal of that of Moses. Among these is an eschatological admonition that refuses to accept the demise of the Prophet before the capitulation of certain Roman cities,[29] an omen that sometimes figures in early Muslim lists of the "signs of the Hour," or eschaton.[30] There is also a declaration put into the mouth of an anonymous group of enthusiasts that "his [i.e., Muḥammad's] soul was taken up just as the soul of Moses was taken up," where intriguingly the verb used for his soul's departure is the same one employed of the Prophet's renowned visit (*mi'rāj*) to heaven.[31] Classical descriptions of the *mi'rāj* often portray Muḥammad encountering and conversing with Moses in the sixth heaven immediately before and after his audience before the throne of God in the seventh heaven,[32] yet it is not unusual in medieval Jewish or Muslim texts for exemplary servants of God to enjoy a blissful existence in Paradise prior to the Day of Resurrection, regardless of their actual earthly fate.

Another *ḥadīth* attributed to Ibn 'Abbās has the Prophet himself pronounce upon the historical veracity of the death and burial of Moses. After Moses realizes that he is fated to die before the people of Israel enter the Promised Land, he begs God for his tomb "to be brought as close to the Holy Land

27. For the rhetorical juxtapositioning of these two successors to Muḥammad in this early tradition, see especially Stephen J. Shoemaker, *The Death of a Prophet: The End of Muhammad's Life and the Beginnings of Islam* (Philadelphia: University of Pennsylvania Press, 2012), 179–88.

28. Ṭabarī, *Ta'rīkh* (ed. de Goeje), vol. 1, bk. 4, 1817.1–2. 'Umar's resistance to the notion of the Prophet's demise prior to the fulfillment of eschatological hopes is also noted by Fred M. Donner, *Muhammad and the Believers: At the Origins of Islam* (Cambridge, Mass.: Harvard University Press, 2010), 97.

29. Ibn Sa'd, *ṭabaqāt*, vol. 2, bk. 2, 38.4–6; Arjomand, "Islamic Apocalypticism," 247.

30. For an initial discussion with bibliographic references, see John C. Reeves, *Trajectories in Near Eastern Apocalyptic: A Postrabbinic Jewish Apocalypse Reader* (Atlanta, Ga.: Society of Biblical Literature, 2005), 108–10.

31. Ibn Sa'd, *ṭabaqāt*, vol. 2, bk. 2, 53.18–19.

32. See for example Ibn Hishām, *Kitāb sīrat rasūl Allāh*, ed. Ferdinand Wüstenfeld (Göttingen: Dieterichsche Universitäts-Buchhandlung, 1858), 1:270–71; Alfred Guillaume, *The Life of Muhammad: A Translation of Ishāq's Sīrat Rasūl Allāh* (Oxford: Oxford University Press, 1955), 186–87.

as one stone's throw." Muḥammad is then represented as stating: "If I had been on the spot, I would have shown you his [i.e, Moses's] grave beside the road at the foot of the red hill."[33] This pronouncement provides a powerful endorsement for the qur'ānic notion that Moses, like Muḥammad himself, was purely a human agent of the Deity and so should not be imagined as somehow exempt from the funeral rituals associated with the passage of the human form from life to death. Three different sites in Syria and the Jordan River valley will later vie with one another for official recognition as the authentic locale for the tomb of Moses.[34]

We however cannot leave this particular facet of our topic without mentioning one of the most popular literary expressions of the removal of Moses from human society: his infamous struggle with the Angel of Death.[35] Variant versions of this legend abound within Jewish literature, and there is no need for us here to engage in a close comparative reading that calls attention to and explicates their differences.[36] Muslim tradition is also familiar with the theme of Moses's ultimately unsuccessful struggle with the Angel of Death. Ṭabarī recounts a tradition in which the Prophet is reported to have said that the Angel of Death had been in the habit of appearing openly before his victims prior to his encounter with Moses. When he attempted to slay Moses, the latter struck his would-be assassin so hard that he "gouged out his eye." Owing to this trauma, the Angel of Death never again publicly confronted people, preferring instead to operate in stealth.[37] This tradition contains some interesting points of contact with the Jewish cycle of legends surrounding the Palestinian amora R. Joshua b. Levi and his own adventures with the Angel of Death.[38]

33. G. H. A. Juynboll, *Encyclopaedia of the Canonical ḥadīth* (Leiden: Brill, 2007), 29.

34. Brannon Wheeler, *Mecca and Eden: Ritual, Relics, and Territory in Islam* (Chicago: University of Chicago Press, 2006), 89.

35. The *locus classicus* for this well-known story is at the end of *Deut. Rab.* 11.10 (ed. Vilna). An early nucleus for this assignation, which tempers the supernatural dimensions of Moses's character, occurs in *Sifre* Deut §305 (ed. Finkelstein, 326–27).

36. These have been exhaustively and brilliantly surveyed in Kushelevsky, *Moses and the Angel of Death*, 107–278.

37. Ṭabarī, *Ta'rikh* (ed. de Goeje), vol. 1, bk. 1, 505.1–10; Juynboll, *Encyclopaedia*, 29. See also Kushelevsky, *Moses and the Angel of Death*, 136, who suggests that the motif of the blinding (and healing) of the Angel of Death originates in Islamic sources.

38. The narrative kernel for their encounter is *b. Ketub.* 77b, an aggadic anecdote, which subsequent storytellers expand into a detailed tour of heaven and hell under the incipit *Ma'aseh R. Joshua ben Levi*. See Israël Lévi, "Le conte du *Diable dupé* dans le folklore juif," *Revue des Études Juives (REJ)* 85 (1928): 137–63, esp. 142–44. There are a large number of manuscript and print versions of the *Ma'aseh*,

R. Joshua b. Levi cunningly tricks the Angel of Death into handing over his sword into his own care, and refuses to return it until the Angel swears that he will no longer "show it to any person at the time you are taking their soul."[39] One might also note that the curious motif of the "blinding" of the Angel of Death—a disability that seemingly would render that entity a much more dangerous adversary, and which, incidentally, is also a feature of the *Deuteronomy Rabbah* story—aligns surprisingly well with his proper name "Samael," a cognomen whose etymological association with blindness is at least as old as the Nag Hammadi treatise known as the *Hypostasis of the Archons*.[40]

In the later collection of Muslim prophetic legends attributed to al-Kisā'ī, we also find a story that possesses some verbal overlaps with the cognate tale recounted in the medieval *Deuteronomy Rabbah* midrash and its congeners. There we read:

Then the Angel of Death descended to Moses, who was seated reading the Torah. He said: "Greetings [lit. "Peace"] unto you, O Moses!" He responded: "And greetings unto you. Who are you?" He said: "I am the Angel of Death. I have come now to take your soul." Moses replied: "From where will you take it?" He said: "From your mouth." He answered: "I spoke with my Lord through it!" He said: "Then from your hands." He replied: "I held the tablets with them!" He said: "Then from your ears." He answered: "I heard with them the discourse from my Lord and the sound of the Pen on the Preserved Tablets."[41] He said: "Then from your eyes." He replied: "I saw with them the Light of my Lord." He said: "Then from your feet." He replied: "I stood with them on the mountain—Mount Sinai—under the protection of my Lord."[42] Then the

of which the *editio princeps* is the second work in the unpaginated anthological volume *Liqquṭim we-ḥibburim* (Constantinople: Astruc de Toulon, 1519). For a different version, see Adolph Jellinek, ed., *Bet ha-Midrasch: Sammlung kleiner Midraschim und vermischter Abhandlungen aus der jüdischen Literatur* (repr., Jerusalem: Bamberger & Wahrmann, 1938), 2:48–49. This collection is subsequently referenced as *BHM*.

    39. "Prior to this, at every place where a particular person was leaving [this world], he [the Angel of Death] would slaughter them in full view of everyone, even if they were [an infant] asleep in the bosom of their mother. At that time he [the Angel] swore to him [R. Joshua], and so he gave him back the sword."

    40. *Hyp. Arch.* 94.9–95.13 (NHC 2.4), where "Samael" is glossed as "god of the blind."

    41. According to some traditions, the first thing created by God was the pen. On the tablet, see Q 85:22; A. J. Wensinck and C. E. Bosworth, "Lawḥ" *Encyclopaedia of Islam, New Edition* (Leiden: Brill, 1983), 5:698; and Daniel A. Madigan, "Preserved Tablet," *EncQur* 4:261–63.

    42. A similar somatic protest is registered within the Armenian *Life of Moses* quoted by Michael E. Stone, "The Metamorphosis of Ezra: Jewish Apocalypse and Medieval Vision," *Journal of Theological Studies* n.s. 33 (1982): 10. Note also the abbreviated list of exit points (face, hands, or feet) from where Samael proposes to extract the soul of Moses in the *Peṭirat Mosheh* midrash published by Jellinek, *BHM* 6:75.20–25.

Angel of Death said to him: "O Moses, I see that you speak to me in the style of one who has drunk alcohol!" Thereupon his mind was confused, and he said: "I have never drunk wine!" but the Angel of Death approached him and took his soul.[43]

Of primary interest here is the opening scene wherein the Angel of Death and Moses politely exchange greetings: "Greetings unto you, O Moses," said the Angel. "And greetings unto you," replied Moses. A similar opening scene is present in the contest between Moses and the Angel of Death in *Deuteronomy Rabbah*:

Even before Samael showed himself to Moses, Moses was aware that Samael had arrived. While Samael gazed at Moses, trembling and shaking seized him like that of a woman giving birth, and he could not muster the courage to speak to Moses until Moses addressed him, saying, "There is no peace [here probably "greeting"], says the Lord, for the wicked" [Isa 48:22; cf. 57:21]. What are you doing here?[44]

It is intriguing and certainly worthy of more reflection than we can give it here that the positive expressions of cordiality and hospitality articulated by Moses and the Angel in the Muslim tale are expropriated, and using almost an identical set of vocables, turned on their head to formulate a one-sided stinging rebuke in the Jewish midrash. It is little linguistic gems like this that betray the existence of a lively textual commerce among those religious communities sharing a basic scriptural lexicon of characters, locales, and events in the Islamicate world during late antiquity and the medieval era.[45] Scholars of the parascriptural lore that surround these lemmata are slowly beginning to recognize that the luxurious growth of this tangled thicket of legendry cannot be properly appreciated if one's gaze is restricted to the various motifs and themes that are iterated in only one religious tradition, or, perhaps worse, if one uncritically or stubbornly assumes that these cultural processes of authorship, trans-

---

43. Muḥammad b. ʿAbd Allāh, *Qiṣaṣ al-anbiyāʾ: Vita prophetarum*, ed. Isaac Eisenberg (Leiden: Brill, 1922), 1:239.12–21. See also W. M. Thackston Jr., *The Tales of the Prophets of al-Kisāʾi* (Boston: Twayne Publishers, 1978), 257–58.

44. *Deut. Rab.* 11.10 (ed. Vilna): וטרם שהראה סמאל את עצמו למשה היה משה יודע שבא סמאל וכיון שראה סמאל את משה אחזתו רעדה וחיל כיולדה ולא מצא פתחון פה לדבר עם משה עד שאמר משה לסמאל אין שלום אמר ה' לר־ שעים מה תעשה בכאן. Moses's inhospitable address to Samael is paralleled in the two *Peṭirat Mosheh* midrashim published by Jellinek, *BHM* 1:127.32–33; 6:75.34–76.1.

45. Works like *Deuteronomy Rabbah*, the *Peṭirat Mosheh* texts, and the tales of the prophets (*qiṣaṣ al-anbiyāʾ*) collection ascribed to al-Kisāʾi share a general vagueness with regard to their geographical and chronological provenances.

mission, adoption, adaptation, and reformulation are unidirectional in their movement and application and monolingual in their expression.

Confronting the Eschatological Moses

One of the seemingly enduring maxims of the Jewish apocalyptic *mentalité* is the notion that what is termed the "first redemption" of Israel, the one that unfolded under the orchestration of Moses at the Sea of Reeds, prescribes a paradigm for the "final redemption," which will occur at the End of Days.[46] It seems likely that the conceptual twinning of exodus and eschaton could have been exegetically generated from the divine promise made in Micah 7:15: "I will show him [i.e., My people][47] marvels, just like the days of your going forth from Egypt." Given the signal role played by Moses in the bringing to fruition of the "first redemption," we should probably not be too surprised to remark that a number of eschatological traditions make room for him in their formulations of the events that will mark the End of Days.[48]

An expectation that Moses will return, for example, plays a notable role in some early Christian works. Such a hope determines the structure of the transfiguration pericopae in the synoptic gospels (Mark 9:2–8 and its parallels) where Moses and Elijah are said to join a transmogrified Jesus on the summit of the revelatory mountain. It is also likely that the mysterious pair of anonymous prophetic witnesses presented in Revelation 11:3–14, in spite of their identification within later Eastern apocalyptic sources as Enoch and Elijah, encode a second coming for Moses and Elijah.[49] One of the more interesting examples of a Christian text that incorporates the notion of a returning Mo-

---

46. Note *b. Roš. Haš.* 11a; S. Landauer, ed., *Kitâb al-Amânât wa'l-I'tiqâdât von Sa'adja b. Jûsuf al-Fajjûmî* (Leiden: Brill, 1880), 224.19; cf. also 225.1, 13–14; Saadia Gaon, *The Book of Beliefs and Opinions*, trans. Samuel Rosenblatt, Yale Judaica Series 1 (New Haven, Conn.: Yale University Press, 1948), 282–83.

47. Cf. the commentary of Ibn Ezra *ad loc.*

48. A point eloquently made by Naphtali Wieder, "The Idea of a Second Coming of Moses," *Jewish Quarterly Review* n.s. 46 (1955–56): 358–59. See especially *Pesiq. Rab Kah.* 5.8 (ed. Mandelbaum, 92): "The final redeemer will be just like the first redeemer [i.e., Moses]"; also the remarks of Ronit Meroz, "Zoharic Narratives and Their Adaptations," *Hispania Judaica Bulletin* 3 (2000): 3–63, at 35. An identical symmetry between Moses and the so-called Taheb (i.e., "returning one" or "restorer") would appear to characterize Samaritan Jewish eschatology; see Meeks, *The Prophet-King*, 246–54. For the occasional identification of Moses and the Taheb, see John Bowman, "Early Samaritan Eschatology," *Journal of Jewish Studies* 6 (1955): 63–72.

49. See Loewenstamm, "Death of Moses," 214n28; James C. VanderKam, *Enoch: A Man for All Generations* (Columbia: University of South Carolina Press, 1995), 180–81.

ses is the recurrent yet relatively obscure account about a messianic huckster named Serene or Severus who deliberately misled and financially despoiled a number of Syrian Jewish communities during the early eighth century.[50] According to the report about this episode in the so-called *Zuqnīn Chronicle*, he claimed: "I am Moses, the one who formerly brought Israel forth from Egypt and who was with them at the sea and in the wilderness for forty years. I have now come to save Israel and to bring them out to the desert. Afterwards I will make them again enter to take possession of that Promised Land!" The report goes on to state that "all of them [i.e., the Jews] went astray after him."[51] But instead of supervising a new Exodus and conquest, he caused many of his followers to perish in the wilderness and embezzled the cash and material goods that they had been duped into contributing to his mission. This story is remarkably similar to the curious anecdote that is told by the fifth-century church historian Socrates about a "pseudo-Moses" (ὁ ψευδομωυσῆς) who likewise deluded the Jewish community in Crete during the 430s into thinking that he, like Moses, could lead them safely across the sea that separated them from the Promised Land, but who actually led a number of them off the rocky cliffs to death and destruction.[52]

A tradition recounted in the traditional biography (*Sīra*) of the Prophet also bears witness to the expectation among a Jewish group that Moses, or at least a prophet charged with a commission analogous to that of the lawgiv-

---

50. For the primary sources that record the story of Serene/Severus, see *Theophanis Chronographia*, ed. Carolus de Boor (Leipzig: B. G. Teubner, 1883), 1:617; *Incerti auctoris Chronicon Pseudo-Dionysianum vulgo dictum*, CSCO 104 (ed. J.-B. Chabot; Paris: Reipublicae, 1933), 2:172.25–174.22; Agapius, *Kitāb al-'Unwān* (see Alexandre Vasiliev, "*Kitāb al-Unvān*: Histoire universelle écrite par Agapius (Mahboub) de Menbidj," *Patrologia Orientalis* 8 [1912]: 504); *Chronique de Michel le Syrien, patriarche jacobite d'Antioche, 1166–1199*, ed. J.-B. Chabot (repr., Brussels: Culture et Civilisation, 1963), 4:456c; *Anonymi auctoris Chronicon ad annum Christi 1234 pertinens*, 2 vols., ed. J.-B. Chabot, CSCO 81–82 (Paris: Reipublicae, 1916–20), 308. Important discussions are Heinrich Graetz, *Geschichte der Juden von den ältesten Zeiten bis auf die Gegenwart*, 3d ed. (Leipzig: Oskar Leiner, 1895), 5:400–403; J.-B. Chabot, "Trois episodes concernant les Juifs tirés de la chronique syriaque de Denys de Tell Mahré," *REJ* 28 (1894): 290–94; Israel Friedlaender, "Jewish-Arabic Studies," *Jewish Quarterly Review* n.s. 1 (1910): 210–11; Joshua Starr, "Le mouvement messianique au début du VIIIe siècle," *REJ* 102 (1937): 81–92; Aaron Ze'ev Aescoly, *Messianic Movements in Israel*, vol. 1, *From the Bar-Kokhba Revolt until the Expulsion of the Jews from Spain*, ed. Yehudah Even-Shmuel, 2nd ed.(Jerusalem: Mosad Bialik, 1987), 124–25, 152–55.

51. *Zuqnīn Chronicle* (ed. Chabot), 2:173.22–26; 174.4–5 (translation my own). For a recent English translation of the entire episode, see Amir Harrak, *The Chronicle of Zuqnīn, Parts III and IV: A.D. 488–775* (Toronto: Pontifical Institute of Mediaeval Studies, 1999), 163–64.

52. Socrates, *Hist. eccl.* 7.38.1–12. This episode is also recounted in the *Zuqnīn Chronicle* (ed. Chabot), 1:211.11–212.24. See also Starr, "Le mouvement," 83–84.

er, would make a future appearance on earth. Ibn Isḥāq preserves a valuable first-person account about the circumstances that led to the conversion to Islam of 'Abd Allāh b. Salām, a prominent scholar within the large Jewish community in Medina:

['Abd Allāh b. Salām said]: When I heard about the Apostle of God, I recognized from his portrayal, his name, and his timing that he was the one for whom we were waiting, and I was joyful about this, [although] remaining silent about it until the Apostle of God had arrived in Medina ... then when I heard the news about the arrival of the Apostle of God, I vocally extolled God, and my aunt said to me: "When I heard you extolling God, you would not have said more even if you had heard that Moses b. 'Imrān had arrived!" I said to her: "By God, O aunt, he is the brother of Moses b. 'Imrān and belongs to his religion. He has been sent with what he [i.e., Moses] was sent." She then asked: "O my nephew! Can he be the prophet who we have been told will be sent at this very time?" I answered her: "Yes!"[53]

Passages such as these suggest that the notion of a second coming of Moses was not absent from the Jewish apocalyptic mindset. But when one seeks actual textual corroboration for these Christian or Muslim portrayals, the evidence is somewhat meager. The biblical verses relating God's promise to provide Israel with a "Moses-like" prophet (Dt 18:15, 18) after Moses's departure are suggestive, but they do not attract much attention in classical rabbinic literature.[54] Those verses moreover do not predict a return for Moses himself, a circumstance that seems operative in the Christian tales about the "pseudo-Moses" above. It turns out there are a handful of such notices, although it remains uncertain how early they can be dated. One good example is found in *Deuteronomy Rabbah* where a tradition in the name of R. Yoḥanan b. Zakkai represents God as swearing to Moses that "just as you devoted your life to them [i.e., the people of Israel] in this world, so too in the world to come when I bring the prophet Elijah to them, the two of you will come together."[55] Although he is expected to arrive, nothing is said here however about from where Moses will come; the language suggests he presently occupies the same supernal space as his confrere Elijah. Hebrew language apocalypses from late antiquity and the medieval era also occasionally feature a curtain call for

53. Ibn Hishām, *Sīra* (ed. Wüstenfeld), 1/1:353.3–5, 7–11. See also Guillaume, *Life*, 240–41.
54. Also noted by Meeks, *The Prophet-King*, 199–200.
55. *Deut Rab.* 3.17 (ed. Vilna). Cited by Naphtali Wieder, "The 'Law-Interpreter' of the Sect of the Dead Sea Scrolls: The Second Moses," *Journal of Jewish Studies* 4 (1953): 169.

Moses. For example, Moses unexpectedly appears as a butcher at the messianic banquet that is described in Jellinek's edition of the *Nistarot* (or *Secrets)*
of Rabbi Shim'ōn b. Yoḥai.[56] In the detailed calendar of apocalyptic events for
the final year of redemption that is provided by many versions of *Sefer Zerub-
babel*, a work that probably ranks as the most influential Jewish apocalypse
after the book of Daniel, there is a somewhat peculiar notice about how the
congregation of Qorah (cf. Nm 16:1–35)[57] will reemerge from the underworld
on the plains of Jericho and assemble themselves around Moses.[58] It pointedly
does not tell us how Moses happens to be there, nor does Moses have any further role to play in this particular apocalypse. We should probably follow the
advice of Louis Ginzberg and think here of a "resurrected Moses,"[59] one who
will finally get to experience life in the Promised Land along with the rest of
the wilderness generation, a scenario similar to that present in Pseudo-Philo
above.

A question is posed in the Bavli as to whether the bodies of the resurrected dead require treatment with the potion for purification from corpse uncleanness, whose manufacture from the ashes of the red heifer and prescriptive
use is described in Numbers 19. Fortunately the solution to this potentially
baffling conundrum will be provided "when Moses our teacher is resurrected
along with them."[60] A similar scenario is discussed in *b. Yoma* 5b, where puzzlement over the proper order to be observed in the donning of the priestly
garments in the Temple of the messianic age will not be problematic because
"Moses will be with them." The later apocalyptic anthology published by Jellinek under the title *Pirqe Mashiaḥ* has the prophet Elijah perform as his first
miracle "the bringing back of Moses and his generation from the wilderness,
as scripture states: 'Gather together My pious ones for Me' [Ps 50:5]."[61] A similar explanation for the latter-day advent of Moses probably lies behind the

56. Jellinek, *BHM* 3:80.32; Reeves, *Trajectories*, 86.

57. For a dispute about their ultimate fate, see *m. Sanh.* 10.3; *b. Sanh.* 109b–110a.

58. Israel Lévi, "L'apocalypse de Zorobabel et le roi de Perse Siroès," *REJ* 68 (1914): 139.2; Eli Yassif, ed., *Sefer ha-Zikronot hu' Divrey ha-Yamim le-Yeraḥme'el* (Tel Aviv: Tel Aviv University, 2001), 432;
Reeves, *Trajectories*, 61.

59. The part played by Moses "as the forerunner or assistant of the Messiah does not presuppose
Moses' immortality, but his resurrection at the very beginning of the Messianic time." Louis Ginzberg,
Legends of the Jews (Philadelphia: Jewish Publication Society of America), 5:96n67.

60. B. *Niddah* 70b; see also Saadia, *Book of Beliefs*, 282.

61. Reeves, *Trajectories*, 158.

laconic wording of the so-called Fragment Targum to Exodus 12:42 according to Ms. Vat. Ebr. 440, where Moses is to lead a "flock" of refugees out of the desert to the Promised Land at the same time that the King Messiah is approaching from the west at the head of an analogous "flock" from Rome.[62]

Sometimes stories about the assumed return of Moses from the dead envision a forensic role for the Israelite lawgiver, in which he is to serve in the capacity of a witness or an advocate for the newly resurrected at the final judgment. This seems to be his primary responsibility on the Samaritan Day of Judgment, when he will reportedly be resurrected to mediate between the righteous and the wicked.[63] When at Saul's behest the witch of Endor conjured up the shade of Samuel for oracular consultation, the Hebrew text describing this séance reports that the witch actually beheld a plurality of ghosts flitting up from the underworld.[64] According to a talmudic interpretation of the incident, Samuel compelled Moses to accompany him on this unexpected journey because he mistakenly assumed that God was raising him for judgment: he wanted Moses present to offer testimony on his behalf that he had not neglected to fulfill every precept that was written in the Torah.[65] This specific kind of evaluative role resembles that attributed to Enoch as the "scribe of righteousness" in the *Apocalypse of Paul* and the *Testament of Abraham*, two parascriptural works that display a keen interest in the fate of the dead and the mechanisms of reward and punishment.[66] Interestingly such an intercessory role on the Day of Judgment is explicitly denied to Moses by some of the Latin witnesses to 4 Ezra 7:102–15.[67]

Vagueness about a final appearance for Moses is also present in Islamic tradition. In one *ḥadīth* that features Muḥammad mediating a dispute between a Jew and a Muslim about the respective merits of their prophetic teachers, we

---

62. See Michael L. Klein, *The Fragment-Targums of the Pentateuch according to their Extant Sources* (Rome: Biblical Institute Press, 1980), 1:167; cf. also Klein, *Genizah Manuscripts*, 1:220–21.

63. Arthur Cowley, "The Samaritan Doctrine of the Messiah," *The Expositor* 1, no. 5 (March 1895): 161–74, at 171.

64. 1 Sm 28:13: "I see <u>divine beings emerging</u> from the underworld." [אלהים ראיתי עלים מן הארץ.]

65. *B. ḥag.* 4b; cf. Rashi, *ad* 1 Sam 28:13.

66. *Apoc. Paul* §20, for which see Montague Rhodes James, *Apocrypha Anecdota: A Collection of Thirteen Apocryphal Books and Fragments*, TS 2.3 (Cambridge: Cambridge University Press, 1893), 21.22–31; *T. Ab.* recension B 11:1–10, for which see Montague Rhodes James, *The Testament of Abraham: The Greek Text Now First Edited with an Introduction and Notes*, TS 2.2 (Cambridge: Cambridge University Press, 1892), 115–16.

67. Meeks, *The Prophet-King*, 161.

have the following statement put into the mouth of the Prophet: "Do not favor me above Moses. On the Day of Resurrection, all people will die and I will be the first to regain consciousness, and lo, there will be Moses holding on to one of the sides of the Throne. I do not know whether he is one of those who died and regained consciousness before me, or whether he was one of those for whom God had made an exception."[68] Or, in other words, Moses will put in an appearance at the final hour, but whether his presence at that temporal margin is due to a resurrection or a restoration after a lengthy period of occultation remains frustratingly opaque.

Material and Nominal "Moses-Surrogates"

Although the notion of an actual "Moses-ophany" seems to be attested in a handful of reports and traditions, an especially popular and recurrent theme is the seemingly miraculous recovery of certain material relics associated with the career of the first Moses. Items such as the "ark of the covenant" and the "miracle-working staff," although recovered and wielded by other figures, seem to function as material Moses surrogates—symbolic place-fillers, if you will—to signal the essential role that the original lawgiver must play in the final consummation of what has become a scripturally determined age. Whether retrieved from long sealed caverns in Syria, Palestine, or the Transjordan (Moses's tomb?),[69] dredged up from the bottom of the Lake of Tiberias, or militarily liberated from the clutches of apostate emperors, these sacred objects legitimize their new bearers as authentic and divinely sanctioned agents of the cataclysmic changes taking place in the natural and political orders. I have previously written at length about the religiously entangled lore surrounding the

68. Juynboll, *Encyclopaedia*, 234. Also referenced by Samuel Rosenblatt, "Rabbinic Legends in Hadith," *Muslim World* 35 (1945): 245–46.

69. According to the Syriac *Book of the Bee* (ed. Budge), 51.2–6 (text); 50 (translation), Jethro comes across the staff while rifling the "Cave of Treasures" located in the hill country of Moab, presumably the site of the future grave of Moses. Note also 2 Macc 2:4–8; *Cave of Treasures* §45.12, according to Ri's Manuscript M (see Andreas Su-Min Ri, ed., *La Caverne des Trésors: Les deux recensions syriaques*, scrip. syri 207–8, 2 vols., CSCO 486–487 [Leuven: Peeters, 1987]); *Yeraḥmeʾel* (ed. Yassif), 266, which is in turn dependent here upon *Sefer Yosippon*. These latter Syriac and medieval Hebrew sources situate the cave of the Ark's concealment on Mt. Nebo; cf. Dt 32:49; 34:1. See especially the remarks of Andreas Su-Min Ri, *Commentaire de la Caverne des Trésors: Étude sur l'histoire du texte et de ses sources*, CSCO 581 (Leuven: Peeters, 2000), 452–53; also Loewenstamm, "Death of Moses," 203–4, who remarks on this motif's affinities with Samaritan traditions.

miracle-working staff of Moses and its end-time manifestations,[70] and hope to do something similar in the near future with regard to the ark and some of its contents, especially the copies of the "lost scriptures" supposedly contained therein.[71]

In addition to these *tangible* signs of a Moses connection, there are also persistent rumors, especially within Jewish and Muslim accounts of the events associated with the End, of a *nominal* "Moses-surrogate"; namely, the "people of Moses," who inhabit the eastern margins of the inhabitable world and who supposedly possess the original Mosaic teachings couched in a linguistically and religiously purer form than those which were being used by the scripturally allied communities of the time.[72] I bring them up in this context simply because a small number of religious provocateurs (e.g., 'Anan b. David), messianic pretenders (e.g., Abū 'Īsā al-Iṣfahānī), and even established Messengers of God like Muḥammad claim to have made pilgrimage to the East to consult this group, copy or otherwise pilfer their archives, or receive their endorsement before launching their own programs of religious reform.[73] The restoration of the ark and the tablets of the Law that is anticipated in the Byzantine Christian *Vita Prophetarum* also may belong to this trajectory of legitimation.[74] It is as if some sort of verbal connection with the name of the Jewish lawgiver, however tenuous it might seem to modern eyes, is *de rigueur* for

70. Reeves, *Trajectories*, 187–99.

71. For the meantime, see the excellently nuanced treatment of the traditions about the fate of the Temple vessels by Ra'anan S. Boustan, "The Spoils of the Jerusalem Temple at Rome and Constantinople: Jewish Counter-Geography in a Christianizing Empire," in *Antiquity in Antiquity: Jewish and Christian Pasts in the Greco-Roman World*, ed. Gregg Gardner and Kevin L. Osterloh (Tübingen: Mohr Siebeck, 2008), 327–72; also, with a more limited focus, Steven Fine, "'When I Went to Rome ... There I Saw the Menorah.... ' The Jerusalem Temple Implements during the Second Century C.E.," in *The Archaeology of Difference: Gender, Ethnicity, Class and the "Other" in Antiquity: Studies in Honor of Eric M. Meyers*, ed. Douglas R. Edwards and C. Thomas McCollough, AASOR 60/61 (Boston: American Schools of Oriental Research, 2006/2007), 169–80.

72. See Reeves, *Trajectories*, 200–24; Brannon M. Wheeler, *Moses in the Quran and Islamic Exegesis* (New York: Routledge Curzon, 2002), 93–117.

73. Primary source references are assembled in John C. Reeves, "Manichaeans as *Ahl al-Kitāb*: A Study in Manichaean Scripturalism," in *Light against Darkness: Dualism in Ancient Mediterranean Religion and the Contemporary World*, ed. Armin Lange et al. (Göttingen: Vandenhoeck & Ruprecht, 2011), 249–65, at 253–54.

74. *Liv. Pro.* "Jeremiah"; see Charles Cutler Torrey, *The Lives of the Prophets: Greek Text and Translation* (Philadelphia: Society of Biblical Literature and Exegesis, 1946), 22 (text); 36 (translation). The Christian provenance of the *Liv. Pro.* has been convincingly demonstrated by David Satran, *Biblical Prophets in Byzantine Palestine: Reassessing the Lives of the Prophets* (Leiden: Brill, 1995).

those who see themselves as playing an intimate part in a scripturally modu-lated apocalyptic drama.

What then can we say about the final disposition of the figure of Moses for textual communities who construct their separate identities out of what is at root a common base of scriptural characters, themes, and events? A dead and buried Moses can rejoin a redeemed Israel or community of Believers, but only at the outer edge or margin of the approaching future age whose bound-ary is marked by the Day of Resurrection. A supernal Moses, whether engaged in heavenly service, sequestered under the Divine Throne,[75] or installed in a celestial *Gan Eden*, similarly inhabits a locale that lies just beyond the lim-its or margins of the physical universe. Even the powerfully charged relics of Moses and the utopian "people of Moses" are tethered to places that lie out of reach and times that hover beyond our experience of the present cosmos. This recurring pattern of his bi-dimensional banishment—situating Moses at the margins of space and time—is apparently not an accidental but instead a de-liberately crafted narratological strategy, one that is inter-religiously appreciat-ed, cultivated, and manipulated along a continuum of exegetes, thinkers, tra-dents, commentators, and assorted troublemakers who extend from Philo to the Qur'ān and points beyond.

75. According to *Abot R. Natan* A §12, the "soul of Moses" is closeted beneath the Throne of Glo-ry along with the souls of all the righteous. See Solomon Schechter, ed., *Massekhet Avot de-Rabbi Natan* (Vienna: Ch. D. Lippe, 1887), 50.

GENERAL BIBLIOGRAPHY

This bibliography contains secondary works referred to in one or more of the chapters. Primary works have been omitted, except where a contributor has referred to an editorial or translator's comment.

Adang, Camilla P. "Hypocrites and Hypocrisy." In McAuliffe, *Encyclopaedia of the Qur'ān*, 2:468–72.

Adler, William. "The *Chronicle* of Eusebius and Its Legacy." In *Eusebius, Christianity, and Judaism*, edited by Harry W. Attridge and Gohei Hata, 467–91. Detroit, Mich.: Wayne State University Press, 1992.

———. "Eusebius' Critique of Africanus." In *Julius Africanus und die christliche Weltchronik*, edited by Martin Wallraff, 147–57. Texte und Untersuchungen 157. Berlin: de Gruyter, 2006.

Aescoly, Aaron Ze'ev. *Messianic Movements in Israel*. Vol. 1, *From the Bar-Kokhba Revolt until the Expulsion of the Jews from Spain*. Edited by Yehudah Even-Shmuel. 2nd ed. Jerusalem: Mosad Bialik, 1987.

Albl, Martin C. *"And Scripture Cannot Be Broken": The Form and Function of the Early Christian Testimonia Collections*. Novum Testamentum, Supplements 96. Leiden: Brill, 1999.

Alexander, Patrick H., John F. Kutsko, James D. Ernest, Shirley A. Decker-Lucke, and David L. Petersen, eds. *The SBL Handbook of Style for Ancient Near Eastern, Biblical, and Early Christian Studies*. Peabody, Mass.: Hendrickson, 1999.

Alexander, Philip S. "The Dualism of Heaven and Earth in Early Jewish Literature and Its Implications." In Lange et al., *Light against Darkness*, 169–85.

Allegro, J. M. "Fragments of a Qumran Scroll of Eschatological Midrashim." *Journal of Biblical Literature* 77 (1958): 350–54.

Amerise, Marilena. "Costantino il 'Nuovo Mosè.'" *Salesianum* 67, no. 4 (2005): 671–700.

Anderson, Gary A. "Towards a Theology of the Tabernacle and Its Furniture." In *Text, Thought, and Practice in Qumran and Early Christianity: Proceedings of the Ninth International Symposium of the Orion Center for the Study of the Dead Sea Scrolls and Associated Literature, 11–13 January, 2004*, edited by Ruth A. Clements and Daniel R. Schwartz, 161–94. Leiden: Brill, 2009.

Annas, Julia. *The Morality of Happiness*. Oxford: Oxford University Press, 1993.

———. "Virtue and Law in Plato." In *Plato's Laws: A Critical Guide*, edited by Christopher Bobonich, 71–91. Cambridge: Cambridge University Press, 2010.

Arjomand, Saïd Amir. "Islamic Apocalypticism in the Classical Period." In *The Encyclopedia of Apocalypticism*, vol. 2, edited by Bernard McGinn, John J. Collins, and Stephen J. Stein, 238–83. New York: Continuum, 1998.

Arweiler, Alexander. *Die Imitation antiker und spätantiker Literatur in der Dichtung* De spiritalis historiae gestis *des Alcimus Avitus, mit einem Kommentar zu Avit. carm. 4,429–540 und 5,526–703*. Berlin: De Gruyter, 1999.

Attridge, Harold. *The Epistle to the Hebrews*. Hermeneia. Philadelphia: Fortress Press, 1989.

Bakke, Odd Magne. *"Concord and Peace": A Rhetorical Analysis of the First Letter of Clement with an Emphasis on the Language of Unity and Sedition*. Wissenschaftliche Untersuchungen Zum Neuen Testament. Tübingen: Mohr Siebeck, 2001.

Barclay, John M. G. "Manipulating Moses: Exodus 2:10–15 in Egyptian Judaism and the New Testament." In *Text as Pretext: Essays in Honour of Robert Davidson*, edited by Robert P. Carroll, 28–46. Sheffield, U.K.: JSOT Press, 1992.

Barnard, L. W. "The Letters of Athanasius to Amoun and Draconius." *Studia Patristica* 26 (1993): 354–59.

Barnes, Timothy D. *Constantine and Eusebius*. Cambridge, Mass.: Harvard University Press, 2006.

———. *Constantine: Dynasty, Religion and Power in the Later Roman Empire*. Chichester, U.K.: Wiley-Blackwell, 2011.

Barrett, C. K. *The Acts of the Apostles*. 2 vols. Edinburgh: T&T Clark, 1994.

Bauer, Walter, Robert A. Kraft, and Gerhard Krodel. *Orthodoxy and Heresy in Earliest Christianity*. Philadelphia: Fortress Press, 1971.

Baumgarten, Albert I. "The Pharisaic *Paradosis*." *Harvard Theological Review* 80 (1987): 63–77.

Beavis, Mary Ann. "Philo's Therapeutai: Philosopher's Dream or Utopian Construction?" *Journal for the Study of Pseudepigrapha* 14 (2004): 30–42.

Becker, Ernst. "Konstantin der Grosse der 'neue Moses': Die Schlacht am Pons Milvius und die Katastrophe am Schilfmeer." *Zeitschrift für Kirchengeschichte* 3 (1910): 161–71.

———. "Protest gegen den Kaiserkult und die Verherrlichung des Sieges am Pons Milvius in der christlichen Kunst der konstantinischen Zeit." In *Konstantin der Große und seine Zeit*, edited by Franz J. Dölger, 155–90. Freiburg im Breisgau: Herder, 1913.

BeDuhn, Jason. *The Manichaean Body in Discipline and Ritual*. Baltimore, Md.: Johns Hopkins University Press, 2000.

Begg, Christopher. "'Josephus's Portrayal of the Disappearances of Enoch, Elijah, and Moses': Some Observations." *Journal of Biblical Literature* 109 (1990): 691–93.

Belleville, Linda L. "Tradition or Creation? Paul's Use of the Exodus 34 Tradition in 2 Corinthians 3.7–18." In *Paul and the Scriptures of Israel*, edited by Craig A. Evans and J. A. Sanders, 165–86. Journal for the Study of the New Testament, Supplement Series 83. Sheffield, U.K.: JSOT, 1993.

Bergjan, Silke-Petra. *Der fürsorgende Gott: Der Begriff der Pronoia Gottes in der apolo-getischen Literatur der Alten Kirche.* Berlin: De Gruyter, 2002.

Bieringer, Reimund, and Jan Lambrecht. *Studies on Second Corinthians.* Bibliotheca Ephe-meridum Theologicarum Lovaniensium, 112. Leuven: Peeters, 1994.

Bird, Michael F., and Joseph R. Dodson, eds. *Paul and the Second Century.* Library of New Testament Studies. New York: T&T Clark, 2011.

Bochet, Isabelle. "Le fondement de l'herméneutique augustinienne." In *Saint Augustin et la Bible: Actes du colloque de l'université Paul Verlaine-Metz (7–8 avril 2005),* edited by Gé-rard Nauroy and Marie-Anne Vannier, 37–57. Bern: Peter Lang, 2008.

Boustan, Ra'anan S. "The Spoils of the Jerusalem Temple at Rome and Constantinople: Jew-ish Counter-Geography in a Christianizing Empire." In *Antiquity in Antiquity: Jewish and Christian Pasts in the Greco-Roman World,* edited by Gregg Gardner and Kevin L. Osterloh, 327–72. Tübingen: Mohr Siebeck, 2008.

Bowman, John. "Early Samaritan Eschatology." *Journal of Jewish Studies* 6 (1955): 63–72.

Boyarin, Daniel. *A Radical Jew: Paul and the Politics of Identity.* Berkeley: University of Cal-ifornia Press, 1994.

———. "'After the Sabbath, at the Moment When the First Day Was About to Shine,' (Matt. 28:1): Once More into the Crux." *Journal of Theological Studies* 52 (2001): 678–88.

———. *Border Lines: The Partition of Judaeo-Christianity.* Philadelphia: University of Pennsylvania Press, 2004.

———. "By Way of Apology; Dawson, Edwards, Origen." *The Studia Philonica Annual* 16 (2004): 188–217.

———. "Rethinking Jewish Christianity: An Argument for Dismantling a Dubious Cate-gory (to Which Is Appended a Correction of My *Border Lines*)." *Jewish Quarterly Re-view* 99, no. 1 (2009): 7–36.

———. *The Jewish Gospel: The Story of the Jewish Christ.* New York: The New Press, 2012.

———. "The Talmud in Jesus: How Much Jewishness in Mark's Christ?" In *Envisioning Judaism: Studies in Honor of Peter Schäfer on the Occasion of His Seventieth Birthday,* edited by Ra'anan Boustan, Klaus Hermann, Reimund Leicht, Annette Yoshiko Reed, and Giuseppe Veltri. Tübingen: Mohr Siebeck, 2013.

———. *Judaism: The Genealogy of a Modern Notion.* Brunswick, N.J.: Rutgers University Press, 2018.

———. "Mark 7:1–23—Finally." In *Re-making the World: Categories and Early Christianity. Essays in Honor of Karen L. King,* edited by Carly Daniel-Hughes, Benjamin Dunning, Laura Nasrallah, AnneMarie Luijendijk, and Taylor Petrey. Tübingen: Mohr Siebeck, forthcoming.

Brakke, David. *Athanasius and the Politics of Asceticism.* Oxford: Clarendon Press, 1995.

Brandenburg, Hugo. *Ancient Churches of Rome.* Turnhout: Brepols, 2004.

Brown, Raymond E., and John P. Meier, eds. *Antioch and Rome: New Testament Cradles of Catholic Christianity.* New York: Paulist Press, 1982.

Budge, Ernest A. Wallis, ed. *The Book of the Bee.* Oxford: Clarendon Press, 1886.

Buell, Denise Kimber. *Why This New Race? Ethnic Reasoning in Early Christianity*. New York: Columbia University Press, 2005.

Burgess, Richard W. "The Dates and Editions of Eusebius's *Chronici canones* and *Historia ecclesiastica*." *Journal of Theological Studies* 48 (1997): 471–504.

———. *Studies in Eusebian and Post-Eusebian Chronography*. Stuttgart: Steiner, 1999.

Cassel, J. David. "Cyril of Alexandria and the Science of the Grammarians: A Study in the Setting, Purpose, and Emphasis of Cyril's Commentary on Isaiah." PhD dissertation, University of Virginia, 1992.

Castelli, Elizabeth A. *Imagining Paul: A Discourse of Power*. Louisville, Ky.: Westminster/ John Knox, 1991.

Cechelli, Carlo, et al., eds. *The Rabbula Gospels: Facsimile Edition of the Miniatures of the Syriac Manuscript Plut. I, 56 in the Medicaean-Laurentian Library*. Lausanne: URS Graf-Verlag, 1959.

Chabot, J.-B. "Trois episodes concernant les Juifs tirés de la chronique syriaque de Denys de Tell Mahré." *Revue des Études Juives* 28 (1894): 290–94.

Chadwick, Henry. "Oracles of the End in the Conflict of Paganism and Christianity in the Fourth Century." In *Mémorial André-Jean Festugière: Antiquité païenne et chrétienne*, edited by E. Lucchesi and H. D. Saffrey, 125–29. Geneva: Patrick Cramer, 1984.

Charlesworth, James H., and Carol A. Newsom. *Angelic Liturgy: Songs of the Sabbath Sacrifice*. Tübingen: Mohr Siebeck, 1999.

Charlier, Noël. "*Le Thesaurus De Trinitate* de Saint Cyrille d'Alexandrie: Questions de critique littéraire." *Revue d'Histoire Ecclésiastique* 45 (1950): 25–81.

Clark, Elizabeth A. *The Origenist Controversy: The Cultural Construction of an Early Christian Debate*. Princeton, N.J.: Princeton University Press, 1992.

Coakley, Sarah. *Re-thinking Gregory of Nyssa*. London: Blackwell, 2003.

Cockerill, Gareth Lee. "Heb 1:1–14, 1 Clem. 36:1–6 and the High Priest Title." *Journal of Biblical Literature* 97 (1978): 437–40.

———. *The Epistle to the Hebrews*. New International Commentary on the New Testament. Grand Rapids, Mich.: Eerdmans, 2012.

Collins, Adela Yarbro. *Mark: A Commentary*. Edited by Harold W. Attridge. Minneapolis, Minn.: Fortress Press, 2007.

Collins, Roger. *Visigothic Spain, 409–711*. Oxford: Blackwell, 2004.

Conway-Jones, Ann. "The Garments of Heaven: Gregory of Nyssa's Interpretation of the Priestly Robe (*Life of Moses* 2,189–191) Seen in the Light of Heavenly Ascent Texts." In *Studia Patristica, Vol. 50—Including Papers Presented at the National Conference on Patristic Studies Held at Cambridge in the Faculty of Divinity under Allen Brent, Thomas Graumann and Judith Lieu in 2009*, edited by Allen Brent and Markus Vinzent, 207–15. Leuven: Peeters, 2011.

———. "Not Made with Hands: Gregory of Nyssa's Doctrine of the Celestial Tabernacle in Its Jewish and Christian Contexts." PhD thesis, University of Manchester, 2012.

———. *Gregory of Nyssa's Tabernacle Imagery in Its Jewish and Christian Contexts*. Oxford: Oxford University Press, 2014.

Conzelmann, Hans. *Acts of the Apostles*. Philadelphia: Fortress Press, 1987.

Cosby, Michael R. *The Rhetorical Composition and Function of Hebrews 11: In Light of Example Lists in Antiquity*. Macon, Ga.: Mercer University Press, 1988.

———. "The Rhetorical Composition of Hebrews 11." *Journal of Biblical Literature* 107, no. 2 (1988): 257–73.

Cowley, Arthur. "The Samaritan Doctrine of the Messiah." *The Expositor* 1, no. 5 (1895): 161–74.

Damgaard, Finn. "Revisiting Eusebius' Use of the Figure of Moses in the *Vita Constantini*." In *Eusebius of Caesarea: Tradition and Innovations*, edited by Aaron P. Johnson and Jeremy Schott, 115–32. Cambridge, Mass.: Harvard University Press/Center for Hellenic Studies Press, 2013.

D'Angelo, Mary Rose. *Moses in the Letter to the Hebrews*. Missoula, Mont.: Scholars Press, 1979.

———. "Women in Luke-Acts: A Redactional View." *Journal of Biblical Literature* 109 (1990): 441–61.

Daniélou, Jean. *Platonisme et théologie mystique: Essai sur la doctrine spirituelle de saint Grégoire de Nysse*. Paris: Aubier, 1944.

———. *The Bible and the Liturgy*. Notre Dame, Ind.: University of Notre Dame Press, 1956.

———. "Le mariage de Grégoire de Nysse et la chronologie de sa vie." *Revue des Études Augustiniennes* 2 (1956): 71–78.

———. *From Shadows to Reality: Studies in the Biblical Typology of the Fathers*. London: Burns and Oates, 1960.

———. Introduction to *From Glory to Glory: Texts from Gregory of Nyssa's Mystical Writings*, edited by Herbert Musurillo, 3–78. New York: Scribner, 1961. Reprinted Crestwood: St Vladimir's Seminary Press, 2001.

Dawson, David. *Allegorical Readers and Cultural Revision in Ancient Alexandria*. Berkeley: University of California Press, 1992.

Dechow, Jon. *Dogma and Mysticism in Early Christianity: Epiphanius of Cyprus and the Legacy of Origen*. Macon, Ga.: Mercer University Press, 1988.

Deckers, Johannes. "Constantine the Great and Early Christian Art." In *Picturing the Bible: The Earliest Christian Art*, edited by Jeffrey Spier, 87–109. New Haven, Conn.: Yale University Press, 2007.

Deerberg, Daniel. *Der Sturz des Judas. Kommentar (5, 1–163) und Studien zur poetischen Erbauung bei Sedulius*. Münster: Aschendorff, 2011.

DeFilippo, Joseph G., and Phillip Mitsis. "Socrates and Stoic Natural Law." In *The Socratic Movement*, edited by Paul Vander Waerdt, 252–71. Ithaca, N.Y.: Cornell University Press, 1994.

Dibelius, Martin. "The Speeches in Acts and Ancient Historiography." In *Studies in the Acts of the Apostles*, edited by Heinrich Greeven, 138–85. London: SCM Press, 1956.

Dimant, Devorah. "Noah in Early Jewish Literature." In *Biblical Figures outside the Bible*, edited by Michael E. Stone and Theodore A. Bergren, 123–50. Harrisburg, Pa.: Trinity Press International, 1998.

Dodd, C. H. *According to the Scriptures: The Sub-structure of New Testament Theology*. New York: Scribner's, 1953.

Dölger, Franz J. "Der Durchzug durch das Rote Meer als Sinnbild des christlichen Taufe." *Antiquité Classique* 2 (1930): 63–69.

Donaldson, T. L. "Moses Typology and the Sectarian Nature of Early Christian Anti-Judaism: A Study in Acts 7." *Journal for the Study of the New Testament* 12 (1981): 27–52.

Donati, Angela. *Pietro e Paolo: La storia, il culto, la memoria nei primi secoli*. Milan: Electa, 2000.

Donner, Fred M. *Muhammad and the Believers: At the Origins of Islam*. Cambridge, Mass.: Harvard University Press, 2010.

Droge, Arthur. *Homer or Moses? Early Christian Interpretations of the History of Culture*. Tübingen: Mohr Siebeck, 1989.

Duff, Paul Brooks. "Glory in the Ministry of Death: Gentile Condemnation and Letters of Recommendation in 2 Cor 3:6–18." *Novum Testamentum* 46 (2004): 313–37.

———. "Transformed 'from Glory to Glory': Paul's Appeal to the Experience of His Readers in 2 Corinthians 3:18." *Journal of Biblical Literature* 127 (2008): 759–80.

Dunn, James D. G. *Paul and the Mosaic Law*. Grand Rapids, Mich.: Eerdmans, 2001.

———. *The New Perspective on Paul: Collected Essays*. Wissenschaftliche Untersuchungen Zum Neuen Testament. Tübingen: Mohr Siebeck, 2005.

Efroymson, D. "The Patristic Connection." In *Anti-Semitism and the Foundations of Christianity*, edited by A. Davies, 98–117. New York: Paulist Press, 1979.

Ellingworth, Paul. "Hebrews and 1 Clement: Literary Dependence or Common Tradition?" *Biblische Zeitschrift* 23, no. 2 (1979): 262–69.

———. *The Epistle to the Hebrews: A Commentary on the Greek Text*. The New International Greek Testament Commentary. Grand Rapids, Mich.: Eerdmans, 1993.

Elm, Susanna. *Sons of Hellenism, Fathers of the Church: Emperor Julian, Gregory of Nazianzus, and the Vision of Rome*. Berkeley: University of California Press, 2012.

Elsner, Jaś. "'Pharaoh's Army Got Drownded': Some Reflections on Jewish and Roman Genealogies of Early Christian Art." In *Judaism and Christian Art: Aesthetic Anxieties from the Catacombs to Colonialism*, edited by Herbert Kessler and David Nirenberg, 10–44. Philadelphia: University of Pennsylvania Press, 2011.

Engberg-Pedersen, Troels. "Philo's *De Vita Contemplativa* as a Philosopher's Dream." *Journal for the Study of Judaism* 30 (1999): 40–64.

———. *Paul and the Stoics: An Essay in Interpretation*. Edinburgh: T&T Clark, 2000.

Epstein, J. *The Babylonian Talmud. Seder Nezikin. Baba Bathra I*. London: Soncino Press, 1935.

Eusebius. *Life of Constantine*. Introduction, translation, and commentary by Averil Cameron and Stuart G. Hall. Oxford: Clarendon Press, 1999.

Falk, Daniel K. "Moses." In *The Eerdmans Dictionary of Early Judaism*, edited by John J. Collins and Daniel C. Harlow, 967–70. Grand Rapids, Mich.: Eerdmans, 2010.

Farag, Lois M. *St. Cyril of Alexandria, a New Testament Exegete: His Commentary on the Gospel of John*. Piscataway, N.J.: Gorgias Press, 2007.

Fee, Gordon. *God's Empowering Presence: The Holy Spirit in the Letters of Paul.* Peabody, Mass.: Hendrickson, 1994.

Fine, Steven. "'When I Went to Rome … There I Saw the Menorah …': The Jerusalem Temple Implements during the Second Century C.E." In *The Archaeology of Difference: Gender, Ethnicity, Class and the "Other" in Antiquity: Studies in Honor of Eric M. Meyers*, edited by Douglas R. Edwards and C. Thomas McCollough, 169–80. Boston, Mass.: American Schools of Oriental Research, 2006/2007.

France, R. T. *The Gospel of Mark: A Commentary on the Greek Text.* Grand Rapids, Mich.: Eerdmans, 2002.

Franke, Peter. "Traditio legis und Petrus primat: Eine Entgegung auf Franz Nikolasch." *Vigiliae Christianae* 26 (1989): 263–71.

Frankfurter, David. "Beyond 'Jewish Christianity': Continuing Religious Sub-cultures of the Second and Third Centuries and Their Documents." In *The Ways That Never Parted: Jews and Christians in Late Antiquity and the Early Middle Ages*, edited by Adam H. Becker and Annette Yoshiko Reed, 131–43. Minneapolis, Minn.: Fortress Press, 2007.

Fredriksen, Paula. "Mandatory Retirement: Ideas in the Study of Christian Origins Whose Time Has Come to Go." *Studies in Religion/Sciences Religieuses* 36 (2006): 231–46.

———. *Augustine and the Jews.* New Haven, Conn.: Yale University Press, 2010.

———. "Augustine on Jesus the Jew." *Augustinian Studies* 42, no. 1 (2011): 1–20.

———. *Sin: The Early History of an Idea.* Princeton, N.J.: Princeton University Press, 2012.

Frend, W. H. C. *Martyrdom and Persecution in the Early Church: A Study of a Conflict from the Maccabees to Donatus.* New York: New York University Press, 1967.

Frey, Jörg. "Paul's Jewish Identity." In *Jewish Identity in the Greco-Roman World / Judische Identität in der griechisch-römischen Welt*, edited by Jörg Frey, Daniel R. Schwartz, and Stephanie Gripenrung, 285–321. Leiden: Brill, 2007.

Freyne, Seán. *Galilee, from Alexander the Great to Hadrian, 323 B.C.E. to 135 C.E.: A Study of Second Temple Judaism.* University of Notre Dame Center for the Study of Judaism and Christianity in Antiquity 5. Notre Dame, Ind.: University of Notre Dame Press, 1980.

Friedlaender, Israel. "Jewish-Arabic Studies." *Jewish Quarterly Review* 1 (1910): 183–215.

Furnish, Victor Paul. *II Corinthians.* Garden City, N.Y.: Doubleday, 1984.

Fürstenberg, Yair. "Defilement Penetrating the Body: A New Understanding of Contamination in Mark 7.15." *New Testament Studies* 54 (2008): 176–200.

Gager, John G. *Moses in Greco-Roman Paganism.* Nashville, Tenn.: Abingdon Press, 1972.

———. "The Gospels and Jesus: Some Doubts about Method." *Journal of Religion* 54 (1974): 256–59.

———. *Kingdom and Community: The Social World of Early Christianity.* Prentice-Hall Studies in Religion Series. Englewood Cliffs, N.J.: Prentice-Hall, 1975.

———. *The Origins of Anti-Semitism: Attitudes toward Judaism in Pagan and Christian Antiquity.* New York: Oxford University Press, 1983.

———. *Reinventing Paul.* New York: Oxford University Press, 2000.

Gamble, Harry Y. *Books and Readers in the Early Church: A History of Early Christian Texts.* New Haven, Conn.: Yale University Press, 1995.

Gardner, I., and S. Lieu. *Manichaean Texts from the Roman Empire*. Cambridge: Cambridge University Press, 2004.

Geljon, Albert C. *Philonic Exegesis in Gregory of Nyssa's* De Vita Moysis. Studia Philonica Monographs 5. Providence, R.I.: Brown Judaic Studies, 2002.

Gibbons, Kathleen. "Moses, Statesman and Philosopher: The Philosophical Background of the Ideal of Assimilating to God and the Methodology of Clement of Alexandria's Stromateis 1." *Vigiliae Christianae*, 69 (2015): 157–85

———. *The Moral Psychology of Clement of Alexandria*. New York: Routledge, 2017.

———. *The Moral Psychology of Clement of Alexandria: Mosaic Philosophy*. Abingdon: Ashgate, 2017.

Ginzberg, Louis. *Legends of the Jews*. 7 vols. Philadelphia: The Jewish Publication Society of America, 1909–38.

Gioia, Luigi. *The Theological Epistemology of Augustine's* De Trinitate. New York: Oxford University Press, 2008.

Goodenough, E. R. *Jewish Symbols in the Greco-Roman Period*. Vol. 9, *Symbolism in the Dura Synagogue*. New York: Pantheon Books, 1965.

Goodman, Martin. "Sacred Scripture and 'Defiling the Hands.'" *Journal of Theological Studies*, 41 (1990): 99–107.

Goodspeed, Edgar J. "First Clement Called Forth by Hebrews." *Journal of Biblical Literature* 30, no. 2 (1911): 157–60.

Grabar, André. *Christian Iconography: A Study of Its Origins*. Princeton, N.J.: Princeton University Press, 1968.

Graetz, Heinrich. *Geschichte der Juden von den ältesten Zeiten bis auf die Gegenwart*. 3rd ed. 11 vols. Leipzig: Oskar Leiner, 1897–1911.

Grafton, Anthony. *Forgers and Critics: Creativity and Duplicity in Western Scholarship*. Princeton, N.J.: Princeton University Press, 1990.

Grafton, Anthony, and Megan Williams. *Christianity and the Transformation of the Book: Origen, Eusebius, and the Library of Caesarea*. Cambridge, Mass.: Belknap Press of Harvard University Press, 2006.

Grant, Robert. "The Decalogue in Early Christianity." *Harvard Theological Review* 40 (1947): 1–17.

Grant, Robert M., and Holt H. Graham. *First and Second Clement*. New York: Nelson, 1965.

Green, Roger P. H. *Latin Epics of the New Testament: Juvencus, Sedulius, Arator*. Oxford: Oxford University Press, 2006.

Gregory, Andrew F., and C. M. Tuckett. *Trajectories through the New Testament and the Apostolic Fathers*. New York: Oxford University Press, 2005.

Grimaldi, Giacomo. *Descrizione della basilica antica di S. Pietro in Vaticano: Codice Barberini latino 2733*, edited by Reto Niggl. Vatican City: Biblioteca Apostolica Vaticana, 1972.

Gruen, Erich. "Jewish Perspectives on Greek Culture and Ethnicity." In *Ancient Perceptions of Greek Ethnicity*, edited by I. Malkin, 347–73. Cambridge, Mass.: Harvard University Press, 2001.

———. *Diaspora: Jews amidst Greeks and Romans*. Cambridge, Mass.: Harvard University Press, 2004.

Guelich, Robert A. *Mark 1–8:26*. Dallas, Tex.: Word Books, 1989.

Guillaume, Alfred. *The Life of Muhammad: A Translation of Isḥāq's Sīrat Rasūl Allāh*. Oxford: Oxford University Press, 1955.

Guj, Melania. "La Concordia Apostolorum nell'antica decorazione di San Paolo fuori le mura." In *Ecclesiae urbis: atti del congress internazionale di studi sulle chiese di Roma, IV–X secolo*, vol. 2, edited by Federico Guidobaldi, 1873–92. Vatican City: Pontificio Istituto di Archeologia Cristiana, 2002.

Gundry, Robert H. *Mark: A Commentary on His Apology for the Cross*. Grand Rapids, Mich.: Eerdmans, 2004.

Habel, Norman C. *The Book of Job*. Philadelphia: The Westminster Press, 1985.

Haenchen, Ernst. *The Acts of the Apostles*. Philadelphia: Westminster Press, 1971.

Hagedorn, Dieter. *Der Hiobkommentar des Arianers Julian*. Patristische Texte und Studien (PTS) 14. Berlin: de Gruyter, 1973.

Hagner, Donald Alfred. *The Use of the Old and New Testaments in Clement of Rome*. Leiden: Brill, 1973.

Hamilton, Mark Wade. "In the Shadow of Leviathan: Kingship in the Book of Job." *Restoration Quarterly* 45 (2003): 33–45.

Hannah, Darrell D. "Isaiah's Vision in the Ascension of Isaiah and the Early Church." *Journal of Theological Studies* 50, no. 1 (1999): 80–101.

Harl, Marguerite. *Origène et la function revélatrice du verbe incarné*. Paris: Seuil, 1958.

———. "Les trois quarantaines de Moïse." *Revue des Études Grecques* 80 (1967): 407–12.

———. "Moïse figure de l'évêque dans l'Eloge de Basile de Grégoire de Nysse (381): Un plaidoyer pour l'autorité épiscopale." In *The Biographical Works of Gregory of Nyssa: Proceedings of the Fifth International Colloquium on Gregory of Nyssa*, edited by Andreas Spira and Christoph Klock, 71–119. Cambridge, Mass.: The Philadelphia Patristic Foundation, 1984.

Harnack, Adolf. *History of Dogma*, vol. 1. Translated by Neil Buchanan. Boston, Mass.: Little, Brown and Company, 1905.

Harrington, Daniel J. "Pseudo-Philo (First Century A.D.)." In *The Old Testament Pseudepigrapha*, vol. 2, edited by James H. Charlesworth, 297–377. Garden City, N.Y.: Doubleday, 1985.

Hays, Richard B. *Echoes of Scripture in the Letters of Paul*. New Haven, Conn.: Yale University Press, 1989.

Hegedus, Tim. *Early Christianity and Ancient Astrology*. New York: Peter Lang, 2007.

Helms, Randel. *Gospel Fictions*. Buffalo, N.Y.: Prometheus Books, 1988.

Hengel, Martin. "Mc 7,3 *pugme*: Die Geschichte einer exegetischen Aproie und der Versuch ihrer Lösung." *Zeitschrift für Neutestamentliche Wissenshaft* 60 (1969): 182–98.

Herzog, Reinhart. *Die Bibelepik der lateinischen Spätantike: Formgeschichte einer erbaulichen Gattung I*. Munich: Fink, 1975.

Heschel, Abraham Joshua. *Heavenly Torah as Refracted through the Generations*. New York: Continuum, 2007.

Hickling, C. J. A. "Paul's Use of Exodus in the Corinthian Correspondence." In *The Corinthian Correspondence*, edited by Reimund Bieringer, 367–76. Leuven: Peeters, 1996.

Himmelfarb, Martha. *Ascent to Heaven in Jewish and Christian Apocalypses*. Oxford: Oxford University Press, 1993.

Hochschild, Paige E. *Memory in Augustine's Theological Anthropology*. Oxford: Oxford University Press, 2012.

Hogeterp, Albert L. A. *Expectations of the End: A Comparative Traditio-Historical Study of Eschatological, Apocalyptic and Messianic Ideas in the Dead Sea Scrolls and the New Testament*. Studies on the Texts of the Desert of Judah 83. Leiden: Brill, 2009.

Hollander, H. W., and M. de Jonge. *The Testaments of the Twelve Patriarchs: A Commentary*. Leiden: Brill, 1985.

Hollerich, Michael. "Hebrews, Jews, and Christians: Eusebius of Caesarea on the Biblical Basis of the Two States of the Christian Life." In *In Dominico Eloquio—In Lordly Eloquence: Essays on Patristic Exegesis in Honor of Robert Louis Wilken*, edited by Paul Blowers et al., 172–84. Grand Rapids, Mich.: Eerdmans, 2002.

Holloway, Ross. *Constantine and Rome*. New Haven, Conn.: Yale University Press, 2004.

Hooker, Morna D. "Beyond the Things That Are Written? St. Paul's Use of Scripture." In *From Adam to Christ: Essays on Paul*, 139–54. Cambridge: Cambridge University Press, 1990.

Huskinson, Janet. *Concordia Apostolorum: Christian Propaganda at Rome in the Fourth and Fifth Centuries*. BAR International Series. Oxford: BAR Publishing, 1982.

Inowlocki, Sabrina. "Eusebius's Appropriation of Moses in an Apologetic Context." In *Moses in Biblical and Extra-biblical Traditions*, edited by Axel Graupner and Michael Wolter, 241–55. Zeitschrift für die alttestamentliche Wissenschaft Supplements 372. Berlin: De Gruyter, 2007.

Inwood, Brad. "Goal and Target in Stoicism." *Journal of Philosophy* 83 (1986): 547–56.

———. *Reading Seneca: Stoic Philosophy at Rome*. Oxford: Clarendon Press, 2005.

———. "Ancient Goods: The Tria Genera Bonorum in Ethical Theory." Chapter 11 in *Strategies of Argument: Essays in Ancient Ethics, Epistemology, and Logic*, edited by Mi-Kyoung Lee. Oxford: Oxford University Press, 2014.

Jaeger, Werner. *Two Rediscovered Works of Ancient Christian Literature: Gregory of Nyssa and Macarius*. Leiden: Brill, 1954.

Jasper, Detlev, and Horst Fuhrmann. *Papal Letters in the Early Middle Ages*. Washington, D.C.: The Catholic University of America Press, 2001.

Jaubert, Annie. *Épître aux Corinthiens Clemens Romanus*. Sources Chrétiennes 167. Paris: Éditions du Cerf, 1971.

Jeffers, James S. *Conflict at Rome: Social Order and Hierarchy in Early Christianity*. Minneapolis, Minn.: Fortress Press, 1991.

Jefferson, Lee. "The Staff of Jesus in Early Christian Art." *Religion and the Arts* 14 (2010): 221–51.

Jensen, Robin M. "Moses Imagery in Jewish and Christian Art." In *SBL Seminar Papers*, edited by Eugene H. Lovering Jr, 389–418. Atlanta, Ga.: Scholars Press, 1992.

———. "The Offering of Isaac in Jewish and Christian Tradition: Image and Text." *Biblical Interpretation* 2 (1994): 42–51.

Jervell, Jacob. "The Divided People of God: The Restoration of Israel and Salvation for the Gentiles." In *Luke and the People of God: A New Look at Luke-Acts*, 41–74. Minneapolis, Minn.: Augsburg Press, 1972.

Johnson, Luke Timothy. *The Acts of the Apostles.* Collegeville, Minn.: Liturgical Press, 1992.

Jones, Christopher P. *Kinship Diplomacy in the Ancient World.* Cambridge, Mass.: Harvard University Press, 1999.

Jones, Peter R. "The Apostle Paul: A Second Moses according to II Corinthians 2:14–4:7." Unpublished PhD thesis, Princeton Theological Seminary, 1973.

Juynboll, G. H. A. *Encyclopaedia of the Canonical ḥadīth.* Leiden: Brill, 2007.

Kahlos, M. *Debate and Dialogue: Christian and Pagan Cultures, c. 360–430.* Aldershot: Ashgate, 2007.

Kazen, Thomas. *Jesus and Purity Halakhah: Was Jesus Indifferent to Impurity?* Stockholm: Almqvist & Wiksell, 2002.

Kerrigan, Alexander. *St. Cyril of Alexandria, Interpreter of the Old Testament.* Rome: Pontificio Istituto Biblico, 1952.

Kéry, Lotte. *Canonical Collections of the Early Middle Ages, ca. 400–1140: A Bibliographical Guide to the Manuscripts and Literature.* Washington, D.C.: The Catholic University of America Press, 1999.

Kessler, Edward. *Bound by the Bible: Jews, Christians, and the Sacrifice of Isaac.* Cambridge: Cambridge University Press, 2004.

Kessler, Herbert. "The Meeting of Peter and Paul in Rome: An Emblematic Narrative of Spiritual Brotherhood." *Dumbarton Oaks Papers* 41 (1987): 265–75.

———. *Old St. Peter's and Church Decoration in Medieval Italy.* Spoleto: Centro Italiano di Studi sull'Alto Medioevo, 2002.

Kirsch, Wolfgang. *Die Lateinische Versepik des 4. Jahrhunderts.* Berlin: Akademie Verlag, 1989.

Kister, Menahem. "Law, Morality and Rhetoric in Some Sayings of Jesus." In *Studies in Ancient Midrash*, edited by James L. Kugel, 145–54. Cambridge, Mass.: Harvard University Press, 2001.

Knust, Jennifer Wright, and Zsuzsanna Várhelyi, eds. *Ancient Mediterranean Sacrifice.* New York: Oxford University Press, 2011.

Kollwitz, Johannes. "Christus als Lehrer und die Gesetzesübergabe an Petrus in der konstantinischen Kunst Roms." *Römische Quartalschrift* 44 (1936): 46–66.

Koltun-Fromm, Naomi. *Hermeneutics of Holiness: Ancient Jewish and Christian Notions of Sexuality and Religious Community.* New York: Oxford University Press, 2010.

Kovacs, Judith. "Divine Pedagogy and the Gnostic Teaching according to Clement of Alexandria." *Journal of Early Christian Studies* 9 (2001): 3–25.

Kraft, Robert A. *Barnabas and the Didache.* New York: Nelson, 1965.

Kugel, James L. *Traditions of the Bible: A Guide to the Bible as It Was at the Start of the Common Era.* Cambridge, Mass.: Harvard University Press, 1998.

Kushelevsky, Rella. *Moses and the Angel of Death.* New York: Peter Lang, 1995.

Laehr, Gerhard. "Ein karolingischer Konzilsbrief und der Fürstenspiegel Hincmars von Reims." *Neues Archiv der Gesellschaft für ältere deutsche Geschichtskunde* 50 (1935): 106–34.

Lambrecht, Jan. "Transformation in 2 Corinthians 3, 18." In *Studies on Second Corinthians*, edited by Reimund Bieringer and Jan Lambrecht, 295–307. Bibliotheca Ephemeridum Theologicarum Lovaniensium 125. Leuven: Peeters, 1994.

Lampe, Peter. *From Paul to Valentinus: Christians at Rome in the First Two Centuries*. Translated by Michael Steinhauser and edited by Marshall D. Johnson. Minneapolis, Minn.: Fortress Press, 2003.

Landwehr, Hugo. "Griechische handschriften aus Fayyum." *Philologus* 44 (1885): 1–29.

Lange, Armin, Eric M. Meyers, Bennie H. Reynolds, and Randall Styers, eds. *Light against Darkness: Dualism in Ancient Mediterranean Religion and the Contemporary World*. Göttingen: Vandenhoeck & Ruprecht, 2011.

Larsen, Kasper Bro. "Mark 7:1–23: A Pauline Halakah." In *Mark and Paul. Part II, For and Against Pauline Influence on Mark: Comparative Essays*, edited by Eve-Marie Becker, Troels Engberg-Pedersen, and Mogens Müller, 169–87. Berlin: De Gruyter, 2014.

Lasine, Stuart. *Knowing Kings: Knowledge, Power, and Narcissism in the Hebrew Bible*. Atlanta, Ga.: The Society of Biblical Literature, 2001.

Lassus, Jean. "Représentations du 'Passage de la Mer Rouge' dans l'art chrétien d'Orient et d'Occident." *Mélanges d'Archéologie et d'Histoire* 46 (1929): 159–81.

Layton, Richard. *Didymus the Blind and His Circle in Late-Antique Alexandria*. Urbana: University of Illinois Press, 2003.

Le Donne, Anthony. *The Historiographical Jesus: Memory, Typology, and the Son of David*. Waco, Tex.: Baylor University Press, 2009.

Lehto, Adam. *The Demonstrations of Aphrahat, The Persian Sage*. Piscataway, N.J.: Gorgias Press, 2010.

Lévi, Israel. "L'Apocalypse de Zorobabel et le roi de Perse Siroès." *Revue des Études Juives* 68 (1914): 129–60.

———. "Le conte du *Diable dupé* dans le folklore juif." *Revue des Études Juives* 85 (1928): 137–63.

Lierman, John. *The New Testament Moses: Christian Perceptions of Moses and Israel in the Setting of Jewish Religion*. Tübingen: Mohr Siebeck, 2004.

Lieu, Judith. "'As Much My Apostle as Christ Is Mine:' The Dispute over Paul between Tertullian and Marcion." *Early Christianity* 1 (2010): 41–59.

Lightfoot, J. B. *The Apostolic Fathers*. Part 1. London: Macmillan, 1890.

Lilla, Salvatore R. C. *Clement of Alexandria: A Study of Christian Platonism and Gnosticism*. Oxford: Oxford University Press, 1971.

Lindemann, Andreas. *Die Clemensbriefe*. Handbuch Zum Neuen Testament 17. Tübingen: Mohr Siebeck, 1992.

———. "Paul's Influence on 'Clement' and Ignatius." In *Trajectories through the New Testament and the Apostolic Fathers*, edited by Andrew F. Gregory and Christopher M. Tuckett, 9–24. Oxford: Oxford University Press, 2005.

Lipsius, R., and M. Bonnet, eds. *Acta Apostolorum Apocrypha*, vol. 1. Leipzig: H. Mendelssohn, 1891.

Loewenstamm, Samuel E. "The Death of Moses." In *Studies on the Testament of Abraham*, edited by George W. E. Nickelsburg Jr., 185–217. Missoula, Mont.: Scholars Press, 1976.

Lona, Horacio. *Der Erste Clemensbrief. Kommentar zu den Apostolischen Vätern.* Göttingen: Vandenhoeck & Ruprecht, 1998.

Long, Anthony. *Epictetus: The Stoic and Socratic Guide to Life.* Oxford: Clarendon Press, 2004.

Longenecker, Bruce W. *The Triumph of Abraham's God: The Transformation of Identity in Galatians.* Edinburgh: T&T Clark, 1998.

Lundberg, Per. *La typologie baptismale dans l'ancienne église.* Leipzig: A. Lorentz, 1942.

Madigan, Daniel A. "Preserved Tablet." In McAuliffe, *Encyclopaedia of the Qur'ān*, 4:261–63.

Malchow, Bruce V. "A Royal Prototype in Job 29." In *The Psalms and Other Studies on the Old Testament. Festschrift J. I. Hunt*, edited by Jack C. Knight and Lawrence A. Sinclair, 178–84. Nashotah, Wisc.: Nashotah House Seminary, 1990.

Malherbe, Abraham J., and Everett Ferguson. *Gregory of Nyssa: The Life of Moses.* New York: Paulist Press, 1978.

Marcus, Joel. *Mark 1–8: A New Translation with Introduction and Commentary.* New York: Doubleday, 2000.

———. "Mark—Interpreter of Paul." *New Testament Studies* 46 (2000): 473–87.

———. "Mark—Interpreter of Paul." In *Mark and Paul: Comparative Essays, 2, For and Against Pauline Influence on Mark*, edited by Eve-Marie Becker, Troels Engberg-Pedersen, and Mogens Müller, 29–49. Berlin: De Gruyter, 2013.

Marguerat, Daniel. "Paul après Paul: Une histoire de réception." *New Testament Studies* 54, (2008): 317–37.

Mariès, Louis. *Études préliminaires à l'édition de Diodore de Tarse sur les Psaumes.* Paris: Édition "Les Belle Lettres," 1933.

Märki-Boehringer, Julie. *Frühchristliche Sarkophage in Bild und Wort.* Olten: Urs Graf-Verlag, 1966.

Markus, Robert A. "Gregory the Great's *Rector* and His Genesis." In *Grégoire le Grand, Colloques internationaux, Chantilly 15–19 septembre 1982*, edited by Jacques Fontaine et al., 137–46. Paris: Éditions du Centre National de la Recherche Scientifique, 1986.

———. "Gregory the Great on Kings: Rulers and Preachers in the Commentary on I Kings." In *The Church and Sovereignty: Essays in Honour of Michael Wilks*, edited by Diana Wood, 7–21. Studies in Church History, Subsidia 9. Oxford: Blackwell, 1991. Reprinted in Markus, *Sacred and Secular*, Paper 8.

———. *Sacred and Secular: Studies on Augustine and Latin Christianity.* Aldershot: Variorum, 1994.

Marshall, J. "Misunderstanding the New Paul: Marcion's Transformation of the *Sonderzeit* Paul." *Journal of Early Christian Studies* 20, no. 1 (2012): 1–29.

Martens, John W. *One God, One Law: Philo of Alexandria on the Mosaic and Greco-Roman Law.* Leiden: Brill, 2003.

Martin, Ralph P. *2 Corinthians.* Waco, Tex.: Word Books, 1986.

Massie, Alban. *Peuple prophétique et nation témoin. Le peuple juif dans le* Contra Faustum manichaeum *de saint Augustin.* Paris: Études Augustiniennes, 2011.

Mateo-Seco, Lucas Francisco. "Epektasis." In *The Brill Dictionary of Gregory of Nyssa*, edited by Lucas Francisco Mateo-Seco and Giulio Maspero, and translated by Seth Cherney. Leiden: Brill, 2010.

Mathews, Thomas. *The Clash of Gods: A Reinterpretation of Early Christian Art.* 2nd ed. Princeton, N.J.: Princeton University Press, 1993.

Mazzega, Michael. *Sedulius, Carmen paschale, Buch III.* Basel: Schwabe, 1996.

McAuliffe, Jane Dammen, ed. *Encyclopaedia of the Qur'ān.* 6 vols. Leiden: Brill, 2001–2006.

McCormack, Sabine. *Art and Ceremony in Late Antiquity.* Berkeley: University of California Press, 1981.

McGinn, Bernard. *The Foundations of Mysticism: Origins to the Fifth Century.* New York: Crossroad, 1991.

McGuckin, John A. "St. Cyril of Alexandria: Bishop and Pastor." In *The Theology of St. Cyril of Alexandria: A Critical Appreciation*, edited by Thomas G. Weinandy and Daniel A. Keating, 205–36. London: T&T Clark, 2003.

———. *St. Cyril of Alexandria and the Christological Controversy: Its History, Theology, and Texts.* Crestwood, N.Y.: St. Vladimir's Seminary Press, 2004.

Meeks, Wayne A. *The Prophet-King: Moses Traditions and the Johannine Christology.* Novum Testamentum Supplements 14. Leiden: Brill, 1967.

Meijering, E. P. *Augustin über Schöpfung, Ewigkeit und Zeit: Das elfte Buch der Bekenntnisse.* Leiden: Brill, 1979.

Meredith, Anthony. *Gregory of Nyssa.* The Early Church Fathers. London: Routledge, 1999.

Meroz, Ronit. "Zoharic Narratives and Their Adaptations." *Hispania Judaica Bulletin* 3 (2000): 3–63.

Miller, D. "Ethnicity Comes of Age: An Overview of Twentieth-Century Terms for *Ioudaios*." *Currents in Biblical Research* 10, no. 2 (2012): 293–311.

Minear, Paul S. *To Heal and to Reveal: The Prophetic Vocation according to Luke.* New York: Crossroad, 1976.

Mitsis, Phillip. "Seneca on Reason, Rules, and Moral Development." In *Passions and Perceptions: Studies in Hellenic Philosophy of Mind*, edited by Jacques Brunschwig and Martha C. Nussbaum, 285–312. Cambridge: Cambridge University Press, 1993.

Moessner, David P. "Luke 9:1–50: Luke's Preview of the Journey of the Prophet Like Moses of Deuteronomy." *Journal of Biblical Literature* 102 (1983): 575–605.

Morlet, Sébastien. *La 'Démonstration évangélique' d'Eusèbe de Césarée: Étude sur l'apologétique chrétienne à l'époque de Constantin.* Paris: Institut d'Études Augustiniennes, 2009.

Mosshammer, Alden A. *The Chronicle of Eusebius and Greek Chronographic Tradition.* Lewisburg, Pa..: Bucknell University Press, 1979.

Muehlberger, Ellen. *Angels in Late Ancient Christianity.* New York: Oxford University Press, 2013.

Najman, Hindy. *Seconding Sinai: The Development of Mosaic Discourse in Second Temple Judaism.* Leiden: Brill, 2003.

Nelson, Janet L. "The Earliest Surviving Royal Ordo: Some Liturgical and Historical Aspects." In *Authority and Power: Studies in Medieval Law and Government Presented to*

Walter Ullmann on His Seventieth Birthday, edited by Brian Tierney and Peter Linehan, 29–48. Cambridge: Cambridge University Press, 1980. Reprinted in Janet L. Nelson, *Politics and Ritual in Early Medieval Europe*, 341–60. London: Hambledon Press, 1986.

Newport, K. C. G. *The Sources and Sitz im Leben of Matthew 23*. Sheffield, U.K.: Sheffield Academic Press, 1995.

Nguyen, V. Henry T. *Christian Identity in Corinth: A Comparative Study of 2 Corinthians, Epictetus and Valerius Maximus*. Tübingen: Mohr Siebeck, 2008.

Niehoff, Maren R. *Jewish Exegesis and Homeric Scholarship in Alexandria*. Cambridge: Cambridge University Press, 2011.

Noga-Banai, Galit. "Visual Prototype versus Biblical Text: Moses Receiving the Law in Rome." In *Sarcofagi tardoantichi, paleocristiani e altomedievali*, edited by Fabrizio Bisconti and Hugo Brandenburg, 175–85. Monumenta di Antichità Cristiana 18 (series 2). Vatican City: Pontificio Istituto di Archaeologia Cristiana, 2004.

Nordström, Carl O. "The Water Miracles of Moses in Jewish Legend and Byzantine Art." *Orientalia Suecana* 7 (1958): 78–109.

Norton, M. A. "Prosopography of Juvencus." In *Leaders of Iberian Christianity*, ed. J. M. F. Maricq, 114–20. Boston: St Paul's, 1962.

O'Donnell, James J. *Augustine: Confessions*. Oxford: Clarendon Press, 1992.

O'Laughlin, Michael W. *Origenism in the Desert: Anthropology and Integration in Evagrius Ponticus*. Doctoral dissertation, Harvard University, 1987.

O'Toole, Robert F. "The Parallels between Jesus and Moses." *Biblical Theology Bulletin* 29 (1990): 22–29.

Orlov, Andrei A. *The Enoch-Metatron Tradition*. Texts and Studies in Ancient Judaism. Tübingen: Mohr Siebeck, 2005.

Oxford Society of Historical Theology. *The New Testament in the Apostolic Fathers*. Oxford: Oxford University Press, 1905.

Pervo, Richard I. *Acts: A Commentary*. Minneapolis, Minn.: Fortress Press, 2009.

Pietri, Charles. "Pierre-Moïse et sa communauté." *Roma Christiana* 1 (1976): 336–40.

Pohlenz, Max. "Klemens von Alexandria und sein hellenisches Christentum." *Nachrichten von der Akademie der Wissenschaften in Gottingen*, phil.-hist. Kl (1943): 103–80.

Poirier, John C. "Why Did the Pharisees Wash Their Hands?" *Journal of Jewish Studies* 47 (1996): 217–33.

Pratt, David. *The Political Thought of King Alfred the Great*. Cambridge: Cambridge University Press, 2007.

Rapp, Claudia. "Imperial Ideology in the Making: Eusebius of Caesarea on Constantine as 'Bishop.'" *Journal of Theological Studies* 49 (1998): 685–95.

———. *Holy Bishops in Late Antiquity: The Nature of Christian Leadership in an Age of Transition*. Berkeley: University of California Press, 2005.

Reed, Annette Yoshiko. "The Trickery of the Fallen Angels and the Demonic Mimesis of the Divine." *Journal of Early Christian Studies* 12 (2004): 141–71.

Reeves, John C. *Trajectories in Near Eastern Apocalyptic: A Postrabbinic Jewish Apocalypse Reader*. Atlanta, Ga.: Society of Biblical Literature, 2005.

———. "Manichaeans as *Ahl al-Kitāb*: A Study in Manichaean Scripturalism." In Lange et al., *Light against Darkness*, 249–65.

Ri, Andreas Su-Min. *Commentaire de la Caverne des Trésors: Étude sur l'histoire du texte et de ses sources.* Leuven: Peeters, 2000.

Richard, Earl. *Acts 6:1–8:4: The Author's Method of Composition.* Missoula, Mont.: Scholars Press, 1978.

———. "The Polemical Character of the Joseph Episode in Acts 7." *Journal of Biblical Literature* 98 (1979): 255–67.

Ridings, Daniel. *The Attic Moses: The Dependency Theme in Some Early Christian Writers.* Göteborg: Acta Universitatis Gothoburgensis, 1995.

Riedinger, Rudolph. "Neue Quellen zu den Erotapokriseis des Pseudo-Kaisarios." *Jahrbuch der Österreichischen Byzantinistik* 19 (1970): 153–84.

Rives, J. "The Theology of Animal Sacrifice in the Ancient Greek World." In Knust and Várhelyi, *Ancient Mediterranean Sacrifice*, 187–202.

Rizzardi, Clementina. *I sarcophagi paleocristiani con rappresentazione del passaggio del Mare rosso* (Faenza, Italy: Fratelli Lega, 1970).

Roberts, Michael. *Biblical Epic and Rhetorical Paraphrase in Late Antiquity.* Liverpool: Cairns, 1985.

Roloff, Jürgen. *Die Apostelgeschichte.* Göttingen: Vandenhoeck & Ruprecht, 1981.

Rose, Paul Lawrence. "Muhammad, the Jews and the Constitution of Medina: Retrieving the Historical Kernel." *Der Islam* 86 (2011): 1–29.

Rosenblatt, Samuel. "Rabbinic Legends in Hadith." *Muslim World* 35 (1945): 237–52.

Rowland, Christopher, and Christopher R. A. Morray-Jones. *The Mystery of God: Early Jewish Mysticism and the New Testament.* Leiden: Brill, 2009.

Rubin, Uri. "Prophets and Prophethood." In McAuliffe, *Encyclopaedia of the Qur'ān*, 4:289–307.

Runia, David T. *Philo in Early Christian Literature: A Survey.* Assen, Netherlands: Van Gorcum, 1993.

Sanders, E. P. *Paul, the Law, and the Jewish People.* Philadelphia: Fortress Press, 1983.

———. *Jesus and Judaism.* Philadelphia: Fortress Press, 1985.

———. *Paul: A Very Short Introduction.* New York: Oxford University Press, 2001.

Sandnes, Karl-Olav. *The Gospel "According to Homer and Virgil": Cento and Canon.* Leiden: Brill, 2011.

Satran, David. *Biblical Prophets in Byzantine Palestine: Reassessing the Lives of the Prophets.* Leiden: Brill, 1995.

Schneider, Gerhard. *Die Apostelgeschichte.* Freiburg: Herder, 1980.

Schöck, Cornelia. "Moses." In McAuliffe, *Encyclopaedia of the Qur'ān*, 3:419–26.

Schurig, Sebastian. *Die Theologie des Kreuzes beim frühen Cyrill von Alexandria, dargestellt an seiner Schrift "De adoratione et cultu in spiritu et veritate."* Tübingen: Mohr Siebeck, 2005.

Schwind, Johannes. *Arator-Studien.* Göttingen: Vandenhoeck & Ruprecht, 1990.

Segal, Alan F. *Paul the Convert: The Apostolate and Apostasy of Saul the Pharisee.* New Haven, Conn.: Yale University Press, 1990.

Shea, George W. *The Poems of Alcimus Ecdicius Avitus: Translation and Introduction.* Tempe, Ariz.: Nabu. 1997.

Shepardson, Christine. *Anti-Judaism and Christian Orthodoxy: Ephrem's Hymns in Fourth-Century Syria.* Washington, D.C.: The Catholic University of America Press, 2008.

Shoemaker, Stephen J. *The Death of a Prophet: The End of Muhammad's Life and the Beginnings of Islam.* Philadelphia: University of Pennsylvania Press, 2012.

Sirinelli, Jean. *Les vues historiques d'Eusèbe de Césarée durant la période prénicéenne.* Dakar: Université de Dakar, 1961.

Skarsaune, Oskar, and Reidar Hvalvik, eds. *Jewish Believers in Jesus: The Early Centuries.* Peabody, Mass.: Hendrickson, 2007.

Spence, Stephen. *The Parting of the Ways: The Roman Church as a Case Study.* Interdisciplinary Studies in Ancient Culture and Religion 5. Leuven: Peeters, 2004.

Springer, Carl P. E. *The Gospel as Epic in Late Antiquity: The "Paschale Carmen" of Sedulius.* Leiden: Brill, 1988.

Starr, Joshua. "Le mouvement messianique au début du VIIIe siècle." *Revue des Études Juives* 102 (1937): 81–92.

Stendahl, Krister. *Paul among Jews and Gentiles, and Other Essays.* Philadelphia: Fortress Press, 1976.

Stephenson, Paul. *Constantine: Roman Emperor, Christian Victor.* New York: Overlook Press, 2010.

Sterk, Andrea. *Renouncing the World Yet Leading the Church: The Monk-Bishop in Late Antiquity.* Cambridge, Mass.: Harvard University Press, 2004.

Stewart, Columba. *Cassian the Monk.* New York: Oxford University Press, 1998.

Stockhausen, Carol K. *Moses' Veil and the Glory of the New Covenant: The Exegetical Substructure of II Cor. 3,1–4,6.* Analecta Biblica 116. Rome: Pontifical Biblical Institute, 1989.

Stocking, Rachel L. *Bishops, Councils, and Consensus in the Visigothic Kingdom, 589–633.* Ann Arbor: The University of Michigan Press, 2000.

Stone, Michael E. "The Metamorphosis of Ezra: Jewish Apocalypse and Medieval Vision." *Journal of Theological Studies* n.s. 33 (1982): 1–18.

Storin, Bradley. "The Letters of Gregory of Nazianzus: Discourse and Community in Late Antique Epistolary Culture." PhD dissertation, Indiana University, 2012.

Straw, Carole E. *Gregory the Great: Perfection in Imperfection.* Berkeley: University of California Press, 1988.

———. "Gregory's Politics: Theory and Practice." In *Gregorio Magno e il suo tempo: XIX Incontro di studiosi dell'antichità cristiana in collaborazione con l'École Française de Rome, Roma 9–12 Maggio 1990,* 1:47–63. Studia Ephemeridis Augustinianum 33. Rome: Institutum Patristicum "Augustinianum," 1991.

Striker, Gisela. *Essays on Hellenistic Epistemology and Ethics.* Cambridge: Cambridge University Press, 1996.

Stroumsa, Guy G. "The Scriptural Movement of Late Antiquity and Christian Monasticism." *Journal of Early Christian Studies* 16 (2008): 61–77.

Stuhlfauth, G. *Die apokryphen Petrus geschichten in der altchristlichen Kunst*. Berlin: de Gruyter, 1925.

Svartvik, Jesper. *Mark and Mission: Mk 7:1–23 in Its Narrative and Historical Contexts*. Conlectanea Biblica, New Testament Series. Stockholm: Almqvist & Wiksell, 2000.

Tabor, James D. "'Returning to the Divinity': Josephus's Portrayal of the Disappearances of Enoch, Elijah, and Moses." *Journal of Biblical Literature* 108 (1989): 225–38.

Tardieu, M. "Principes de l'exégèse manichéenne du Nouveau Testament." In *Les règles de l'interprétation*, edited by M. Tardieu, 123–28. Paris: Éditions du Cerf, 1987.

Taylor, Joan E., and Philip R. Davies. "The So-Called Therapeutae of *De Vita Contemplativa*: Identity and Character." *Harvard Theological Review* 91 (1998): 3–24.

Taylor, Miriam S. *Anti-Judaism and Early Christian Identity: A Critique of the Scholarly Consensus*. Leiden: Brill, 1995.

Thackston, W. M., Jr. *The Tales of the Prophets of al-Kisa'i*. Boston: Twayne Publishers, 1978.

Theissen, Gerd. *Psychological Aspects of Pauline Theology*. Translated by John P. Galvin. Edinburgh: T&T Clark, 1987.

Thrall, Margaret E. *A Critical and Exegetical Commentary on the Second Epistle to the Corinthians*. Edinburgh: T&T Clark, 1994.

Tiede, David L. *Prophecy and History in Luke-Acts*. Philadelphia: Fortress Press, 1980.

Tomson, Peter J. *Paul and the Jewish Law: Halakha in the Letters of the Apostle to the Gentiles*. Compendia Rerum Iudaicarum Ad Novum Testamentum, section 3, Jewish Traditions in Early Christian Literature, vol. 1. Minneapolis, Minn.: Fortress Press, 1990.

———. "Jewish Purity Laws as Viewed by the Church Fathers and by the Early Followers of Jesus." In *Purity and Holiness: The Heritage of Leviticus*, edited by M. J. H. M. Poorthuis and J. Schwartz, 73–91. Leiden: Brill, 2000.

Tonneau, Raymond Marie. "Moïse dans la tradition syrienne." In *Moïse: L'homme de l'alliance*, edited by H. Cazelles, 245–65. Tournai: Desclée, 1955.

Treschow, Michael. "The Prologue to Alfred's Law Code: Instruction in the Spirit of Mercy." *Florilegium* 13 (1994): 79–109.

Tronzo, William. *The Via Latina Catacomb: Imitation and Discontinuity in Fourth-Century Roman Painting*. University Park: Pennsylvania State University Press, 1986.

Tucker, J. Brian. *"You Belong to Christ": Paul and the Formation of Social Identity in 1 Corinthians 1–4*. Eugene, Ore.: Pickwick Publications, 2010.

Ullucci, D. "Contesting the Meaning of Animal Sacrifice." In Knust and Várhelyi, *Ancient Mediterranean Sacrifice*, 57–74.

Van den Hoek, Annewies. *Clement of Alexandria and His Use of Philo in the* Stromateis: *An Early Christian Reshaping of a Jewish Model*. Leiden: Brill, 1988.

Van der Horst, P. "'Thou Shalt Not Revile the Gods:' The LXX Translation of Exodus 22.28(27), Its Background and Influence." *Studia Philonica* 5 (1993): 1–8.

Van Kooten, George H. *Paul's Anthropology in Context: The Image of God, Assimilation to God, and Tripartite Man in Ancient Judaism, Ancient Philosophy and Early Christianity*. Tübingen: Mohr Siebeck, 2008.

Van Unnik, W. C. "Studies on the So-Called First Epistle of Clement: The Literary Genre."

In *Encounters with Hellenism*, edited by Cilliers Breytenbach and Laurence L. Welborn, 115–81. Leiden: Brill, 2004.

Vander Waerdt, Paul. "Philosophical Influence on Roman Jurisprudence? The Case of Stoicism and Natural Law." *Aufstieg und Niedergang der Römischen Welt* 2.26.7 (1994): 4856–58.

———, ed. *The Socratic Movement*. Ithaca, N.Y.: Cornell University Press, 1994.

VanderKam, James C. *Enoch: A Man for All Generations*. Columbia: University of South Carolina Press, 1995.

Vannier, Marie-Anne. *"Creatio", "Conversio", "Formatio" chez S. Augustin*. Fribourg: Éditions Universitaires, 1991.

Vivian, Tim. "'Everything Made by God Is Good': A Letter from Saint Athanasius to the Monk Amoun." *Église et théologie* 24 (1993): 75–108.

Wan, Sze-Kar. "Charismatic Exegesis: Philo and Paul Compared." In *The Studia Philonica Annual: Studies in Hellenistic Judaism*, vol. 6, edited by David T. Runia, 54–82. Brown Judaic Studies 299. Atlanta, Ga.: Scholars Press, 1994.

Wasselynck, René. *L'influence des "Moralia in Job" de S. Grégoire le Grand sur la théologie morale entre le VIIe et le XIIe siècle*. 3 vols. Doctoral thesis, Université de Lille, 1956.

Weedman, Mark. "The Polemical Context of Gregory of Nyssa's Doctrine of Divine Infinity." *Journal of Early Christian Studies* 18 (2010): 81–104.

Weitzman, Kurt, and Ihor Ševčenko. "The Moses Cross at Sinai." *Dumbarton Oaks Papers* 17 (1963): 385–98.

Wensinck, A. J., and C. E. Bosworth. "Lawḥ." In *Encyclopaedia of Islam*, edited by P. Bearman, Th. Bianquis, C. E. Bosworth, E. van Donzel, and W. P. Heinrichs, 5:698. New edition in 11 vols. Leiden: Brill, 1954–2002.

Westerholm, Stephen. *Jesus and Scribal Authority*. Lund, Sweden: Liber Läromedel/Gleerup, 1978.

Wharton, Annabel J. "Good and Bad Images from the Synagogue of Dura Europus." *Art History* 17 (1994): 1–25.

Wheeler, Brannon. *Moses in the Quran and Islamic Exegesis*. New York: Routledge Curzon, 2002.

———. *Mecca and Eden: Ritual, Relics, and Territory in Islam*. Chicago: University of Chicago Press, 2006.

Wieder, Naphtali. "The 'Law-Interpreter' of the Sect of the Dead Sea Scrolls: The Second Moses." *Journal of Jewish Studies* 4 (1953): 158–75.

———. "The Idea of a Second Coming of Moses." *Jewish Quarterly Review* n.s. 46 (1955–56): 356–66.

Wild, Robert A. "The Encounter between Pharisaic and Christian Judaism: Some Early Gospel Evidence." *Novum Testamentum* 27 (1985): 105–24.

Wilken, Robert Louis. *Judaism and the Early Christian Mind: A Study of Cyril of Alexandria's Exegesis and Theology*. New Haven, Conn.: Yale University Press, 1971.

Williams, Michael Stuart. *Authorized Lives in Early Christian Biography: Between Eusebius and Augustine*. Cambridge: Cambridge University Press, 2008.

Wilson, Anna. "Biographical Models: the Constantinian Period and Beyond." In *Constantine: History, Historiography, and Legend*, edited by Samuel N. C. Lieu and Dominic Montserrat, 107–35. London: Routledge, 1998.

Wood, Ian N. "Avitus of Vienne, the Augustinian Poet." In *Society and Culture in Late Antique Gaul: Revisiting the Sources*, edited by Ralph W. Mathisen and Danuta Shanzer, 263–77. Aldershot: Ashgate, 2001.

Wood, Jamie. *The Politics of Identity in Visigothic Spain: Religion and Power in the Histories of Isidore of Seville*. Leiden: Brill, 2012.

Wright, N. T. *The Climax of the Covenant: Christ and the Law in Pauline Theology*. Minneapolis, Minn.: Fortress Press, 1992.

Yassif, Eli, ed. *Sefer ha-Zikronot hu' Divrey ha-Yamim le-Yerahme'el*. Tel Aviv: Tel Aviv University, 2001.

Yates, John W. *The Spirit and Creation in Paul*. Wissenschaftliche Untersuchungen zum Neuen Testament II/251. Tübingen: Mohr Siebeck, 2008.

Young, Robin Darling. "*Xeniteia* according to Evagrius of Pontus." In *Ascetic Culture: Essays in Honor of Philip Rousseau*, edited by Blake Leyerle and Robin Darling Young, 229–52. Notre Dame, Ind.: University of Notre Dame Press, 2013.

Zehnle, Richard F. *Peter's Pentecost Discourse: Tradition and Lukan Reinterpretation in Peter's Speeches of Acts 2 and 3*. Nashville, Tenn.: Abingdon Press, 1971.

Zerubavel, Yael. "The Historical, the Legendary and the Incredible: Invented Tradition and Collective Memory in Israel." In *Commemorations: The Politics of National Identity*, edited by J. R. Gillis, 105–25. Princeton, N.J.: Princeton University Press, 1994.

Zeumer, Karl. "Geschichte der westgotischen Gesetzgebung II." *Neues Archiv der Gesellschaft für ältere deutsche Geschichtskunde* 24 (1899): 41–122.

CONTRIBUTORS

Lee Blackburn is associate professor of history and humanities at Milligan College, Tennessee. His recent publications include the article "Law" in *The Oxford Handbook of Early Christian Biblical Interpretation*, ed. Paul M. Blowers and Peter W. Martens (forthcoming, 2019).

Dulcinea Boesenberg is assistant professor of New Testament at Creighton University in Omaha, Nebraska. Her recent publications include "Philo's Descriptions of Jewish Sabbath Practice," *Studia Philonica Annual* 22 (2010): 143–63; "Moses in Second Temple Jewish Texts" (with James C. VanderKam), in *Parables of Enoch: A Paradigm Shift*, ed. James Charlesworth and Darrell Bock (T&T Clark, 2013), 124–58; and "Retelling Moses's Killing of the Egyptian: Acts 7 in Its Jewish Context," *Biblical Theology Bulletin* 48 (2018): 148–56.

Daniel Boyarin is Hermann P. and Sophia Taubman Professor of Talmudic Culture in the Departments of Near Eastern Studies and Rhetoric, University of California, Berkeley. He is a fellow of the American Academy of Arts and Sciences. His major publications include *A Radical Jew: Paul and the Politics of Identity* (University of California Press, 1994); *Dying for God: Martyrdom and the Making of Christianity and Judaism* (Stanford University Press, 1999); *Border Lines: The Partition of Judaeo-Christianity* (University of Pennsylvania Press, 2004); *The Jewish Gospels: The Story of the Jewish Christ* (The New Press, 2012); *Socrates and the Fat Rabbis* (University of Chicago Press, 2014); and *A Traveling Homeland: The Babylonian Talmud as Diaspora* (University of Pennsylvania Press, 2015). He is co-editor (with Virginia Burrus and Derek Krueger) of the series "Divinations: Rereading Late Ancient Religions," published by the University of Pennsylvania Press.

Ann Conway-Jones is an honorary research fellow at the University of Birmingham (U.K.) and at the Queen's Foundation for Ecumenical Theological Education, also in Birmingham. She is the author of *Gregory of Nyssa's Tabernacle Imagery in Its Jew-*

306   CONTRIBUTORS

ish and Christian Contexts (Oxford University Press, 2014). Her papers include "Interiorised Apocalyptic in Gregory of Nyssa, Evagrius of Pontus and Pseudo-Macarius," *Studia Patristica* 74 (Peeters, 2016), and "'The Greatest Paradox of All': The 'Place of God' in the Mystical Theology of Gregory of Nyssa and Evagrius of Pontus," *Journal of the Bible and Its Reception* 5, no. 2 (forthcoming).

Paula Fredriksen is Aurelio Professor emerita at Boston University and distinguished visiting professor at the Hebrew University, Jerusalem. A fellow of the American Academy of Arts and Sciences, she holds honorary doctorates at Iona College (United States), Lund University (Sweden), and the Hebrew University (Israel). Her major publications include *From Jesus to Christ* (Yale University Press, 1988; 2nd ed. 2000); *Jesus of Nazareth, King of the Jews* (Knopf, 1999); *Augustine and the Jews* (Doubleday, 2008; reprint, Yale University Press, 2010); *Sin: The Early History of an Idea* (Princeton University Press, 2012), and *Paul, The Pagans' Apostle* (Yale University Press, 2017). A notable edited volume was (with Adele Reinhartz) *Jesus, Judaism, and Christian Anti-Judaism: Reading the New Testament after the Holocaust* (Westminster John Knox Press, 2002).

Kathleen Gibbons is the author of *The Moral Psychology of Clement of Alexandria* (Routledge, 2017). Other publications include "Moses, Statesman and Philosopher: Assimilating to God and Clement of Alexandria's Methodology in *Stromateis* I," *Vigiliae Christianae* 69 (2015): 157–85; "Human Autonomy and Its Limits in the Thought of Origen of Alexandria," *Classical Quarterly* 66 (2016): 673–90; "Who Reads the Stars? Origen of Alexandria on Ethnic Reasoning and Astrological Discourse," in *The Routledge Handbook of Identity and the Environment in the Classical and Medieval Worlds*, ed. Rebecca Kennedy and Molly Ayn Jones-Lewis (Routledge, 2015); and "Passions, Pleasures, and Perceptions: Rethinking Evagrius Ponticus on Mental Representation," *Zeitschrift für Antikes Christentum / The Journal of Ancient Christianity* 19 (2015): 297–330. She is currently at work on a book on ancient astrology and early Christianity.

Michael Hollerich is professor of theology at the University of St Thomas, in St Paul, Minnesota. He is the author of *Eusebius of Caesarea's* Commentary on Isaiah: *Christian Exegesis in the Age of Constantine* (Oxford University Press, 1999). His most recent book is a translation, with introduction, of Erik Peterson's *Theological Tractates* (Stanford University Press, 2011). He is completing a study of the reception history of Eusebius's *Ecclesiastical History*. With Catherine Cory and Mark McInroy, he is co-editor of the third and fourth editions of *The Christian Theological Tradition* (Macmillan, 2008; Routledge, 2018).

Robin M. Jensen is the Patrick O'Brien Professor of Theology at the University of Notre Dame. She is a past president of the North American Patristics Society and vice president of the International Catacomb Society. Her major publications in early Christian art and liturgy include *Understanding Early Christian Art* (Routledge, 2000); *The Substance of Things Seen: Art, Faith, and the Christian Community* (Eerdmans, 2004); *Face to Face: The Portrait of the Divine in Early Christianity* (Fortress Press, 2005); *Living Water: The Art and Architecture of Ancient Christian Baptism* (Brill, 2011); *Baptismal Imagery in Early Christianity* (Baker Academic Press, 2012); and *The Cross: History, Art, and Controversy* (Harvard University Press, 2017). She is co-author (with J. Patout Burns) of *Christianity in Roman Africa: The Development of its Practices and Beliefs* (Eerdmans, 2014); co-editor (with Lee Jefferson) of *The Art of Empire: Christian Art in Its Imperial Context* (Fortress Press, 2015); co-editor (with Mark Ellison) of *The Routledge Companion to Early Christian Art*; and co-editor of the forthcoming *Cambridge History of Late Antique Archaeology*.

Naomi Koltun-Fromm is associate professor in the Department of Religion at Haverford College, in Pennsylvania. She is author of *Hermeneutics of Holiness: Ancient Jewish and Christian Notions of Sexuality and Religious Community* (Oxford University Press, 2010); and *Jewish-Christian Conversation in Fourth-Century Persian Mesopotamia: A Reconstructed Conversation* (Gorgias Press, 2011). She is currently studying the mythological representations of Jerusalem in late antique Judaism, Christianity, and Islam.

Richard A. Layton is associate professor of medieval studies, religion, and classics in the Department of Religion at the University of Illinois, Urbana-Champaign. He is the author of *Didymus the Blind and His Circle in Late-Antique Alexandria: Virtue and Narrative in Biblical Scholarship* (University of Illinois Press, 2004).

Ellen Muehlberger is associate professor of Near Eastern studies and of history at the University of Michigan, Ann Arbor. She is the author of *Angels in Late Ancient Christianity* (Oxford University Press, 2013) and of *Moment of Reckoning: Imagined Death and Its Consequences in Late Ancient Christianity* (forthcoming from Oxford University Press, 2019), as well as of significant articles in *Vigiliae Christianae* (2011), *Church History* (2012), *Journal of Early Christian Studies* (2015), and *Past and Present* (2015). She has also edited *Practice*, the second volume of the Cambridge Edition of Early Christian Writings (2017).

Michael Müller, after doctoral study and teaching at the University of Cologne, has accepted a teaching position at the Rabanus-Maurus-Gymnasium in Mainz. He is author of *Tod und Auferstehung Jesu Christi bei Iuvencus (4. 570–812): Untersuchun-*

gen zu Dichtkunst, Theologie und Zweck der Evangeliorum Libri Quattuor (Steiner, 2016).

Emmanuel Nathan is national head of the School of Theology in the Faculty of Theology and Philosophy at the Australian Catholic University in Sydney, where he is also lecturer in biblical studies. His most recent publications include *2 Corinthians in the Perspective of Late Second Temple Judaism* (Brill, 2014); *Is There a Judeo-Christian Tradition? A European Perspective* (De Gruyter, 2016); and *Remembering the New Covenant at Corinth* (Mohr Siebeck, 2019).

Vadim Prozorov is associate professor of late antique and early medieval history at the Lomonosov Moscow State University. His recent papers and articles in English include, "How to Bind the 'Rhinoceros of Earthly Power': Perception of Gregorian Political Ideas in the Ninth Century Europe," in *The Legitimation of Political Power in Medieval Thought*, ed. S. C. López Alcaide, J. Puig Montada, and P. Roche Arnas (Brepols, 2018), 295–310; "The Tenth Century Councils in Split and the Problem of the Reliability of Their Acts," *Crkvene Studije* 10 (2013): 275–87; "'Where He Is Thither Will the Eagles Be Gathered Together': The Metropolitan Status of the Bishop of Spalato from the Decline of Salona until the Councils of Spalato in 925 and 928," in *Saintly Bishops and Bishops' Saints*, ed. John S. Ott and Trpimir Vedriš (Hagiotheca, 2012), 103–22; "The Sixth Century Councils of Salona," *Vjesnikza Arheologijui Povijest Dalmatinsku* 104 (2011): 309–37; and "The Passion of St Domnius: The Tradition of Apostolic Succession in Dalmatia," *Scrinium* 2 (2006): 219–39. He is preparing a study of the works of Gregory the Great in their legal context.

John C. Reeves is Blumenthal Professor of Judaic Studies and professor of religious studies in the Department of Religious Studies at the University of North Carolina, Charlotte. He is author of *Jewish Lore in Manichaean Cosmogony: Studies in the Book of Giants Traditions* (Hebrew Union College Press, 1992); *Heralds of That Good Realm: Syro-Mesopotamian Gnosis and Jewish Traditions* (Brill, 1996); *Trajectories in Near Eastern Apocalyptic: A Postrabbinic Jewish Apocalypse Reader* (Society of Biblical Literature, 2005); *Prolegomena to a History of Islamicate Manichaeism* (Equinox Publishing, 2011); and the co-author (with Annette Yoshiko Reed) of *Enoch from Antiquity to the Middle Ages*, vol. 1: *Sources from Judaism, Christianity, and Islam* (Oxford University Press, 2018). He also edited the collections *Tracing the Threads: Studies in the Vitality of Jewish Pseudepigrapha* (Scholars Press, 1994) and *Bible and Qurān: Essays in Scriptural Intertextuality* (Brill, 2003).

Philip Rousseau is Andrew W. Mellon Distinguished Professor of Early Christian Studies at the Catholic University of America. His major publications include

Ascetics, Authority, and the Church in the Age of Jerome and Cassian (Oxford University Press, 1978), reissued in a second edition with new introduction and updated bibliography (University of Notre Dame Press, 2010), and *The Early Christian Centuries* (Longmans, 2002); monographs on Pachomius (University of California Press, 1985; with a new preface, 1999) and Basil of Caesarea (University of California Press, 1994); and the edited volumes *A Companion to Late Antiquity* (Wiley-Blackwell, 2009), and (with Manolis Papoutsakis) *Transformations of Late Antiquity: Essays for Peter Brown* (Ashgate, 2009). He is general editor of the series CUA Studies in Early Christianity, published by the Catholic University of America Press.

David A. Smith is adjunct instructor of New Testament at Duke University and adjunct assistant professor of religious studies at Elon University. He is author of "'No Poor among Them': Sabbath and Jubilee Years in Lukan Social Ethics," in *Horizons in Biblical Theology* 40 (2018): 142–65, and of a forthcoming monograph on the portrayal of Jewish and Christian identities in the Gospel of Luke.

Janet A. Timbie is adjunct associate professor in the Department of Semitic and Egyptian Languages and Literatures at the Catholic University of America. She is co-editor (with James Goehring) of *The World of Early Egyptian Christianity: Language, Literature, and Social Context: Essays in Honor of David W. Johnson* (The Catholic University of America Press, 2007), together with (most recently) a number of papers on the Egyptian monastic leader Shenoute. She is a member of the editorial board of the series CUA Studies in Early Christianity, published by the Catholic University of America Press.

Virginia Wayland, after an academic career in chemistry, switched her field of interest and completed (in 2017) her doctoral dissertation in the Department of Religious Studies at the University of Pennsylvania, "Following Moses: An Inquiry into the Prophetic Discourse of the First Century C.E." Focusing on Second Temple Judaism and early Christianity, she has delivered several papers on the interplay between historical and legal texts designed to identify and authorize successors of Moses.

INDEX

Aaron: in Christian texts, 150; in golden calf incident, 35, 272; and Jesus, 59–60n43, 228–29; in the Korah Rebellion, 56–59; and Miriam, 59, 266; and Moses, 187, 239, 247, 249–50; and Paul, 171–72

Abraham: in art, 166, 168, 170, 192; in Christian texts, 136; and covenant, 28, 37, 53n10, 75n39, 170; *genos* of, 31, 53n9, 127, 205, 217; and God, 83; and Isaac, 86, 168, 170, 192; and Moses, 168; and Sarah, 222; *Testament of*, 281

Acts: exegesis of, 244; Jesus in, 25–26, 28, 30–31, 37–38, 168–69; Moses in, 25–38, 59n41, 61n47, 168–69; Peter in, 25–26, 28, 31, 168; as source for Arator, 243; Stephen in, 32, 37–38, 169

Adam: and Christ, 41; as cosmopolitan, 87; curse, 231, 270; in Ephrem, 199n16, 205; and God, 83, 199n16, 217; knowledge of Creation, 205

adventus, 178–80

Alcimus Avitus, 237, 245–51

Alfred the Great, 259, 262

allegorical interpretation: by Arator, 243–44; by Clement of Alexandria, 100–102, 106, 109–15; by Gregory the Great, 253–54, by Gregory of Nyssa, 154, 182–83; of Old Testament, 167; by Origen, 125; by Philo, 88–89

Al-Kisa'i, 275–76

Ambrose of Milan, 173, 177, 240n14, 241n19, 249n53

Angel of Death, 274–76

angels: in art, 187; companion, 147; in comparison with Jesus, 69–70, 76, 78; in comparison with Moses, 195, 267; fallen, 209n5, 216; in Genesis, 93, 206; Moses with, 35, 82, 159, 195, 267; as objects of worship, 156

Animal Apocalypse, 267–68

anti-Judaism: in Arator, 244, 251; in art, 173, 175; in Cyril of Alexandria, 232, 234–35; in Eusebius, 121–23, 127; Manichean, 212, 224–25; tradition, 123, 170, 210, 216, 224, 251

apocalypse: and a return of Moses, 42, 277–84; in Paul, 40; its influence on mysticism, 163; Muslim, 273

apostles and Moses, 52–60, 62–63, 76, 125, 170–71, 202–4, 223

Aphrahat, 186–87, 193–97, 206–7

Arator, 243–45, 250–51

Aristotle, 31n9, 81

Ark of the Covenant: in art, 190; in Gregory the Great, 254–55, 259; in Gregory of Nyssa, 159; and the labarum, 132–33; as symbol of Moses, 282–93

ascent: heavenly, 156–64; spiritual, 89

ascetic: community, 15, 144, 148–53; discipline, 145–47, 194–95; elite, 126, 129; leadership, 136, 138–39, 147; life, 144–45; literature, 151

Athanasius of Alexandria, 15, 152

Augustine: allegory in, 173, 184; on Genesis, 91–99; influence on Arator, 243; against Manichaeism, 210, 218–26; on Moses, 169, 256

155, 157, 160, 182; on Law, 14–15, 83, 232; on striking the rock, 242

parable: of Exodus, 43–44; of Good Samaritan, 254; of Law, 5n16, 6–9, 15, 18–20, 22–23, 228; of prophecy, 200–201
parting of ways between church and synagogue, 64, 78–80
passions, 126, 145–46, 151, 182–83, 239
Passover, 29–30, 183, 248–49
Paul: and Aaron, 171; *Apocalypse of*, 281; in Arator, 244–45; in Augustine, 223, 225; on baptism, 182, 244; on Christ, 170, 174, 176–77; in *1 Clement*, 51–53, 56, 62–63, 65; in Clement of Alexandria, 101; conversion of, 40, 45–50; in Cyril of Alexandria, 233; and Judaism, 1–3, 211; and Law, 3, 20–22, 82, 101, 170–71, 225, 232–33; in Mani, 211; and Mark, 1–3, 20–24; and Moses, 20, 39–50, 53, 56, 62–63, 82, 164, 223, 235; and Peter, 52, 170–71, 176, 223; in Sedulius, 240–41
Peter: in Acts, 25–31, 168–69; *Acts of Peter*, 176; in art, 170–71, 172–76; baptizing Roman soldiers, 175; in *1 Clement*, 52–53; as criminal, 214, 223; in Eusebius, 124; and Law, 170–71, 203–4; in Matthew, 19; and Moses, 184, 214, 223; and Old Testament, 244–45; and Paul, 52–53, 170–71, 176, 223; striking the rock, 173–76; and the Transfiguration, 201, 203–4
Pharisees, 3–12, 14–23
Philo of Alexandria: as contemporary of Paul, 39; on death of Moses, 268; influence on Basil of Caesarea, 84–86, 89; influence on Clement of Alexandria, 102, 106, 109; influence on Didymus the Blind, 89–91; influence on Eusebius, 128–29; influence on Gregory of Nyssa, 136, 155, 159, 162n41; influence on Josephus, 85–86, 89; on Moses as author, 84–85, 89–92, 99; on Moses as cosmopolitan, 87–88; on Moses as king, 134n77
plagues, 145, 172, 197, 231, 248
Platonism, 81n2, 111–12, 121–22, 156, 159–60, 163

Poirier, John C., 16n40
Porphyry, 120, 125
prophecy: of Covenants, 109; of Genesis, 205; of Jesus, 25–28, 31, 199–201, 214; keys of, 203–4; Moses as type for, 200–201
prophets, 31, 37–38, 54–55, 69, 73–76, 87, 119, 122, 125, 200–201, 203, 206, 219, 232, 249; Aaron, 239, 247–50; Elijah, 69, 164, 203–4, 279–80; Ezekiel, 36, 43, 69, 160, 164, 206; Isaiah, 11, 19, 157, 160, 164, 176–77, 206; Jesus as, 25–28, 30–31, 38, 215; Moses, 25–28, 30–31, 38, 81, 82–83, 90, 119, 167, 169, 177, 194, 200–201, 205, 213–15, 221, 225–26, 239, 243, 247, 250–51, 264, 266; Muhammad, 264, 271, 273–74; Zecharia (Zekharia), 13, 90
Providence, 101n3, 110–14
punishment, 37, 144, 256–67, 272, 281
purity, 4–10, 12–19, 21–23, 90, 189, 218, 230–32

Qur'ān, 264, 266, 274

Rabbula gospel, 187–90, 193, 195, 206–7
Red Sea crossing, 60, 143, 167, 177–84, 240–41, 245, 250
rule-following vs. right reasoning, 103–15

sacrifice: blood, 13, 29, 54–55, 209–10, 216–17, 220–22, 225; incense, 160; of Isaac, 168, 192; of Jesus, 67, 203, 216–17, 221, 225; self-sacrifice, 61, 76, 129, 256
Samael. *See* Angel of Death
Samuel, 281
Sedulius, 236–37, 240–43, 246, 250
Seneca, 103–5
sexual continence, 29, 195, 218–19, 222
Sīra, 278–79
Songs of the Sabbath Sacrifice, 155–56, 159–60
staff, wonder-working, 133, 172–78, 181, 246–48, 282–83
Stephen, 32, 37–38, 169
Sterk, Andrea, 148–51
Stoicism, 81n2, 102, 103–14
Svartvik, Jesper, 2n4, 7n21, 14–15
Syriac tradition, 186–207

The Christian Moses: From Philo to the Qur'ān was designed in Garamond by Kachergis Book Design of Pittsboro, North Carolina. It was printed on 60-pound House Natural Smooth and bound by Sheridan Books of Chelsea, Michigan.